누구나 매일매일 쓰는

일상영어
표현사전 3300

Chris Suh

MENT◯RS

누구나 매일매일 쓰는

일상영어 표현사전 3300

2022년 11월 21일 인쇄
2022년 11월 28일 발행

지 은 이   Chris Suh
발 행 인   Chris Suh
발 행 처   **MENT◎RS**
　　　　　 경기도 성남시 분당구 분당로 53번길 12 313-1
　　　　　 TEL 031-604-0025 **FAX** 031-696-5221
　　　　　 mentors.co.kr
　　　　　 blog.naver.com/mentorsbook

등록일자   2022년 11월 11일
등록번호   제 2022-000130호
I S B N   979-11-980848-0-4
가　　격   25,000원

어리말

어려운 것보다 쉬운 것이 더 어렵다!

대기업 무역부의 한 과장은 상대 파트너들에게 영어로 프레젠테이션도 능숙하게 하고 업무 대화도 무리없이 잘해냈다. 문제는 미팅 후의 회식자리에서이다. 그 과장은 앞서 선보였던 영어실력을 회식 때는 보여주질 못하고 다른 사람이 된 것처럼 보였다. 원인은 그 과장은 어느 정도 정형화된 프레젠테이션이나 업무영어에는 익숙했지만 망망대해와 같은 일상의 캐주얼한 소재 앞에서는 그만 영어실력이 들통이 난 것이다. 어려운 것보다 쉬운 것이 더 어렵다는 역설이 공식화된 몇 안되는 경우인 셈이다.

영어의 진짜 실력은 일상영어에서 판가름!

그렇다! 영어의 진짜 실력은 업무영어보다 일상영어에서 판가름난다. 자신에 관한 일반적인 소개들, 우리 주변의 소식에 관한 이야기들을 이야기하려면 영어의 기본이 탄탄해야 하기 때문이다. 예를 들어 "우리는 친한 사이라고" 말하는 We're on a first name basis, "아파트 7층에 살고 있다"는 I live on the seventh floor of an apartment building, 그리고 "걘 성격이 좋아서 거의 화를 내지 않아"는 He's easy going and rarely gets upset about anything 라고 하는 것들은 기본적으로 알고 있어야 한다. 그리고 최근의 우리 주변의 소재거리로, "난 넷플릭스와 자막의 도움으로 영어를 공부하고 있어"라고 할 때는 I'm learning English with the help of Netflix and subtitles, "많은 한국 사람들이 프리미어리그를 보고 있는데, 특히 손흥민 때문에 토트넘 경기를 놓치지 않고 봐"라고 할 때는 Many Koreans follow the Premier League, especially Tottenham Hotspur because of Son Heung-Min, 그리고 "요즘 머리가 빠져"라고 할 때는 I'm losing hair these days 등의 표현법에 능숙해져야 진짜 영어실력이 좋아지는 것이다. 그리고 "요즘 배달이 안되는 건 없어"라고 하면 Nothing can be delivered these days라고 하면 된다는 것까지 알아두면 금상첨화!

일상영어를 총정리!

이책 〈일상영어표현사전 3300〉은 이런 자신의 신체, 건강, 취미 등 기본적인 정보 등을 정리하였을 뿐만 아니라 요즘의 핫한 소재인 넷플릭스, 배달문화, 성희롱, 오징어게임 등, 그리고 점, 돌, 추석, 판문점 등 우리나라에 관한 일상적인 소재들을 중심으로 쓰일 수 있는 문장들을 총정리하였다. 그래서 이책을 완독하면 앞서 말한 업무영어만 잘하는 반쪽짜리 비즈니스맨이 아니라 업무영어 뿐만아니라 일상영어도 잘하는 그래서 회의에서 뿐만 아니라 회식에서도 영어로 화제를 이끌어갈 수 있는 진정한 비즈니스맨이 될 수 있을 것으로 확신한다.

1. 언제 어디서나 쓰일 수 있는 일상영어회화표현 3300개를 수록하였다.

2. 자기의 정보말하기, 건강, 취미, 스포츠 그리고 Korea 등 알기 쉽게 테마별로 분류하였다.

3. 각 넘버링마다 다섯개의 대표문장과 그와 비슷하게 쓰이는 문장들을 함께 볼 수 있다.

4. 각 대표문장에는 현지 네이티브가 작성한 생생한 다이알로그가 수록되었다.

5. 모든 문장과 다이알로그는 현장감 넘치는 네이티브들의 목소리로 담았다.

1. 전체 표현을 Unit 01~ Unit 10까지로 분류 수록하였다.

2. 각 Unit에는 넘버링 페이지(2페이지)가 평균 2–30개 들어 있다.

3. 각 넘버링 페이지에는 다섯개의 대표문장을 실었으며 그 밑에 유사한 표현을 2–3개 넣었다.

4. 각 대표문장에서는 생동감 넘치는 현지 다이알로그를 하나씩 수록하여 이해를 도왔다.

5. 각 넘버링에는 오른쪽 페이지에 대표사진을 넣어 어떤 내용을 학습하는지 한눈에 알아볼 수 있도록 하였다.

자기 이름 말하기

001

Most people just call me Su-hyun

대부분 '수현'이라고 불러

초면일 때는 Hi. Nice to meet you. How are you? 등의 인사를 하면서 자신의 이름을 말한다. 이름(first name)만 말해도 되거나 혹은 성(last name)까지 함께 말한다.

 01 Nice to meet you. I'm Chris Suh
만나서 반가워. 내 이름은 크리스 서야

- My name is Yeon-hwa Choi. How are you? 내 이름은 최연화야. 안녕하세요?
- Hi, I'm Man-jin, Mi-sue's brother. 안녕, 난 민진이라고 해, 미수의 오빠야.
- Hello, my name is David 안녕하세요, 데이빗이라고 합니다
- Hello, I am Mr. Brown. It's good to meet you.
  안녕하세요, 브라운이라고 합니다. 만나서 반갑습니다.

A: Hi, I think you must be new in our office. I'm Miss Stevens.
사무실 신입인 것 같군요. 전 미스 스티븐스예요.
B: Hello, I am Mr. Brown. It's good to meet you.
안녕하세요, 전 브라운이라고 합니다. 만나서 반갑습니다.

02 I'm Su-hyun Kim. Most people just call me Su-hyun
난 김수현이야. 대부분 '수현'이라고 불러

- Chris has told me so much about you. 크리스로부터 얘기 많이 들었습니다.
- It's nice to know you. 알게 되어서 반가워요.
- My name is Jonathan Keller, but please just call me John.
  이름은 조나단 켈러지만 그냥 존이라고 부르세요.

A: My name is Jonathan Keller, but please just call me John.
이름은 조나단 켈러지만 그냥 존이라고 부르세요.
B: It's a pleasure to meet you, John. Please call me Tammy.
만나서 반가워요, 존. 난 태미라고 불러요.

| 24 | 일상영어 표현사전 3300

넘버링

각 Unit에 2페이지씩 들어가는 것으로 보통 2-30개의 넘버링이 포함된다.

넘버링 제목

각 넘버링에서 다루고자 하는 내용이 뭔지 한번에 이해할 수 있도록 우리말 제목을 간략하게 달았다.

넘버링 타이틀

각 넘버링에 있는 내용을 대표하는 문장을 제목으로 하였다.

넘버링 우리말 설명

좀 더 친절하게 각 넘버링에서 다루고 있는 내용을 우리말로 설명하였다.

대표문장

각 넘버링에는 5개의 대표문장이 수록되었다.

유사문장

5개의 대표문장에는 각각 유사한 문맥에서 사용될 수 있는 관련 문장을 2-3개 수록하였다.

다이알로그

각 대표문장에 어울리는 AB다이알로그를 통해서 현장감있게 문장을 이해할 수 있다.

Contents

Contents

Unit 2   나의 건강

3 가족과 주변상황

Contents

4 직장생활

Contents

취미생활

Contents

인터넷/SNS

Contents

자동차 등

Contents

Unit 8 스포츠

Unit 9 퇴직

Contents

Unit

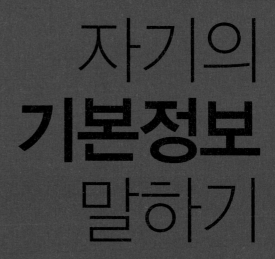

자기의
기본정보
말하기

001

Most people just call me Su-hyun

대부분 '수현'이라고 불러

초면일 때는 Hi. Nice to meet you. How are you? 등의 인사를 하면서 자신의 이름을 말한다. 이름(first name)만 말해도 되거나 혹은 성(last name)까지 함께 말한다.

01 Nice to meet you. I'm Chris Suh

만나서 반가워. 내 이름은 크리스 서야

- My name is Yeon-hwa Choi. How are you? 내 이름은 최연화야. 안녕하세요?
- Hi, I'm Man-jin, Mi-sue's brother. 안녕. 난 만진이라고 해. 미수의 오빠야.
- Hello, my name is David 안녕하세요, 데이빗이라고 합니다
- Hello, I am Mr. Brown. It's good to meet you.
  안녕하세요, 브라운이라고 합니다. 만나서 반갑습니다.

A: Hi, I think you must be new in our office. I'm Miss Stevens.
사무실 신입인 것 같군요. 전 미스 스티븐스예요.

B: Hello, I am Mr. Brown. It's good to meet you.
안녕하세요, 전 브라운이라고 합니다. 만나서 반갑습니다.

02 I'm Su-hyun Kim. Most people just call me Su-hyun

난 김수현이야. 대부분 '수현'이라고 불러

- Chris has told me so much about you. 크리스로부터 얘기 많이 들었습니다.
- It's nice to know you. 알게 되어서 반가워요.
- My name is Jonathan Keller, but please just call me John.
  이름은 조나단 켈러이지만 그냥 존이라고 부르세요.

A: My name is Jonathan Keller, but please just call me John.
이름은 조나단 켈러이지만 그냥 존이라고 부르세요.

B: It's a pleasure to meet you, John. Please call me Tammy.
만나서 반가워요, 존. 난 태미라고 불러요.

03 Hi, Shaun, my name is John
안녕, 션, 내 이름은 존이야

* I've been wanting to meet you. 만나뵙고 싶었습니다.
* I'd like to introduce myself. **My name is Peter.** 내 소개를 하죠. 피터라고 해요.
* **My name is Steve, it's nice to meet you.** 내 이름은 스티브야. 만나서 반가워.

A: I have seen you hanging around, but we were never introduced.
주변에서 봤는데 소개를 한 적이 없어.

B: Oh, really? My name is Steve, it's nice to meet you.
오, 정말? 내 이름은 스티브야. 만나서 반가워.

04 I don't think we've met before. My name is Paul
초면인 것 같은데요. 난 폴이라고 해요

* We've never met before. 우린 초면예요.
* Have we met? **I don't think I know you.** 우리 만난 적 있어요? 초면인 것 같은데요.
* I haven't met you before. **Are you new here?** 만난 적이 없는데요. 여기 처음예요?

A: I haven't met you before. Are you new here?
만난 적이 없는데요. 여기 처음예요?

B: Yeah, I just moved into town and don't know many people here.
예, 방금 이사와서 아는 사람이 많지 않아요.

05 May I ask[have] your name, please?
이름을 여쭤봐도 될까요?

* **This is my business card.** 제 명함입니다. (Here is my card)
* **Sorry, but I'm out of cards.** 명함이 떨어져서요.
* **Could you let us know your name?** 이름을 알 수 있을까요?

A: I have a reservation to stay at this hotel this week.
이번 주 이 호텔에 숙박이 예약되어 있어요.

B: I will check the reservation list. Could you let us know your name?
예약자 리스트를 확인해볼게요. 성함 좀 알려주실래요?

002

Jessica, are you busy as usual?

제시카, 여느 때처럼 바빠?

인사로는 보통 How are you?. How are you doing?. What's up? 등이 쓰이며 특히 아는 사람을 다시 만나서 반갑다고 할 때는 see 동사를 써서 Nice to see you again이라고 한다.

01 How are you, Mr. Smith?

스미스 씨, 안녕하세요?

- Hey, Mike, What's up? 마이크 , 안녕?
- What's new? 무슨 일 있어?
- John, Anything new? 존, 무슨 일 있어?
- I haven't seen you in a long time. How have you been?
  오랜만이네. 어떻게 지냈어?

A: I haven't seen you in a long time. How have you been?
   오랜간만야. 어떻게 지냈어?

B: I've been busy with my family. Did you know my wife gave birth to a daughter? 집안 일로 바빴어. 내 아내가 딸 출산한거 알고 있어?

02 How're you doing, Chris?

크리스, 안녕?

- Tim, how're you getting along? 팀. 어떻게 지내?
- Katie, how's everything going with you? 케이티, 별일 없지?
- How have things been going for you? 어떻게 지내고 있어?

A: We haven't crossed paths in a while. How have things been going for you? 한동안 보지 못했네. 어떻게 지내고 있어?

B: I've been having a hard time. I lost my job and now I'm broke.
   어려움을 겪고 있어. 실직해서 빈털터리야.

03 Nice to see you again, Ms. Brown
브라운 씨, 다시 만나 반가워요

- I'm happy to see you again. 다시 만나서 기뻐.
- Good to see you again. 다시 만나서 좋아.
- It's great to catch up with you again. 다시 만나게 돼서 아주 좋아.

A: I don't think we've seen each other since we attended high school.
고등학교 때 이후로 서로 만난 적이 없는 것 같아.

B: What a long time ago. It's great to catch up with you again.
참 오랜 전 일이네. 다시 만나게 되어서 아주 기뻐.

04 How's your family, Mike?
마이크, 가족들 잘 지내?

- We're all fine[well], thank you. 우리 모두 다 잘 지내, 고마워.
- Everyone's fine, thank you. 다들 잘 지내, 고마워.
- They are all doing well, I'm happy to say. 기쁘게 말하지만 다들 잘 지내고 있어.

A: How have your sisters and brothers been during the pandemic?
전염병이 도는데 너희 형제자매는 어떻게 지내?

B: They are all healthy and doing well, I'm happy to say.
다행이지만, 다들 건강히 지내고 있어.

05 Jessica, are you busy as usual?
제시카, 여느 때처럼 바빠?

- Not so much. 그렇게 바쁘지 않아.
- It's been a long time since the last time I saw you. 너 본지 정말 오랜간만이다.
- I haven't seen you for a long time. 오랫동안 만나지 못했네.
- It seems like it's been forever since we last met. 우리 만난지 아주 오래된 것 같아.

A: It seems like it's been forever since we last met. 우리 만난지 아주 오래된 것 같아.
B: You're right. It's been at least a decade since I saw you.
맞아. 한 10년은 된 것 같아.

003

We're on a first name basis

우리는 친한 사이야

성은 last name, family name, 이름은 first name, given name, 전체는 full name이라고 하며 어려운 사람이 아니면 보통 이름, 즉 first name으로 부르는 것이 일반적이다.

01 My name is Suh Sung-duck. Suh is my family name, and Sung-duck is my first name

내 이름은 서성덕이야. '서'는 성이고 '성덕'은 이름이야

- Which is your family name, **Suh or Hong?** '서'와 '홍' 중에서 어떤게 성이니?
- A given name which ends in '-ja' **is usually used by women.** '-자'로 끝나는 이름은 보통 여자야.
- **Is Kim** your given name or your family name? 김은 이름이야 아니면 성이야?

A: I'm confused. Is Kim your given name or your family name? 헷갈려. 김은 이름이야 성이야?

B: Kim is my family name, but I know Kim is often a woman's given name in the West. 김은 성이야 하지만 서양에서는 김이 종종 여성의 이름으로 쓰여.

02 What's your first name?

이름이 뭐예요?

- My friends call me **Hong.** 친구들은 나를 홍이라고 불러.
- **Excuse me,** is your name Sally? 실례지만, 이름이 샐리예요?
- What name **would you like to have us use for you?** 어떤 이름으로 불러주기를 바래요?

A: What name would you like to have us use for you? 어떤 이름으로 불러주기를 바래?

B: You might as well just call me Carl. Everyone else does. 칼이라고 불러도 돼. 다들 그렇게 불러.

03 We're on a first name basis
우리는 친한 사이야

- You can call me by **my first name**. 이름으로 불러.
- Just call me Sandy. **That's my first name.** 그냥 샌디라고 불러. 그게 내 이름이야.

A: Would you prefer that we call you Mrs. Platt, or Sandy?
플래트 부인 아니면 샌디 중 어떻게 불러드릴까요?

B: Just call me Sandy. That's my first name. 그냥 샌디라고 불러요. 내 이름에요.

04 My name, Chul-soo, is the most common male name in Korea
내 이름은 철수인데, 우리나라에거 가장 흔한 남자 이름이야

- Sung-hee is often mistaken for **a woman's name.** 성희는 종종 여자 이름으로 생각되어져.
- Choi is common family name in Korea. 최는 우리나라에서 흔한 성이야.
- My family name, 'Dong' is pretty rare in Korea. 내 성은 '동'인데 한국에서 드문 성이야.
- Kim is one of the oldest family names in Korea. 김은 한국에서 아주 오래된 성중의 하나야.

A: Why are there so many people named Choi working here?
여기 일하는 사람중에 최씨가 왜 그렇게 많은거야?

B: They are all Korean. Choi is common family name in Korea.
다들 한국인인데요. 최씨는 한국에서 흔한 성입니다.

05 What does your name mean?
너의 이름이 의미하는 것은 뭐야?

- My name, Suh Hong means a big seagull flying slow.
내 이름, 서홍은 커다란 갈매기가 천천히 난다는 의미야.
- Last names starting with Mac **mean they descended from a particular person.** 맥으로 시작하는 성은 어느 특정한 사람의 자손이라는 것을 의미해.

A: Many people from Britain and Ireland have names that start with Mac. 영국과 아일랜드 출신 중 많은 사람들이 맥으로 시작해.

B: Last names starting with Mac mean they descended from a particular person. 맥으로 시작하는 성은 어느 특정한 사람의 자손이라는 것을 의미해.

004

He is in his early thirties

걔는 30대 초반이야

My birthday is October 4th.처럼 구체적으로 생년월일을 말할 수도 있다. 그리고 ~십대 초[후]반이라고 할 때는 be one's early[late] ~를 써서 He is his early forties(40대 초반이야)라고 할 수 있다.

01 I was born in 2002
난 2002년도에 태어났어

- I was born on **November 07, 2002.** 난 2002년 11월 7일에 태어났어.
- I was born on **August 10, 2003,** 난 2003년 8월 10일에 태어났어
- **When were you born?** 언제 태어났어?
- **What's the date of your birth?** 너 생일은 언제야?

A: You don't seem very old. When were you born?
넌 나이들어보이지 않아. 언제 태어났어?

B: No, I'm not old. I was born on November 07, 2002.
그래, 난 젊어. 2002년 11월 7일에 태어났어.

02 My birthday is October 4th.[October fourth]
내 생일은 10월 4일이야

- **What's your age?** 나이가 어떻게 돼?
- My birthday falls on **Sunday this year.** 금년도 내 생일은 일요일이야.
- **The 18th of this month will be my twenty-fourth birthday.**
이번 달 18일이 내 24번째 생일이야.

A: The 18th of this month will be my twenty-fourth birthday.
이번 달 18일이 내 24번째 생일이야.

B: Happy birthday! Are you planning to have a big celebration?
생일축하해! 거하게 기념할거니?

03 I'm twenty-eight
난 28살이야

- I'm thirty-three **years old**. 난 서른 세살이야.
- I'm fifty six **years of age**. 난 나이가 56세이야.
- I am twenty-two **years old right now**. 난 지금 22세이야.

A: I thought you were still a teenager. 난 네가 아직 10대인 줄 알았어.

B: Not anymore. I am twenty-two years old right now.
이제 아니야. 난 지금 스물두살이야.

04 He is in his early thirties
걔는 30대 초반이야

- I'm **going to be** thirty next Monday. 난 다음주에 30세가 돼.
- I **turned** 41 **last week**. 지난주에 41세가 되었어.
- I'm **in my late twenties**, but I'm **pushing** 30. 이십대 후반으로 곧 30이 돼.

A: Have you had your thirtieth birthday yet? 너 30살이 되었어?

B: I'm in my late twenties, but I'm pushing 30. 이십대 후반으로 곧 30이 돼.

05 I'm three years older than her
난 걔보다 3살 더 많아

- My **age is top secret**. 내 나이는 일급비밀이야.
- He's only **a year older than** his wife. 걘 자기 아내보다 단지 한 살 많아.
- I was **born a few years before** my sister. 난 여동생보다 훨씬 일찍 태어났어.

A: You never told me that Helen was younger than you.
헬렌이 너보다 젊다는 것을 말한 적이 없어.

B: I was born a few years before my sister. 난 여동생보다 몇년 일찍 태어났어.

005

You're fairly good-looking

너 꽤 잘 생겼다

구체적으로 키가 몇 센티인지 몸무게 몇 킬로인지 말하는 법, 그리고 아울러 혈액형이 뭔지, 시력이 어떻게 되는지 말해본다.

01 I'm 175 centimeters tall

난 키가 175야

● How tall are you? 키가 어떻게 돼?(What's your height?)

● I'm about 5 feet, 5 inches tall. 키는 한 5피트 5인치야.

● I'm 170 centimeters, **that is**, about 5.5 feet tall. 내 키는 170cm인데 5.5 피트 정도 돼.

A: You look like a basketball player. How tall are you?
넌 농구선수같아. 키가 어떻게 돼?

B: I'm about 6 feet, 6 inches tall, but I don't play basketball.
6피트 6인치이지만 농구를 하지 않아.

02 I weigh 74 kilograms now

지금 74킬로 나가

● I have a pot belly. 나 배가 좀 나왔어.

● **My stomach** is getting fat. 뱃살이 점점 나오고 있어.

● How much do you weigh? 몸무게가 어떻게 돼?(What's your weight?)

A: My stomach is getting fat. I'm really out of shape.
뱃살이 나오고 있어. 몸매가 엉망이야.

B: You should stop eating fried foods every day.
넌 매일 먹는 튀김음식을 중단해야 돼.

03   I have type B blood
내 혈액형은 B형이야

- **My eyes** are getting weak, **so it's hard for me to read small print.**
  내 시력이 점점 약해져서 작은 글자는 읽기가 힘들어.

- **I can't see as well as I could when I was young.** 젊었을 때처럼 잘 읽을 수가 없어.

A: I haven't ever seen you wearing glasses before.
전에 너 안경쓴 모습을 보지 못했어.

B: My eyes are getting weak, so it's hard for me to read small print.
내 시력이 점점 약해져서 작은 글자는 읽기가 힘들어.

04   My eyesight for both my eyes is 20-20
내 시력은 양쪽 다 2.0이야

- **My vision isn't as good as it used to be.** 내 시력은 예전만 못해.

- **I'm right-handed.** 난 오른손잡이야.

- **I'm left-handed.** 난 왼손잡이야.

A: I've got to see an eye doctor. My vision isn't as good as it used to be. 안과의사 진료를 받아야 돼. 시력이 예전만 못해.

B: Yeah, it's best to get glasses if you can't see well.
잘 보이지 않으면 안경을 쓰는게 최고야.

05   You're fairly good-looking
너 꽤 잘 생겼다

- **He looks like Ashton Kutcher.** 걔는 애쉬튼 커쳐처럼 생겼어.

- **You look younger than me.** 너는 나보다 젊어보여.

- **He looks older than he is** 걔는 실제보다 나이가 들어보여.

- **You look young for your age.** 너는 나이에 비해 어려보여.

A: I'll be turning fifty next year. 나 내년에 50세에 들어서.

B: That is hard to believe. You look young for your age.
믿기지 않네. 넌 나이에 비해 어려보여.

006 I'm from Daegue

난 대구출신이야

이번에는 자신이 태어난 해, 태어난 고향으로 어디서 자랐는지 말해보고, 자신의 고향의 지리적 위치, 그리고 고향이 뭘로 유명한지 설명하는 법을 배워본다.

01 I was born in Seoul in 1992

난 1992년 서울에서 태어났어

- I was born in Ahnsung in Gyeunggi-do. 난 경기도 안성에서 태어났어.
- I was born in Seoul in 2006. 난 2006년 서울에서 태어났어.
- Where were you born? 어디서 태어났어?

A: I was born in Busan. Where were you born? 난 부산에서 태어났는데, 넌?
B: I was born in Canada, while my parents were working there.
난 캐나다, 부모님이 거기서 일하시다가.

02 I'm from Daegue

난 대구출신이야

- I'm from America, born and raised in New York.
난 미국출신인데 뉴욕에서 태어나서 자랐어.
- Seoul is my second hometown. 서울은 내 두번째 고향이야.
- I grew up in Daegue, but I moved here for university.
난 대구에서 자랐지만 대학 때문에 이리로 이사왔어.

A: I was raised in the suburbs of Mok-po. Where do you come from?
난 목포외곽에서 자랐는데 넌 어디 출신이야?
B: Hey, we were almost neighbors. I was raised nearby, in Gwang-ju.
야, 우리 거의 이웃이었네. 난 근처 광주에서 자랐어.

03 I lived there until the age of 18
난 18살까지 거기서 살았어

- I've lived there since **I was born.** 난 태어난 이래로 거기서 살았어.
- I left my hometown when **I was twelve.** 난 12살에 고향을 떠났어.
- When did you leave your hometown? 넌 언제 고향을 떠났어?

A: I left my hometown when I was twelve. My father got a job elsewhere. 난 12살에 고향을 떠났어. 아버지가 다른 곳에 직장을 가지셔서.

B: You must have been sad to leave all of your friends behind.
친구들을 뒤에 놔두고 떠나다니 아주 슬펐겠구나.

04 It's located about 30 kilometers from Gwang-ju
광주에서 한 30킬로 미터 지점에 있어

- It's about 50 miles from **New York.** 그곳은 뉴욕으로부터 약 50마일 떨어진 곳이야.
- It is around 11 miles to **the stadium.** 경기장까지는 약 11마일 떨어진 곳이야.
- **The university** is 4 kilometers from here. 그 대학은 여기서 4킬로미터 떨어진 곳에 있어.

A: Aren't we going to be late for the orientation?
오리엔테이션에 늦지 않을까?

B: Don't worry, the university is only 4 kilometers from here.
걱정마. 그 대학교까지는 여기서 4킬로 남았어.

05 My hometown is famous for its beautiful scenery
내 고향은 멋진 풍경으로 유명해

- **Apples** are a specialty[special product] of **my hometown.**
사과는 내 고향의 특산물이야.
- I miss my hometown friends. 난 고향친구들이 그리워.
- What's your birthplace like? 너의 고향은 어떤 곳이니?

A: I miss my hometown friends. I haven't been there in a while.
고향친구들을 보고 싶어. 오랫동안 가보지 않았거든.

B: Should we go for a visit next weekend? 다음 주말에 가볼까?

주소 및 연락처

007 I live in Donam-dong, Seoul

난 서울 돈암동에 살아

역시 자신의 정보에 대해 말하는 것으로 지금 자기가 사는 지역을 대강 동이나 구로 말하거나 혹은 구체적인 주소를 말하는 것과 자신의 연락처를 줄 때는 숫자를 어떻게 말하는지 잘 귀기울여 들어본다.

01 I live in Donam-dong, Seoul

난 서울 돈암동에 살아

- I live in **Bundang in the surburbs of Seoul**. 난 서울의 외곽인 분당에 살고 있어.

- I live in **Gangnam**. 난 강남에 살아.

- I live with **my family in Suhhyun-dong. You've probably heard about that area, right?** 난 식구들하고 서현동에 살아. 그 동네에 관해서 들어봤을거야. 그렇지?

A: You never told me where your apartment was.
네 아파트가 어디인지 말하지 않았어.

B: I'm living over in Jong-am Dong, near Korea University. Do you know that neighborhood? 고려대학교 근처의 종암동에 살아. 그 동네 알아?

02 My address is 590 Backhyun-dong, Bundang-gu, Song-nam City

내 주소는 성남시 분당구 백현동 5900이야

- My email address is **sillage@nate.com**. 내 이메일 주소는 sillage@nate.com이야.

- What's your e-mail address? 이메일 주소가 어떻게 돼?

- Let's keep in touch. My e-mail address is syduck2@nate.com.
계속 연락하고 지내자. 내 이메일 주소는 syduck2@nate.com이야.

A: Let's keep in touch. My e-mail address is syduck2@nate.com.
연락하고 지내자. 내 이멜주소는 syduck2@nate.com이야.

B: That sounds good. I'll send you an e-mail next week.
좋아, 다음주에 이멜을 보낼게.

04 My house is in a residential area
내 집은 주거지역에 있어

- My house is in **a commercial area[district]**. 내 집은 상업지구에 있어.

- What's your new house like? 네 새 집은 어때?

- What[Which] is the nearest station? 가장 가까운 역이 어디야?

A: It's easiest to get to the venue using the subway.
전철을 이용하면 행사장에 가장 쉽게 올 수 있어.

B: What is the nearest station? I'll look it up online.
가장 가까운 역은 어디야. 인터넷에서 찾아볼게.

04 It's about 500 meters to the station
역까지 약 500미터 거리야

- It takes ten minutes to **get to the station on foot**. 걸어서 역까지 10분걸려.

- How long does it take to **get to your house from the station?**
역에서 집까지 가는데 얼마 걸려?

- How far is it from **the station to your house?** 역에서 집까지 얼마나 멀어?

A: How far is it from the station to your house? 역에서 집까지 얼마나 멀어?
B: It's not far at all. It only takes me five minutes to walk there.
그렇게 멀지 않아. 걸어서 5분밖에 안걸려.

05 My phone number is 010-3794-5450
내 핸드폰번호는 010-3794-54500|야

- May I have **his cell phone number?** 그 사람 핸드폰번호 좀 알 수 있을까요?

- Can I have **your phone number?** 전화번호 좀 알려줄래?

- Could you tell me **your phone number?** 네 전화번호 좀 알려줄래?

A: I'll call you later. Could you tell me your phone number?
나중에 전화할게. 전번 좀 알려줘.

B: No problem. My cell number is 607-339-5209.
그래. 내 핸드폰번호는 607-339-52090|야.

Unit 01 자기의 기본정보 말하기 | 37 |

008

You can use T-map or Naver map to find my house

티맵이나 네이버맵을 이용해서 우리집을 찾아

집을 말했으면 이번에는 집이나 사무실을 찾아오는 방법을 말해본다. 지하철이나 버스의 경우, …에서 내려라(Get off at~), …에서 좌회전해(Turn left at~)를 쓰고 모르면 그냥 요즘 유행하는 티맵 등을 이용해서 찾아오라고 하면 된다.

01 Get off at Jung-ja Station on the Bundang line
분당라인 정자역에서 내려

- Get on bus No.18. 18번 버스를 타.
- Take the 4th exit of the station. 역의 4번출구로 나가.
- Take the subway for one stop and get off at Yoksam Station.
  지하철로 한 정거장 가서 역삼역에서 내려요.

A: Should I take the subway to the art gallery? 미술관가는데 지하철을 타야되나요?
B: No, it's very close. You can just catch a cab. 아뇨, 아주 가까워요. 그냥 택시타세요.

02 Walk along the street until you see a coffee shop
커피숍이 보일 때까지 쭉 걸어가세요

- Go straight until you come to the post office. 우체국에 갈 때까지 직진해서 가세요.
- Go about 100 meters from the convenience store. 편의점으로부터 약 100미터 가세요.
- Walk Sara home so that you are sure that she got there safely.
  새라가 안전하게 집에 가도록 확실히 하기 위해 집까지 걸어서 데려다 줘.

A: Sara told me that her ex-boyfriend has been stalking her.
   새라가 그러는데 전남친이 자신을 스토킹하고 있대.
B: Walk Sara home so that you are sure that she got there safely.
   새라가 안전하게 집에 가도록 확실히 하기 위해 집까지 걸어서 데려다 줘.

03 Turn left at the fourth traffic light[signal]
4번째 교통신호등에서 좌회전하세요

- Cross the intersection. 교차로를 건너가세요.
- After passing by a convenience store, you'll see a dry cleaner's on the right. 편의점을 지나고 나면 오른편에 세탁소가 보일겁니다.
- Just go three blocks and turn left. 세 블럭 내려가서 왼쪽으로 돌기만 하면 돼요.

A: Is there a shop where I can get my cell phone repaired?
내 핸드폰을 수리할 수 있는 가게가 있나요?

B: Just go three blocks and turn left. You'll see the shop right there.
3블럭 간 다음 좌회전하세요. 바로 거기에 가게가 보일거예요.

04 You can't miss it
바로 보일거예요

- You can find it easily. 쉽게 찾을 수 있을거예요.
- If you get lost, please call me. 길을 잃으면 나한테 전화해.
- Where are you calling from? 어디서 전화하는거야?

A: There's no way that I can find the immigration office.
이민국 사무소 전혀 못찾겠어.

B: If you get lost, please call me. I'll help you out.
길을 잃으면 전화해. 내가 도와줄게.

05 You can use T-map or Naver map to find my house
티맵이나 네이버맵을 이용해서 우리집을 찾아

- Many people use a GPS if they can't find what they are looking for.
많은 사람들이 찾는 것을 찾지 못할 때 GPS를 이용해.
- We can look online for a quicker route. 더 빠른 길을 찾기 위해 우린 인터넷을 볼 수 있어.

A: How can you find which roads we need to drive on?
우리가 어느 도로로 가야 되는지 어떻게 찾을 수 있어?

B: Many people use a GPS if they can't find what they are looking for.
많은 사람들이 찾는 것을 찾지 못할 때 GPS를 이용해.

009

I live on the second floor of an apartment building

난 아파트 2층에서 살고 있어

집이 아파트인지 주택인지도 말해보고 방이 몇 개인지 말하는 법도 알아본다. 또한 자가가 아니라 전세일 때 그리고 또 월세일 때의 말하는 법도 함께 익혀본다.

01 I live in an apartment
난 아파트에서 살고 있어

- I live in **a dorm.** 난 기숙사에서 살고 있어.
- I live in **a house.** 난 주택에서 살고 있어.
- I live in **an officetel.** 난 오피스텔에서 살고 있어.
- I have lived there **for five years.** 거기서 5년째 살고 있어.

A: This is my third year attending the local university.
올해가 지방 대학에 다닌지 3년이 돼.

B: Do you live in the dorm? Or do you live at home with your parents?
기숙사에서 사니 아니면 집에서 부모님과 함께 사니?

02 I live on the second floor of an apartment building
난 아파트 2층에서 살고 있어

- It's 15-story **apartment house.** 그건 15층차리 아파트야.
- It was built **23 years ago.** 그건 지은지 23년 됐어.
- **Which floor do you live on?** 넌 몇층에 살고 있니?

A: How large is the building your mom and dad live in?
너의 부모님이 살고 있는 아파트는 얼마나 커?

B: There are about 60 families in the apartment building, so it's pretty big. 약 60가구가 살고 있으니 무척 크지.

03 My house has three rooms
집에는 방이 3개야

- There are four rooms **in my house.** 우리 집에는 방이 4개야.
- How many rooms **does your house have?** 너희 집에는 방이 몇 개야?
- I'd like to buy a house **with at least seven rooms.**
  난 적어도 방이 7개 되는 집을 사고 싶어.

A: You want to find a house that is big enough for your family?
가족이 살기에 충분히 큰 집을 원한다고?

B: I'd like to buy a house with at least seven rooms.
난 적어도 방이 7개 되는 집을 사고 싶어.

04 You'll need to leave a security deposit to rent this house 이 집을 렌트하려면 전세금을 맡겨야 돼

- I'm going to rent a larger room. 더 큰 방을 얻으려고 해.
- A student only needs to rent a small space. 학생이라면 작은 집을 렌트하면 돼.
- They decided to rent an apartment together. 걔들은 함께 아파트를 렌트하기로 했어.

A: They decided to rent an apartment together, but it didn't work out.
걔들은 함께 아파트를 렌트하려고 했지만 잘 안됐어.

B: It's difficult to live together with people, even if they are your
friends. 비록 친구라 할지라도 함께 사는 것은 힘들어.

05 I pay 1,000,000 won a month for rent
월세로 100만원을 내고 있어

- I rent a room for **500,000 won a month.** 한달 월세 50만원짜리 방을 렌트했어.
- I pay 700,000 won **a month in rent.** 월세로 한달에 70만원을 내고 있어.
- How much is your rent? 월세가 얼마야?

A: How much is your rent? 월세가 얼마나 돼?
B: I pay 1,000,000 won a month for rent. 월세로 100만원 내고 있어.

010

She's a good mixer
개는 매우 잘 어울려

자신의 성격이 어떠한 지 네번에 걸쳐 알아본다. 이번에는 그 처음으로 easy-going, a good mixer, outgoing, 그리고 reserved의 단어들에 주목해본다.

01 I'm an easy-going person
난 성격이 좋은 사람야

- He's very friendly. 걔는 매우 우호적이야.
- She's kind to **everyone she meets**. 걘 누구에게나 친절해.
- Larry is a pleasant person. 래리는 유쾌한 사람이야.

>
>
> A: I think Sheila and Larry make a nice couple.
> 쉴라와 래리는 좋은 커플이 될 것 같아.
>
> B: Larry is a pleasant person. He'll be a good husband.
> 래리는 성격이 유쾌해서 좋은 남편이 될거야.

02 He's easy to get along with
걔는 어울리기 쉬운 친구야

- He's a warm-hearted guy. 걘 맘이 따뜻한 친구야.
- She's always willing to help out. 걔는 항상 도와줄려고 해.
- He's easy going and rarely gets upset about anything.
걘 성격이 좋아서 거의 화를 내지 않아.

>
>
> A: I'm always impressed with how calm your boss is.
> 난 네 사장이 참 차분한 것이 인상적이야.
>
> B: He's easy going and rarely gets upset about anything.
> 성격이 좋아서 거의 화를 내지 않아.

03 She's a good mixer
걔는 매우 잘 어울려

- You're so generous. 너는 정말 너그러워.

- He just can't turn down a request. 걔는 단지 거절을 못하는거야.

- He's a thoughtful person who has many friends. 걘 친구가 많은 사려깊은 사람이야.

A: People say that Kara's boyfriend is really nice.
사람들이 그러는데 카라는 남친은 매우 착하다고 해.

B: I like him. He's a thoughtful person who has many friends.
난 걔가 좋아. 친구가 많은 사려깊은 사람이야.

04 He's the outgoing type
걔는 외향적이야

- He's a two-faced person. 걘 성격이 이중적이야.

- He's a dishonest old man. 그는 부정직한 노인네야.

A: What do you think about the political candidate?
그 정치 후보자에 대해 어떻게 생각해?

B: He's a dishonest old man. No one trusts him.
부정직한 노인네야. 아무도 신뢰하지 않아.

05 He's so reserved
걔는 매우 내성적이야

- He's shy. 걔는 수줍어 해.

- You're too timid. 너는 너무 소극적이야.

- She's an introvert who is uncomfortable around people.
걘 내향적이어서 주변에 사람들이 있을 때 불편해 해.

A: Why doesn't your sister ever join us when we go out?
왜 내 누이는 우리가 나가 놀 때 함께 하지 않는거야?

B: She's an introvert who is uncomfortable around people.
내향적이어서 주변에 사람들이 있을 때 불편해 해.

자기 성격 2

011 She's a smooth talker

쟤는 정말 말을 잘해

두번째 자신의 성격을 말하는 공간으로 현명할 때는 wise, 쓸데없이 완벽주의자일 때는 perfectionist, 대담할 때는 have a lot of nerve 그리고 센스가 빠를 때는 catch on quickly 등이 쓰이는 점을 기억해둔다.

01 He's a wise guy
쟤는 현명한 친구야

● He's wise for **his age**. 쟤는 나이에 비해 현명해.

● She's very sharp. 쟤는 매우 날카로워.

● He's got a good head **on his shoulders**. 쟤는 분별력이 있는 사람이야.

A: Brian's very smart. He's got a good head on his shoulders.
브라이언은 매우 현명해. 분별력이 있는 사람이야.

B: I know. He has the top grades in his class. 알아. 반에서 성적이 상위권이야.

02 He's a perfectionist
쟤는 진짜 완벽주의야

● He has good judgment. 쟤는 분별력이 좋아.

● He's a real go-getter. 쟤는 정말 수완가야.

● He's very self motivated. 쟤는 매우 자율적인 사람이야.

A: Our boss started his own company when he was in his twenties.
우리 사장은 20대에 사업을 시작했어.

B: He's very self motivated. That's why he's rich.
스스로 동기를 부여하는 사람이구나. 그래서 부자인거야.

03 You have a lot of nerve
너는 아주 대담해

- **He's got a lot of nerve.** 걔는 아주 대담해.
- **You're** very brave. 넌 매우 용감해.
- **You're** bold. 너는 대담해.

A: I grabbed the snake and threw it off into the bushes.
난 뱀을 잡아서 숲속으로 집어던졌어.

B: You're very brave. I never would have done that.
너 용감하구나. 나라면 절대로 그렇게 못했을거야.

04 She's a smooth talker
쟤는 정말 말을 잘해

- **He's** flexible in his thinking. 걔는 생각이 유연해.
- **He is** good humored. 걔는 유머감각이 좋아.
- **He's** a very modest man. 걔는 점잖은 사람야.

A: Bill never brags about how much money he has made.
빌은 자기가 번 돈을 자랑하지 않아.

B: He's a very modest man. He doesn't like attention.
매우 점잖은 사람으로 관심끄는 것을 싫어해.

05 He catches on quickly
걔는 빨리 알아들어

- **Once he makes a promise, he** never goes back on his word.
걔는 약속을 일단 하면 절대로 말을 바꾸지 않아.
- **He's not the type to** break his word. 약속을 깨는 타입은 아니야.

A: I didn't like Carl at first, but I've grown to respect him.
처음엔 칼을 싫어했지만 걔를 존경하게 되었어.

B: He has a rough manner, but deep down, he's a nice guy.
걔는 매너가 좀 거칠지만 실은 괜찮은 녀석이야.

012

He's very outspoken

걔는 말을 거침없이 해

계속해서 사람이 이기적일 때는 selfish, self-centered, 거침없이 말할 때는 outspoken, 민감할 때는 sensitive, 멍청할 때는 거의 우리말화된 a loser를 이용해서 쓰면 된다.

01 He's selfish
걔는 이기적이야

● **He's self-centered.** 걔는 자기 중심적이야.

● **He only cares about himself.** 걔는 오직 자기만 생각해.

● **He's stingy.** 걔는 인색해.

A: Why didn't he help his family when they needed it?
가족이 도움을 필요로 할 때 왜 걘 돕지 않았어?

B: He only cares about himself. He's just very selfish.
걘 자기 생각만 해. 매우 이기적이야.

02 He's very outspoken
걔는 말을 거침없이 해

● **He's sarcastic.** 걔는 냉소적이야.

● **He's talkative.** 걔는 수다쟁이야.

● **He's very offensive.** 걔는 매우 공격적이야.

A: He's very offensive. I don't think anyone likes him.
걘 매우 공격적이야. 걜 좋아하는 사람이 아무도 없을 것 같아.

B: I don't think he knows he is being rude. 걘 자신이 무례하다는 것을 모르는 것 같아.

He isn't so smart
개는 똑똑하지가 않아

- **He** has poor judgment. 개는 분별력이 없어.

- **He's** simpleminded. 개는 단순해.

- **His** best days are behind **him**. 그 사람 좋은 시절은 다 갔어.

A: That actor has gotten old. His best days are behind him.
그 배우는 나이가 들었어. 좋은 시절은 다 갔어.

B: Yeah, it has been years since he was in a popular movie.
그래. 인기있는 영화에 나온지 꽤 오래됐어.

You're (such) a loser
너는 한심한 놈이야

- **He's** a loser. 개 골통야.

- **You are** not so great. 그렇게 잘난 것도 없으면서.

- **You really** suck. 넌 정말 밥맛이다.

A: I can't repay any of the money that you loaned me.
네가 빌려준 돈 일푼도 갚을 수가 없어.

B: You really suck! You promised me you would pay it back!
밥맛이야! 갚겠다고 약속했잖아!

She's so sensitive
개는 매우 민감해

- **She** shows her feelings easily. 개는 쉽게 자기 감정을 노출해.

- **He** loses his temper quickly. 개는 쉽사리 성질을 부려.

- **He** has a bad[short] temper. 개는 성질이 못됐어.

A: I'm scared of your dad. He has a short temper.
난 네 아빠가 무서워. 성격이 벼락같아.

B: I know. I try to avoid him when he is getting upset.
알아. 난 아빠가 화났을 때는 마주치지 않으려고 해.

013

One of my strong points is that I'm cautious

내 강점중의 하나는 신중하다는거야

사교적일 때는 sociable, 낙천적일 때는 optimistic, 수동적일 때는 passive, 그리고 신중할 때는 cautious란 단어를 사용한다. 또한 ~ person이라는 표현형태인 morning person, dog person 등에 대해 알아본다.

01 I'm a sociable person
난 사교적이야

- **I'm patient.** 참을성이 있는 사람이야.
- **I'm optimistic.** 난 낙천적이야.
- **I'm pessimistic.** 난 부정적이야.

A: Why are you always complaining about everything?
넌 왜 항상 매사에 불평인거야?

B: I'm pessimistic, and I tend to see the negative side of things.
난 부정적이어서 매사에 부정적인 면을 보는 성향이 있어.

02 I'm too passive
난 너무 수동적이야

- **Being passive is one of my weak points.** 수동적인게 내 약점중 하나야.
- **I've become quite conservative lately.** 최근 내가 아주 보수적으로 되었어.
- **She is lackadaisical and can never make good decisions.**
걔 부주의해서 제대로 된 결정을 내리지 못해.

A: You need to take some risks or you will waste your life.
넌 모험을 좀 해야지 아니면 인생을 낭비하게 될거야.

B: I'm afraid of risks. Being passive is one of my weak points.
난 위험을 무서워 해. 수동적인게 내 약점중의 하나야.

03
One of my strong points is that I'm cautious
내 강점중의 하나는 신중하다는거야

- I really like jokes **very much**. 정말 조크를 아주 좋아해.
- She lacks seriousness. 걘 진지함이 결여되어 있어.
- She's always criticizing others. 걘 항상 다른 사람을 비난해.

A: Sam drives me nuts. She's always criticizing others.
샘 때문에 내가 미쳐. 항상 다른 사람을 비난해.

B: I know. It's very hard to listen to her bitching about everything.
알아. 걔가 매사에 불평하는 것을 듣는게 괴롭지.

04
I rarely sleep before 3am because I'm a night person
난 야행성이어서 새벽 3시전에는 거의 잠을 자지 않아

- She's a morning person **who gets up early**. 걘 일찍 일어나는 아침형 인간이야.
- He's half awake **in the morning**. 걘 아침에는 비몽사몽이야.
- Mom has always been an early riser. 엄마는 항상 일찍 일어나는 사람이야.

A: It's 5am. Is your mom downstairs already?
새벽 5시인데 네 엄마는 벌써 아래층에 있는거야?

B: Yeah. Mom has always been an early riser.
그래. 엄마는 항상 일찍 일어나는 사람이야.

05
Cats are OK, but honestly, I have always been a dog person
고양이도 괜찮지만, 솔직히 말해서 난 언제나 개를 좋아해

- He seems like a mamma's boy. 걘 마마보이처럼 보여.
- He acts like a woman. 걘 여자처럼 행동해.
- She always looks lonely. 걘 항상 외로워보여.

A: Jerry is a wimp. He seems like a mamma's boy.
제리는 약골이야. 마마보이처럼 보여.

B: I have heard that he calls his mother whenever he has problems.
걘 문제있을 때마다 엄마한테 전화한다는 얘기를 들었어.

자신의 신조

014

I like the slogan, "Just do it"

난 "그냥 해봐"라는 슬로건을 좋아해

자신의 삶의 원칙이나 신조 등에 말하는 법이다. 유명한 Seize the day. Just do it 등을 인용해서 말하거나 아니면 …가 중요하다. …하는 것은 예의가 아니다라고 하면 서 자신의 원칙을 언급할 수 있다.

01 My favorite saying is "Seize the day!"
내가 좋아하는 말은 "현재를 즐겨라!"야

- My teacher used to say "I think, therefore I am."
  선생님은 예전에 "난 생각한다. 고로 존재한다"라는 말씀을 하셨어.

- Hunger is like a sauce that makes everything taste good.
  허기는 모든 것을 맛있게 해주는 양념같은거야.

A: You have eaten a huge amount of food tonight. 너 오늘 저녁 정말 많이 먹는다.
B: I'm starving. Hunger is like a sauce that makes everything taste good. 배고팠어. 허기는 모든 것을 맛있게 해주는 양념같은거야.

02 I like the slogan, "Just do it"
난 "그냥 해봐"라는 슬로건을 좋아해

- Please tell me what your principles are. 너의 원칙이 뭔지 말해봐.

- How would you describe your life's philosophy? 네 인생철학이 뭔지 말해볼래?

- What creed guides you in your life? 네 인생을 이끄는 신념은 뭐야?

A: How would you describe your life's philosophy?
   네 인생철학이 뭔지 말해볼래?

B: I try to work hard, be happy, and not hurt anyone.
   열심히 일하고 즐겁게 살고, 그리고 남에게 피해를 끼치지 않으려는거야.

03 "Get real" is my motto
"현실을 직시하라"가 내 모토야

- What's the most important thing for you? 네게 가장 중요한 것은 뭐야?

- I tell people that too much free time is bad for the soul.
  난 사람들에게 너무 한가한 시간이 많으면 영혼에 좋지 않다고 말해.

- Time is money, so you'd better hurry up. 시간은 돈이야. 그러니 너 서둘러야 돼.

A: I have had to delay finishing the business report.
비즈니스 레포트 마무리하는 것을 늦춰야했어.

B: Time is money, so you'd better hurry up. 시간은 돈이야. 그러니 너 서둘러야 돼.

04 It's important to be punctual
시간을 지키는 게 중요해

- It's my principle to enjoy everything. 모든 것을 즐기자는게 내 신조야.

- It's my principle to get along well with others. 다른 사람들과 잘 지내자는게 내 신조야.

- Keeping someone waiting is against my principles. 사람기다리게 하는건 내 신조가 아냐.

A: You have a reputation for always being on time. 넌 시간 잘 지키는 것으로 평판있어.

B: Keeping someone waiting is against my principles.
사람을 기다리게 하는건 내 신조가 아냐.

05 I think it's impolite to use cell phones on trains
열차에서 핸드폰을 하는 것은 예의가 아닌 것 같아

- I make it a point to live comfortably. 맘 편안하게 살기로 했어.

- I'm sure having good health is the most important thing.
  건강한 것이 가장 중요한 것이라는게 확실해.

- You should have a good job before you get married. 결혼전에 좋은 직장을 가져야 돼.

A: Some people are very rich, but they get cancer and die.
어떤 사람들은 무척 부유하지만, 암에 걸려 죽기도 해.

B: I'm sure having good health is the most important thing.
건강한 것이 가장 중요한 것이라는게 확실해.

015 자고 일어나기

I usually go to bed late

난 보통 늦게 잠자리에 들어

늦게 잘 때는 go to bed late, work up late, stay up late 등을 사용하고 늦잠 자다는 wake up late, sleep in, 반면 일찍 일어나다는 get up early라는 표현을 사용하면 된다.

01 I usually go to bed late
난 보통 늦게 잠자리에 들어

- **How come you are going to bed early tonight?** 오늘 밤에 왜 일찍 자려는거야?
- **I went to bed at 10:00.** 난 10시에 잤어.
- **I didn't go to bed last night.** 간밤에 잠을 못잤어.
- **I hate to get out of bed.** 난 일어나는게 싫어.

A: You look like shit. What happened to you? 너 몰골이 왜 그래. 무슨 일이야?
B: I didn't go to bed last night. I stayed up drinking.
지난 밤에 잠을 못잤어. 자지않고 술을 마셨어.

02 I gotta go and get some sleep
가서 잠 좀 자야겠어

- **You look sleepy today.** 너 오늘 피곤해 보여.
- **I always get enough sleep.** 난 항상 충분한 수면을 취해.
- **I didn't get much sleep.** 잠을 많이 못 잤어.

A: Scientists say you should sleep 7-8 hours a night.
과학자들이 그러는데 하루에 7시간내지 8시간은 자야 된대.
B: I always get enough sleep. It's the key to a long life.
난 항상 잠을 충분히 자. 그게 장수의 비결이야.

03
Even though she woke up late, she caught her bus on time 걘 늦게 일어났지만, 버스를 늦지 않게 탔어

- I wanted to sleep in tomorrow. 내일은 늦잠 좀 자려고 했단 말야.
- I hope I didn't wake you up this morning. 아침 잠을 깨운 게 아니었으면 싶은데.
- I plan to lie in bed until noon. 정오까지 침대에 누워있을거야.

A: My exams are finished. I plan to lie in bed until noon.
시험이 끝났어. 정오까지 침대에 누워있을거야.

B: Don't you want to go outside for a while? 잠시 밖에 나가고 싶지 않아?

04
Do you need to get up early tomorrow morning?
내일 아침 일찍 일어나야 돼?

- Set the alarm for 6 am. 6시로 알람을 맞춰.
- I thought I told you to go to bed. 가서 자라고 말한 것 같은데.
- I'll call to wake you up around 8 am. 아침 8시에 전화해서 널 깨울게.

A: I have a feeling I might oversleep and miss my flight.
늦잠자서 비행기를 놓칠 것 같아.

B: I'll call to wake you up around 8am. 아침 8시에 전화해서 널 깨울게.

05
My friends like to stay up late on the weekends
내 친구들은 주말마다 밤늦게까지 자지 않는 것을 좋아해

- I think I will stay up all night, instead. 대신 그냥 밤을 꼬박 새야겠어.
- We stayed up talking until the sun came up.
우리는 해가 뜰 때까지 안자고 얘기를 했어.
- I'm having trouble sleeping at night, lately. 요즘, 밤에 잠을 자는데 애를 먹고 있어.

A: How was the camping trip you went on? 갔던 캠핑여행 어땠어?
B: Great. We stayed up talking until the sun came up.
아주 좋았어. 우리는 해가 뜰 때까지 안자고 얘기를 했어.

016

It's time to eat breakfast

아침먹을 시간이야

아침, 점심, 그리고 저녁식사를 말할 때는 관사없이 have+식사라고 쓴다는 점을 유의
해둔다. 그리고 생리적인 현상에서 소변은 number 1, 대변은 number 2로 쓴다는
것도 재미삼아 알아둔다.

01 Are you ready for breakfast?
아침먹을 준비됐어?

- It's time to eat breakfast. 아침먹을 시간이야.
- Would you like to have breakfast together? 함께 아침을 먹을래?
- You'll have to wait until I finish my breakfast. 내가 아침 다 먹을 때까지 넌 기다려야 돼.

A: It's Sunday morning. Let's go for a walk in the park.
일요일 아침이야. 공원에 산책하러 가자.

B: You'll have to wait until I finish my breakfast.
내가 아침 다 먹을 때까지 넌 기다려야 돼.

02 Some of us are going out for lunch
우리들 중 일부는 점심먹으러 외출할거야

- He just stepped out for lunch. 걘 점심먹으러 나갔어.
- I'd be pleased if you could join us for dinner. 우리와 함께 저녁을 먹을 수 있으면 좋겠어.
- What's for dinner tonight? 저녁식사 메뉴가 뭐지?
- I want to take you out to dinner tomorrow night.
내일 저녁 널 데리고 나가 저녁을 먹고 싶어.

A: I want to take you out to dinner tomorrow night.
내일 저녁 널 데리고 나가 저녁을 먹고 싶어.

B: I can't do it. I already have other plans. 나 안돼. 다른 계획이 이미 있어.

03 Where's the toilet? I need to do number 2
화장실이 어디야? 대변을 봐야 돼

- Excuse me for a minute, I have to take a leak. 잠깐 실례, 소변을 봐야 돼.

- I gotta pee, and I can't hold it in any longer. 오줌싸야 돼. 더 이상 참지 못하겠어.

A: You drank three cups of coffee this morning. 너 오늘 아침에 커피 3잔을 마셨어.
B: Yeah. Excuse me for a minute, I have to take a leak.
그래. 잠깐 실례, 소변을 봐야 돼.

04 It looks like you never wash yourself
너 전혀 안 씻는 것 같아

- Make sure you wash your face before going to bed.
자기 전에 세수하는거 확실히 해.

- I always wash my hands to get rid of germs. 난 세균을 없애려고 항상 손을 씻어.

A: I always wash my hands to get rid of germs.
난 세균을 없애려고 항상 손을 씻어.

B: Good idea. There are a lot of germs that can make us sick.
좋은 생각이야. 많은 세균들이 우리를 병들게 하지.

05 Let me help you finish washing the dishes
설거지 도와줄게

- She does the dishes every night. 걘 매일 저녁 설거지를 해.

- I can wash the dishes in a few minutes. 난 금방 설거지를 할 수 있어.

- I'll help you finish washing the dishes if you like.
원한다면 설거지 마무리하는 것 도와줄게.

A: Oh dear, this place is a mess and I have no time to clean up.
이런. 여기가 엉망인데 치울 시간이 없네.

B: No problem. I can wash the dishes in a few minutes.
걱정마. 내가 설거지를 금방 할 수 있어.

017

아침에 일어나서 2

Can you help me get dressed?

옷 입는 거 좀 도와줄래?

옷을 입는 것은 get dressed, 반대로 옷을 벗다는 get undressed가 많이 쓰이며, 양말이나 신발을 당겨 신을 때는 pull on, 그리고 셔츠를 바지 속에 넣을 때는 tuck your shirt into~라고 쓰인다는 점을 기억해둔다.

01 Can you help me get dressed?
옷 입는 거 좀 도와줄래?

● It's time to get dressed **and go to school.** 옷입고 학교에 갈 시간이야.

● You should **put on a sweater.** 너 스웨터를 입어라.

● I need to tie my necktie **before we go.** 나가기 전에 넥타이를 매야 돼.

A: Is everyone ready to go to the wedding? 다들 결혼식장에 갈 준비됐어?
B: Not yet. I need to tie my necktie before we go.
아직. 나가기 전에 넥타이를 매야 돼.

02 I put on too much make-up
화장을 너무 많이 했어

● Doris takes a long time to put on her make-up.
도리스는 화장을 하는데 많은 시간이 걸려.

● She uses make-up **to hide her blemishes.** 걘 잡티를 감추기 위해 화장을 해.

● What brand of make-up **do you use?** 넌 어느 브랜드 화장품을 써?

A: She uses make-up to hide her blemishes. 걘 잡티를 감추기 위해 화장을 해.
B: I still think she's the most attractive woman here.
그래도 걔가 여기서는 가장 매력적이라고 생각해.

03 Let me pull on my shoes
잠깐만, 내 신발을 좀 당겨 신을게

- Pull on some boots **because it's snowing outside**. 밖에 눈이 오니까 부츠를 당겨 신어.
- I'll pull on some shoes **when we leave.** 우리가 나갈 때 신발을 당겨 신을게.

A: Have you checked to see what the weather is? 날씨가 어떤지 확인해봤어?
B: Pull on some boots because it's snowing outside.
밖에 눈이 오니까 부츠를 당겨 신어.

04 Tuck your shirt into your pants before going out
나가기 전에 셔츠를 바지 속에 집어 넣어

- Tuck your hair into **your hat.** 머리를 모자안으로 밀어넣어.
- Tuck some money into **your wallet for later.** 나중을 대비해서 돈을 좀 지갑에 집어 넣어.
- Tuck these papers into **that folder.** 이 서류들은 저 폴더에 집어 넣어.

A: I have a feeling we'll be going to some clubs tonight.
우리가 오늘밤 클럽에 갈 것 같아.
B: Tuck some money into your wallet for later.
나중을 대비해서 돈을 좀 지갑에 집어 넣어.

05 She brushes her teeth twice a day
걘 하루에 두 번 양치질을 해

- I forgot to brush my teeth **last night.** 난 지난밤에 깜박 잊고 양치질을 안했어.
- **When he doesn't brush his hair, it's messy.** 걘 머리를 빗지 않으면, 머리가 엉망이야.
- **You better fix your hair before pictures are taken.** 사진을 찍기 전에 머리를 손봐라.

A: You better fix your hair before pictures are taken.
사진을 찍기 전에 머리를 손봐라.
B: That's a good idea. Can I borrow a comb? 좋은 생각이야. 빗 좀 빌려줄테야?

식사하기 1

018

I like meat better than fish

난 생선보다 고기를 좋아해

식성에 관한 표현들로 다른 나라 음식을 좋아한다고 할 때, 그리고 natural foods나 spicy foods를 좋아하거나 싫어하는 것을 말해본다. 그리고 음식을 가리지 않을 때, 즉 음식에 진심일 때 어떻게 말하는 지도 알아둔다.

01 I like Mexican food very much
난 멕시코 음식을 아주 좋아해

- **Many models** eat Japanese food **to stay thin.**
  많은 모델들은 날씬함을 유지하기 위해 일본식을 먹어.

- **Korean food is known for its health benefits.** 한국음식은 건강식으로 알려져 있어.

- I've had Chinese food **twice this week.** 난 이번주에 중국식을 두번이나 먹었어.

A: Many models eat Japanese food to stay thin.
많은 모델들은 날씬함을 유지하기 위해 일본식을 먹어.

B: I've heard that sushi doesn't contain many calories.
초밥에는 칼로리가 많지 않다는 얘기를 들었어.

02 I prefer to eat natural foods over fast food
난 패스트푸드보다 자연식을 더 좋아해

- **This restaurant features natural foods.** 이 식당은 자연식을 특징으로 해.

- Eating organic foods **is one way to avoid pesticides.**
  유기농 음식을 먹으면 농약을 피할 수 있어.

A: I worry about the amount of chemicals that farmers use.
농부들이 사용하는 화학물질의 양에 대해 걱정이 돼.

B: Eating organic foods is one way to avoid pesticides.
유기농 음식을 먹는게 농약을 피할 수 있는 한 방법이야.

03 I like spicy foods
양념을 많이 한 음식을 좋아해

- I only eat vegetable. 난 야채만 먹어.

- I don't eat instant foods. 난 즉석 음식은 먹지 않아.

- She follows a strict vegan diet. 걘 채식식단을 엄격히 따르고 있어.

A: Why doesn't your sister ever eat with us?
네 누이는 왜 우리와 함께 식사를 하지 않는거야?

B: She follows a strict vegan diet. She doesn't eat meat.
걘 채식식단을 엄격히 따르고 있어. 고기를 먹지 않아.

04 I like meat better than fish
난 생선보다 고기를 좋아해

- I prefer fish to meat. 난 고기보다 생선을 더 좋아해.

- I think fish is healthier than meat. 난 생선이 고기보다 더 건강에 좋은 것 같아.

- Meat tends to be more expensive than fish. 고기가 생선보다 더 비싼 것 같아.

- Meat and fish both contain a lot of protein.
고기나 생선 모두 많은 양의 단백질을 포함하고 있어.

A: I notice that you eat more fish than meat. 너 고기보다 생선을 많이 먹더라.
B: Meat tends to be more expensive than fish. 고기가 생선보다 더 비싼 것 같아.

05 I eat every kind of food
나 음식을 가리지 않고 먹어

- I eat anything. 난 아무거나 다 먹어.

- I like various kinds of food. 난 다양한 종류의 음식을 좋아해.

- I eat whatever is put in front of me. 내 앞에 놓여 진 음식은 뭐든 다 먹어.

A: I notice that Greg is a fussy eater. 그렉은 식성이 까다로운 사람이야.
B: I eat whatever is put in front of me. 난 내 앞에 놓여 진 음식은 뭐든 다 먹는데.

019

I sometimes skip breakfast
때때로 아침은 건너 뛰어

이번에는 하루에 몇 끼를 먹는지, 아침을 거르는지 여부 등을 말해본다. 그리고 점심은 어디서 먹는지, 외식은 하는지 등을 어떻게 영어로 말하는지 배워본다.

01 I have[eat] two meals a day
난 하루에 두 끼 먹어

● **Do you have breakfast every day?** 넌 매일 아침 식사를 해?

● **What are your favorite dishes?** 좋아하는 음식은 뭐야?

● **What vegetable do you like?** 무슨 야채를 좋아해?

A: Do you have breakfast every day? 넌 매일 아침 식사를 해?
B: Yeah, I generally eat bread and cheese with some coffee.
   어, 보통 커피와 함께 빵과 치즈를 먹어.

02 I sometimes skip breakfast
때때로 아침은 건너 뛰어

● **I have[eat] something light for breakfast.** 아침으로는 간편식을 먹어.

● **I like to eat a big breakfast.** 아침을 거하게 먹는 것을 좋아해.

● **Breakfast is the most important meal of the day.** 아침은 하루 중 가장 중요한 식사야.

A: Breakfast is the most important meal of the day.
   아침은 하루 중 가장 중요한 식사야.
B: I know. I try to eat healthy food in the morning.
   알아. 아침에 건강식을 먹으려고 해.

03 I usually have[eat] lunch in the company cafeteria
보통 회사 구내식당에서 점심을 먹어

- I like to have lunch with my fellow students. 난 동기들과 함께 점심먹는 것을 좋아해.
- He eats lunch during his thirty minute break. 걘 30분 휴식시간에 점심을 먹어.
- I often don't have time to eat a full lunch. 가끔 점심을 제대로 먹을 시간이 없어.

A: Working in this shop must keep you busy. 이 가게에서 일하면 무척 바빠.
B: I often don't have time to eat a full lunch. 가끔 점심을 제대로 먹을 시간이 없어.

04 I always eat out for dinner on weekends
난 항상 주말마다 저녁은 외식을 해

- I'm planning to take Mindy out for dinner. 난 민디를 데리고 나가서 저녁을 먹을 생각이야.
- We didn't go out for dinner during the pandemic.
  우리는 전염병 상황에서 저녁먹으러 나가지 않았어.
- I came by to see if you could go out for dinner with me.
  네가 나랑 저녁 먹을 수 있는지 확인하러 왔어.

A: Can I help you with something, Mr. Johnson? 존슨 씨. 뭐 도와드릴까요?
B: I came by to see if you could go out for dinner with me.
  나랑 저녁 먹을 수 있는지 확인하러 왔어요.

05 Enjoy your meal
식사 맛있게 해

- Are you ready to order your meal yet? 이제 식사를 주문하시겠어요?
- The restaurant offers a larger side dish with each meal.
  이 식당에서는 식사와 함께 많은 반찬들이 달려 나와.
- You have a choice of either soup or salad with your meal.
  식사에 더해서 수프 혹은 샐러드 중 하나를 선택할 수 있습니다.

A: Do you offer any side dishes with these meals? 식사에 함께 곁들어 나오는게 있나요?
B: You have a choice of either soup or salad with your meal.
  식사에 더해서 수프 혹은 샐러드 중 하나를 선택할 수 있습니다.

020

Will they make a delivery on Sunday?

걔네들 일요일에도 배송을 한대?

배달의 시대. 우편부터 음식까지 배달 안 되는게 없는 세상이 되었다. 여기서는 포장(~ to go; takeout)부터 배달되는 것(have ~ delivered)에 대해 다양하게 말해보는 법을 배워본다.

01

They ordered sandwiches for lunch

걔네들은 점심으로 샌드위치를 주문했어

- I ordered **two cups of coffee to go**. 난 테이크아웃으로 커피 두 잔을 주문했어.

- We ordered **20 minutes ago but still haven't gotten food.**
  음식을 20분 전에 주문했는데 아직 나오지 않았어.

- He ordered **a few beers for his friends.** 걘 친구들 먹으라고 맥주 몇 잔을 주문했어.

A: What did you get while you were at Starbucks?
스타벅스에 있는 동안 뭐 먹었어?

B: I ordered two cups of coffee to go. 난 테이크아웃으로 커피 두 잔을 주문했어.

02

It's common for people to order foods to be delivered to their homes

사람들이 집으로 음식을 배달시켜먹는 것은 흔한 일이야

- I ordered **some medicine to** be delivered **to my apartment.**
  난 약을 좀 주문해서 아파트로 배송시켰어.

- Will that be all the food you are ordering for **the party?**
  이게 파티용으로 주문한 음식 전부입니까?

- Many people in the US order items to be delivered from **Amazon.**
  미국의 많은 사람들은 아마존에서 물품을 주문배송 받아.

A: Can I have these delivered to this address? 이 주소로 이것들을 배달시킬 수 있나요?
B: Sure, just fill out this form and I'll bring you a receipt.
물론이죠. 이 양식서를 작성하시면 영수증을 가져다 드리죠.

03 They had the pizza delivered to their office
개네들은 피자를 사무실로 배달시켰어

● She can buy these groceries and have them delivered to her house.
걘 식료품들을 사서 집으로 배달시킬 수가 있어.

● Was the birthday cake delivered to you? 생일 케익이 너에게 배달되었어?

A: How can I get a vehicle that I buy on the Internet?
인터넷으로 차를 사면 어떻게 내가 받죠?

B: If you buy a car online, it will be delivered to your home.
온라인으로 차를 구입하시면 댁으로 배송됩니다.

04 It is common to see people on scooters making deliveries in Korea 한국에서 스쿠터를 타고 배달하는 것을 보는 것은 흔한 일이야

● The postman makes deliveries to my mailbox daily.
우체부는 매일 메일함에 배송을 해.

● Will they make a delivery on Sunday? 개네들 일요일에도 배송을 한대?

A: You can order groceries to be delivered to your house.
넌 식료품을 집으로 주문배송할 수 있어.

B: Will they make a delivery on Sunday? 일요일에도 배송을 한대?

05 Drones will be used to deliver packages to households 드론은 각 가정에 물품을 배송하는데 사용될거야

● Your pizza will be delivered in 10 minutes. 피자는 10분안에 배달될거예요.

● Would you like these items delivered? 이 물건들을 배달해 드릴까요?

● When do you want it delivered? 그걸 언제쯤 배달해 드리면 될까요?

A: How far do you deliver items purchased from your store?
가게에서 구입한 물건들은 어디까지 배달이 되죠?

B: We deliver in the city free of charge, but outside of the city costs extra. 시내는 무료로 배달해드리지만 시외는 별도 비용을 내셔야 합니다.

술먹기 1

021

I can't drink at all

난 술을 전혀 못마셔

술을 전혀 못마실 때는 not drink at all. 술을 좋아할 때는 enjoy drinking~ 그리고 술고래일 때는 a heavy drinker라고 하면 된다. 그리고 술마시고 말이 많아지면 get talkative, 잠이 오면 get sleepy라고 하면 된다.

01 I like to drink at my favorite bar
내가 좋아하는 바에서 술을 마시고 싶어

● I like to drink **some wine before going to bed.** 난 자기 전에 와인을 좀 마시는 걸 좋아해.

● **Let's head for the bar, I need a drink!** 술집에 가자. 한 잔 해야겠어!

● **We'll** have some drinks with **old friends.** 우리는 옛 친구들과 술을 좀 할거야.

A: What are your plans for this weekend? 이번 주말에는 뭘 할거야?
B: We'll have some drinks with old friends. 우리는 옛 친구들과 술을 좀 할거야.

02 I enjoy drinking wine
난 와인 마시는 것을 즐겨해

● **I'm a wine lover.** 난 와인을 무척 좋아해.

● **I like to drink wine very much.** 난 와인 마시는 것을 아주 좋아해.

● **I prefer red wine over white.** 난 백포도주보다는 적포도주를 좋아해.

A: What sort of alcohol do you like to drink? 어떤 종류의 술을 마셔?
B: I prefer red wine over white. It has more flavor.
난 백포도주보다는 적포도주를 좋아해. 맛이 더 좋아.

03 I get talkative quickly
난 바로 말이 많아져

- When I drink, **I get sleepy quickly.** 술을 마시면, 바로 잠이 들어.
- When I drink, **I get a headache.** 술을 마시면, 머리가 아파.
- Drinking alcohol **makes me feel more relaxed.** 술을 마시면 내가 긴장을 더 풀게 해줘.

A: Beer is very popular in most countries around the world.
맥주는 전세계 대부분의 나라에서 매우 인기가 있어.

B: Drinking alcohol makes me feel more relaxed.
술을 마시면 내가 긴장을 더 풀게 해줘.

04 I can't drink at all
난 술을 전혀 못마셔

- I can't drink **a drop of alcohol.** 난 술을 입에 대지도 못해.
- I'm not drinking **these days.** 난 요즘 술을 마시지 않아.
- I'm off liquor **these days.** 난 요즘 술을 끊었어.
- **You need to** cut back on **beer drinking.** 너 맥주 마시는 것 좀 줄여야 돼.

A: I quit drinking after having health problems. 건강문제로 술을 끊었어.
B: My doctor said it was OK if I had a drink occasionally.
내 의사는 가끔 술을 마신다면 괜찮을거라고 말했어.

05 I'm a heavy drinker
난 술고래야

- I drink all kinds of **alcoholic drinks, but I like soju the best.**
난 모든 종류의 술을 마시지만 소주를 가장 좋아해.
- Peter is drinking a lot of alcohol **these days.** 피터는 요즘 술을 아주 많이 마셔.
- I was hung over **after the New Year's party.** 신년회 후에 숙취로 고생했어.

A: Peter is drinking a lot of alcohol these days. 피터는 요즘 술을 아주 많이 마셔.
B: I think he's stressed out about issues in his marriage.
걘 결혼문제로 스트레스가 쌓인 것 같아.

022

술먹기 2

Have you ever been dead drunk?

고주망태가 되어본 적이 있어?

술마시면 긴장이 풀린다는 얘기, 술을 좋아하냐고 물어볼 때 쓰는 표현, 술마시면 어떻게 행동하는지 등을 어떻게 말하는지, 그리고 과음을 해본 적이 있는지 궁금할 때 사용하면 되는 표현들이다.

01 Liquor relaxes me
술은 마시면 긴장이 이완 돼

- **Liquor eases my tension.** 술을 마시면 긴장이 풀려.
- **I can't say no when I'm asked to drink.** 술을 먹으라고 권해지면 난 거절할 수가 없어.
- **I like to have a drink when I get home from work.**
  퇴근해 집에 와서 술한잔 하는 것을 좋아해.

A: When do you usually drink cocktails? 넌 보통 언제 칵테일을 마셔?
B: I like to have a drink when I get home from work.
　　퇴근해 집에 와서 술한잔 하는 것을 좋아해.

02 Are you fond of drinking?
술마시는 것을 좋아해?

- **She never drinks alcohol.** 걘 절대로 술을 마시지 않아.
- **I've always enjoyed drinking socially.** 난 항상 사교적으로 술마시는 것을 즐겨했어.
- **Jim likes to drink but he usually overdoes it.**
  짐은 술마시는 것을 좋아하지만 보통 과음을 해.

A: Jim likes to drink but he usually overdoes it.
　　짐은 술마시는 것을 좋아하지만 보통 과음을 해.
B: People say they think he is becoming an alcoholic.
　　사람들이 걔가 알코올 중독자가 될거라 생각한다고 그래.

How do you act when you drink?
술마시면 넌 어떻게 행동해?

- He became aggressive after drinking too much. 걘 과음 후에는 공격적으로 변해.
- Some people become mean when they drink. 어떤 사람들은 술마시면 비열해져.
- Drinking tends to make me more sociable. 술마시면 난 더 사교적으로 돼.

A: You said you liked to have a few beers when you're out.
너 외출하면 맥주 몇 잔하는 것을 좋아했다고 했지.

B: I'm kind of introverted. Drinking tends to make me more sociable.
난 좀 내향적인데 술을 마시면 난 더 사교적으로 돼.

Have you ever been dead drunk?
고주망태가 되어본 적이 있어?

- She blacked out after drinking too much. 걘 과음 후에 필름이 끊겼어.
- If you drink 5 beers, you'll be hung over. 맥주 5잔을 마시면, 넌 숙취로 고생할거야.
- You'd better limit your drinking. 마시는 술의 양을 정해놔.

A: My girlfriend's parents are here tonight. 여친 부모님이 오늘밤에 여기 오신대.
B: You'd better limit your drinking and behave yourself.
술의 양을 정해놓고 행동거지 바르게 해라.

We went out for drinks last night
우리는 지난밤에 나가서 술을 마셨어

- I go out for drinks a few times a week. 난 일주일에 몇 번 나가서 술을 마셔.
- Do you want to go out for drinks? 나가서 술을 마실까?
- Can we still go out for drinks together? 함께 나가서 술 할 수 있을까?

A: Your friends want you to join them at the bar.
네 친구들이 바에서 함께 하기를 바래.

B: I've been so busy that I haven't had time to go out for drinks.
너무 바빠서 술마시러 나가 보지를 못했어.

023

I can't drink today because I have to drive

운전해야 돼서 오늘 술 못마셔

술마시러 잠깐 들르라고 하거나 운전을 해야 하기 때문에 술을 마실 수 없을 때, 그리고 상대방에게 축하를 하기 위해서 건배하는 법 등을 알아본다.

01 I told him to drop by for a drink
걔한테 술 한잔하게 잠깐 들르라고 했어

- **What do you say we** get together for a drink? 만나서 술한잔 하면 어때?
- **She** invited me in to have a drink. 걔는 들어와서 한 잔 하자고 초대했어.
- **Let's** have a drink **when this is finished.** 이게 끝나면 술을 마시자.

> A: I can't wait until this boring meeting ends. 이 지겨운 회의가 빨리 끝났으면 해.
> B: Let's have a drink when this is finished. 끝나면 술 마시자.

02 I can't drink today because I have to drive
운전해야 돼서 오늘 술 못마셔

- **I** got arrested for drinking and driving **last night.** 나 어젯밤에 음주운전으로 체포됐어.
- **The cops** catch a lot of people who drink and drive.
  경찰들이 음주운전하는 많은 사람을 잡고 있어.
- **You'd better use a taxi** if you drink a lot. 술을 많이 마시면 택시를 타.

> A: My new car is parked right outside the nightclub.
>   나이트클럽 바로 밖에 내 차가 주차되어 있어.
> B: You'd better use a taxi if you drink a lot. 술을 많이 마시면 택시를 타.

03 I proposed a toast and we all clinked glasses
난 건배를 했고 우리 모두는 잔을 부딪혔어

- Bottoms up! Let's all toast the married couple. Bottoms up!
  원샷! 신혼부부를 위하여 건배하자. 원샷!
- Cheers! Cheers! Everybody drink to our friend who is retiring.
  위하여! 위하여! 퇴직하는 우리 친구를 위하여 건배하자.
- I'm so proud of your recent promotion. Here's to you!
  얼마 전 승진한 거 정말 자랑스러워. 너를 위하여!

A: I'm going to receive a larger salary and a new office.
   난 급여도 더 많아지고 새로운 사무실도 생길거야.

B: I'm so proud of your recent promotion. Here's to you!
   얼마 전 승진한 거 정말 자랑스러워. 너를 위하여!

04 I paid for the drinks using a credit card
난 신용카드로 술값을 냈어

- Whiskey and soda disagrees with me. 위스키 소다는 난 못마시겠어.
- Hard alcohol gives me a tremendous hangover. 독한 술 마시면 엄청난 숙취가 와.
- Order a few whiskey shots for our table. 우리 테이블에 위스키 몇 잔 주문해.

A: How'd you like a shot of rum? 럼주 한 잔 어때?

B: I can't. Hard alcohol gives me a tremendous hangover.
   안돼. 독한 술 마시면 엄청난 숙취가 와.

커피 1

024
I'd love some coffee
커피 좀 주세요

대중화된 아니 없어서는 안되는 일상이 되어버린 커피를 마시고 싶다고 할 때, 혹은 상대방에 커피를 마시겠냐고 의향을 물어볼 때 쓰는 방법을 들여다본다.

01 I like iced coffee
난 아이스 커피를 좋아해

- I like black coffee. 난 블랙커피를 좋아해.
- **She prefers** sugar and cream in her coffee.
  걘 자기 커피에 설탕과 프림 넣는 것을 더 좋아해.
- I want a strong cup of coffee. 난 진한 커피로 한 잔 줘.

A: You look sleepy. Can I get you something to wake up with?
넌 졸려보인다. 잠깰 뭐 좀 줄까?

B: I want a strong cup of coffee. And make it black.
진한 커피로 한 잔 줘. 블랙으로 해줘.

02 I'd love some coffee
커피 좀 주세요

- The coffee will arrive **in a few minutes.** 커피가 금방 도착할거야.
- I'm making some coffee **for everyone.** 모두들 먹을 커피를 만들고 있어.
- Can I get a cup of coffee? 커피 한 잔 줄래요?

A: It's time to serve cake and pie. 케익과 파이를 서빙할 때야.
B: Give me a minute. I'm making some coffee for everyone.
잠깐만. 지금 모두들 마실 커피를 만들고 있어.

03 Would you like to have coffee?
커피 마실래?

- I asked her to have coffee with me. 난 걔에게 함께 커피마시자고 했어.

- Many couples go out to have coffee on their first date.
많은 커플들은 첫데이트에서 나가서 커피를 마셔.

- We were only having coffee. 우리는 커피마셨을뿐야.

A: What can I do after I ask a girl to go out with me?
여자애에게 데이트 신청하고는 어떻게 해야 돼?

B: Many couples go out to have coffee on their first date.
많은 커플들은 첫데이트에서 나가서 커피를 마셔.

04 Hold on, I need to get a coffee
잠깐, 나 커피 한잔 마셔야 돼

- You can get a cup of coffee from the vending machine.
자동판매기에서 커피를 마실 수도 있어.

- I need to get me some coffee because I'm exhausted. 지쳤기 때문에 커피 좀 줘.

- Let's break for coffee. 쉬면서 커피 한잔 하자.

A: I just can't seem to wake up this morning. 오늘 아침 잠이 깨지 않는 것 같아.
B: You can get a cup of coffee from the pot. 커피 포트에서 커피 한잔 마셔.

05 Drink some coffee and it will warm you up
커피를 좀 마시면 몸이 따뜻해질거야

- He is sitting drinking some coffee. 걘 앉아서 커피를 좀 마시고 있어.

- He is sitting at a desk, drinking a cup of coffee. 책상에 앉아서 커피 한잔 마시고 있어.

- I've been drinking coffee all night. 난 밤새 커피를 마셨어.

A: How come you're still awake? It's midnight.
넌 어떻게 그렇게 멀쩡하냐? 밤 12시인데.

B: I've been drinking coffee all night. I can't sleep.
밤새 커피를 마셨어. 잠이 안와.

025

Bring me a coffee on your way back

돌아오는 길에 커피를 가져와

커피를 사다주거나 갖다줄 때, 혹은 커피 마실 시간이 되냐고 물어볼 때 어떻게 문장을
만드는지 살펴본다. 그리고 커피숍에서 커피 마시기와 사무실 등에서 커피가 떨어졌을
때 말하는 표현들을 알아본다.

01 Bring Ray some coffee from the break room
휴게실에서 커피를 가져다 레이에게 줘

- **Bring me a coffee** on your way back. 돌아오는 길에 커피를 가져와.
- **You have to grab the boss some coffee.** 넌 상사에게 커피를 좀 사다 줘야 돼.
- **I usually grab a coffee** while smoking a cigarette. 난 담배를 필 때 보통 커피를 마셔.

A: When is your favorite time to drink coffee? 언제가 커피마시기에 가장 좋아?
B: During my breaks. I usually grab a coffee while smoking a cigarette. 휴식 때에. 담배를 필 때 보통 커피를 마셔.

02 She can pick up a coffee at the caf?
걘 카페에서 커피를 픽업할 수 있어

- **Do you** have time for a coffee? 커피 마실 시간 있어?
- **I'm going to** pick up a coffee, **do you want one?** 커피 한잔 마셔야겠어. 너도 마실래?
- **He can** pick up a coffee **for his partner.** 걘 동료를 위해 커피를 픽업할 수 있어.

A: I'm going to pick up a coffee, do you want one?
커피 한잔 마셔야겠어. 너도 마실래?
B: No, I think I will stick with drinking tea today.
아니. 오늘은 차만 계속 마실 생각이야.

03 I'm working on my coffee
난 커피를 마시고 있어

- Oops! I just spilled coffee on my new dress. 아뿔싸! 내 새 옷에 커피를 쏟았어.

- He tipped over a cup of coffee when he was upset. 걘 당황했을 때 커피를 엎질렀어.

- Someone brewed fresh coffee for the employees.
누군가 직원들을 위해 신선한 커피를 만들었어.

A: Why does Dan have a coffee stain on his shirt?
댄은 왜 셔츠에 커피자국이 있는거야?

B: He tipped over a cup of coffee when he was upset.
걘 당황했을 때 커피를 엎질렀어.

04 Let's go to the coffee shop around the corner
모퉁이 지나 있는 커피숍에 가자

- The group met at the coffeehouse to discuss their plans.
그 그룹은 그들의 계획을 논의하기 위해서 커피숍에서 만났어.

- There are hundreds of coffee shops in Seoul. 서울에는 많은 커피숍이 있어.

A: Have you been to a coffeehouse that serves specialty drinks?
특제 음료를 내놓는 커피숍에 가본 적이 있어?

B: Yeah, we have one located near my university.
어, 내가 다니는 대학교 근처에 하나 있어.

05 We're out of coffee
커피가 다 떨어졌어

- We're out of coffee in the staff room. 직원 휴게실에 커피가 떨어졌어.

- I brought coffee for everyone. 여러분들을 위해 내가 커피 좀 가져왔어요.

- Could you show me where your coffee makers are? 커피 메이커 좀 보여주시겠어요?

A: Could you show me where your coffee makers are?
커피 메이커 좀 보여주시겠어요?

B: Sure, just follow me. 물론이죠. 따라오세요.

026

Do you mind if I smoke in here?

여기서 담배 펴도 돼?

담배를 좋아하는지, 펴도 되는지, 혹은 끊었는지 여부에 관해 묻고 답해본다. 그리고 밖에 나가서 담배를 핀다고 할 때 어떻게 말하는지도 알아본다.

01 I don't like smoking
난 담배피는 것을 좋아하지 않아

- I'm a heavy smoker. 난 담배를 많이 피는 골초야.
- He was smoking several packs a day. 걘 하루에 담배 몇 갑을 폈어.
- I gave up smoking because it wasn't healthy. 건강에 좋지 않아서 담배를 끊었어.

A: I thought you liked to take cigarette breaks.
담배피면서 휴식하는 것을 좋아하는 걸로 알았는데.

B: I gave up smoking because it wasn't healthy. 건강에 좋지 않아서 담배를 끊었어.

02 Do you mind if I smoke in here?
여기서 담배 펴도 돼?

- You'll have time to smoke a cigarette. 넌 담배 필 시간이 있을거야.
- I need to go outside and smoke. 난 나가서 담배를 펴야 돼.
- My wife asked me not to smoke. 아내가 나보고 담배 피지 말라고 했어.

A: My wife asked me not to smoke. But I miss smoking.
아내가 나보고 담배 피지 말라고 했어. 하지만 담배가 그립네.

B: Are you allowed to smoke while you're at work?
직장에서 일할 때 흡연할 수 있지?

When did you stop smoking?
언제 담배 끊었어?

- I quit[gave up] smoking **two years ago**. 난 2년 전에 금연했어.
- Smoking is not allowed in **public places**. 흡연은 공공장소에서는 금지되고 있어.
- He was smoking outside **my apartment**. 걘 내 아파트 밖에서 담배를 피고 있었어.

A: Smoking is not allowed in public places. 공공장소에서 흡연은 금지되고 있어.
B: I know. I'm not able to smoke at my favorite bar.
　　알아. 내가 좋아하는 바에서 담배를 필 수가 없어.

Are you still smoking?
아직도 담배를 피니?

- **What kind** do you smoke? 무슨 담배를 피워?
- Do you smoke cigarettes or cigars? 담배를 피니, 아니면 시가를 피니?
- Does he smoke when **he is stressed**? 걘 스트레스 받으면 담배를 피니?

A: Does he smoke when he is stressed? 걘 스트레스 받으면 담배를 피니?
B: Yeah, he smokes tons of cigarettes when he's upset. 어, 화나면 담배를 엄청 펴.

She just left for a smoke outside
걘 담배피러 밖으로 나갔어

- **I need to leave the building for a cigarette.** 난 담배를 피우기 위해 빌딩에서 나가야 돼.
- Smokers must wait until their break time to leave the building for a cigarette. 담배피는 사람들은 휴식시간까지 기다렸다가 담배피러 빌딩을 나가야 돼.

A: Will the boss mind if I smoke in here? 내가 여기서 담배를 펴도 상사가 가만 있을까?
B: Smokers must wait until their break time to leave the building for a cigarette. 담배피는 사람들은 휴식시간까지 기다렸다가 담배피러 빌딩을 나가야 돼.

027

There is no smoking allowed in the building

이 빌딩에서 흡연장소는 없어

엄격해진 흡연공간의 상징적인 문장으로 이 빌딩안에서는 흡연공간이 없다고 말해보고 다음 유행하는 전자담배(e-cigarette)를 알아보고, 마지막으로 흡연이 건강에 안좋다는 당연한 말을 해본다.

01 He shouldn't be allowed to smoke in the building

걘 이 빌딩에서는 담배를 피면 안돼

- Smoking isn't allowed in **the office**. 사무실에서 금연이야.
- **There is no smoking allowed in the building** 이 빌딩에서 흡연장소는 없어.
- Mom doesn't allow smoking in **her house.** 엄마는 집에서 담배를 못피게 해.

A: Why doesn't your dad stay inside when he smokes?
왜 너희 아빠는 집안에서 담배를 못펴?

B: Mom doesn't allow smoking in her house. 엄마는 집에서 담배를 못피게 해.

02 E-cigarettes are becoming more popular than regular cigarettes

전자담배는 일반담배보다 더 인기가 있어

- Do you smoke? 너 담배피니?
- **Have you tried** the new style of e-cigarettes?
새로운 스타일의 전자담배를 펴본 적 있어?
- E-cigarettes **come in many different flavors.** 전자담배는 많은 다양한 맛으로 나와.

A: E-cigarettes come in many different flavors. 전자담배는 많은 다양한 맛으로 나와.
B: Yes, I know. I smoked one that was strawberry flavored.
어, 알아. 딸기맛나는거 하나 펴봤어.

03 It's more convenient to smoke e-cigarettes

전자담배를 피는게 더 편리해

- **Many students** are smoking e-cigarettes. 많은 학생들이 전자담배를 펴.
- **E-cigarettes can cause lung cancer like regular cigarettes.**
  전자담배는 일반담배처럼 폐암을 초래할 수 있어.
- **Is there a store I can buy e-cigarettes at?** 내가 전자담배를 살 수 있는 가게가 있어?

A: Is there a store I can buy e-cigarettes at? 전자담배를 살 수 있는 가게가 있어?
B: Yeah, try the store that is just down the street. 어, 거리 아래 있는 가게에 가봐.

04 Health problems made me cut down on smoking

건강문제로 난 담배를 줄여야했어

- **How many cigarettes** do you smoke a day? 하루에 담배 몇 개를 펴?
- **I'm trying to** cut down on smoking. 난 담배를 줄이려고 하고 있어.
- **You should really** cut down on **the number of cigarettes you smoke.**
  네가 피는 담배 개수 좀 정말 줄여야겠어.

A: You should really cut down on the number of cigarettes you smoke.
   네가 피는 담배 개수 좀 정말 줄여야겠어.

B: Yes, that's true, but I really enjoy smoking.
   어, 맞는 말이야. 하지만 난 정말 담배피는 것을 좋아해.

05 Cigarette smoke can lead to lung cancer

흡연은 폐암으로 갈 수가 있어

- **I know smoking isn't good for my health, but it helps with my stress.**
  흡연이 건강에 안좋다는 것을 알지만 스트레스를 푸는데는 도움이 돼.
- **Some people** hate the smell of cigarette smoke. 일부 사람들은 담배연기냄새를 싫어해.

A: Why do you think smoking indoors was banned?
   실내흡연이 왜 금지되었다고 생각해?

B: Some people hate the smell of cigarette smoke.
   담배연기냄새를 아주 싫어하는 사람들도 있거든.

028

Chris wore a casual shirt to the meeting

크리스는 회의에 일상복을 입고 왔어

회의나 결혼식 때 혹은 개인적으로 만남을 하는 경우에 각각 어떤 옷을 입는지에 관한 문장들을 들여다본다. 그리고 옷을 갈아입고, 옷을 벗고, 입는다고 할 때의 표현들도 함께 읽어본다.

01 I like wearing skirts

난 치마 입는 것을 좋아해

- I wore a sweater because the weather was chilly. 날씨가 서늘해서 스웨터를 입었어.
- Wear something loose and comfortable to the beach.
  해변에서는 헐거운 그리고 편안한 옷을 입어.
- Chris wore a casual shirt to the meeting. 크리스는 회의에 일상복을 입고 왔어.

A: Chris wore a casual shirt to the meeting. 크리스는 회의에 일상복을 입고 왔어.
B: I think the boss was expecting him to wear a tie.
   사장은 걔가 넥타이를 매고 오기를 기대했을거야.

02 You'd better wear a suit to the wedding

결혼식에는 정장을 입어라

- Wear a jacket if you decide to go outside. 밖에 나가기로 했으면 자켓을 입어.
- I have never forgotten to wear underwear. 난 속옷입는 것을 잊어본 적이 없어.

A: Have you ever forgotten to put on undergarments?
   속옷입는 것을 깜박한 적이 있어?
B: I have never forgotten to wear underwear. 난 속옷입는 것을 잊어본 적이 없어.

03 You look nice in white
하얀 옷을 입으니 멋져 보인다

- Black may suit me. 검은 색 옷이 내게 맞는 것 같아.
- The blue shirt makes you look sexy. 파란색 셔츠를 입으니 너 섹시해보여.
- You look best when you wear black. 넌 검은 색 옷을 입을 때 최고로 보여.

A: You look best when you wear black. 넌 검은 색 옷을 입을 때 최고로 보여.
B: I like black clothes, but they are hard to keep clean.
검은 색 옷을 좋아하지만 깨끗이 입기가 힘들어.

04 The kids will change into their swim clothes
아이들은 수영복으로 갈아입을거야

- Time to wake up and get dressed for school. 일어나서 옷입고 학교에 갈 시간이야.
- She took off her clothes before taking her bath. 걘 목욕을 하기 전에 옷을 벗었어.
- You'd better put on a raincoat before leaving. 나가기 전에 우의를 입어라.

A: I've got to go, but the rain is coming down in torrents.
나 가야 되는데 비가 엄청 쏟아지네.
B: You'd better put on a raincoat before leaving. 나갈 때 우의를 입어.

05 What size do you wear?
입는 옷 사이즈가 어떻게 돼?

- Kevin wears an extra large size. 케빈은 엑스라지 사이즈 옷을 입어.
- These clothes will never fit you. 이 옷들은 너한테 절대로 맞지 않을거야.
- I need pants that are medium length. 중간 길이 정도의 바지가 필요해.

A: What size pants are going to fit you best?
어떤 사이즈의 바지가 너한테 가장 잘 맞아?
B: I need pants that are medium length. 중간 길이 정도의 바지가 필요해.

029

I'd like to try this on

이거 입어보고 싶어요

이어서 옷을 구매할 때 필요한 사이즈를 영어로 말해보는 훈련. 두개의 의상 등이 서로 어울리지는 여부에 관해 영어로 말해본다. 다음으로는 가장 일반적인 문장으로 옷이나 신발 등을 입거나 신어볼 때는 on를 써서 try~ on이라고 한다는 점을 꼭 기억해둔다.

01   I usually wear size 9 1/2
보통 9와 2분의 1 사이즈를 입어

- My clothing is smaller than **most people.** 내 옷은 대부분의 사람들 옷보다 작아.
- See if they have dresses in size 6. 사이즈 6의 옷이 있는지 알아봐.
- My boots are men's size 13. 내 부츠는 남성용 사이즈 13이야.

A: My boots are men's size 13. 내 부츠는 남성용 사이즈 13이야.
B: That's very large. Do you have trouble finding that size?
    매우 큰건데. 그 사이즈 찾는데 어려움이 있어?

02   Anne wears her glasses when reading books
앤은 책을 읽을 때 안경을 써

- I love it when women wear perfume. 난 여성들이 향수를 뿌렸을 때 좋더라.
- She wears skin lotion **to prevent wrinkles.** 걘 주름을 예방하기 위해 스킨로션을 발라.
- You should wear dark sunglasses **whenever you are out in the sun.**
햇볕쬐는데 나갈 때는 언제나 짙은 선글라스를 써야 해.

A: Your mom always looks much younger than her age.
    너희 엄마는 항상 나이보다 훨씬 젊게 보이셔.
B: She wears skin lotion to prevent wrinkles.
    엄마는 주름을 예방하기 위해 스킨로션을 발라.

03 Her shoes even matched her suit
걔 신발은 정장과 매치가 됐어

- I put on my running shoes and headed to the track.
  난 운동화를 신고 트랙으로 향했어.

- A new pair of jogging shoes will make you more comfortable.
  새로운 조깅화로 넌 더 편안함을 느낄거야.

- I bought shoes that I could wear to work. 일할 때 신을 신발을 샀어.

A: Lately my feet have been painful after I exercise.
최근에 운동을 한 후에 발이 아팠어.

B: A new pair of jogging shoes will make you more comfortable.
새로운 조깅화로 넌 더 편안함을 느낄거야.

04 May I try on a pair of shoes?
신발 좀 신어봐도 될까요?

- I'd like to try this on. 이거 입어보고 싶어요.

- Would you like to try it on? 이거 입어볼래요?

- What size do you need? 사이즈가 어떻게 되시는데요?

A: I want to purchase a new pair of sweat pants. 운동복 바지를 새로 사고 싶은데요.
B: Of course. What size do you need? 그럼요. 사이즈가 어떻게 되나요?

05 These shoes are killing my feet
이 신발을 신으면 발이 아주 아파

- It will take a couple of days to break them in. 신발을 길들이려면 2–3일 걸릴거야.

- These boots are too large for my feet. 이 부츠는 내 발에 너무 커.

- It's difficult to find shoes that fit my feet. 내 발에 맞는 신발을 찾는게 어려워.

A: It's difficult to find shoes that fit my feet. 내 발에 맞는 신발을 찾는게 어려워.
B: Have you tried ordering shoes on the Internet? 인터넷으로 신발을 주문해봤어?

030

I'm losing my hair these days

요즘 머리가 빠져

머리에 관한 표현들로 먼저 머리스타일, 머리깎기, 그리고 머리가 흰색으로 되어서 염색하게 될 때의 표현을 살펴본다. 끝으로는 머리하는데 걸리는 시간 그리고 머리가 빠지고 있다고 말하는 것을 연습해본다.

01 I used to keep my hair short
난 머리를 짧게 해왔어

- I don't like your new haircut. 너 머리자른거 맘에 안들어.
- You have really great hair. 너 머리가 정말 멋지네
- His hair was short because he was in the military. 걔는 군인이어서 머리가 짧았어.

A: John's hair was cut very close to his scalp.
존의 아주 짧게 깎아서 두피가 보일 정도야.

B: His hair was short because he was in the military.
걔는 군인이어서 머리가 짧았어.

02 I dyed my hair black because it was turning gray
머리가 희어져서 검은색으로 염색했어

- Do you think I should change my hair style? 내 머리스타일을 바꿔야 한다고 생각해?
- She dyed her hair and made it a lighter color. 걘 머리염색을 좀 밝은 색으로 했어.
- I went to a beauty parlor to have my hair trimmed. 미장원에 가서 머리를 가다듬었어.

A: I went to a beauty parlor to have my hair trimmed today.
난 오늘 미장원에 가서 머리를 정리했어.

B: Really? It looks almost the same to me. 정말? 내게는 똑같아 보이는데.

03 I got[had] my hair cut
난 머리를 잘랐어

- How often do you get your hair cut? 머리를 얼마나 자주 잘라?
- Your hair looks great since you got that perm. 파마하니까 네 머리 멋있어 보여.
- It has become fashionable to have a beard. 턱수염 기르는게 유행이 되었어.

A: It has become fashionable to have a beard. 턱수염 기르는게 유행이 되었어.
B: I tried to grow a beard, but it doesn't look good.
턱수염을 길러봤지만 그리 좋아보이지 않아.

04 It took her an hour to do her hair
걔 머리하는데 한 시간 걸렸어

- Oscar always parts his hair on the left side. 오스카는 항상 왼쪽으로 가르마를 타.
- I need to do my hair before we go. 가기 전에 머리를 해야 되는데.
- Do you really hate my hairdo? 내 머리모양이 그렇게 마음에 안들어?

A: Your hair style doesn't suit your face. 네 머리 스타일은 네 얼굴에 어울리지 않아.
B: Do you really hate my hairdo? 내 머리모양이 그렇게 마음에 안들어?

05 I'm losing my hair these days
요즘 머리가 빠져

- You'd better not use my hair dryer. 내 헤어드라이어기 쓰지 마라.
- My grandfather still has a full head of hair. 할아버지는 아직도 머리가 풍성하셔.
- You'd better not cut your long hair. 네 긴 머리를 자르지 마라.

A: Does my hair look better when it's long or when it's short?
내 머리모양이 길 때 아니면 짧을 때, 어느 때가 더 좋아보여?
B: You'd better not cut your long hair. 네 긴 머리를 자르지마.

031 I need to go wash off my make up

난 가서 화장을 지워야 돼

화장을 하는 것, 늦지 않게 화장을 서둘러 하는 것 그리고 자기 전에는 화장을 지워야 되는 것 등을 어떻게 영어로 말하는지 알아본다. 그리고 하루에 화장에 소요되는 시간, 그리고 비용들을 말해보자.

01 Sara had to put on make up before leaving

새라는 나가기 전에 화장을 해야 했어

- She's wearing a lot of makeup. 걔는 화장을 떡칠해.
- I put on too much make-up. I look like a clown. 화장을 너무 많이 했나봐. 광대처럼 보여.
- Just wait a few minutes while I put on makeup. 내가 화장을 할 때까지 좀만 기다려.

A: Hurry up, we are going to miss the train. 서둘러. 기차놓치겠어.
B: Just wait a few minutes while I put on makeup.
  내가 화장을 할 때까지 좀만 기다려.

02 Better remove your make up before going to bed

자기 전에는 화장을 지워라

- I need to go wash off my make up. 난 가서 화장을 지워야 돼.
- She removes her eyeliner every night. 걘 매일밤 아이라이너를 지워.
- They're not allowed to wear make-up to school. 학교에서는 화장하는게 허용되지 않아.

A: Do you think Nellie goes to bed wearing make up?
  넬리가 화장을 한 채 자는 것 같아?
B: She removes her eyeliner every night. 걘 매일밤 아이라이너를 지워.

03 Every day I spend 30 minutes on my make up

매일 난 30분 걸려서 화장을 해

- I spend only a few minutes putting on my makeup. 난 화장하는데 단 몇 분이면 돼.
- Don't spend so much time putting on your makeup.
  화장하는데 너무 많은 시간을 쓰지마라.
- It will take hours for the models to put on makeup. 모델들은 화장하는 몇 시간이 걸려.

A: It will take hours for the models to put on makeup.
   모델들은 화장하는데 몇 시간이 걸릴거야.

B: Will they be ready for the fashion show? 패션쇼를 준비하는거야?

04 It's common for young women to spend 200,000 won a month on cosmetics

젊은 여성이 한달에 화장품값으로 20만원을 쓰는 것은 흔한 일이야

- Makeup has grown more expensive over the years.
  화장품은 수년간 가격이 더 비싸졌어.
- Older women spend less on cosmetics. 나이든 여성은 화장품에 비용을 덜 써.
- My girlfriend buys cosmetic supplies every week. 여친은 매주 화장품을 사.

A: My girlfriend buys cosmetic supplies every week. 여친은 매주 화장품을 사.
B: I didn't know she was so concerned with fashion.
   걔가 그렇게 패션에 관심있는 줄은 몰랐어.

032

I started Korea University in 2015

2015년에 고려대학교에 진학했어

학교에 들어가거나 다녔다고 할 때는 과거형시제로 got into+학교와 went to college[school]를 주로 이용하면 된다. 아주 쉬운 단어로 start를 쓰기도 하며 반대로 그만둔다고 할 때는 quit을 쓴다.

01

She got into the college she wanted to go to

걘 자기가 원하는 대학에 들어갔어

- I wasn't able to get into Seoul National University. 서울대에 못들어갔어.

- I got into the police academy! 경찰학교에 합격했어요!

- Did you hear that I got into the training program?
  내가 그 교육 프로그램에 들어가게 됐다는 말 들었니?

A: I wasn't able to get into Seoul National University. 서울대에 못들어갔어.
B: Don't feel so bad about it. You can get into Korea University or Yonsei. 넘 기분나빠하지마. 고려대나 연세대 들어가면 되잖아.

02

I went to college in a small school in New York

난 뉴욕의 조그만 학교에 들어갔어

- Most students go to college when they are eighteen.
  모든 학생들은 18살에 대학에 가.

- Frank went to school on an academic scholarship.
  프랭크는 장학생으로 학교에 들어갔어.

- Are you planning to go to college when you finish high school?
  고등학교 마친 후에 대학교에 갈 생각이야?

A: Frank went to school on an academic scholarship.
  프랭크는 장학생으로 학교에 들어갔어.
B: He must be smart and have had very good grades. 걘 영리하고 성적이 좋았겠다.

03 I went to school with an actress who became famous
난 유명해진 여배우와 함께 학교를 다녔어

- I went to school with her brother years ago. 난 오래전에 걔 오빠와 학교를 같이 다녔어.
- They went to school with other students from their hometown.
  걔네들은 같은 고향의 학생들과 함께 학교를 다녔어.
- He went to school with the woman he would later marry.
  걘 나중에 결혼하게 될 여자와 함께 학교를 다녔어.

A: Why does Ted think that university life is romantic?
왜 테드는 대학생활이 낭만적이라고 생각하는거야?

B: He went to school with the woman he would later marry.
걘 나중에 결혼하게 될 여자와 함께 학교를 다녔어.

04 They went to Harvard together from 2014 to 2018
걔네들은 2014년부터 2018년까지 함께 하버드를 다녔어

- Did you go to university together? 너희 함께 대학교에 들어갔니?
- I went to university together with my sister. 난 내 누이와 함께 대학교를 다녔어.
- We went together to Seoul National University but had different majors.
  우리는 서울대를 함께 다녔지만 전공은 서로 달랐어.

A: Didn't you go to university together? 너희 함께 대학교에 다니지 않았어?
B: Yes, we did but my major was business and hers was biology.
아니, 함께 다녔지만 내 전공은 경영학이었고, 걘 생물학이었어.

05 Chris started Yonsei University in 1999
크리스는 1999년에 연세대학교에 들어갔어

- I began studying at the institute 3 years ago. 난 3년전에 학원에서 공부를 시작했어.
- I started Korea University in 2015. 2015년에 고려대학교에 진학했어.
- I quit college after 2 years. 난 대학 2년 다닌 후에 그만뒀어.

A: I began studying at the institute 3 years ago. 난 3년전에 학원에서 공부를 시작했어.
B: Have you been able to improve your language skills?
언어실력을 늘릴 수 있었어?

033

Pete is in his second year at law school

피트는 로스쿨 2년차야

몇 학년인지 말할 때는 be one's freshman, be one's second-year at~ 등으로 표현하면 되며 전공이 뭔지 말하려면 study+전공 혹은 major in을 쓰면 된다. 중간고사는 mid-term exams, 수업을 빼먹다라고 할 때는 cut classes, skip[ditch] class라고 하면 된다.

01 I'm a third-year student at Chosun University
난 조선대학교에 다니고 3학년이야

- This is my freshman year at school. 올해는 내가 학교에 들어온 해야.
- Pete is in his second year at law school. 피트는 로스쿨 2년차야.
- Larry started his senior year in university. 래리는 대학교 4년차를 시작했어.

A: Larry started his senior year in university. 래리는 대학교 4년차를 시작했어.
B: He must be happy that he's almost finished. 거의 끝나가서 좋겠구만.

02 I'm studying law at Seoul National University
서울대학교에서 법학을 공부하고 있어

- He wants to study biology when he enters university.
  걘 대학교 들어가서 생물학을 배우고 싶어해.
- Many students study business at Harvard University.
  많은 학생들이 하버드 대학교에서 비즈니스를 공부해.
- Do you plan to study at a medical school? 넌 의대에서 공부할 생각이니?

A: You're smart. Do you plan to study at a medical school?
너 똑똑해. 의대에서 공부할 생각이니?
B: Yes, I would really like to become a doctor. 어. 의사가 무척 되고 싶어.

03 Korea University is well known for its law program
고려대학교는 법대 쪽이 유명해

- **Most universities** have a program for **nursing**. 대부분의 대학교는 간호학과가 있어.
- **This school** has the most prestigious MBA program.
  이 학교에는 일류 MBA프로그램이 있어.

A: I selected my university because it has an international studies degree. 난 국제학 학위가 있어서 이 대학을 선택했어.

B: I understand. So you want to work overseas?
알겠어. 그럼 넌 해외에서 일하는 것을 원해?

04 Our university is having mid-term exams this week
이번주 우리 대학은 중간고사 기간야

- **Very few students** did well on the exams. 시험을 잘 치른 학생은 거의 없어.
- **We will be up all night** studying for the test. 시험준비하느라 우리는 밤을 샐거야.
- **The exams will begin at 8 o'clock in the morning.** 시험은 아침 8시에 시작될거야.

A: You must do well in school so you can graduate.
너 졸업하려면 학교다닐 때 잘 해야 돼.

B: We will be up all night studying for the test. 시험준비하느라 우리는 밤을 샐거야.

05 I often cut classes when I was in college
학교 다닐 때 수업을 종종 빼먹었어

- **You'll get into trouble** if you skip class. 수업을 빼먹으면 곤경에 빠질거야.
- **Sometimes I feel like** ditching class. 때때로 난 수업을 빼먹고 싶어.
- **She was very good and** never cut classes. 걘 아주 잘하고 있고 절대 수업을 빼먹지 않아.

A: How did your sister get such high grades?
네 누이는 어떻게 그렇게 높은 점수를 받은거야?

B: She was very good and never cut classes.
걘 아주 잘하고 있고 절대 수업을 빼먹지 않아.

034 학교 3

I'm a Yonsei graduate

연세대학교 졸업했어

졸업하다는 graduate from~이라고 한다. from를 빼먹으면 안된다. 또한 졸업생이라고 할 때는 위에서처럼 I'm a+학교명+graduate라고 한다. 여기서 graduate는 명사이다.

01 I graduated from college in 2018

2018년에 대학교를 졸업했어

- **My dad finished school back in 1995.** 나의 아버지는 1995년에 학교를 마치셨어.

- **They will graduate a few years from now.** 걔네들은 지금부터 몇 년 지나서 졸업할거야.

- **Kelly got her degree in the summer of 2016.** 켈리는 2016년 여름학기에 학위를 땄어.

A: Kelly got her degree in the summer of 2016.
켈리는 2016년 여름학기에 학위를 땄어.

B: Has she found work that is related to her studies?
학과와 관련된 일자리를 구했어?

02 I'm a Yonsei graduate

연세대학교 졸업했어

- **I'm a graduate from Yonsei University.** 난 연세대학교를 졸업했어.

- **I received a degree from Cambridge University.** 난 캠브리지 대학 학위를 받았어.

- **They finished their studies at Princeton University.**
걔네들은 프린스턴 대학교에서 공부를 마쳤어.

A: Where did your friends graduate from? 걔네들 어느 대학을 졸업했어?
B: They finished their studies at Princeton University.
걔네들은 프린스턴 대학교에서 공부를 마쳤어.

03 I'm hoping to graduate this year
금년도에 졸업하기를 바래

- We can't wait until we are finished with school. 학교를 빨리 마쳤으면 해.
- I'd like to graduate and start my career. 졸업하고 직장생활을 시작하고 싶어.
- Preston expects to graduate within the next year. 프레스톤은 내년안에 졸업을 기대해.

A: I'd like to graduate and start my career. 졸업하고 직장생활을 시작하고 싶어.
B: A lot of university seniors are anxious to begin working.
많은 대학 4학년생들은 몹시 일을 시작하고 싶어해.

04 I'm planning to study for a master's degree
공부를 해서 석사학위를 받으려고 해

- Dave always wanted to get a law degree. 데이브는 항상 법학학위를 받고 싶어했어.
- You should obtain an MBA and work in the business world.
넌 MBA를 따서 직장생활을 해야 돼.
- I want to return to school to finish my degree. 학위를 마치려고 학교로 돌아가고 싶어.

A: You had to drop out because the tuition was too expensive?
등록금이 너무 비싸서 중퇴해야 했어?
B: That's right. But I want to return to school to finish my degree.
맞아. 하지만 학위를 마치려고 학교로 돌아가고 싶어.

035

I am studying chemistry at the moment

난 지금 화학을 공부하고 있어

학교에서 뭐를 공부하는지 말하려면 ~수강을 듣다라는 뜻의 take a ~ class 혹은 study+공부의 형태로 써주면 된다. 재미있으면 be much fun, 재미없으면 be a little bit boring이라고 한다.

01 She took a computer programming class
걘 컴퓨터 프로그래밍 수업을 들어

- I'm taking an English conversation class on Mondays and Wednesdays. My teacher is really great and always makes us laugh.
  매주 월요일과 수요일에 영어회화 수업을 듣고 있는데, 강사가 굉장히 잘 가르치고 학생들을 항상 웃게 만들지.

- My teacher wants me to take extra classes after school to help me do better on my tests.
  내 선생님은 내가 테스트에서 더 좋은 결과가 나오도록 수업후의 과외수업을 듣기를 원해.

> A: Want to see a movie tonight? 오늘밤 영화볼래?
> B: I can't. I'm taking an English conversation class at 7pm.
>   안돼. 저녁 7시에 영어회화반 수업을 들어.

02 I'm studying chemistry on my own
난 혼자 힘으로 화학을 공부하고 있어

- We're studying Korean in the library together.
  우리는 함께 도서관에서 한국어를 학습하고 있어.

- My sister is studying piano every day after school.
  내 누이는 방과후 매일 피아노를 학습하고 있어.

- I am studying chemistry at the moment. 난 지금 화학을 공부하고 있어.

> A: What is he studying at the moment? 지금 걘 무슨 공부해?
> B: He's studying Korean. 걘 한국어를 공부하고 있어.

03 I wish I had studied math harder
수학공부를 더 열심히 했더라면 좋았을텐데

- I wish I hadn't studied piano. 내가 피아노를 배우지 않았더라면 좋았을텐데.
- She wishes she had studied more last night.
  걘 지난밤에 공부를 더 열심히 했더라면 하고 있어.
- They wish they had studied together. 걔네들은 함께 공부를 했더라면 좋았을텐데.

A: How was the test? 시험은 어땠어?

B: Not good. I wish I had studied harder last night.
  좋지 않아. 지난밤에 공부를 더 열심히 할 걸.

04 The class was very good
수업은 아주 좋았어

- The biology class wasn't much fun. 생물수업은 정말 재미없었어.
- The English class was a little bit boring. 영어수업은 좀 따분했어.
- The Physical Education class was tiring. 체육수업은 피곤하게 해.

A: How was that new computer class? 새로운 컴퓨터 수업은 어땠어?

B: It was OK. The teacher is a little boring though.
  괜찮았어. 비록 선생님이 좀 따분했지만.

05 The class went very well
수업은 아주 잘됐어

- My new class didn't go very well. 내 새로운 수업은 아주 잘 되지 않았어.
- The class is usually good but today it didn't go very well.
  그 수업은 보통 좋지만 오늘은 안그랬어.
- The yoga class went well today. 요가수업은 오늘 좋았어.

A: How did the class go yesterday? 어제 그 수업은 어땠어?

B: It went very well. We all learned a lot. 잘됐어. 우리는 많은 것을 배웠어.

036

I'm majoring in economics

경제학을 전공하고 있어

앞서 언급한 것처럼 전공을 말할 때는 major in, My major is~ 이라고 하고 전공을 바꾼다고 할 때는 change A to B의 형태로 말하면 된다. 참고로 논문은 thesis 라는 것도 알아둔다.

01 I majored in business administration
난 경영학을 전공했어

- I'm majoring in **economics**. 경제학을 전공하고 있어.

- My major was **English literature**. 내 전공은 영문학이었어.

- My major is **political science but I'm thinking of changing it to economics.**
  내 전공은 정치학이지만 경제학으로 바꿀 생각이야.

A: What was your major in university? 대학교 때 전공이 뭐였어?
B: I majored in English Lit. 영문학을 전공했어.

02 My graduation thesis was about "The Big Bang"
내 졸업논문은 "빅뱅"에 대한거야

- My thesis is going to be on the role of religion in the French Revolution.
  내 전공은 프랑스 혁명에서 종교의 역할이 될거야.

- I still haven't decided what my thesis is going to be about.
  어떤 주제로 논문을 쓸지 아직 결정하지 못했어.

- Her thesis sounds **very interesting**. 걔의 논문은 매우 흥미롭게 들려.

A: My thesis is about the influence of Buddhism in Korean politics during the Park Chunghee era.
내 전공은 박정희 시대 동안 한국정치에서의 불교의 영향력에 관한거야.

B: Wow! That sounds very interesting. 왜! 무척 흥미롭게 들린다.

03 I want to qualify as a lawyer
변호사 자격을 따고 싶어

- I hope to be a criminal defense lawyer **someday**.
  언젠가 형사 사건 전문 변호사가 되고 싶어.

- I want to get a pharmacist's license. 난 약사증을 따고 싶어.

- My dream is to be a chemical engineer **one day**. 내 꿈은 언젠가 화학기사가 되는거야.

A: What are your plans for the future? 너 미래의 계획은 뭐야?

B: I want to pass my bar exam and practice criminal law.
변호사가 되어서 형사변호사가 되는거야.

04 I wish I could change my major to a more interesting subject
전공을 바꿔서 다른 흥미로운 전공을 택했으면 해

- What was your major **in college**? 대학교 때 전공이 뭐였어?

- What did you study **in university**? 대학교에서 뭐를 배웠어?

- What did you major in **in college**? 대학교에서 전공을 뭘로 했어?

A: What did you study in university? 대학교에서 뭐를 공부했어?

B: My major was civil engineering. 내 전공은 토목공학이야.

05 I'm studying biology at Sogang University. I'm really interested in environmental science
난 서강대학교에서 생물학을 공부하고 있는데, 환경과학에 굉장히 흥미가 있어

- **Tell me** your educational background. 네 학력에 대해 말해줘봐.

- What is your field of study? 너의 연구분야는 뭐야?

A: Can you tell me a bit about your educational background?
학력에 대해 좀 내게 얘기해줄래?

B: I studied biology for my undergrad then did a master's degree in biochemical engineering. 학부 때는 생물학을 공부했고 생화학공학에서 석사학위를 땄어.

037

I am studying English these days

난 요즘 영어공부를 하고 있어

영어공부를 한다고 할 때는 전형적으로 study English 그리고 영어를 배우다는 learn English를 쓰면 된다. 영어를 말하는 speak English 그리고 TOEIC시험을 보다는 take the TOEIC test라는 것도 함께 알아둔다.

01 I'm going to study English
난 영어공부할거야

- I've been studying English. 난 영어공부를 해오고 있어.
- I am studying English **these days**. 난 요즘 영어공부를 하고 있어.
- **My plan** is to study English. 내 계획은 영어를 공부하는거야.
- I studied English **in high school**. 난 고등학교에서 영어를 공부했어.

A: Have you ever studied English? 영어공부를 해본 적이 있어?
B: Yes, I studied it in high school. 어. 고등학교에서 영어를 공부했어.

02 I have studied English for about 10 years
난 약 10년간 영어를 공부했어

- I started to study English **again in September**. 난 9월에 다시 영어공부를 시작했어.
- I haven't studied English **since my school days**.
  학교다닐 때 이후로는 영어를 공부하지 않았어.
- I started studying English **when I was 10 years old**. 난 10살 때 영어공부를 시작했어.

A: When did you start to study English? 언제 영어공부를 시작했어?
B: I have been studying English since I was in elementary school.
초등학교 다닐 때부터 영어공부를 해왔어.

03 This is my first time for me to speak English
이번이 내가 처음으로 영어를 말하는 순간이야

- **Please tell me** the best way of learning English.
  영어를 배우는 가장 좋은 방법이 뭔지 내게 말해줘.

- **What are** some good ways to learn English? 영어를 배우는 좋은 방법들로 뭐가 있어?

- **Do you know** any effective ways to learn English?
  영어를 효과적으로 배우는 방법을 혹 알고 있어?

A: How is your English class going? 너 영어수업 어떻게 돼가?
B: Not well. Please tell me the best way to learn English.
   잘 안돼. 영어를 배우는 최고의 방법을 내게 말해주라.

04 I study every day for the TOEIC test
난 TOEIC 시험공부를 매일 하고 있어

- **I'm going to** take the TOEIC test **this Summer.** 이번 여름에 TOEIC 시험을 볼거야.

- **I am preparing for the TOEIC test this weekend.**
  이번 주말에 있을 TOEIC 시험을 준비하고 있어.

- **I've taken the TOEIC test many times.** 난 TOEIC 시험을 여러 번 봤어.

A: What are you studying for? 너 뭐 공부해?
B: I'm going to take the TOEIC test this Saturday.
   이번 토요일에 있을 TOEIC시험을 볼거야.

05 A high TOIEC score will get me a good job
TOEIC점수가 높으면 좋은데 취직할 수 있을거야

- A good score on the TOIEC test **will help land me a job.**
  TOEIC 점수가 좋으면 내가 취직하는데 도움이 될거야.

- Getting a good score on the TOIEC test **will make it easier to find a good**
  job. TOEIC 점수에서 고득점을 얻으면 좋은 직장에 취직하는게 쉬워질거야.

A: Why is the TOIEC score so important? 왜 TOEIC 시험이 이렇게 중요한거야?
B: Doing well on it is important for finding a good job.
   고득점은 좋은 직장을 찾는데 중요하거든.

038

I study English using Mentors books

난 멘토스 교재들로 영어공부를 해

이번에는 영어를 공부하는 방법을 말해본다. 자기가 좋아하는 출판사를 언급할 수도 있고, 새로운 영어학습의 수단으로 여겨지는 YouTube 그리고 학원에 갈 때는 go to an English Institute라고 하면 된다.

01 I study English using Mentors books
난 멘토스 교재들로 영어공부를 해

● **Mentors is famous for** publishing very useful English learning books.
멘토스는 매우 유용한 영어교재를 출판하는 것으로 유명해.

● **Mentors is a very well-known ESL publishing company.**
멘토스는 유명한 영어출판 회사야.

● **My favorite ESL books are** published by **the Mentors publishing company.**
내가 좋아하는 영어교재들은 멘토스 출판사가 출판한거야.

A: Which books do you recommend for learning English?
영어공부를 하는데 어떤 책을 추천하겠어?

B: Mentors is very famous for ESL books. I recommend any of their stuff. 멘토스는 아주 유명한 영어교재 출판사야. 멘토스가 출판한 아무 도서나 추천해.

02 YouTube is a good way to learn English
유튜브는 영어를 배우는 좋은 방법이야

● **He's so eager to learn English.** 걔는 영어배울려고 열 올리고 있어.

● **His enthusiasm for** learning English **is incredible.**
걔의 영어공부 열정은 믿을 수 없을 정도야.

● **I've never met anyone** with his passion for studying English **before.**
걔만큼 영어를 열정적으로 공부하는 사람은 전에 본 적이 없어.

A: Every time I see him he is studying English. 걘 언제봐도 영어공부를 하고 있어.
B: Yes, he is very eager to learn English. 맞아. 걘 영어공부에 매우 열정적이야.

03

English apps are also popular to learn active English 영어회화어플 또한 실제 영어를 배우는데 매우 인기가 있어

- These days there are many different kinds of apps you can use to study English. 요즘 영어공부하는데 활용할 수 있는 다양한 종류의 어플이 있어.

- I found some really good YouTube channels for studying English. 난 영어공부를 하는데 좋은 유튜브채널을 몇 개 찾았어.

A: What are some different ways I can learn English? 영어배울 수 있는 다른 방법이 있어?

B: These days you can use apps, YouTube channels and podcasts to study English. 요즘에는 어플, 유튜브 그리고 팟캐스트를 활용해 영어를 공부할 수 있어.

04

I go to an English Institute twice a week 난 주에 두번 영어학원에 다녀

- I'm learning English with the help of Netflix and subtitles. 난 넷플릭스와 자막의 도움으로 영어를 공부하고 있어.

- It's hard for me to enjoy movies without Korean subtitles. 난 한글자막없이 영화를 즐기기가 어려워.

A: Are you watching TV shows to help improve your English? 영어실력향상을 위해 TV 프로그램들을 보고 있어?

B: Yes, I've been watching Netflix comedies with subtitles. It's really been useful. 어, 난 넷플릭스 코미디를 자막으로 보고 있는데 매우 도움이 돼.

05

I do free talking with a native speaker 난 네이티브와 자유로이 영어로 말해

- I think this is the best way to learn living English. 이게 산 영어를 배우는 최고방법이라 생각해.

- If possible, practice speaking with a native speaker to help improve. 가능하다면, 영어를 향상시키기 위해 네이티브와 대화를 하도록 해.

A: I do free talking with a native speaker from America. 난 미국출신의 네이티브와 자유로이 대화를 나눠.

B: Nice! That's a very useful way to learn to speak naturally. 잘하고 있어! 자연스럽게 말하는 법을 배우는데 아주 유용한 방법이야.

039

My English isn't good enough
영어가 달려서요

해도해도 말이 안나오는게 영어다. 그래서 영어실력이 부족하다고 말할 때가 많은데 이때는 can't speak English very well, 혹은 not be good enough, be poor at speaking English 혹은 be broken 등의 표현을 사용한다.

01 I'm sorry, but I can't speak English very well
미안하지만 영어가 서툴러요

- You'd better check with **someone else.** 다른 사람에게 물어보세요.

- I can't speak English very well. **Could you ask someone else?**
  저기 영어를 잘 말 못해요. 다른 사람에게 물어볼래요?

- My English isn't very good. **You should probably ask someone else.**
  영어가 서툴러서요. 다른 사람에게 물어보세요.

A: Excuse me, could you help translate this for me?
실례지만, 이거 통역하는거 도와줄래요?

B: Sorry but my English ability isn't very good. You'd better ask someone else to help you. 미안하지만, 영어가 서툴러요. 다른 사람에게 물어 도움받으세요.

02 My English isn't good enough
영어가 달려서요

- I'm embarrassed. **My English isn't good enough.** 당황했어요. 영어가 달려서요.

- I feel ashamed about my level of English. 난 내 영어수준이 창피해.

- My English isn't as good as it should be. 내 영어는 그렇게 좋지 못해요.

A: How is your English? 네 영어실력은 어때?
B: I'm embarrassed to say that it isn't very good.
말하기 창피하지만 그렇게 좋지 못해.

03 I'm poor at speaking English.

난 영어 말하는데 서툴러

- I'm not good at **speaking English.** 난 영어를 말하는데 잘하지 못해.
- I'm not strong in **spoken English.** 난 구어체 회화에 약해.
- I'm very weak when **it comes to speaking English.**
  난 영어말하는데 있어서는 매우 약해.

A: Can you call the school for me? 나 대신 학교에 전화해줄래?

B: Sorry but I'm very weak when it comes to speaking English.
미안하지만 영어말하기에는 서툴러서 밀야.

04 My English is broken. It's more Konglish than

English 내 영어는 유창하지 못해. 영어라기보다는 콩글리시에 가까워

- My English skills **are very poor.** 내 영어실력은 정말 형편없어.
- My Konglish **is better than my English.** 난 영어보다 콩글리시를 더 잘해.
- I have terrible English skills. 난 영어실력이 끔찍하게 형편없어.

A: My English is so broken. All I know is Konglish.
내 영어는 유창하지 못해. 아는 거라고는 콩글리시뿐이야.

B: No! Your English is very good. 아냐! 네 영어는 아주 훌륭해.

05 Please correct my errors when I use wrong English

내가 틀린 영어를 쓸 때 바로 잡아줘요

- Let me know when I make a mistake **using English.**
  영어하다 실수할 때가 있으면 알려줘요.
- If I say something incorrectly, **please tell me.** 내가 뭔가 틀리게 말하면 내게 말해줘요.
- When I say something wrong, **please correct me.**
  내가 틀리게 뭔가 말하면 바로 잡아줘요.

A: Your English is really good. 너의 영어는 아주 훌륭해.

B: Yes, but when I make a mistake, please let me know.
그래, 하지만, 내가 실수하게 되면 알려줘.

Unit 01 자기의 기본정보 말하기 | **101** |

040

What do you call this in English?

이걸 영어로 뭐라고 해요?

네이티브와 대화를 하다 보면 특정단어를 영어로는 어떻게 말하는지 궁금해질 때가 있다. 전형적으로 쓰이는 표현은 What do you call A in English?, 혹은 How do you say A in English?라고 하면 된다.

What do you call this in English?

이걸 영어로 뭐라고 해요?

- What's 'chobop' in English? 초밥이 영어로 뭐야?
- What's the English word for "chobop"? 초밥을 영어로 하면 어떻게 돼?
- We really don't have a word for it in English.
  영어에는 사실 그것에 해당되는 단어가 없어.
- In English, what word do you use for 'chobob?"

A: What's the English word for "chobop?" 초밥에 해당되는 영어단어는 뭐야?
B: In English "chobop" is "sushi." 영어로는 초밥은 스시야.

How do you say 'dubu' in English?

두부를 영어로 뭐라고 하지요?

- How do you say that in English? 저것을 영어로 뭐라고 해?
- In English, how do I say "dubu?" 영어로 두부를 뭐라고 해?
- Could you tell me how to say "dubu" in English?
  두부를 영어로 뭐라고 하는지 알려줄래?

A: Excuse me but could you tell me how to say "dubu" in English?
   실례지만 영어로 두부를 뭐라고 하나요?
B: Tofu! 토푸요!

03 What's the word for that in English?
영어로 그걸 말하는 단어는 뭔가요?

- What word do you use for **that in English?** 영어로 그걸 말할 때는 어떤 단어를 쓰나요?
- In English, could you tell me what word you use for this? 영어로 이걸 뭐라고 하나요?
- If I want to say this in English, what word would I use? 이걸 영어로 말하려면 어떤 단어를 써야 하나요?

A: What word do you use for that in English?
영어로 그걸 말할 때 어떤 단어를 쓰나요?

B: We say "tuna sushi." 참치 스시라고 해요.

04 I don't know how to say it in English
이걸 영어로 뭐라고 하는지 모르겠어

- I'm not sure how to say this **in English.** 이걸 영어로 뭐라고 하는지 잘 모르겠어.
- I can't remember how to say this **in English.** 이걸 영어로 뭐라고 하는지 잊어버렸어.

A: Excuse me but what's this in English? 미안하지만 영어로 이게 뭔가요?

B: Sorry but I can't remember how to say it in English.
미안하지만 영어로 뭐라고 하는지 잊어버렸어요.

05 How long have you been studying English?
영어공부를 한지 얼마나 됐어?

- How do you study English? 영어공부를 어떻게 해?
- Why are you studying English? 영어공부를 왜 해?
- If I could speak English well, **I'd get a pay raise.**
내가 영어회화를 잘 한다면, 급여인상을 받을텐데.

A: Why are you studying English? 너는 왜 영어를 공부해.

B: Because I want to travel. If I could speak English well, I'd enjoy traveling more. 해외여행을 하고 싶어서. 영어를 잘 말한다면, 해외여행을 더 즐길 수 있을거야.

041

I'd happy if I could stay in good health

내가 건강한 상태로 지낼 수 있다면 기쁠거야

Unit 01의 마지막으로 나의 장래희망에 대해 말해본다. 삼성에 입사하거나, 자기 사업을 하거나, 변호사나 회계사 자격증을 따고 싶다고 할 때의 표현을 알아본다. 하지만 가장 중요한 것은 위의 제목처럼 건강이 아닐까…

I want to have my own business
내 사업을 하고 싶어

● I want to run a Korean restaurant. 난 한식당을 운영해보고 싶어.

● My dream is to work for Samsung. 내 꿈은 삼성에 입사하는거야.

● Are you satisfied with the present job? 현재 직장에 만족해?

A: What are your plans for the future? 미래의 계획은 뭐야?
B: My dream is to work for Google. 내 꿈은 구글에서 일하는거야.

I want to get a certified public accountant
난 공인회계사 자격증을 따고 싶어

● I want to qualify as a lawyer. 난 변호사가 되고 싶어.

● I want to get my pharmacist's license. 난 약사자격증을 따고 싶어.

● I want to get my tax accounting certification. 난 세무사 자격증을 따고 싶어.

A: Do you have any plans this year? 금년에 뭐 계획이 있어?
B: Yes, I want to get my pharmacist's license. 어, 약사자격증을 따고 싶어.

03 I'd like to live in a house with a large yard
큰 마당이 있는 집에서 살고 싶어

- I'd like to live in a large apartment. 대형평수 아파트에서 살고 싶어.
- I want to live in a penthouse in Gangnam. 강남의 펜트하우스에서 살고 싶어.
- I'd love to live in a traditional Korean home in the countryside.
  교외의 전통한옥에서 살고 싶어.

A: What is your dream home? 너의 꿈의 집은 뭐야?
B: I'd like to live in a large house in the countryside.
   전원지역의 큰 집에서 살고 싶어.

04 I'd like to be promoted to office manager
난 실장으로 승진하고 싶어

- My dream is to get married and then work together.
  나의 꿈은 결혼해서 직장을 계속 다니는거야.
- Have you ever wanted to work overseas? 해외에서 근무를 원했던 적이 있어?
- I'd love to be promoted to the position of manager. 난 매니저로 승진하고 싶어.

A: Do you have any career ambitions? 직장에서의 야망이 뭐 있어?
B: Yes, I'd love to be promoted to office manager. 어, 난 실장으로 승진하고 싶어.

05 I'd happy if I could stay in good health
내가 건강한 상태로 지낼 수 있다면 기쁠거야

- Health is more important to me than a high salary.
  건강은 급여를 많이 받는 것보다 더 중요해.
- If I am healthy, I'll be happy. 내가 건강하면, 기쁠거야.
- I want to stay healthy. 난 건강한 상태를 유지하고 싶어.

A: What's more important to you, a big salary or good health?
   고임금과 건강을 누리는 것중 어떤게 더 중요해?
B: I'll be happy if I can stay in good health. 내가 건강을 누릴 수 있다면 행복할거야.

Unit

2

나의
건강

건강해

I'm in good shape

난 건강이 좋아

건강이 좋다(healthy, in good shape)거나, 반대로 몸이 좀 안좋거나(be not feeling well), 쉽게 피곤해지거나(get tired easily) 그리고 활력이 없거나(have no energy) 등의 표현을 기억해둔다.

01 I am healthy

난 건강해

● **What's your secret for staying healthy?** 건강을 유지하는 비결이 뭐야?

● **What do you do to stay so healthy?** 건강을 유지하기 위해서 뭘 하고 있어?

● **How do you stay in such good shape?** 어떻게 양호한 건강을 유지하고 있어?

A: What's your secret for staying so healthy?
건강을 그렇게 유지하고 있는 비결이 뭐야?

B: I eat well and exercise a little bit each day. 잘 먹고 매일 조금씩 운동을 해.

02 I'm trying to live a healthier life these days

난 요즘 더 건강한 삶을 살려고 하고 있어

● I am doing my best to stay in shape these days.
난 요즘 건강을 유지하려고 최선을 다하고 있어.

● I am really watching what I eat this year.
나는 금년에 먹는 것에 정말 주의를 기울이고 있어.

● I am trying to watch my weight. 난 살찌지 않도록 먹는거에 신중하려고 하고 있어.

A: Why aren't you drinking any beer? 넌 왜 맥주 한모금도 마시지 않는거야?

B: I'm really trying to watch my weight this year.
올해에는 살찌지 않게 먹는거에 조심하려고 하고 있어.

03 I'm in good shape[health]
난 건강이 좋아

- My parents are in good health. 내 부모님의 건강상태는 좋아.

- I get up early to help keep me in good health. 건강을 유지하기 위해 일찍 일어나고 있어.

- Are you in good shape? 너 건강상태가 좋아?

A: Both my parents are in good shape. 내 부모님 두 분 다 건강상태가 양호해.
B: That's great. You look like you are in good shape too.
잘됐네. 너도 역시 건강상태가 좋은 것처럼 보여.

04 I'm not feeling well
난 몸상태가 안좋아

- I don't feel well. 몸이 좋지 않아.

- I'm feeling a little under the weather. 난 몸상태가 좀 좋지 않아.

- I think I might be ill. 내가 병에 걸린 것 같아.

A: What's wrong? 왜 그래?
B: I don't feel well. I think I might be ill. 몸상태가 안좋아. 병에 걸린 것 같아.

05 I get tired easily
쉽게 피곤해져

- I get tired easily these days. Something's wrong with me.
요즘 쉽게 피곤해져. 내 몸상태가 좀 이상해.

- These days I have no energy. 요즘은 활력이 없어.

- I feel absolutely exhausted this week. 난 이번주에 정말이지 완전히 녹초가 됐어.

A: Are you OK? 너 괜찮아?
B: I'm not sure why but I feel absolutely exhausted today.
이유를 모르겠지만 오늘 완전히 녹초가 됐어

002 I'm on a diet

다이어트 하는 중이야

건강의 적신호인 살이 쪘다고 할 때는 get fat, put on[gain] weight를 쓰고, 반대로 살이 빠진다고 할 때는 lose (some) weight라고 하면 된다. 살이 찐 사람은 다이어트를 하게 마련인데 이때는 be on a diet라 한다.

01 I'm getting fat
살이 쪄

- I've gotten fat **these days**. 난 요즘 살쪘어.

- **These days I've put on a few kilograms.** 요즘, 몇 킬로 살이 쪘어.

- I've really gained a lot of weight **this month**. 이번 달에 정말로 살이 많이 쪘어.

A: You look a bit bigger than before. 넌 전보다 좀 살이 찐 것 같아.
B: Yeah, I've put on a few kilograms since we last met.
어, 지난번 만난 이후로 몇 킬로 살이 쪘어.

02 I've put on[gained] weight
살쪘어

- I tend to put on weight **easily**. 난 살이 쉽게 찌는 스타일이야.

- It doesn't take much for me to gain some weight. 난 금방 살이 쪄.

- I pack on the pounds **really easily**. 난 정말이지 쉽게 몇 파운드 살이 쪄.

A: Why aren't you eating more? 왜 더 먹지 않는거야?
B: Because I tend to put on weight easily. 난 살이 쉽게 찌는 스타일이어서.

03 I lost some weight
난 살이 좀 빠졌어

- I lost some weight because I go to a gym to work out.
  체육관에 가서 운동을 해서 살이 좀 빠졌어.

- I've slimmed down a bit because I've stopped eating sweets.
  단것을 그만 먹었더니 살이 좀 빠졌어.

- I've dropped a few kilograms because I'm exercising more regularly.
  정기적으로 운동을 하니 몇 킬로 살이 빠졌어.

A: You look fantastic. Have you lost some weight?
너 멋져 보인다. 살이 좀 빠진거야?

B: Yes, I've slimmed down a bit because I'm exercising more regularly.
어, 정기적으로 운동을 하니까 살이 좀 빠졌어.

04 I'm dieting
나 다이어트하고 있어

- These days I'm really watching what I eat. 요즈음에는 정말 먹는거 조심하고 있어.

- I've cut down on sugar in my diet. 식단에서 설탕을 줄였어.

- I'm trying to eat less carbohydrates these days. 난 요즘 탄수화물 섭취를 줄이려 하고 있어.

A: You look fantastic these days! 너 요즘 멋져 보인다!
B: Thanks, I've cut down sugar in my diet and I feel so much better.
고마워, 식단에서 설탕을 줄였더니 기분이 더 좋아져.

05 I'm on a diet
다이어트하는 중이야

- A lot of women go on diets. 많은 여성들이 다이어트를 하고 있어.

- My boyfriend is going on a low fat diet. 내 남친은 저지방식 식이요법을 하고 있어.

- I am on the Atkin's no carb diet. 난 앳킨의 탄수화물을 섭취하지 않는 다이어트를 하고 있어.

A: Why aren't you eating any rice or bread? 넌 왜 밥과 빵을 먹지 않는거야?
B: I'm on the Atkin's diet. 난 앳킨의 다이어트를 하고 있어.

003

건강상태

My hair is turning gray
내 머리가 점점 하얗게 변하고 있어

머리가 빠지기 시작하면 lose one's hair, 기억이 깜빡깜빡 잊어버리면 be forgetful, 그리고 시력이 나빠지면 One's eyesight is getting worse라 한다. 참고로 원시는 farsighted, 근시는 nearsighted라고 하면 된다.

01 I'm losing my hair these days
요즘 머리가 빠져

- He's bald. 걔는 대머리야.

- My hair is turning gray. 내 머리가 점점 하얗게 변하고 있어.

- I'm getting a bald spot **on the top of my head.** 난 정수리 부분이 탈모가 되고 있어.

  A: Why does he always wear a hat? 왜 걔는 항상 모자를 쓰고 있는거야?
  B: Because he's bald I guess. 내 생각에 대머리라서 그러는 것 같아.

02 I'd like to gain some weight
살이 쪘으면 해

- I've gained three kilograms **in five months.** 5개월에 3킬로 살이 쪘어.

- I'm a little overweight. 난 조금 과체중이야.

- I've put on a few kilograms **this past winter.** 지난 겨울에 몇 킬로 살이 쪘어.

  A: You look different. 너 좀 달리 보인다.
  B: Yes, I've gained some weight the past few months.
     어, 지난 몇 달동안 살이 좀 쪘어.

03 I'm rather skinny
난 다소 날씬해

- I'm on a diet. 난 다이어트 중이야.

- I'd be happy if I had a more slender figure. 좀 더 날씬한 몸매였으면 좋을텐데.

- I hope to lose a little weight. 살이 좀 빠지기를 바래.

A: Why are you only eating salad? 왜 넌 샐러드만 먹어?
B: I want to lose a little weight. 살을 좀 빼고 싶어.

04 I'm afraid I'm becoming forgetful
점점 깜박하는게 걱정돼

- My memory is starting to go! 내 기억력이 점점 감퇴되고 있어!

- I can't remember things as well as I used to. 난 기억력이 예전만 못해.

- As I get older, I forget things more often. 나이가 들어감에 따라 더 자주 깜빡해.

A: You lost the car keys again? 자동차 키 어디에 두었는지 또 잊었어?
B: Yes. My memory is starting to go! 어. 내 기억력이 맛이 가고 있어!

05 My eyesight is getting worse
내 시력이 점점 나빠지고 있어

- My eyesight is much weaker than it used to be. 내 시력이 예전보다 훨씬 나빠졌어.

- I wear glasses because I am farsighted. 내가 원시여서 안경을 쓰고 있어.

- She is nearsighted. 걔는 근시야.

A: Why do you wear glasses? 왜 안경을 쓰는거야?
B: I'm nearsighted. 근시여서.

004

I usually go to the gym after work

보통 퇴근 후에 체육관에 가

살을 빼기 위해서 혹은 건강을 유지하기 위해서 많은 사람들이 운동을 한다. 가장 쉬운 jogging를 하거나, 혹은 go to the gym하고 work out을 하게 된다. 운동이 필요하다고 할 때는 need exercise라고 하면 된다.

01 I jog every day for my health
건강을 위해 매일 조깅해

- I am working out three or four times a week to stay in shape.
  건강을 유지하기 위해 일주일에 3–4번 운동을 하고 있어.

- I ride a bicycle to work every day to keep in shape.
  난 건강을 유지하기 위해 매일 자전거 타고 출근해.

- I am trying to walk for 30 minutes a day to get some regular exercise.
  정기적으로 운동을 좀 하려고 매일 30분씩 걸으려고 하고 있어.

A: Do you take the subway to work? 전철타고 출근해?
B: No, I ride a bicycle to work to help stay in shape.
   아니, 건강을 유지하려고 자전거로 출근해.

02 I usually go to the gym after work
보통 퇴근 후에 체육관에 가

- I go to the sports[fitness] club twice a week. 일주일에 두 번 헬스클럽에 가.

- I try to go swimming a few times a week. 일주일에 몇번 수영을 하려고 해.

- I've been going to a rock climbing gym these days.
  난 요즘은 체육관에 암벽등반을 하러 다녀.

A: How do you stay in shape? 넌 어떻게 건강을 유지해?
B: I go to the swimming pool two or three times a week.
   일주일에 두세번 수영장에 가.

03 I usually work out after work
퇴근 후에 보통 운동을 해

- I always go jogging **on weekends.** 난 항상 주말마다 조깅을 하러 가.
- I like to do push-ups and sit-ups **every morning before I go to work.**
  난 매일아침 출근 전에 푸시업과 윗몸일으키기 하는 것을 좋아해.
- My mother goes to aerobics **every Monday and Wednesday.**
  엄마는 매주 월요일과 수요일에 에어로빅을 하러 다니셔.

A: What do you usually do on your weekends? 주말에는 보통 뭘 해?
B: I always go jogging with my best friend. 난 젤 친한 친구와 항상 조깅을 해.

04 I haven't been getting enough exercise lately
요즘 충분한 운동을 못하고 있어

- You need exercise. 넌 운동 좀 해야 돼.
- I'm so out of shape **these days.** 난 요즈음 건강상태가 아주 안좋아.
- I haven't done any kind of physical activity **in a long time.**
  난 오랫동안 어떤 종류의 운동도 하지 않았어.

A: Have you gained a bit of weight? 너 살이 좀 찐거야?
B: Yes, I need exercise. I haven't done any physical activity in ages.
어, 난 운동을 해야 돼. 오랫동안 어떤 운동도 하지 않았어.

05 I'm really into health food now
난 요즘 건강식에 관심이 정말 많아

- I'm really into health food and yoga **now.**
  내가 요즘 건강식하고 요가에 정말 관심이 많거든.
- I've really gotten into eating healthy. 난 건강식을 하고 있어.
- I am passionate about staying in shape. 난 건강을 유지하는데 아주 열정적이야.

A: You look fantastic! 너 멋져 보인다!
B: Yes, I'm passionate about eating healthy foods and staying in shape
these days. 어, 요즘 난 건강식을 하고 건강을 유지하는데 아주 열정적이야.

005

I took up golf two months ago

골프를 두달 전에 시작했어

구체적인 운동을 하는 경우를 본다. 요가를 하다는 do yoga. 테니스 동호회에 가입하다는 belong to a tennis club. 그리고 골프를 잘한다고 할 때는 be good at playing golf. 그리고 운동이나 취미를 시작한다고 할 때는 take up이나 start를 쓰면 된다.

01 I'm interested in the new yoga class

새로 생긴 요가교실에 관심이 있어

- I'm going to start doing aerobics next month. 다음 달에 에어로빅을 시작할거야.

- I'm trying pilates this week. 난 이번주에 필라테스를 해보려고.

- I'm interested in trying out hot yoga. 난 핫요가를 해보는데 관심이 있어.

A: I'm trying out pilates this Wednesday. 이번 수요일에 필라테스를 해보려고.
B: Interesting. Please let me know what it's like. I may try it too.
흥미롭네. 어떤지 알려줘. 나도 해볼 수 있으니까.

02 I belong to a tennis club

테니스 클럽에 들었어

- I am joining a hiking club that goes on trips twice a month.
한달에 두번 하이킹하는 등산클럽에 가입할거야.

- I am on an ice hockey team that plays twice a week.
난 일주일에 두번 경기하는 아이스하키 팀에 들어갔어.

- My girlfriend is in a rock climbing club that takes trips once a month.
내 여친은 한달에 한번 하는 암벽등반클럽에 가입했어.

A: My girlfriend is in a rock climbing club that takes trips once a month. 내 여친은 한달에 한번하는 암벽등반클럽에 들어갔어.
B: I couldn't do that. I'm scared of heights. 나라면 못할거야. 고소공포증이 있어서.

03 I'm good at playing golf
난 골프를 잘 쳐

- I'm into golf. 난 골프에 빠졌어.
- My brother is crazy about golf. 내 형은 골프를 엄청 좋아해.
- I am passionate about golf. 난 골프치는 것을 정말 좋아해.

A: What's your favorite sport? 가장 좋아하는 스포츠가 뭐야?
B: I'm really into golf. 난 정말이지 골프에 빠져 있어.

04 I took up golf two months ago
골프를 두달 전에 시작했어

- It's only been a year since I started playing golf. 골프를 친 지가 1년 밖에 안됐어.
- I've just started learning golf. 난 골프치는 것을 배우기 시작했어.
- I've been playing golf since I was 8 years old. 난 8살 때부터 골프를 쳐왔어.

A: How long have you been playing golf? 골프친지 얼마나 됐어?
B: I've just started learning it. 이제 배우기 시작했어.

05 My score was 3-under-par 69
3언더파로 69타야

- My golf handicap is 20. 핸디캡이 20야.
- I finished the round at 2 under par. 2언더파로 라운드를 마쳤어.
- My golf game is terrible. 내 골프게임은 아주 으악야.

A: Are you any good at golf? 혹 골프를 잘 쳐?
B: No, my golf game is terrible. I usually get between 20 to 30 over par. 아니. 으악야. 보통 규정타수보다 20-30타 더 쳐.

006
I enjoy camping with my family

난 가족과 함께 캠핑하는 것을 좋아해

운동을 위하여 …강습을 받는다고 할 때는 take ~ lessons, 하이킹을 좋아한다고 할 때는 like to go hiking, 그리고 캠핑[스키]을 좋아한다고 할 때는 enjoy camping[skiing] 등의 표현으로 말하면 된다.

I'm taking swimming lessons
수영강습을 들어

- I like to go rafting. 난 래프팅하는 걸 좋아해.
- I enjoy water sports. 난 수상스포츠를 즐겨.
- I'm learning how to water ski. 수상스키하는 법을 배우고 있어.

A: Why are you packing your swimming suit? 왜 수영복을 챙기는거야?
B: I'm taking swimming lessons today after work. 오늘 퇴근 후에 수영강습을 받아.

I don't like to go hiking
난 하이킹가는 것을 좋아하지 않아

- How do you feel these days? 요즘 기분이 어때?
- I am not a fan of hiking. 난 하이킹을 좋아하지 않아.
- I really don't like being outdoors. 난 정말이지 야외활동은 좋아하지 않아.

A: Do you like going to the mountains? 넌 산에 가는거 좋아해?
B: No, I don't like hiking or being outdoors.
아니, 하이킹이나 야외활동은 좋아하지 않아.

03 I enjoy camping with my family
난 가족과 함께 캠핑하는 것을 좋아해

- I really enjoy being outside in nature with my family.
  난 가족과 함께 자연 속에 나가는 것을 즐겨.

- I love going on camping trips with family or friends.
  난 가족이나 친구들과 캠핑가는 것을 좋아해.

- Being outdoors is very enjoyable for me. 야외에 나가는게 난 아주 즐거워.

A: You are going camping again this weekend? 이번 주말에 또 캠핑가?

B: Yes, I really enjoy camping with my family.
어, 난 정말 가족과 함께 캠핑가는 것을 즐겨.

04 I enjoy skiing every winter
매 겨울마다 스키를 타

- I can't wait to go skiing. 스키타고 싶어 죽겠어.

- I am crazy about skiing. 난 스키타는 것을 정말 좋아해.

- I love skiing more than anything. 난 다른 어떤 것보다 스키타는 것을 좋아해.

A: Can you ski? 스키탈 수 있어?

B: Of course! I am crazy about skiing. 당연하지! 난 스키타는 것을 정말 좋아해.

05 I stretch every morning
난 매일 아침 스트레칭을 해

- What do you do to stay healthy? 건강을 유지하기 위해 뭘 해?

- What's the secret of your good health? 네 양호한 건강의 비결은 뭐야?

- How do you stay in such good shape? 어떻게 건강한 상태를 유지하고 있는거야?

A: What's your secret to staying so healthy?
그렇게 건강함을 유지하고 있는 비결은 뭐야?

B: I eat right and exercise a little bit every day.
적정하게 먹고 매일 조금씩 운동하는거야.

007

I'm so burned out

난 정말 뻗었어

먼저 식욕이 없다고 할 때는 have a poor appetite, 혹은 have no appetite, 특
정식품에 앨러지가 있다고 할 때는 be allergic to+식품이라고 한다. 그리고 지쳤을
때는 exhausted, burned out 등의 표현을 쓴다.

I have a poor appetite these days
요즘 입맛이 없어

- **What's wrong with you?** 어디가 아프세요?
- **I have no appetite today.** 오늘 입맛이 없어.
- **I can't keep any food down today.** 오늘 먹는 음식은 다 토하고 있어.

A: **What's wrong with you?** 어디가 안좋아?
B: **I don't know why but I have no appetite today.**
이유를 모르겠지만 오늘 입맛이 없어.

I'm allergic to peaches
난 복숭아 앨러지가 있어

- **I have an allergy to grapes.** 난 포도 앨러지가 있어.
- **Are you allergic to apples?** 사과 앨러지가 있어?
- **I have dust allergies.** 난 먼지 앨러지가 있어.
- **He has a serious peanut allergy.** 걘 땅콩 앨러지가 아주 심해.

A: **Make sure there are not peanuts in that candy.**
그 사탕에 땅콩 들어있지 않는거 확인해.
B: **Right! He has a serious allergy to peanuts.** 맞아! 걘 땅콩에 앨러지가 심하지.

03 You look exhausted
넌 지쳐보여

- **You** look **pale. What's the matter with you?** 창백해보여. 무슨 일이야?
- **You** look **like death!** 넌 몹시 지쳐보여!
- **She** looks **green.** 걘 창백해보여.

A: You look like death. What's wrong? 넌 지쳐보여. 무슨 일 있어?
B: I drank 3 bottles of soju last night. 지난밤에 소주 3병을 마셨어.

04 I'm so burned out
난 정말 뻗었어

- **I'm** stressed out. 난 스트레스를 많이 받았어.
- **These days I'm** going crazy. 요즈음 미치겠어.
- **Work** is driving me up the wall **these days.** 요즘 일 때문에 미치겠어.

A: What's the matter? 무슨 일이야?
B: I'm stressed out because of my boyfriend. 남친 때문에 스트레스를 많이 받았어.

05 I feel sick
토할 것 같아

- **I** feel cold. 추워.
- **I** feel chill. 좀 추워.
- **I** feel dizzy. 어지러워.
- **I** feel okay. 난 괜찮아.

A: Why are you lying down? 왜 누워있는거야?
B: I suddenly felt dizzy. 갑자기 어지러워서.

008

I caught a cold from you

감기 너한테 옮았어

감기 걸렸을 때는 get a cold 혹은 catch a cold를 쓴다. 다만 독감에 걸렸을 때는 get the flu라고 한다는 점을 기억해둔다. 콧물이 흐르면 have a runny nose, 목이 부었으면 swollen, 그리고 코가 막혔을 때는 congested라는 단어를 쓴다는 것을 알아둔다.

01 I have a fever
열이 나

- I have a slight fever. 난 열이 조금 나.
- My fever has gone down. 열이 좀 내려갔어.
- I'm running a fever. 난 열이 나.

A: Are you coming to work today? 오늘 출근하는거야?
B: No, I'm running a high fever so it's best I stay home.
아니, 열이 많이 나서 집에 있는게 최선인 것 같아.

02 I got a cold
난 감기에 걸렸어

- I've had a cold **for two weeks**. 난 2주전에 감기에 걸렸어.
- I rarely catch colds. 난 거의 감기에 걸리지 않아.
- I got the flu. 난 독감에 걸렸어.
- I caught a cold **from you**. 감기 너한테 옮았어.

A: I think I caught my cold from you. 감기를 너한테 옮은 것 같아.
B: Sorry! 미안해!

03 I have a runny nose
콧물이 흘러

- My nose is running. 콧물이 흘러.
- My nose won't stop running. 콧물이 멈추지 않고 계속 흘러.
- I can't stop coughing. 기침이 멈추지 않아.

A: You sound horrible. 너 목소리가 이상하게 들려.
B: Yes, I can't stop coughing. 어. 기침이 멈추지를 않아.

04 My throat is swollen
목이 부었어

- I've got a really sore throat. 목이 정말 아파.
- My throat's sore. 목이 아파요.
- I have a sore throat **due to a cold**. 감기 때문에 목이 아파.

A: You sound hoarse. 너 목소리가 쉰 것 같아.
B: Yes, I've got a really sore throat. 어. 목이 정말이지 아파.

05 I'm very congested
난 코가 많이 막혔어

- **My nose** is very stuffed up. 코가 정말이지 많이 막혔어.
- My sinuses are plugged up. 내 코가 꽉 막혔어.
- My sinuses are congested. 코가 막혔어.

A: You sound different. 너 목소리가 다르게 들려.
B: Yes, it's because my nose is completely stuffed up. 어. 코가 꽉 막혀서 그래.

009

Did you get your PCR test?

너 PCR 테스트 했어?

유행하는 코로나에 대해서 말해본다. 확진자는 a confirmed case for Covid19, 자가격리는 be a self-quarantine 그리고 외출할(when going out) 때나 공공 장소에서(in public places) 마스크를 쓰다는 wear a mask이다.

I'm a confirmed case for Covid19

난 코로나 확진자야

- I tested positive for COVID **yesterday.** 난 어제 코로나 확진판정을 받았어.
- I got COVID from **my co-worker.** 난 동료로부터 코로나에 걸렸어.
- I'm **not sure how I** contracted COVID. 내가 어떻게 코로나에 걸렸는지 모르겠어.

A: Did you get your PCR test? 너 PCR 테스트 했어?
B: Yes, I tested positive for COVID this morning.
어, 오늘 아침에 확진판정을 받았어.

I'm contagious so I'm under a self-quarantine

난 확진되어서 자가격리 중이야

- I tested positive for COVID **so I have to** self-quarantine at home.
  난 코로나 확진판정을 받아서 집에서 자가 격리해야 돼.
- I have COVID symptoms **so I need to get tested as soon as possible.**
  코로나 증상이 있어서 가능한 한 빨리 검사를 받아야 돼.
- I had a close contact with a friend who had COVID so I need to self-quarantine. 코로나에 걸린 친구와 밀접접촉을 해서 자가격리를 해야 돼.

A: Why are you doing a self-quarantine? 넌 왜 자가격리를 하는거야?
B: Because I tested positive for COVID three days ago.
3일전에 확진판정을 받아서 그래.

03 I need to wear a mask when going out
외출할 때는 마스크를 써야 돼

- The government decided to enforce a lockdown to stop the spread of COVID. 정부는 코로나 확산을 막기 위해서 법적으로 봉쇄를 하기로 했어.

- There are many restrictions people have to follow under the lockdown guidelines. 봉쇄정책하에서는 사람들이 따라야 하는 많은 제한조치가 있어.

A: Do you remember the lockdown when only 6 people could meet for private gatherings under the government guidelines? 정부지침으로 사적모임이 6명으로 제한되었던 봉쇄정책이 기억나?

B: Yes, I'm glad those days are behind us. 어, 그런 날들이 지나가서 기뻐.

04 Everyone must wear a mask in public places
모든 사람은 공공장소에서 마스크를 반드시 써야 돼

- Masks are required to use public transportation.
대중교통을 이용할 때는 마스크를 써야 돼.

- Masks help prevent the spread of COVID. 마스크는 코로나확산을 방지하는데 도움이 돼.

- There is a mandate to wear masks in public places.
공공장소에서는 마스크를 써야 하는 지침이 있어.

A: Do I have to wear a mask there? 거기서 마스크를 써야 돼?
B: Yes, masks are required indoors. 어, 실내에서 마스크를 써야 돼.

05 My temperature is very high
내가 열이 아주 많이 나

- I have a high temperature. 고열이 나.

- I need to check my temperature. 내 체온을 재야 돼.

- My temperature is running high. 내 체온이 높아.

A: You don't look well. 너 안색이 좋지 않아.
B: My temperature is very high. 내 체온이 매우 높아.

아플 때 4 - 머리 1

010

I have a migraine headache

난 편두통을 앓고 있어

머리가 아플 때는 기본적으로 have a headache. 편두통은 have a migraine headache. 그리고 머리가 깨질듯이 아플 때는 have a splitting headache라고 한다. 한편 목이나 어깨가 뻐근할 때는 stiff를 쓰면 된다.

01 I have a headache
머리가 아파

- My head was hurt **in an accident.** 사고로 머리를 다쳤어.
- I have a migraine headache. 난 편두통을 앓고 있어.
- I've got a terrible headache. 머리가 아파 죽겠어.

A: I have a terrible migraine. 편두통으로 아파 죽겠어.
B: Take some aspirin. 아스피린을 먹어.

02 I've had a bad cough since yesterday
어제부터 기침이 아주 많이 나

- I've been coughing **all day long.** 하루 온종일 기침을 했어.
- I can't stop coughing. 기침이 멈추지가 않아.
- I have a terrible cough. 끔찍하게 기침이 나.

A: I've been coughing all day long. 온종일 기침을 했어.
B: You should take some cough syrup. 너 기침약을 좀 먹어야겠다.

03 I have a stuffy nose
난 코가 막혔어

- **My nose** is really stuffed up. 코가 정말이지 꽉 막혔어.
- **My nose** is plugged up. 내 코가 막혔어.
- **My sinuses** are completely blocked up. 내 코가 꽉 막혔어.

A: You look tired. 너 피곤해보인다.
B: Yes, my nose is really stuffed up so I couldn't sleep well last night.
어, 코가 꽉 막혀서 지난밤에 잠을 잘 못잤어.

04 I have a stiff neck
목이 뻐근해

- I have stiff shoulders. 어깨가 뻐근해.
- **My shoulders** are stiff. 어깨가 뻣뻣해.
- **My knees** are really stiff. 내 무릎이 뻣뻣해.

A: What's wrong with you? 너 왜 그래?
B: I woke up with a really stiff neck. 아침에 일어났는데 목이 정말이 뻐근했어.

05 I have a pain in my head
머리가 아파

- I have a splitting headache. 머리가 깨질듯이 아파.
- I have a terrible headache. 머리가 지독히 아파.
- **My head** is throbbing with pain. 머리가 욱신욱신거려.

A: I have a splitting headache. 머리가 깨질듯이 아파.
B: You should go see a doctor. 병원에 가봐.

011
I have high blood pressure
난 고혈압이야

눈이 아플 때는 My eyes ache, 고혈압일 때는 have high blood pressure, 반대로 저혈압이라고 할 때는 have low blood pressure라고 한다. a를 붙이지 않도록 주의한다.

01 My eyes ache when reading books
책을 읽을 때 눈이 아파

- **My eyes are sore.** 내 눈이 아파.
- **I think I have pinkeye.** 유행성 결막염에 걸린 것 같아.
- **My vision is a little blurry.** 시력이 좀 흐릿해.

A: Why are you squinting? 왜 눈을 가늘게 뜨고 찡그리고 있어?
B: My vision is becoming blurry these days. 시력이 요즘 나빠졌어.

02 I have high blood pressure
난 고혈압이야

- **I have low blood pressure.** 난 저혈압이야.
- **The doctor says I have to watch my blood pressure.**
  의사가 그러는데 난 혈압을 조심해야 한대.
- **My blood pressure isn't good these days.** 내 혈압이 요즘 좋지 않대.

A: I can't eat this. It's too salty. 나 이건 먹으면 안돼. 너무 짜.
B: Right, you have to watch your blood pressure! 맞아. 너 혈압을 신경써야 되지!

My neck hurts, so I can't turn it
목이 아파서 돌릴 수가 없어

- I have a really stiff neck **this morning**. 오늘 아침에 정말 목이 뻣뻣했어.

- I can't move my neck. 목을 움직일 수가 없어.

- I have to wear a neck brace **because** I got whiplash in the car accident.
교통사고로 목뼈 손상을 입었기 때문에 목깁스를 해야 돼.

A: Why are you wearing a neck brace? 왜 목깁스를 하고 있는거야?
B: I got bad whiplash from the car accident.
교통사고로 목뼈를 심각하게 손상을 입었어.

I have a bad hangover
숙취가 심해

- I have a killer hangover **this morning**. 오늘 아침 아주 심한 숙취가 있어.

- My hangover is **really bad today**. 오늘 숙취가 정말이지 지독해.

- I've never had a hangover **this bad before**. 전에 이처럼 심한 숙취를 겪어본 적이 없어.

A: You look horrible! 너 몰골이 끔찍해!
B: Yes, I have a terrible hangover. 어, 숙취가 아주 심해.

012

I have a backache
난 허리가 아파

허리가 아플 때는 have a backache, 관절통을 앓고 있을 때는 have a joint pain, 그리고 "…가 안좋아"할 때는 have trouble with~란 표현을 즐겨 쓴다. 배가 아플 때는 have a stomachache, 식중독은 food poisoning이라고 한다.

01 I have a backache
난 허리가 아파

- I have lower back pain. 난 허리 아래쪽이 안좋아.
- I have a stiff back. 난 허리가 뻣뻣해.
- I tweaked something in my back. 난 허리를 좀 삐걱했어.

A: What's wrong? 왜 그래?
B: I tweaked something in my back. 난 허리를 좀 삐걱했어.

02 I have joint pain
난 관절통을 앓고 있어

- I have bad arthritis in my knees. 무릎관절염을 심하게 앓고 있어.
- My grandfather's joints are really creaky.
  할아버지 관절은 정말이지 제 기능을 못하고 있어.
- I have inflammation in my knees. 난 무릎에 염증이 있어.

A: Why is she walking so slowly? 걔는 왜 저렇게 느리게 걷는거야?
B: She has arthritis in her knees. 무릎관절염을 앓고 있어.

03 I have liver trouble
내 간에 문제가 있어

- My liver **isn't good.** 내 간이 좋지 않아.

- I have trouble with **my liver.** 내 간이 나빠.

- I'm suffering from **liver trouble.** 내 간에 문제가 있어.

A: Why are you taking that medicine? 그 약은 왜 먹는거야?

B: I am having trouble with my liver. 내 간에 문제가 있어.

04 My stomach is upset
속이 안좋아

- I have a **stomachache.** 배가 아파.

- I am having **stomach troubles.** 배가 안좋아.

- My stomach **is making funny noises.** 내 배에서 이상한 소리가 나.

A: What's that sound? 그거 무슨 소리야?

B: Sorry, my stomach is really upset. 미안. 내 배속이 안좋아서.

05 I have food poisoning
난 식중독에 걸렸어

- I ate some **bad street food.** 난 불량 거리음식을 좀 먹었어.

- It feels like I **might** have food poisoning. 식중독에 걸렸을지도 모를 것 같아.

- I ate an old sandwich and now I feel like I'm going to be sick.
오래된 샌드위치를 먹었는데 이제 토할 것 같아.

A: You look green. 너 얼굴이 창백하다.

B: I ate some bad street food and think I have food poisoning.
불량거리음식을 좀 먹었는데 식중독에 걸린 것 같아.

013

I sprained my wrist

손목을 삐었어

속이 안좋아 토할 것 같다고 할 때는 throw up, puke, 그리고 vomit란 동사를 사용한다. 또한 설사는 get the runs라는 쉬운 형태로 표현한다. 그리고 뭔가 삐었을 때는 sprain, 뭔가 부러졌을 때는 break란 동사를 사용한다.

01 I feel like throwing up
토할 것 같아

- I feel nauseated. 토할 것 같아.

- I am going to puke. 나 토할거야.

- I am going to vomit. 나 토할거야.

> A: I feel like throwing up. 나 토할 것 같아.
> B: Here's a vomit bag. 자 여기 멀미봉투 있어.

02 I've got the runs
설사했어

- I have diarrhea. 설사했어.

- I have to go poo. 나 똥싸러가야 돼.

- I need to pee. 나 오줌싸야 돼.

> A: I need to pee real bad! 나 정말이지 오줌싸야 돼!
> B: The restroom is over there. 화장실이 저쪽에 있어.

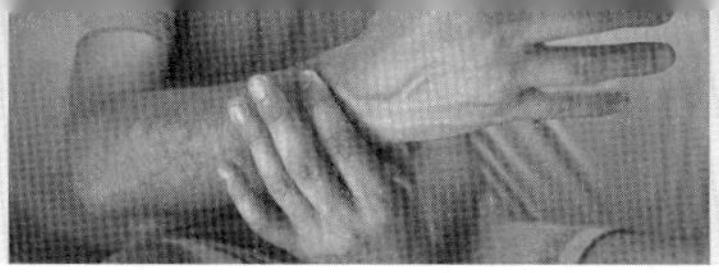

03 Something is wrong with my stomach
뱃속이 뭔가 잘못 된 것 같아

- There's something wrong with my stomach. 배가 뭔가 잘못된 것 같아.
- I have been having stomach problems. 나 복통에 시달리고 있어.
- My stomach has been bothering me. 배가 계속 아파.

A: Something is wrong with my stomach. 배가 뭔가 잘못된 것 같아.
B: You should see a doctor. 병원에 가봐.

Unit 02

04 I sprained my wrist
손목을 삐었어

- I twisted my ankle and sprained it. 발목을 겹질러서 삐었어.
- I fell and sprained my wrist. 넘어져서 손목을 삐었어.
- My ankle is swollen. 발목이 부었어.

A: I think I sprained my ankle. 발목을 삔 것 같아.
B: Yes, it looks swollen. 그래, 부운 것 같아.

05 I broke my collarbone
쇄골이 부러졌어

- I broke my leg. 다리가 골절됐어.
- I broke my arm. 팔이 골절됐어.
- I broke my finger. 손가락이 골절됐어.

A: I heard she had a bad car accident. 걔 교통사고를 심하게 당했다며.
B: Yes, she broke some ribs, her left arm and her collarbone.
어, 갈비뼈, 왼쪽팔 그리고 쇄골이 골절됐어.

014

My fingers are aching

손가락에 통증이 있어

손에 통증이 있을 때는 have a pain in one's hand. 그리고 손목터널 증후군은 have carpal tunnel syndrome이라고 하면 된다. …을 다쳤을 때는 I've hurt+ 다친 부위, 뭔가 베었을 때는 cut, 데웠을 때는 burn이라는 단어를 이용한다.

01 I have a pain in my hand
손에 통증이 있어

- **I have carpal tunnel syndrome.** 난 손목터널 증후군을 앓고 있어.
- **My fingers** are aching. 손가락들에 통증이 있어.
- **I can't** bend my finger. 손가락을 구부릴 수가 없어.

A: What's wrong with your hand? 너 손이 왜 그래?
B: I can't bend my fingers. 손가락을 구부릴 수가 없어.

02 My muscles feel sore from yesterday's hard work
어제 일을 많이 했더니 내 근육이 아파

- **My muscles** are killing me. 근육통 때문에 죽겠어.
- **My back muscles** are aching from carrying the packages all day.
  종일 짐을 날랐더니 등근육이 아파.
- **My muscles** are tired. 내 근육이 지쳤어.

A: I can't do any more work. My muscles are killing me.
더 이상 일을 할 수가 없어. 근육통 때문에 죽겠어.
B: Take a 20 minute break and then try again. 20분 쉬었다가 다시 일해봐.

03 I've hurt my thumb
엄지 손가락을 다쳤어

- I stubbed my thumb **on the door.** 문에 내 엄지손가락을 찧었어.
- I sprained my thumb **when I fell down.** 넘어졌을 때 엄지손가락을 삐었어.
- I broke my thumb **when she closed the door on my hand.**
  걔가 내 손 위로 문을 닫았을 때 엄지손가락이 골절됐어.

A: What happened to your thumb? 네 엄지손가락 어떻게 된거야?
B: I broke it playing basketball. 농구하다가 골절됐어.

04 The cut in my finger hurts
손가락이 베어서 아파

- I cut the tip of my finger **on a piece of glass.** 손가락 끝이 유리조각에 베었어.
- I sliced open my finger **with the razor.** 면도칼에 내 손가락이 베었어.
- I nicked my finger **with the pocketknife.** 주머니칼로 내 손가락이 베었어.

A: You're bleeding! 너 피난다!
B: Yes, I accidentally sliced open my finger with the razor.
   어, 면도칼에 내 손가락이 베었어.

05 I just burned my finger
방금 손가락을 데었어

- I burned my hand **on the stove.** 난로에 내 손을 데었어.
- I had a 2nd degree burn on my arm from the boiling water.
  끓는 물에 데어서 2도 화상을 입었어.
- The burn on my finger blistered. 손가락 화상입은 부분에 물집이 생겼어.

A: That looks painful! 그거 통증이 심하겠다!
B: Yes, I burned my hand on the stove last night.
   맞아, 지난밤에 난로에 내 손을 데었어.

015

I had a heart attack
난 심장마비를 겪었어

심장마비는 heart attack. 부정맥은 get an irregular pulse, 불면증을 앓다는 suffer from insomnia 혹은 have a sleep disorder 그리고 당뇨병이라고 말할 때는 be a diabetic이라고 하면 된다.

01 I'm a diabetic
나 당뇨야

- I'm suffering from diabetes. 나 당뇨병을 앓고 있어.
- I had a blood sugar test. 혈당검사를 했어.
- My blood sugar levels **are low.** 내 혈당수치는 낮아.

A: You have diabetes? 너 당뇨병 있어?
B: Yes, I have to watch my blood sugar levels carefully.
어, 난 혈당수치를 조심해야 돼.

02 My chest is killing me
가슴이 너무 아파요

- I have a sharp pain in my chest. 가슴에 날카로운 통증이 있어요.
- My chest feels very tight. 가슴이 꽉 쪼이는 느낌예요.
- Every time I breathe my chest hurts. 숨쉴 때마다 가슴이 아파요.

A: Why are you holding your chest? 왜 너 가슴을 쥐고 있어?
B: I have a sharp pain in it. Please call an ambulance.
가슴에 날카로운 통증이 있어서. 앰뷸런스를 불러줘.

03 I've got an irregular pulse
난 부정맥이 있어

- My pulse is all over the place. 내 맥박이 일정하지 않아.
- My pulse is hard to find. 내 맥박을 찾기가 힘들어.
- My heart rate is very fast. 내 심박수가 매우 빨리 뛰고 있어.

A: Can you check your own pulse? 너 네 맥박을 확인해봤어?
B: Yes, but mine is very hard to find. 어. 하지만 내 맥박을 찾기가 힘들어.

04 I'm suffering from insomnia
난 불면증에 시달리고 있어

- I have a serious sleep disorder. 나 불면증이 심해.
- She sleepwalks sometimes. 걔는 가끔 몽유병 증세를 보여.
- He snores very loudly. 걘 코를 아주 심하게 골아.

A: Why do you sleep in separate rooms? 왜 너희들은 각방을 쓰는거야?
B: Because he snores loudly. 걔 코골이가 아주 심해서.

05 I had a heart attack
난 심장마비를 겪었어

- I had a heart failure. 난 심장마비를 앓았어.
- She suffered a massive heart attack. 걘 심각한 심장마비를 겪었어.
- I am having a heart attack. 나 심장마비가 오고 있어.

A: Are you alright? 괜찮아?
B: No, I think I'm having a heart attack. Please call 911.
아니, 심장마비가 오는 것 같아. 911에 연락해.

016

I got lung cancer
나 폐암이야

뇌졸증은 stroke, 어지럼증은 feel dizzy, 그리고 심박수는 heart rate라고 한다. 그리고 암은 cancer로 tumor라고 해도 되는데 암이 전이 되었다고 할 때는 ~spread to~라고 하면 된다.

My father had a stroke
아버지가 뇌졸증을 겪으셨어

- He looks like he is having a stroke. 걘 뇌졸증을 겪는 것 같아.
- I suffered a minor stroke last year. 난 작년에 뇌졸증을 가볍게 겪었어.
- She had a major stroke one month ago. 걘 한달전에 아주 심한 뇌졸증을 앓았어.

A: What's wrong with his face? 걘 얼굴이 왜 그래?
B: He suffered a major stroke a few months ago. 몇 달전에 심한 뇌졸증을 앓았어.

I'm having a dizzy spell
난 어지럼증이 있어

- I suddenly feel dizzy. 난 갑자기 어지러웠어.
- My head is spinning. 머리가 빙빙 돌아.
- I'm losing my sense of balance. 난 균형감각을 잃는 것 같아.

A: You look like you're suffering from a dizzy spell. 너 어지럼증을 겪는 것 같아.
B: Yes, I need to sit down. 어. 나 앉아야겠어.

03 Check your heart rate
심박수를 확인해봐

- My heart rate is too high. 내 심박수가 너무 높아.

- Her resting heart rate is 65. She's very healthy.
  걔의 안정시 심박수는 65야. 아주 건강한거지.

- His heart rate is too low. 45 is not safe. 걔의 심박수는 너무 낮아. 45는 안전하지가 않아.

A: What's your heart rate? 네 심박수는 어떻게 돼?
B: Let me check. It's 85. A bit high but I just finished exercising.
   확인해보고. 85야. 조금 높지만 방금 운동을 마쳤거든.

04 I got lung cancer
나 폐암이야

- She was diagnosed with lung cancer. 걘 폐암진단을 받았어.

- The doctors found some tumors in his lung. 의사들은 걔의 폐에서 종양을 일부 발견했어.

- The cancer spread to his lungs. 암이 걔의 폐로 전이 됐어.

A: Did you hear the bad news? 안좋은 소식을 들었니?
B: Yes, she was diagnosed with lung cancer. 어. 걔가 폐암진단을 받았어.

05 She is being treated for a chronic illness
걘 만성질환을 치료받고 있어

- He has chronic back pain. 걘 만성요통에 시달리고 있어.

- She has chronic sinus problems. 걘 만성비염을 앓고 있어.

- He is chronically ill. 걘 만성질환을 앓고 있어.

A: Is he sick again? 걔가 다시 아파?
B: Yes, he is chronically ill. 어. 걘 만성질환을 앓고 있어.

017

My legs have been cramping up

다리에 쥐가 났어

쥐는 cramp라는 단어를 절대적으로 쓴다. 심한 경련은 get bad cramps. 다리에 난 쥐는 leg cramps. 그리고 근육이 올라왔다고 할 때는 pull a muscle이라는 표현을 쓴다. 그리고 복습하는 의미에서 삐는 것은 sprain, 부러졌을 때는 break를 쓴다는 점 다시 한번 기억해둔다.

01 My legs have been cramping up
다리에 쥐가 났어

- I get bad cramps if I don't drink enough water. 물을 충분히 섭취않으면 심한 경련이 와.
- She is suffering from leg cramps. 걘 다리에 쥐가 났어.
- My hand suddenly cramped up. 내 손이 갑자기 경련이 일어났어.

A: What's wrong? 왜 그래?
B: My leg has a bad cramp. 다리에 쥐가 심하게 났어.

01 I have a cramp in my thigh
허벅지에 쥐가 났어

- I pulled a muscle in my leg. 내 다리 근육이 올라왔어.
- She pulled a muscle in her shoulder while exercising.
  걘 운동하다가 어깨근육이 올라왔어.
- He pulled his hamstring badly. 걘 햄스트링이 심하게 올라왔어.

A: Why can't he play soccer this week? 왜 걘 이번주에 축구경기를 못하는거야?
B: He pulled his hamstring last game. 지난 게임에서 햄스트링 부상을 당했어.

03 I sprained my ankle
발목이 삐었어

- I sprained my finger. 손가락이 삐었어.
- I twisted my ankle. 발목이 겹질러졌어.
- I dislocated my shoulder. 내 어깨가 탈구됐어.

A: Why are you wearing an arm sling? 넌 왜 팔걸이 붕대를 하고 있어?
B: I dislocated my shoulder yesterday. 어제 어깨가 탈구됐어.

04 I broke my leg
다리가 부러졌어

- I just put my leg in a cast. 내 다리에 깁스를 했어.
- I have to wear a knee brace. 난 무릎보조기를 해야 해.
- I wrap up my ankle before I play basketball. 난 농구를 하기 전에 발목을 감싸.

A: Why are you wrapping up your ankle? 넌 왜 발목을 감싸고 있는거야?
B: I sprained it a few weeks ago so it's still a little weak.
몇 주전에 삐어서 아직 약한 상태여서.

05 It's itchy
가려워요

- It's bleeding. 피가 나요.
- It hurts. 아파요.
- It's swollen. 부었어.

A: I need a bandaid please. 난 반창고가 필요해.
B: Yes, you're bleeding a lot! 그래. 너 피가 많이 난다!

018

I went to the doctor today

오늘 병원에 갔다왔어

우리는 병원에 갔다왔다라고 하지만 영어에서는 의사선생님을 만나고 왔다라는 표현을 즐겨쓴다. go to the doctor 혹은 see the doctor라고 하면 된다. 정기점검은 physical check up, MRI 찍다는 get an MRI scan이라고 한다.

01 I went to the doctor today
오늘 병원에 갔다왔어

● I see the doctors **on Mondays.** 난 월요일마다 병원에 가.

● I have an appointment with **the doctor this afternoon.**
난 오늘 오후에 병원예약이 되어 있어.

● I made an appointment to see the doctor **next week.** 난 담주에 병원예약을 잡았어.

A: Let's go see a movie after lunch. 점심먹고 영화보러 가자.
B: Sorry, I have an appointment with the doctor this afternoon.
미안, 오후에 병원예약되어 있어.

02 I get physical check ups regularly
난 정기적으로 정기검진을 받아

● I have my annual check up **with the doctor this week.**
난 이번주에 의사와 연례정기검진을 받아.

● I'm due for a check up **soon.** 난 곧 정기검진을 받을거야.

● **She skipped her check up** this year. 걘 금년에 정기검진을 받지 않았어.

A: I need to get a check up soon. 난 곧 정기검진을 받아야 돼.
B: Yeah, didn't you skip it last year? 그래, 작년에는 건너뛰지 않았어?

03 I will get an MRI scan this week
이번주에 MRI 검사를 할거야

- My X-ray didn't show anything so they are going to do a CT scan.
  엑스레이에서 아무것도 나오지 않아서 CT촬영을 할거래.
- I need an MRI done on my shoulder. 난 어깨 MRI를 찍어야 돼.
- The CT scan showed I have torn ligaments in my shoulder.
  CT로 내 어깨인대가 찢겨진 것을 발견했어.

A: What did the X-ray show? 엑스레이는 어떻게 나왔어?
B: I have a small fracture in my arm. 팔에 조그마한 골절이 있대.

04 He will perform surgery on a patient today
그는 오늘 환자수술을 할거야

- The doctor performed surgery on my heart last year.
  그 의사가 작년에 내 심장수술을 했어.
- Do I need an operation? 제가 수술해야 하나요?
- I underwent surgery yesterday. 난 어제 수술을 했어.

A: Why are you going to the hospital today? 왜 너는 오늘 병원에 가는거야?
B: I am having surgery on my eye. 눈수술을 받을거야.

05 He stitched up the patient
그는 환자의 수술부위를 봉합했어

- I needed ten stitches for the cut on my head. 머리상처난 곳에 열바늘을 꿰맸어.
- He has twenty stitches on his leg. 걘 다리에 20바늘을 꿰맸어.
- The cut required over thirty stitches. 그 벤 상처는 30바늘 이상을 꿰매야 했어.

A: That was a bad cut. 그거 심하게 베었네.
B: Yes, it required over twenty stitches. 그래. 20바늘 이상 꿰매야 했어.

019

He was taken to the hospital

그는 병원으로 옮겨졌어

병원에 데려가거나 옮겨졌을 때는 be taken to the hospital, get[take] sb to the hospital이라고 한다. 병원에 입원할 때는 be hospitalized, 그리고 병원에서 퇴원할 때는 간단히 leave the hospital이라고 하면 된다.

01 He was taken to the hospital
그는 병원으로 옮겨졌어

- He was admitted into the hospital. 걘 병원에 입원했어.
- The ambulance rushed him to the Emergency Room.
  그 앰뷸런스는 걔를 급하게 응급실로 날랐어.
- I took my father to the hospital today. 난 오늘 아버지를 병원에 모시고 갔어.

A: He was admitted to the hospital? 걘 병원에 입원한거야?
B: Yes, he has really bad food poisoning. 어. 걘 심한 식중독에 걸렸어.

02 She needs to get her baby to the hospital
걘 아기를 병원에 데려가야 해

- He needs to be admitted to the ICU right away. 걘 바로 중환자실로 옮겨야 돼.
- She had to take her mother to the ER this morning.
  걘 오늘 아침 어머니를 응급실로 데려가야 했어.
- She was rushed to the hospital. 걘 급하게 병원으로 이송됐어.

A: Why aren't they at home now? 왜 걔네들이 지금 집에 없는거야?
B: She had to take her mother to the hospital. She had a heart attack.
   걘 어머니를 병원으로 모셔야 했어. 심장마비가 왔거든.

03 Should I be hospitalized?
제가 입원해야 하나요?

- **You think I need to** be admitted to the hospital?
  내가 병원에 입원해야 된다고 생각하세요?
- **Should I go to the ER?** 내가 응급실로 가야 하나요?
- **Shall I admit myself into the hospital?** 내가 병원에 입원을 해야 되나요?

A: You don't look well. 상태가 안좋게 보여요.
B: Should I be hospitalized? 입원해야 하나요?

04 How long will you be in the hospital for?
얼마나 오래 입원해 있어야 하는거야?

- **When are you** getting out of the hospital? 넌 언제 퇴원하는거야?
- **How much longer are you** going to be in the hospital?
  얼마나 더 오래 병원에 입원해 있을거야?
- **When will the doctors** let you leave the hospital? 언제 의사가 퇴원하라고 할까?

A: I can't meet you. I'm still in the hospital. 널 만날 수가 없어. 아직 병원에 입원중이야.
B: Really? When are you getting out? 정말? 언제 퇴원하는데?

05 Has she been released from the hospital?
걔 병원에서 퇴원했어?

- **When are you** getting released from the hospital? 넌 언제 병원에서 퇴원하는거야?
- **The doctors said she could** leave the hospital today.
  의사들이 그러는데 넌 오늘 퇴원할 수 있대.
- **I was let out of the hospital** yesterday. 난 어제 퇴원했어.

A: When does she get out of the hospital? 걔는 언제 퇴원하는거야?
B: The doctors released her this morning. 의사들이 오늘 아침에 퇴원시켰어.

020

I'm not taking any medicine
먹는 약 아무것도 없어

약을 먹는다는 take medicine, 한방약을 먹는다는 try herbal medicine. 그리고 주사를 맞는다고 할 때는 get an injection~이라고 하면 된다. 독감주사를 맞는 get one's flu shot, 백신주사를 맞다는 get one's vaccination shot이라고 한다.

01 I'm not taking any medicine
먹는 약 아무것도 없어

- He is on sedatives. 그는 진정제를 먹고 있어.

- I need a painkiller for this toothache. 난 치통 때문에 진통제를 먹어야 돼.

- She is trying herbal medicine for her headaches. 걘 두통으로 한방약을 먹어보고 있어.

A: I can't stand this backache any longer! 난 더 이상 이 요통을 참을 수가 없어!
B: Here. Take this painkiller. 자 여기. 이 진통제를 먹어.

02 I got an injection of morphine for my pain
통증을 없애 줄 모르핀 주사를 맞았어

- Please put this thermometer in her mouth to measure her temperature.
체온을 재게 걔의 입에 체온계를 넣어주세요.

- The doctors are vaccinating the children against polio.
의사들은 소아마비 백신주사를 아이들에게 놓고 있어.

- I got my flu shot this year. 난 금년에 독감주사를 맞았어.

A: Did you get your vaccination shot? 백신맞았어?
B: Yes, I got it last month. 어. 지난달에 맞았어.

The doctor prescribed medicine for my cold
의사가 감기약 처방해줬어

- I needed to take the prescription to the pharmacist. 약사에게 줄 처방전이 필요했어.
- You can't buy it over-the-counter. You need a prescription.
넌 그거 처방전이 없이 살 수 없어. 처방전이 필요해.
- Can you prescribe me some painkillers please? 진통제를 좀 처방해주실 수 있나요?

A: Can I see your prescription? 처방전을 볼 수 있을까요?
B: Here you are. 여기 있습니다.

Acupuncture is very good for anemia
침은 빈혈에 매우 효과가 있어

- Oriental medicine is very popular these days. 요즘 한방약은 매우 인기가 있어.
- I've tried massage therapy and found it very relaxing.
마사지 요법을 해봤는데 매우 안정시켜주더라.
- Alternative medicine is something you should consider.
대체의학은 네가 고려해봐야 할거야.

A: What kind of alternative medicine have you tried?
넌 어떤 대체의학을 시도해봤니?

B: I've tried acupuncture and cup therapy. 침과 부항을 시도해봤어.

I'm trying to avoid eating greasy food
기름진 음식 먹는 것을 피하려 하고 있어

- You should avoid foods rich in sugar. 당이 풍부한 음식은 피해야 돼.
- Snacking between meals isn't healthy. 식간에 간식을 먹는 것은 건강에 좋지 않아.
- Try not to eat too many carbohydrates. 너무 많이 탄수화물을 먹지 않도록 해.

A: Are you trying a new diet? 새로운 식이요법을 시도하고 있어?
B: No, but I'm not snacking between meals anymore.
아니, 하지만 더 이상 식간에 간식을 하지 않아.

021

I have a very sensitive tooth

이가 정말이지 시려

충치는 cavity, 치통은 toothache. 충치를 뽑다는 have a rotten tooth pulled out, 스켈링하다는 have one's teeth scaled라고 한다. 또한 신경치료는 root canal, 임플란트를 하다는 get implants라고 하면 된다.

01 I have a cavity
충치가 생겼어

- I have a toothache. 치통이 있어.

- I have a very sensitive tooth. 이가 정말이지 시려.

- It's time for my annual check up with **the dentist.** 치과에 가서 연례 정기점검을 할 때야.

A: Why are you going to the dentist? Do you have a toothache?
왜 치과에 가는거야? 치통이 있어?

B: Yes, it hurts really bad when I eat sweets. 어. 단것을 먹을 때 정말이지 아파.

02 I had a rotten tooth pulled out
난 충치를 뽑았어

- I needed a few teeth pulled out. 난 이를 몇 개 뽑아야 했어.

- **The dentist** fixed my chipped tooth. 치과의사는 내 부러진 이를 치료했어.

- **I had to** have my teeth scaled. 난 이를 스케일해야 했어.

A: Why did you go to the dentist? 왜 치과에 갔어?
B: I needed a few teeth pulled. 이를 몇 개 뽑아야 했어.

03 I have rotten teeth now
난 지금 썩은 이가 있어

- I have a few cavities. 충치가 몇 개 있어.
- His teeth are rotten because he eats too much candy.
  걔 사탕을 너무 많이 먹더니 이가 썩었어.
- I have a bad cavity in one of my back teeth. 어금니 중 하나에 충치가 심하게 생겼어.

A: You're going to the dentist again? 넌 또 치과에 가는거야?
B: I have a lot of cavities. 충치가 많이 있어.

04 Do I need a root canal?
신경치료를 받아야 하나요?

- I'm afraid you need a root canal. 신경치료를 받아야 될 것 같아요.
- Root canals aren't fun. 신경치료는 장난이 아냐.
- I'm getting a root canal tomorrow. 난 내일 신경치료를 받을거야.

A: Why do you look so scared? 왜 그렇게 겁에 질린 표정이야?
B: I'm getting a root canal today. 오늘 신경치료를 받거든.

05 I'm going to get implants
임플란트를 할거야

- The implants will make my teeth look better.
  임플란트를 하면 네 이가 더 좋게 보이게 될거야.
- I got these implants last year. 난 작년에 이 임플란트들을 했어.
- You should get implants. 너 임플란트를 해야겠어.

A: Why aren't you going on a holiday this year? 왜 금년에 휴가를 가지 않는거야?
B: I need implants and they are really expensive.
   임플란트를 해야 되고 매우 비싸거든.

022

She's got Alzheimer's disease
그녀는 알츠하이머에 시달리고 있어

기억이 깜박할 때는 become forgetful, 기억력이 상실되는 것은 memory loss라고 한다. 치매는 get dementia, 그리고 그중 알츠하이머에 시달리고 있을 때는 get Alzheimer's disease라고 한다.

01 I'm afraid I'm becoming forgetful
점점 깜박하는게 걱정돼

● **My memory** is starting to go. 내 기억력이 점점 약해지고 있어.

● **Forgetfulness is becoming a problem for me.** 건망증은 내게 큰 문제가 되고 있어.

● **My memory** isn't what it used to be. 내 기억력이 예전만 못해.

A: What did I do with my car keys? 내가 자동차 키를 어떻게 했더라?
B: Your memory is starting to go. 네 기억력이 약해지고 있구나.

02 I suffer from memory loss
난 기억상실을 겪고 있어

● **The concussion** is causing memory loss. 뇌진탕은 기억상실을 초래해.

● **As I get older I am getting memory loss.** 나이가 들어감에 따라 기억상실을 겪고 있어.

● **Memory loss is part of getting old.** 기억상실은 노화의 한 부분이야.

A: The car accident caused memory loss? 자동차 사고가 기억상실을 초래했다고?
B: Yes, I hit my head very hard. 어, 머리를 심하게 부딪혔거든.

She's got Alzheimer's disease
그녀는 알츠하이머에 시달리고 있어

- Alzheimer's disease is very hard for the family.
  알츠하이머는 가족에게는 매우 고통스러운 일이야.

- There is no cure for Alzheimer's yet. 아직 알츠하이머 치료제가 없어.

- My father is suffering from Alzheimer's. 아버지는 알츠하이머를 앓고 있어.

A: I think she is starting to get Alzheimer's.
그녀가 알츠하이머를 앓기 시작하는 것 같아.

B: Yes, she sometimes forgets where she is and who she is with.
맞아. 가끔 자신이 어디에 있는지 누구와 있는지 깜박해.

 04

Am I getting dementia?
내가 치매를 앓는건가?

- His family has a history of mental illness. 걔의 가족은 정신질환 이력이 있어.

- Dementia runs in his family. 치매는 그의 집안내력이야.

- She is having a mental breakdown. 걔는 신경쇠약을 앓고 있어.

A: Why did he have to go to the mental hospital? 걘 왜 정신병원에 가야 했어?
B: He had a mental breakdown. 신경쇠약을 앓고 있었어.

023

Are you getting plastic surgery?

성형수술을 받을거야?

성형수술을 cosmetic surgery 혹은 plastic surgery라고 하고 성형수술을 받다는 동사로 get을 사용하면 된다. 코수술은 nose job, 가슴성형수술은 boob job이라고 한다.

01 She is getting cosmetic surgery
개는 성형수술을 받을거야

- Cosmetic surgery is very common these days. 요즘 성형수술은 매우 성행해.
- She is thinking of having some cosmetic surgery done.
  그녀는 성형수술 몇가지를 할 생각이야.
- Cosmetic surgeons make good money. 성형의는 많은 돈을 벌어.

A: Why does she have a bandage on her nose?
   그녀는 왜 코에 반창고를 붙이고 있어?
B: She had some cosmetic surgery done on her nose yesterday.
   어제 코에 성형수술을 좀 했대.

02 Are you getting plastic surgery?
성형수술을 받을거야?

- There are many plastic surgeons in Gangnam. 강남에 많은 성형의가 있어.
- Plastic surgery isn't expensive these days. 요즘 성형수술을 그렇게 비싸지 않아.
- My mother had some plastic surrey done on her chin.
  어머니는 턱에 성형수술을 좀 받았어.

A: Do you want to get plastic surgery? 성형수술을 받고 싶어?
B: Yes, I'm thinking of getting breast implants. 어. 유방확대수술을 받을까 하고 있어.

03 He got a nose job
걔 코성형수술을 받았어

- **She** got a boob job. 그녀는 가슴성형수술을 받았어.
- **He** got calf implants. 걔 종아리 확대성형수술을 받았어.
- **My father** got his tummy liposuctioned. 아버지는 복부지방흡입술을 받았어.

A: Your father looks so thin! 네 아버지는 아주 날씬해 보인다!
B: Yes, he got his tummy liposuctioned. 어, 복부지방흡입술을 받았어.

04 I'd like to change my appearance
내 겉모습을 바꾸고 싶어

- I want a new look. 난 새로운 모습으로 보이기를 원해.
- I'd like to look different. 난 좀 지금보다 좀 다르게 보이기를 원해.
- **She** wants to alter her appearance. 그녀는 자신의 외모를 바꾸고 싶어해.

A: Why is he going to the plastic surgeon? 그는 왜 성형외과에 갈려고 하는거야?
B: He wants to alter his appearance. 걘 자신의 외모를 바꾸고 싶어해.

05 The plastic surgery was successful
그 성형수술은 성공적이었어

- The doctor botched her surgery and she looks awful.
  의사는 그녀의 성형수술을 망쳐서 그녀는 외모는 으악이야.
- The plastic surgery **turned out well**. 그 성형수술은 잘되었어.
- The nose job **was successful**. 그 코성형수술을 성공적이었어.

A: Why does his face look so strange? 왜 그의 얼굴이 그렇게 이상하게 보이는거야?
B: A doctor botched his nose job. 의사가 코성형수술을 망쳐놨대.

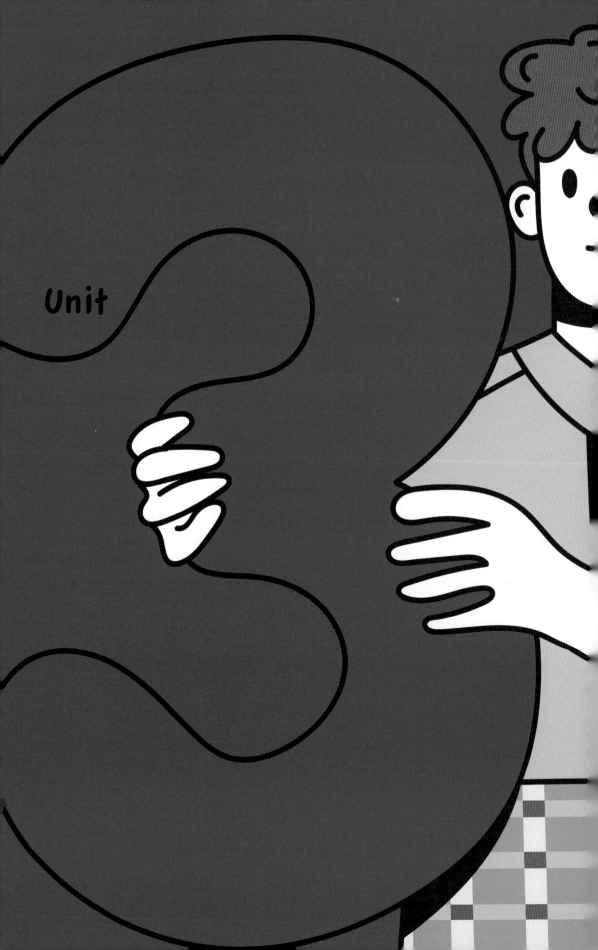

Unit

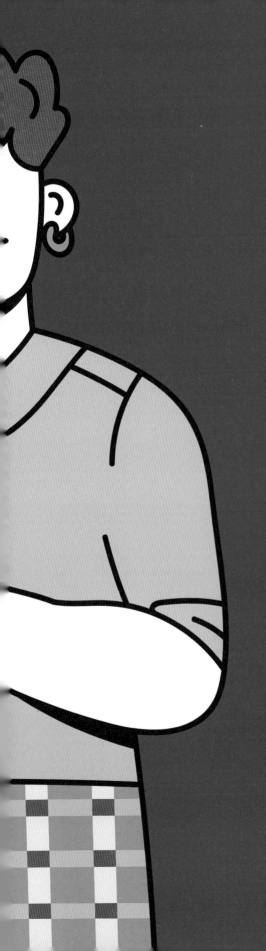

가족과
주변상황

001

We are a family of three

우리 가족은 3명이야

우리 가족은 …야라고 할 때는 There are~ in my family 혹은 We are a family of~ 라고 표현한다. ~에는 가족수를 넣으면 된다. 대가족은 a large family, 가족모임은 a family reunion이라고 하면 된다.

01 There are 3 in my family
우리 가족은 3명이야

- **We are** a family of three. 우리 가족은 3명이야.
- **There are** three members in my family. 우리 가족은 3명이 있어.
- **I have** three people in my family. 가족으로는 3명이 있어.

A: How many are there in your family? 가족이 몇 명이야?
B: There are three: my mother, my older sister and me.
3명이야. 엄마, 누나 그리고 나.

02 We have a large family
우리는 대가족이야

- **Tell me** about your family. Is it big or small? 네 가족에 대해 말해봐. 소가족야 대가족야?
- **How big** is your family? 가족이 몇 명이나 돼?
- **Do you** have a large family? 너희네는 대가족이야?

A: How big is your family? 너희는 가족이 몇 명이나 돼?
B: There are 4 people: my parents, my younger brother and me.
4명이야. 부모님, 남동생 그리고 나.

03 Where are the Smiths?
스미스 가족은 어디 있어?

- The Smiths **just got back** from vacation. 스미스 네 가족이 휴가를 끝내고 막 돌아왔어.
- The entire family **is coming** for the long weekend.
  전 가족이 긴 주말 동안 와 있을 예정이야.
- The family **is returning** from their trip tomorrow. 가족은 내일 여행에서 돌아올거야.

A: Why are you cleaning the house? 넌 왜 집을 청소하고 있어?
B: The entire family is coming to visit tomorrow. 가족 전체가 내일 방문하러 와.

04 Are you having a family reunion?
너는 가족모임을 갖아?

- **When is** the family reunion? 가족모임이 언제야?
- We have a family reunion **every five years**. 우리는 5년마다 가족모임을 하고 있어.
- **Who is** hosting the family reunion **this time**? 이번에는 누가 가족모임을 주관하는거야?

A: My family reunion will be this summer. 우리 가족모임은 이번 여름이 될거야.
B: Who is hosting it? 누구 집에서 하는데?

05 How's the[your] family?
가족들은 다 잘 지내?

- How's the wife[your kid]? 부인[애들]은 잘 지내?
- Give my best to **your folks**. 가족들에게 안부 전해줘.
- All the best to **everyone**. 모두에게 안부 전해줘.

A: Very nice to see you again. 다시 봐서 정말 반가웠어.
B: Yes it was! Please give my best to your wife. 정말 그래! 네 아내에게 안부 전해줘.

002

I'm an only child

난 외동이야

형제를 말할 때는 I have ~ brothers and ~ sisters, 형제가 없을 때는 I have no brothers and sisters라고 한다. 또한 sibling은 형제자매를 말하는 단어임을 기억해둔다. 동생이라고 할 때는 little[kid, baby] 등의 단어를 활용한다.

01 I have three brothers and two sisters

남자형제가 셋 있고, 누이가 둘이야

- I have two brothers. 난 형이 둘이야.
- I have no brothers or sisters. 형제가 없어.
- I have a twin sister. 난 쌍둥이 자매가 있어.
- **Do you** have any siblings? 형제자매가 어떻게 돼?

A: Do you have any siblings? 형제자매가 어떻게 돼?
B: Yes, I have one older sister. 어, 누이가 한 명 있어.

02 I'm an only child

난 외동이야

- **Do you** have any brothers and sisters? 형제자매가 어떻게 돼?
- How many brothers and sisters **do you have**? 형제자매가 어떻게 돼?
- I am an only child. 난 외동이야.

A: How many brothers and sisters do you have? 형제가 어떻게 돼?
B: None. I am an only child. 없어. 외동이야.

I'm the second of five brothers and sisters
난 5형제 중 둘째야

- I am the eldest child. 난 맏이야.
- I am the baby of the family. 난 우리 집의 막내야.
- I am the third of four children. 4형제중 3번째야.

A: Are you the eldest child? 넌 맏이야?
B: No, I'm the baby. 아니. 난 막내야.

I'm the oldest
난 맏이야

- I'm the youngest of three sisters. 3자매 중에서 막내야
- I don't have any brothers. **How about you?** 난 형제가 없어. 넌 어떻게 돼?
- I'm a middle child. 난 중간이야.

A: I'm not the eldest or the youngest. 난 맏이도 막내도 아니야.
B: Oh! You're a middle child like me. 아! 나처럼 중간이구나.

I'm Tony's kid brother
난 토니의 남동생이야

- I'm his little sister. 난 그의 여동생이야.
- He's my older brother. 그는 내 형이야.
- She's my baby sister. 걘 내 여동생이야.

A: She's so pretty! 걘 너무 귀엽다!
B: Stay away from her! She's my baby sister. 가까이 가지 마! 걘 내 여동생이라고.

Unit 03

003

I'm on a date with him

난 걔와 데이트하는 중이야

데이트하다는 date sb, 결혼하다는 getting married라고 한다. 데이트 신청은 ask sb out on a date, 데이트하고 있다고 할 때는 go out with sb, 혹은 be seeing sb라고 하면 된다.

01 I'm dating her in the hope of getting married

난 결혼할 희망으로 걔와 데이트하고 있어

- I plan on getting married to **her one day.** 난 언젠가 그녀와 결혼할 계획이야.
- It's my dream to **marry her.** 그녀와 결혼하는게 내 꿈이야.
- She is my dream bride. 그녀는 내 꿈의 신부야.

A: You really love her? 너 정말로 그녀를 사랑해?
B: Yes, I plan on getting married to her one day.
그럼, 언젠가 그녀와 결혼할 생각이야.

02 I asked her out on a date the other day

요전날 걔에게 데이트 신청을 했어

- We went on a date **last weekend.** 우리는 지난 주말에 데이트를 했어.
- I asked him to **watch a movie with me.** 난 걔에게 나와 함께 영화를 보자고 했어.
- I took her out **last night.** 난 지난밤에 그녀를 데리고 외출했어.

A: Where were you last night? 너 지난밤에 어디 있었어?
B: I asked Mary out on a date. We saw a movie.
메리에게 데이트신청을 했고 우린 영화를 봤어.

03 I'm on a date with him
난 걔와 데이트하는 중이야

- I'm seeing someone **these days**. 난 요즘 누구 만나는 중이야.
- We're a couple **these days**. 우리는 요즘 사귀는 중이야.
- She's my girlfriend **now**. 그녀는 이제 내 여친이야.

A: Are you friends with her? 넌 그녀와 친구야?
B: No, she's my girlfriend now. 아니. 그녀는 이제 내 여친이야.

04 I'm going out with your sister
난 네 여동생과 데이트할거야

- Are **you** seeing anyone **these days**? 요즘 만나는 사람있어?
- Who are **you** going out with? 누구와 데이트해?
- Do **you** have a girlfriend **these days**? 너 요즘 여친있니?

A: I'm going out with one of my classmates. 같은 반이랑 데이트하고 있어.
B: Wow! I thought you were single. 와! 너 애인없는 줄 알았는데.

05 I've got a date with her tonight
난 오늘밤 그녀와 데이트가 있어

- I am seeing my girlfriend **tonight**. 난 오늘밤 여친을 만날거야.
- She is going out with her boyfriend **tonight**. 그녀는 오늘밤 남친과 데이트를 할거야.
- He is taking her out **to the movies**. 걔는 그녀를 데리고 영화관에 갈거야.

A: Where is she tonight? 걘 오늘밤 어디 있는거야?
B: She went out with a new boyfriend. 새로운 남친과 데이트나갔어.

004

I have a crush on him

난 그에게 홀딱 반했어

…의 타입이다는 be one's type, 사랑에 빠지다는 fall in love with sb 혹은 be into sb라고 하면 된다. 반대로 헤어진다고 할 때는 break up with, split up 등의 표현을 사용한다.

01 She's not my type

갠 내 타입이 아냐

- **He's not marriage material.** 갠 결혼상대감이 안돼.
- **She is out of my league.** 그녀는 내게 과분해.
- **He is my ideal man.** 갠 내 이상형이야.

A: Stop staring at him! 걔 그만 쳐다봐!
B: He's my type! 갠 내 타입이야!

02 I fell in love with a girl in Japan

난 일본에서 한 소녀와 사랑에 빠졌어

- **It was love at first sight.** 그건 첫눈에 빠진 사랑이었어.
- **I fell head over heels in love with her.** 난 그녀에게 홀딱 반했어.
- **She fell for him hard.** 갠 그에게 무척이나 빠졌어.

A: Look at the way she is staring at him. 그녀가 걔를 쳐다보는 것 좀 봐.
B: Yes, she is falling for him hard. 맞아. 그녀는 걔에게 무척 빠져있어.

03 I have feelings for her
난 그녀를 좋아해

- I have a crush on him. 난 그에게 홀딱 반했어.
- I have very deep feelings for him. 난 걔에게 아주 깊은 감정이 있어.
- I can't get her out of my head. 난 그녀를 생각하지 않을 수가 없어.

A: Forget about her. 걔는 잊어버려.
B: I can't! I have very deep feelings for her.
안돼! 걔에게 아주 깊은 감정을 가지고 있다고.

04 I'm going to miss her so much
그녀가 무척 보고 싶을거야

- I tried Internet dating. 난 인터넷 데이팅을 시도해봤어.
- I'm afraid of blind dates. 난 소개팅을 무서워해.
- Tinder is the best way to meet guys. 틴더앱은 친구들을 만나는 가장 좋은 방법이야.

A: How did you two meet? 너희 둘은 어떻게 만났어?
B: We met on a dating website. 우리는 데이팅사이트에서 만났어.

05 I broke up with her
난 그녀와 헤어졌어

- She dumped him. 그녀는 걔를 차버렸어.
- They split up. 걔네들은 헤어졌어.
- They mutually parted ways. 걔네들은 서로 각자의 길을 가기로 했어.

A: Did she dump him? 그녀가 걔를 찼어?
B: No, they mutually agreed to break up. 아니. 걔네들은 합의 하에 헤어졌어.

결혼 1

I have been married for 10 years

난 결혼한지 10년됐어

결혼행위는 앞서 나온 get married, 결혼한 상태는 be married를 사용한다. 그래서 결혼생활한 세월을 얘기하려면 현재완료를 써서 have been married for~라고 하면 된다. 돌싱은 I'm single again, 이혼했다고 할 때는 I'm divorced라고 하면 된다.

01 I'm married
난 결혼했어

- I'm engaged. 난 약혼했어.
- I'm single (again). 난 싱글[돌싱]이야.
- I'm divorced. 난 이혼했어.

A: Are you married? 너 결혼했어?
B: I was. I divorced and now I'm single again. 했었지. 이혼해서 지금은 돌싱이야.

02 I'm getting married next week
난 담주에 결혼해

- I want to spend my life with you. 난 너와 함께 인생을 보내고 싶어.
- I hope you can attend our wedding. 네가 우리 결혼식에 참석하기를 바래.
- Our wedding is next month. 우리 결혼식은 담달이야.

A: They want to spend the rest of their lives together.
걔네들은 함께 남은 평생을 함께 보내고 싶어해.
B: That's so beautiful. 참 아름답네.

03 I got married when I was 32
난 32세에 결혼했어

- I got married **at the age of 30**. 난 30세에 결혼했어.
- I got married **in 1992**. 난 1992년에 결혼했어.
- I got married **after graduating from university**. 난 대학교를 졸업하고 결혼했어.

A: **When did you get married?** 언제 결혼했어?
B: **In 2018.** 2018년에.

Unit 03

04 I have been married for 10 years
난 결혼한지 10년됐어

- It's **7 years** since I got married. 난 결혼한지 7년 지났어.
- We've had a long marriage. 우리 결혼생활 오래됐지.
- We've been married since 2008. 우리는 2008년도에 결혼했어.

A: It's been 10 years since I got married. 내가 결혼한지 10년이 지났어.
B: Time really flies. 세월은 정말 빨리 지나가.

05 We'll have been married for 5 years this March
이번 3월이면 결혼한지 5년 돼

- How long will it **have been since you got married next year**?
  내년이면 결혼한지 몇 년 돼?
- They'll **have been together for 20 years on May 3**. 5월 3일이면 결혼 20주년이야.
- It will **have been 5 years** since we met **tomorrow**! 내일이면 우리가 만난지 5년 될거야!

A: What is the special occasion on Friday? 금요일이 무슨 특별한 날이야?
B: It will have been 10 years since we met! 우리가 만난지 10년 되는 날이야!

006 결혼 2

We went to Hawaii for our honeymoon

우리는 신혼여행으로 하와이에 갔어

이번에는 구체적으로 결혼식을 하다는 hold the wedding, 결혼기념일은 our wedding anniversary라고 한다. 신혼여행지는 honeymoon resort 등의 표현을 알고 있으면 된다.

01 Our wedding anniversary is November 3
우리 결혼기념일은 11월 3일이야

- Our wedding anniversary **is coming up soon.** 우리 결혼기념일이 곧 다가와.
- It's going to be their silver wedding anniversary. 그들 결혼 25주년 기념일이 될거야.
- I am looking forward to my grandparent's 50th wedding anniversary **next month.** 담달 할아버지 할머니의 결혼 50주년을 기다리고 있어.

A: I heard it will be your 10th wedding anniversary this Friday. Congrats! 이번 금요일이 결혼 10주년이 된다며. 축하해!

B: Thanks! I can't believe it's been 10 years already.
고마워! 벌써 10년이 되다니 믿기지 않아.

02 We held the wedding in Gangnam
우리는 강남에서 결혼식을 치뤘어

- We are having our wedding outdoors. 우리는 야외결혼식을 열거야.
- The wedding is being held **at a church.** 결혼식은 교회에서 열릴거야.
- **They** had their wedding on a cruise ship. 걔네들은 크루즈 선에서 결혼식을 했어.

A: Where are they holding their wedding? 걔네들 결혼식 어디서 했어?
B: In Gangnam. 강남에서.

03 We went to Hawaii for our honeymoon
우리는 신혼여행으로 하와이에 갔어

- Where are you going for your honeymoon? 신혼여행 어디로 갈거야?
- Jeju used to be a popular honeymoon resort.
  제주도는 신혼여행지로 인기있는 곳이었어.
- They are postponing their honeymoon until they finish university.
  대학마칠 때까지 신혼여행을 미루기로 했어.

A: Where are you going for your honeymoon? 신혼여행 어디로 갈거야?
B: To Hawaii. 하와이로.

04 How's your married life?
결혼생활 어때?

- How is marriage treating you? 결혼생활이 어때?
- Is married life what you thought it would be? 결혼생활이 생각했던거와 같아?
- How are you two adjusting to married life? 너희 둘 결혼생활 어떻게 적응해가고 있어?

A: Are you adjusting to married life? 결혼생활에 적응하고 있어?
B: Yes, it's even better than I imagined it would be.
    어, 내가 예상했던 것보다 더 좋은걸.

05 I'm not sure I want to get married
내가 결혼을 하고 싶어하는지 확신이 안서

- I'm having second thoughts about getting married.
  난 결혼하는 것을 다시 생각해볼거야.
- I am starting to have doubts about my wedding. 내 결혼에 의혹이 들기 시작했어.
- Why are you unsure about getting married? 왜 결혼하는거에 확신이 안 서는거야?

A: What's wrong? 왜 그래?
B: I know the wedding is this week but I'm not sure I want to get
    married now. 이번주 결혼식인데 결혼을 하고 싶은건지 아직 확신이 안서서.

We're getting along well with each other

우리는 서로 사이가 좋아

사이가 좋다라고 할 때는 get along well each other를 전형적으로 사용하며 a well-matched couple이라는 표현도 알아두면 좋다. 취미가 같다고 할 때는 have the same taste in~, 자주 싸운다고 할 때는 We fight a lot, 맞벌이 부부라고 할 때는 We're a working couple이라고 한다.

01 Why did you choose to get married to your wife?
왜 네 아내와 결혼하기로 한거야?

● **What made you decide to** marry your wife? 네 아내와 결혼을 결심한 이유가 뭐야?

● **What was it about your husband that** made you want to marry him?
남편의 어떤 점이 네가 남편과 결혼하고 싶어하게 한거야?

● **When did you realize you** wanted to marry your wife?
네가 네 아내와 결혼하고 싶어하는 것을 언제 깨달았어?

A: When did you realize you wanted to marry your wife?
네가 네 아내와 결혼하고 싶어하는 것을 언제 깨달았어?

B: When I saw how much she loved playing with my brother's children. 아내가 조카들과 노는 것을 엄청 좋아하는 것을 봤을 때.

02 We have the same taste in music
우리는 음악취향이 같아

● We share the same love of sports. 우리는 둘 다 스포츠를 좋아해.

● We love the same hobby- traveling. 우리는 똑같은 취미를 좋아하는데, 여행이야.

● My wife is a full-time housewife. 내 아내는 전업주부야.

A: What does she do? 그녀의 직업은 뭐야?
B: My wife is a full-time housewife. 내 아내는 전업주부야.

03 We like to eat out for dinner on the weekends
우리는 주말마다 저녁외식하는 것을 좋아해

- We're a working couple. 우리는 맞벌이 부부야.
- We're DINK(Double Income, No kids). 우리는 아이없는 맞벌이 부부야.
- We work at the same office. 우리는 같은 회사에서 일해.

A: Does your wife stay at home with the children?
네 아내는 아이들과 집에서 지내니?

B: No, we both work in the same office. 아니. 우리 같은 회사에서 일해.

04 We're getting along well with each other
우리는 서로 사이가 좋아

- I think we are a well-matched couple. 우리는 잘 어울리는 한 쌍인 것 같아.
- Sometimes we argue over child raising. 때때로 우리는 아이들 양육문제로 다퉈.
- We are very compatible with each other. 우리는 서로 매우 사이좋게 지내.

A: Do you fight often? 종종 싸우니?
B: No, we are very compatible. 아니. 우리는 매우 사이좋게 지내.

05 We're pretty happy together
우린 함께 무척 행복해

- We fight a lot. 우리는 많이 싸워.
- Do you sometimes argue with your husband? 넌 네 남편과 가끔 다투니?
- How's your married life? 결혼생활이 어때?
- Does your wife nag? 네 아내가 바가지 긁어?

A: We fight a lot. 우리는 많이 싸워.
B: That's too bad but not uncommon. 안됐지만 흔한 일이지.

008 이혼

I got divorced 3 three years ago
난 3년전에 이혼했어

헤어지는 건 break up with, break it off, split up 등이 있고 별거는 separate, live separately 등의 표현을 사용한다. 이혼하다는 get a divorce 혹은 get divorced라고 하면 된다.

01 Ted and Jill have split up
테드와 질이 헤어졌어

- Have you split up with your wife? 너 부인과 헤어졌어?
- Did your wife leave you? 네 아내가 너를 떠났니?
- My wife and I are separated but not divorced yet.
  아내와 난 별거중이지만 아직 이혼전이야.

A: Did you get a divorce? 너 이혼했니?
B: No, but we separated. 아니. 하지만 별거중이야.

02 We're living separately now
우린 현재 별거하고 있어

- I'm separated from my wife. 아내와 별거하고 있어.
- We aren't living together anymore. 우린 더 이상 같이 살지 않아.
- We are in the process of getting separated. 우리는 별거과정을 밟고 있어.

A: Have you moved out yet? 너 이사해 나갔어?
B: No, but we are in the process of getting separated.
   아니. 하지만 별거과정에 있어.

03 I got divorced 3 three years ago
난 3년전에 이혼했어

* I got divorced **two years ago, so I'm single now.** 2년 전에 이혼했고 지금은 혼자야.
* **My wife's cheating on me.** 내 아내가 바람을 피고 있어.
* **That was my first, and her second marriage.** 난 첫번째고 아내는 두번째 결혼었어.

A: Why did you get divorced? 너 왜 이혼했어?
B: Because my husband cheated on me. 남편이 바람을 폈기 때문에.

04 I wish I had never met you
널 안 만났더라면 좋았을텐데

* **I regret meeting you.** 널 만난 걸 후회해.
* **I'm sorry that I met you.** 널 만난게 유감이야.
* **It would have been better if we'd never met.** 우리가 만나지 않았더라면 더 좋았을텐데.

A: I deeply regret meeting you. 널 만난 걸 깊이 후회하고 있어.
B: The feeling is mutual. 나도 그래.

05 The divorce of elderly couples is increasing
노년부부의 이혼이 증가하고 있어

* **Divorce rates are going up.** 이혼율이 올라가고 있어.
* **These days everyone is getting divorced.** 요즘에는 아무나 다 이혼을 해.
* **When I was young, divorce was very uncommon.**
내가 어렸을 때는 이혼은 아주 드문 일이었어.

A: Did you hear they got divorced? 걔네들 이혼했다는 말 들었어?
B: Yes, these days, everyone is getting divorced.
어, 요즘에는 아무나 다 이혼한다니까.

009

We're going to have a baby in June

우리는 6월에 아이를 낳아

임신 ~개월이다는 be ~ months pregnant. 애가 움직이는게 느껴질 때는 feel the baby moving[kicking]으로 말한다. 또한 미국인들은 be expecting이란 표현으로 임신중임을 표현한다. 입양은 adopt란 단어를 사용하면 된다.

01 We're going to have a baby in June
우리는 6월에 아이를 낳아

- My baby's fine. I can feel her kicking. 내 애는 괜찮아. 걔가 발로 차는게 느껴져.
- I'm five months pregnant. 난 임신 5개월이야.
- I can feel the baby moving. 아이가 움직이는걸 느낄 수 있어.

A: Put your hand on my tummy. 내 배위에 손을 올려놔봐.
B: Wow! I can feel the baby moving. 와! 아이가 움직이는게 느껴져.

02 She is expecting now
그녀는 지금 임신중이야

- I'm expecting. 난 임신중야.
- What did she have? 남자였어 여자였어?
- She gave birth to baby girl. 그녀는 여자아이를 낳았어.

A: She is expecting. 그녀는 임신중이야.
B: That's fabulous news. 아주 멋진 소식이네.

03 I'm never going to have a baby
절대로 애는 안 갖을거야

- I don't want any children. 난 아이를 원하지 않아.

- I wouldn't be a good parent. 난 좋은 부모가 되지 못할거야.

- The idea of having a baby **scares me.** 아이를 갖는다는 생각에 무서워져.

A: Why don't you want any children? 왜 아이를 원하지 않는거야?
B: The idea of having a baby scares me. 아이를 갖는다는 생각에 무서워져.

04 I don't have any children
난 애가 없어

- **I'm not planning on** having any children. 난 애를 갖을 생각을 하고 있지 않아.

- We don't want any children **until after we work for a few years.**
우리는 몇 년간 맞벌이를 한 후에 아이를 갖을거야.

- We have no plans for children. 우리는 아이를 갖을 계획인 없어.

A: How many children do you two want? 아이는 몇이나 원해?
B: We have no plans for children right now. 지금 당장은 아이를 낳을 생각이 없어.

05 We are adopting a baby from China
우리는 중국아이를 입양할거야

- Our son **was adopted from** an orphanage in China.
우리 아들은 중국의 고아원에서 입양되었어.

- Adoption **is something we are thinking about.** 우리는 입양을 생각하고 있어.

- We want to adopt a couple of children. 우리는 두세명의 아이들을 입양하고 싶어.

A: We want to adopt a couple of children. 우리는 두세명의 아이들을 입양하고 싶어.
B: That's great. 아주 좋으네.

010

I have a son in elementary school

초등학교 다니는 아들 하나야

자식들에 대해 말하는 방법. 흔히 묻는 "네 아들은 몇 학년이니?"는 What grade is your son in?이라고 한다. 자식들이 다 초등학생이면 My children are both in elementary school 그리고 "미래에 뭐가 될거래?"라고 물을 때는 What does she want to be?라고 하면 된다.

01 I have a son and two daughters

아들 하나고 딸이 둘야

- My son has started speaking **recently**. 내 아들이 최근에 말을 하기 시작했어.
- What grade is **your son in**? 네 아들은 몇 학년이야?
- My daughter took her first steps **last week**. 내 딸은 지난주에 첫걸음을 떼었어.

A: My son said his first words yesterday. 내 아들이 어제 처음으로 말을 했어.
B: What were they? 무슨 말을 했는데?

02 I have a son in middle school

중학교 다니는 아들 하나야

- My son is a high school student. 아들은 고등학생야.
- My daughter is in university. 내 딸은 대학교에 다녀.
- My children are both in elementary school. 내 아이들은 둘 다 초등학생이야.

A: How old is your son? 네 아들 나이가 몇이야?
B: He's 17. He is in high school now. 17살. 지금 고등학생이야.

03 He goes to grad school
걘 대학원에 진학한대

- What is your son interested in? 네 아들이 뭐에 흥미를 가지고 있어?
- What does she want to be? 걔는 앞으로 뭐가 되고 싶대?
- What are his plans for the future? 걔의 미래계획은 뭐야?

A: My daughter is graduating from high school this year.
내 딸은 금년에 고등학교를 졸업해.

B: What are her plans for the future? 걔의 미래계획은 뭐래?

04 My son won't listen to us at all
아들이 우리말을 전혀 듣지 않으려고 해

- I'm worried about my son because he doesn't like to study.
  내 아들이 공부하기 싫어해서 걱정야.
- She doesn't like to study. 걔는 공부하는 걸 싫어해.
- My son hangs out with the wrong kind of people.
  내 아들은 그릇된 종류의 아이들과 어울려.

A: Why is he doing poorly in school? 왜 걔 학교성적이 형편없는거야?
B: He is hanging out with the wrong kind of people.
걘 삐뚤어진 아이들과 어울리고 있어.

05 Today, my son skipped school
오늘, 아들이 학교를 빼먹었어

- She was playing truant today. 걔는 오늘 무단결석했어.
- He left school during school hours. 걘 학교를 조퇴했어.
- They cut classes and went to a singing room. 걔네들은 수업을 빼먹고 노래방에 갔어.

A: Why are you angry at your son? 넌 왜 아들에게 화가 난거야?
B: He skipped school today and went to the waterpark with his friends.
오늘 학교를 빼먹고 친구들과 워터파크에 갔어.

My father has worked on his own

아버지는 사업을 해오셨어

반대로 이번에는 자식들이 부모에 대해 말할 때의 표현들이다. 자기사업을 한다고 할 때는 work on his own, run his own business 등으로 표현한다. 두 분 다 살아 계신다고 할 때는 My parents are alive and well이라고 한다.

01 My father has worked on his own
아버지는 사업을 해오셨어

- **My father** is still active in business. 아버지는 아직도 비즈니스를 활발히 하고 계셔.
- **My dad** runs his own business. 아버지는 자신의 사업체를 운영하셔.
- **My mother** is an independent business woman. 엄마는 독립적인 비즈니스 여성이셔.

A: What does your mother do? 너희 엄마 뭐하시니?
B: She runs her own clothing business. 의류업체를 운영하고 계셔.

02 My parents are in good health
부모님은 다 건강하셔

- **My parents** are alive and well. 부모님 두 분 다 살아계시고 잘 지내시고 있어.
- **My parents** are really healthy for their age. 부모님은 나이에 비해서 아주 정말 건강하셔.
- **My parents** stay in great shape. 부모님은 아주 건강하셔.

A: Your mom and dad look so healthy. 네 엄마와 아빠는 아주 건강해보여.
B: Yes, they stay in great shape for their age. 어, 연세에 비해 아주 건강하셔.

03 My mother looks young for her age
엄마는 나이에 비해 젊어 보이셔

- I thought your mother was your sister. 난 네 엄마가 네 누나인 줄 알았다.

- Your father looks like he's in his 30s. 네 아버지는 30대인 것처럼 보여.

- Your mother looks so young. What's her secret?
  네 엄마는 아주 젊어 보이셔. 비결이 뭐래?

A: Your father looks so young. What's his secret?
네 아버지는 아주 젊어 보여. 비결이 뭐야?

B: He doesn't smoke or drink and he gets 8 to 9 hours sleep every night. 음주와 흡연을 안하시고 매일 8시간에서 9시간 잠을 주무셔.

04 My father retired last year
아버지는 작년에 퇴직하셨어

- My parents live on their pensions. 부모님은 연금으로 사셔.

- My father has aged a lot in the past few years.
  아버지는 지난 몇 년간 아주 나이를 드셨어.

- My parents are both getting up there in years. 부모님은 두분 다 수년간 늙으셨어.

A: What does your father do? 너희 아버지는 뭐하셔?
B: He retired last year but before that he was a bus driver.
작년에 퇴직하셨는데 버스기사셨어.

05 My father's favorite pastime is hiking
아버지가 가장 좋아하는 소일거리는 하이킹이야

- My mother loves hiking in her free time. 엄마는 시간날 때 하이킹하는 것을 좋아하셔.

- When he isn't busy my father enjoys playing computer games.
  아버지는 바쁘지 않으실 때 컴퓨터 게임을 즐겨하셔.

- My parents are both crazy about hiking. 부모님 두 분 다 하이킹을 무척 좋아하셔.

A: What do your parents do for fun? 네 부모님은 여가시간에 뭐하셔?
B: Their favorite pastime is doing puzzles. 부모님이 젤 좋아하는 취미는 퍼즐맞추기야.

012 I'm from a one-parent family

난 한부모 가정에서 자랐어

한부모 가정은 a one-parent family. 혹은 a single parent를 이용해 표현하고 핵가족이라고 말할 때는 have a typical nuclear family라고 하면 된다. 사고로 돌아가셨다고 하려면 die in a car accident을 사용한다.

01 I'm from a one-parent family
난 한부모 가정에서 자랐어

- **My mom** is a single parent. 내 엄마는 한부모 가정이셔.

- **I have** a typical nuclear family. 나의 집은 전형적인 핵가족이야.

- **My mom** passed away, so my father is a widower.
  어머니는 돌아가셔서 아버지는 홀아비이셔.

A: Your mother is a widow? 네 엄마는 홀어머니이시니?
B: Yes, my father passed away 2 years ago. 어, 아버지가 2년전에 돌아가셨어.

02 My father has been suffering from lung cancer
아버지는 폐암을 앓고 계셔

- **My mother** has breast cancer. 엄마는 유방암이셔.

- **My brother** has type 1 diabetes. 내 형은 제 1형 당뇨병이야.

- **My sister** was diagnosed with skin cancer. 내 누이는 피부암을 진단받았어.

A: My mother was just diagnosed with breast cancer.
   엄마는 유방암으로 진단받았어.
B: I'm so sorry to hear that. 정말 안타까운 소식이네.

03 My mother died in a car accident
엄마는 차사고로 돌아가셨어

- My grandfather died of **natural causes.** 할아버지는 자연사하셨어.
- My grandmother died from **a heart attack.** 할머니는 심장마비로 돌아가셨어.
- A blood clot in the heart **killed my father.** 아버지는 심장의 혈전으로 돌아가셨어.

A: How did she die? 그녀는 어떻게 돌아가신거야?
B: Of natural causes. 자연사야.

04 My father died in an accident a long time ago
아버지는 오래전에 사고로 돌아가셨어

- My grandparents all died **years ago.** 조부모는 오래전에 다 돌아가셨어.
- When did your grandfather **pass away?** 네 할아버지는 언제 돌아가셨어?
- My mother in-law died **before I met my wife.**
  장모님은 내가 아내를 만나기 전에 돌아가셨어.

A: What's your mother in-law like? 장모님은 어떤 분이셔?
B: I never knew her. She died before I met my wife.
만나뵙질 못했어. 아내를 만나기 전에 돌아가셨어.

05 He was killed in a ski accident
걘 스키타다 사고로 죽었어

- He was killed in **the war in Afghanistan.** 걘 아프가니스탄 전쟁에서 사망했어.
- She was murdered by **a jealous girlfriend.** 걘 질투심많은 여자 친구에 의해 살해당했어.
- He was tortured to death **by the soldiers.** 걘 군인들로부터 고문을 당해서 죽었어.

A: How did he die? 걘 어떻게 죽은거야?
B: He was killed by a bomb in Afghanistan. 아프가니스탄에서 폭탄이 터져서 죽었어.

013

He is a little bit senile
그는 조금 노쇠하셨어

아무래도 조부모님을 얘기할 때는 아프시거나 돌아가셨다거나 혹은 노쇠하시다 (senile)라는 표현을 자주 쓸 수 밖에 없다. 병으로 돌아가셨으면 die of~를 쓴다. 아직 건강하시거나 젊어보이신다고 할 때는 strong. look for one's age 등의 표현을 쓴다.

01

My grandfather died of lung cancer two years ago
할아버지는 2년전에 폐암으로 돌아가셨어

● My grandmother died of a stroke **last month.** 할머니는 지난달 뇌졸증으로 돌아가셨어.

● My grandfather almost died of a heart attack.
할아버지는 심장마비로 거의 돌아가실뻔했어.

● She died from head trauma **when she fell from the ladder.**
그녀는 사다리에서 떨어졌을 때 입은 머리외상으로 사망했어.

A: She died from head trauma when she fell while rock climbing.
그녀는 암벽등반하다 떨어져 머리외상으로 죽었어.

B: That's so tragic. 참 안됐네.

02

My grandmother looks happiest when she's with
us 할머니는 우리와 있을 때 가장 즐거워보이셔

● My grandparents are always happy to see us.
조부모님은 우리를 만날 때 항상 즐거워하셔.

● My uncle never looks happy **when he's with my aunt.**
삼촌은 숙모와 있을 때 즐거워한 적이 없어.

● I've never seen her so happy **as she was at her wedding.**
그녀가 자기 결혼식 때 가장 행복해보였어.

A: My grandparents are always happy to see us.
조부모님은 우리는 만날 때 즐거워하셔.

B: Of course they are. 물론 그러시지.

03 My grandmother is becoming senile
할머니는 점점 노쇠해지셔

- My grandparents are becoming more forgetful. 조부모님은 점점 깜박깜박 하셔.

- He is a little bit senile. 그는 조금 노쇠하셨어.

- She isn't senile at all. She's quite sharp. 그녀는 전혀 노쇠하지 않았어. 매우 명민하셔.

A: Is your grandmother senile? 네 할머니는 노쇠하셨어?
B: No at all. She's actually quite sharp. 전혀 안그래. 실은 매우 명민하셔.

04 My grandmother is taking care of us instead of my mother
할머니가 엄마를 대신해서 우리를 돌보셔

- My grandmother is going to look after us while our parents are away.
할머니는 부모님이 외출시 우리를 돌보실거야.

- I am taking care of my baby sister tonight. 난 오늘밤 여동생을 돌볼거야.

- Who is going to watch the baby while I go shopping?
내가 쇼핑간 사이에 누가 아이를 돌볼거야?

A: Who is going to watch the baby while I go shopping?
내가 쇼핑간 사이에 누가 아이를 돌볼거야?
B: I'll take care of him. 내가 돌볼게.

05 My grandfather is still strong and healthy at ninety-four
할아버지는 94세인데도 아직 건강하셔

- For his age, my grandfather is in fantastic shape.
할아버지는 나이에 비해 몸매가 멋지셔.

- My grandfather looks very healthy for his age.
할아버지는 나이에 비해 매우 건강해 보이셔.

A: Your grandmother is 70 years old? I don't believe it!
네 할머니가 70세이시라고? 믿기지 않네!
B: Yes, she looks great for her age. 맞아. 연세에 비해 아주 좋아보이시지.

014

I have a turtle as a pet
애완동물로 거북이를 길러

단순히 have+애완동물해도 되지만 have+애완동물 as a pet이라는 표현도 함께 알아둔다. 유기견은 an abandoned dog. 길잃은 고양이는 a stray cat이라고 하면 된다.

01 I have two dogs
난 개 두 마리를 길러

- I have a turtle as a pet. 애완동물로 거북이를 길러.

- I have a pet hamster. 햄스터를 애완동물로 길러.

- I have a pet cat. 난 애완동물로 고양이를 길러.

A: Do you have any pets? 애완동물 뭐 길러?
B: Yes, a cat and a snake. 어, 고양이와 뱀.

02 I love little birds
난 작은 새들이 좋아

- What kind of animal do you have? 무슨 동물을 길러?

- Have you ever had a dog? 개를 길러본 적이 있어?

- Have you ever owned a pet? 애완동물을 길러본 적이 있어?

A: What kind of pet do you have? 어떤 종류의 애완동물을 길러?
B: A Jindo dog. 진돗개.

03 It's a female mini pin
미니핀 여자아이야

- We call her Ari. 우리는 걔의 이름을 아리라고 불러.
- What do you call it? 걔 이름이 뭐야?
- What is his name? 걔의 이름이 뭐야?

A: What's your dog's name? 너희 집 개 이름이 뭐야?
B: We call him Blue. 블루라고 불러.

04 She was an abandoned dog
걘 유기견이었어

- It's a stray cat. 집없는 고양이였어.
- Do you have any pets? 애완동물 기르는거 있어?
- He was a rescue shelter cat. 구조보호소에 있는 고양이였어.

A: Where did you get your dog? 너희 집 강아지는 어디서 구한거야?
B: From a rescue shelter. He was an abandoned dog they found on the street. 구조보호소에서. 길거리에서 발견된 유기견이었어.

05 She is very friendly to me
걔는 매우 나와 친해

- Your dog is a little skittish. 너희 개는 조금 겁이 많아.
- What a friendly cat! 참 다정한 고양이다!
- Your cat is a bit aloof. 너희 고양이는 좀 어울리지 않아.

A: Why isn't your cat friendly to me? 왜 네 고양이는 내게 살갑게 대하지 않는거야?
B: She's a bit aloof! 걔 좀 외톨이야!

015

I walk my dog every night
매일밤 강아지를 산책시켜

똥오줌을 가리는 건 know where to poop[pee] 혹은 house-train이라고 하고, 산책을 시킨다고 할 때는 walk를 타동사로 써서 walk my dog이라고 하면 된다.

01 My dog knows where to poop[or pee]
내 강아지는 똥[오줌]을 가려

- You need to take care of the dog's poop. 강아지 대변을 처리해야 돼.
- Is your dog house-trained? 네 개는 똥오줌 가리니?
- Do you have a pee pad for your puppy? 강아지용 오줌패드가 있어?

A: Is your dog house-trained yet? 네 강아지는 똥오줌 가리니?
B: No, but we just bought a pee pad and are training her.
아니, 하지만 오줌패드를 샀고 훈련시킬거야.

02 I walk my dog every night
매일밤 강아지를 산책시켜

- Who walks the dog? 누가 개를 산책시켜?
- Who takes the dog out for a walk? 누가 개를 데리고 나가 산책을 하니?
- Who is responsible for walking the dog? 강아지 산책은 누구 담당이야?

A: Who usually walks the dog? 누가 주로 개를 산책시켜?
B: We take turns. 교대로 해.

03 I don't have any pets now
난 지금 아무런 애완동물도 기르지 않아

- We used to have a dog but not now. 강아지를 길렀지만 지금은 아냐.
- Currently we don't have any pets but we're thinking of getting a cat.
  현재 기르는 애완동물이 없지만 고양이를 기를까 생각중이야.
- We had a dog but right now we have no pets.
  강아지를 길렀지만 지금은 아무런 애완동물을 기르지 않아.

A: We used to have a cat but not now. 고양이를 길렀지만 지금은 아냐.
B: Are you thinking of getting another one? 다른 고양이를 기를 생각이야?

04 The hotel doesn't allow pets
호텔은 애완동물 입실불가야

- This is a dog friendly hotel. 이 호텔은 애완견 입실이 가능해.
- No pets are permitted in this park. 공원에는 어떤 애완동물도 들어올 수가 없어.
- This is an off-leash dog park. 여기는 목줄없이 다닐 수 있는 강아지 공원이야.

A: Can I bring my dog there? 거기에 강아지를 데려갈 수 있어요?
B: Sorry. This hotel doesn't allow pets.
   죄송합니다만 저희 호텔은 애완동물 입장불가입니다.

05 My dog knows how to rank the family members
내 강아지는 가족들 서열 매길 줄 알아

- My dog can shake a paw. 내 강아지는 손을 흔들 수 있어.
- Our dog can roll over and play dead. 우리 개는 뒤집어져서 죽은 척할 수 있어.
- The dog knows how to bark on command. 개는 명령에 따라 짖는 법을 알고 있어.

A: What tricks can your dog do? 너희 개는 어떤 장난을 칠 수 있어?
B: She can shake a paw and play dead. 손을 흔들고 죽은 척을 할 수 있어.

016 It's a female named Ari

여자아이이고 이름은 아리야

애완동물을 키우지 않는다고 할 때는 I don't have any pets. 그리고 강아지는 가족같아(be like a family member)서 사람의 가장 친한 친구라고 불리운다.

01 I have a dog

난 강아지를 키워

- **I don't have any pets.** 난 애완동물을 기르지 않아.
- **I'm taking him to the veterinarian later on today.**
  오늘 늦게 걔를 동물병원에 데려갈거야.
- **I am thinking of buying a dog.** 난 강아지를 분양받을까 생각중이야.

A: Do you have any pets? 애완동물 뭐 길러?
B: No, but I'm thinking of buying a cat. 안기르지만 고양이를 기를까 생각중이야.

02 She is female but was spayed

걘 여자아이인데 난소를 제거했어

- **He is a male dog but he's been fixed.**
  걘 남자 강아지인데 중성화수술을 받았어.
- **Are you going to get your dog fixed?** 네 강아지 중성화수술시킬거야?

A: Are you going to breed any puppies with your dog?
   너네 강아지가 새끼를 낳게 할거야?
B: We can't. She's been spayed. 그럴 수 없어. 난소를 제거했거든.

03   I guess a dog really is man's best friend
강아지는 사람의 가장 친한 친구인 것 같아

- In many ways a dog is better than a human. 많은 면에서 강아지는 사람보다 더 나아.
- The bond between humans and dogs is very strong.
사람과 강아지의 유대관계는 매우 두터워.
- My dog knows me better than my wife does. 내 강아지가 내 아내보다 나를 더 잘 알아.

A: You and your dog seem very close. 너와 네 강아지는 매우 가까워 보여.
B: Yes, my dog knows me better than my wife does.
맞아, 내 강아지는 내 아내보다 나를 더 잘알아.

05   A dog is like a family member
강아지는 가족같아

- My dog and I can communicate well with each other.
강아지와 난 서로 의사소통을 잘할 수 있어.
- My dog and I are closer than family. 내 강아지와 난 가족보다 더 가까워.
- My dog is well-trained. 내 강아지는 잘 훈련되어 있어.

A: He is such an obedient dog. 너네 강아지는 복종심이 아주 강하네.
B: Yes, my dog is well-trained. 어, 내 강아지는 잘 훈련되어 있어.

05   I had a kakariki named Sungsuni but she died
나 성순이라는 카카리키가 있었는데 죽었어

- Bird watching is very interesting to me.
새를 바라다보는 것은 내게는 무척 흥미로운 일이야.
- I've been bird watching for years. 난 수년동안 새들을 관찰해왔어.
- Bird watching is very popular in England.
새를 관찰하는 것은 영국에서는 매우 인기있는 일이야.

A: That book is about birds? 저 책은 새들에 관한거야?
B: Yes, bird watching is very interesting to me.
어, 새를 관찰하는 것은 내게 매우 흥미로운 일이야.

017

Are you a cat or a dog person?
넌 고양이를 좋아해 강아지를 좋아해?

요즘 강아지에는 몸에 칩을 삽입하게 되어 있는데 이때는 have a microchip이라고 하면 되고, 목줄을 매다는 leash a dog 혹은 keep a dog on a leash라고 한다. 유기하다는 abandon one's dog이라고 하면 된다.

01 My dog has a microchip in his body
우리집 강아지 몸에는 마이크로칩이 삽입되어 있어

- **My dog** has been microchipped. 내 강아지는 몸에 칩이 삽입되어 있어.

- It's the law that all dogs must have a microchip so they can be identified if they are lost.
  모든 강아지는 잃어버렸을 경우 확인하기 위해 내장칩을 삽입하는 것은 법으로 정해져 있어.

A: I didn't realize you need to get a microchip for your dog in this country. 이 나라에서 강아지 칩이 의무라는 것을 몰랐어.

B: Yes, it's the law. That way the dog's owner can be located if the dog gets lost or does some harm to somebody.
맞아, 법이야. 그렇게 해서 강아지가 길을 잃거나 사람에게 해꼬지를 할 때 주인을 찾을 수 있어.

02 When walking a dog, we must leash him
개를 산보시킬 때는 항상 목줄을 해야 돼

- Keep **your dog** on a leash. 네 개의 목에 목줄을 채워.

- In this park you can let your dogs off their leashes.
  이 공원에서 목줄없이 개가 들어올 수 없어.

A: Is this an off-leash park? 여기는 개목줄없이 다닐 수 있는 공원이야?

B: No, all dogs must be leashed here. If you want to walk off-leash, you can take them to a dog park.
아니, 모든 개는 여기서 목줄을 해야 돼. 목줄없이 산보시키고 싶으면 개공원으로 데리고 가면 돼.

03 My dog won't eat his food
우리집 강아지는 사료를 먹지 않으려고 해

- My dog is a fussy eater. 우리집 강아지는 식성이 까다로와.
- Her dog only eats human food. 걔의 강아지는 인간의 음식만 먹어.
- Their dog doesn't eat kibble, it only eats canned dog food.
  걔네들 강아지는 알갱이로 된 사료는 안먹고 캔에 들어있는 것만 먹어.

A: His dog is a real fussy eater. 걔네 강아지는 정말이지 식성이 까다롭다며.

B: I heard it only eats canned dog food or human food.
캔에 들어있는 음식이나 인간의 음식만 먹는다고 들었어.

04 People tend to abandon their dogs
사람들은 강아지를 유기하는 경향이 있어

- Bad owners often abandon or neglect their pets.
  나쁜 주인은 자신의 애완동물을 유기하거나 제대로 돌보지 않아.
- People who get caught abandoning their pets should be arrested and never allowed to own pets again. 유기하다 걸린 사람은 체포해서 다신 애완동물을 기르지 못하도록 해야 돼.

A: I was just at the rescue shelter. It's so sad because it's full of abandoned cats and dogs.
동물보호소에 있었는데, 거기에 유기된 고양이와 강아지로 가득차있는게 슬펐어.

B: That makes me so angry. Owners who abandon their pets should be arrested. 화나게 만드네. 애완동물 유기한 주인은 체포되어야 해.

05 Are you a cat or a dog person?
고양이 좋아해 강아지 좋아해?

- She is a real dog person. She can't stand cats.
  걘 정말이지 강아지를 좋아해. 고양이는 못 견뎌.
- He isn't a cat or a dog person. He is an animal lover. He loves all animals.
  걘 어떤 사람도 아니야. 모든 동물을 사랑하는 사람이야.

A: Are you a cat or a dog person? 고양이 좋아해 강아지 좋아해?

B: Dog but I still love cats too. 강아지이지만 그래도 역시 고양이를 좋아해.

Unit 03 가족과 주변상황 | 189 |

018

The dog needs a muzzle

그 개는 입마개가 필요해

입마개는 a muzzle, 중성화수술은 spay, neuter 등의 동사를 사용한다. 또한 안락사시키다는 put ～ down 혹은 put～ to sleep이란 표현으로 나타낸다.

01 The dog needs a muzzle
그 개는 입마개가 필요해

● **You must muzzle your dog** if it is more than 10kgs.
네 개가 10킬로가 넘으면 입마개를 해야 돼.

● **I bought a muzzle for my dog** but it hates to wear it.
개를 위해 입마개를 샀는데 하는 걸 무척 싫어해.

● **Why do you need a muzzle for your dog?** Is it dangerous?
네 개에 왜 입마개가 필요한거야? 위험한 개야?

A: Why does your dog have a muzzle? Does it bite?
네 개는 왜 입마개를 하고 있어? 무니?

B: No, but this park has a rule that all dogs over 10kgs must wear muzzles. 아니, 하지만 공원규정에 10킬로가 넘는 모든 개는 입마개를 해야 돼.

02 My female dog was spayed last month
내 여자 강아지는 지난달에 중성화수술을 했어

● **If you don't plan on having puppies** you should have your dog spayed.
새끼 강아지를 볼 생각이 없으면 중성화수술을 시켜.

● **He took his dog into the vet** to have it neutered last week.
갠 지난주에 중성화수술시키려고 동물병원에 갔어.

A: I have to take Rex into the vet tomorrow to have him neutered.
난 렉스를 중성화시키려고 낼 동물병원에 가야 돼.

B: Poor boy! I hope it isn't too traumatic for him.
안됐네! 너무 충격을 받지 않기를 바래.

03 I had to put the dog down this week
난 이번주에 강아지를 안락사시켜야 했어

- I had to put the dog down this week. 난 이번주에 강아지를 안락사시켜야 했어.
- We have to take him to the vet and put him to sleep.
  우리는 걔를 동물병원에 데려가서 안락사시켜야 돼.

A: What's wrong? Why are you crying? 왜 그래? 왜 울고 있는거야?

B: I just got back from the vet's. We had to put Sport down. He had cancer and was in a great deal of pain but it was still hard to do.
동물병원에서 오는 길야. 스포트를 안락사시켜야 했어. 암으로고통을 받았지만 그래도 그렇게 하기가 어려웠어.

04 She's taking them for a walk to the dog park
걔 강아지 공원에 산보시키려 강아지들을 데리고 갈거야

- She takes her dog for a walk twice a day, even if it's raining.
  걔 비가 오더라고 하루에 2번 강아지를 산책시켜.
- That dog loves going for walks, especially to the off-leash dog park.
  저 강아지는 특히 목줄안해도 되는 개공원에서 산책하는 것을 좋아해.
- His dog loves going for walks. 걔의 강아지는 산책나가는 것을 좋아해.

A: Is she taking her dog for a walk again? 걔 또 강아지를 산책시키는거야?

B: Yes, she loves going for walks and so does her dog.
어. 걔 산책하는 것을 좋아하고 강아지도 그래.

05 You need to house train your dog
넌 배변훈련을 시켜야 돼

- You need to house train your dog. 넌 강아지에게 배변훈련을 시켜야 돼.
- We are doing potty training these days for the puppy.
  우리는 요즘 강아지 배변훈련을 시키고 있어.
- How hard is it to house train a puppy? 강아지 배변훈련이 얼마나 어려워?

A: Wow! It looks like you have him potty trained already!
와! 네 강아지 배변훈련을 이미 시킨 것 같아.

B: Yes! He's a smart dog and only 2 months old too. 어! 똑똑하고 겨우 2달된 강아지야.

019

Her dog loves to play fetch
걔 강아지는 물고 오는 것을 좋아해

눕거나 죽은 척하기(play dead) 등의 장난(trick)를 할 수 있는지 혹은 던지면 물고 오는 것(play fetch)을 좋아하는 지 등을 서로 물어볼 수 있다.

01 Does your dog do any tricks?
네 강아지는 뭐 장난하는거 있어?

- **Does your dog** do any tricks? 네 강아지는 뭐 장난하는거 있어?

- **He** plays dead **and** shakes a paw, rolls over, sits, lies down.
  죽은 척하고 손흔들기, 뒹굴기, 앉고 벌렁 눕는 것을 해.

- **This breed** is easy to train. 이 품종은 훈련시키기가 쉬워.

A: This breed is very easy to train. 이 품종은 훈련시키기가 쉬워.
B: Nice. I saw it shaking paws and playing dead. What other tricks does it know? 멋지다. 걔가 손을 흔들고 죽은 척하는 것을 봤어? 다른 장난할 수 있는 건 뭐야?

02 Her dog loves to play fetch
걔 강아지는 물고 오는 것을 좋아해

- **Her dog loves to** play fetch. 걔 강아지는 물고 오는 것을 좋아해.

- **My dog and I usually** play fetch with a frisbee.
  강아지와 난 보통 프리스비를 던지고 물고 오는 놀이를 해.

- **I tire my dog out by** playing fetch with it. 난 그것을 물고 오는 것으로 강아지를 지치게 해.

A: Your dog looks really tired. 네 강아지는 정말 지쳐 보여.
B: We just finished playing fetch for the past hour with a baseball.
야구공으로 지난 한 시간 동안 물고 오는 것을 했어.

03 That dog is always barking
저 강아지는 항상 짖어

- **That dog** is always barking. 저 강아지는 항상 짖어.
- **The neighbors** have been complaining about the barking.
이웃들이 강아지 짖는 소리에 항의하고 있어.

A: The neighbors complained again about your dog barking?
이웃이 네 강아지 짖는 소리에 항의했다며?

B: Yes, so I had to buy an anti-barking collar to train it to stop.
어, 그래서 짖는 것을 멈추게 하는 전기충격방지칼라를 사야 했어.

04 Your dog has a beautiful coat
네 강아지 털이 예쁘다

- **How often do you** brush your dog? 얼마나 자주 네 강아지 빗질을 해줘?
- **Do you go to a** dog groomer's? 애견미용사에게 가?
- **Does your dog shed?** 네 강아지는 털갈이를 해?

A: Your dog has such a beautiful fur coat. Do you take it to a groomer's? 네 강아지 털이 참 예뻐. 애견미용사에게 데려가?

B: No, we brush it 3 times a day and feed it special food.
아니, 하루에 3번 빗질해주고 특별한 사료를 먹이고 있어.

05 What kind of breed is that?
그건 무슨 품종이야?

- **Is it a** German Shepherd? 독일산 셰퍼드야?
- **I love** smaller breeds. 소형품종이 좋아.
- **What kind of breed is** that? 그건 무슨 품종이야?

A: What kind of breed is that? It looks a little like a Schnauzer.
그건 무슨 품종이야? 슈나이저 같아.

B: No, it's a Scottish Terrier. They look similar but Scotty's have shorter legs and thicker bodies.
아니, 얜 스카치테리어야. 둘 다 비슷하지만 스카치테리어는 다리가 더 짧고 몸이 더 두터워.

직장생활

001 구직활동

She is looking for a job

갠 일자리를 찾고 있어

실직중이라고 할 때는 between jobs, out of work 등의 표현을 쓰고, 일자리를 찾는다고 할 때는 look for a job, find a job, job-hunt 등의 표현들을 사용하면 된다.

01 I'm in between jobs right now
나 지금은 실직중이야

- I'm currently out of work. 난 현재는 일을 안하고 있어.
- He is unemployed at the moment. 갠 지금은 실직중이야.
- He has no job right now. 갠 지금은 직업이 없어.

A: Is he working these days? 걔 요즘 일해?
B: No, he's unemployed at the moment. 아니. 지금은 실직중이야.

02 What kind of job are you seeking?
넌 어떤 일자리를 구하고 있어?

- I am seeking work in the entertainment industry. 연예계 쪽 일을 구하고 있어.
- She is looking for a job in the restaurant industry. 식당업계 쪽 일을 찾고 있어.
- What kind of employment are you looking for? 어떤 종류의 취업을 구하고 있어?

A: What kind of employment are you looking for?
어떤 종류의 취업을 구하고 있어?
B: Something in the construction industry. 건설업계 쪽 일을.

03 He is looking for a job
갠 일자리를 찾고 있어

- I'm looking for work **in Seoul.** 난 서울에서 일자리를 찾고 있어.

- She was looking for **work in Australia and found a job in Melbourne.**
  갠 호주에서 일을 찾고 있었고 멜버른에서 일자리를 구했어.

- What kind of **work** are you looking for? 어떤 종류의 일을 구하고 있어?

A: I'm looking for work in the Seoul area. 난 서울지역에서의 일을 구하고 있어.
B: Good luck. 행운을 빌어.

02 I'm job-hunting right now
난 지금 구직활동을 하고 있어

- **How is the** job hunt **going?** 구직활동은 어떻게 돼가?

- **He is hunting for a job** in the movie business. 갠 영화업계에서의 일자리를 구하고 있어.

- **Is your** job hunt **going well?** 네 구직활동은 잘되고 있어?

A: How is the job hunt going? 구직활동은 어떻게 돼가?
B: Good. I have two interviews this week. 좋아. 이번 주에 면접이 두개 잡혀 있어.

05 I need to find a job
난 일자리를 찾아야 해

- He needs to **find a job soon.** 갠 빨리 일자리를 찾아야 돼.

- I found a good job **near my home.** 난 집근처에 좋은 일자리를 구했어.

- She wants to find a job **at a clothing store.** 갠 의류가게 일자리 찾기를 원해.

A: Does he have a job yet? 걔는 일자리를 구했어?
B: No, he needs to find a job soon. 아니. 갠 빨리 일자리를 찾아야 돼.

002

I am rewriting my resume
난 이력서를 다시 작성하고 있어

이력서는 resume 혹은 curriculum vitae(CV)라고 한다. 이력서를 써서 이력서를 보내거나 제출한다고 하려면 send나 submit의 동사를 활용하면 된다.

01 Our company is currently accepting resumes
우리 회사는 현재 이력서를 접수받고 있습니다

- I sent my resume to **five different companies.** 난 이력서를 다섯군데 회사에 보냈어.
- **I am rewriting my resume.** 난 이력서를 다시 작성하고 있어.
- **Do you** have a good resume? 넌 이력서가 괜찮아?

A: Our company is currently accepting resumes.
우리 회사는 현재 이력서를 받고 있습니다.

B: I'll send mine today. 오늘 이력서를 보낼게요.

02 We are reviewing applicants' curriculum vitae(CV)
우리는 지원자의 이력서를 검토하고 있습니다

- His curriculum vitae shows that he volunteered for several organizations.
그 사람의 이력서에는 몇몇 기관에 자원봉사했다고 되어 있어.
- **Please submit your curriculum vitae ASAP.** 이력서를 가능한 빨리 제출하시기 바랍니다.
- I am writing up my curriculum vitae **tonight.** 난 오늘밤 이력서 작성을 마무리할거야.

A: The company is hiring. 저 회사는 지금 채용중이래.
B: I will update my CV and send it in tomorrow.
이력서를 업데이트해서 내일 제출할거야.

Our company is starting to e-recruit
우리 회사는 인터넷으로 사원을 모집하기 시작했습니다

- E-recruiting **has become more popular recently.** 최근 인터넷으로 사원모집 더 많이 해.
- I was hired through an e-recruiting **company.** 인터넷 사원모집하는 회사를 통해서 취직했어.
- I am using e-recruiters **to find a job.**
  난 인터넷으로 사원을 모집하는 회사를 이용해서 일자리를 찾고 있어.

A: How did you get your job? 지금 일자리를 어떻게 구했어?
B: Through an e-recruiting company. 인터넷 구직회사를 통해서.

I must submit my resume by Friday
난 금요일까지 이력서를 제출해야 돼

- When will you submit your CV? 언제 이력서를 제출하실 건가요?
- They are asking applicants to submit their resumes by April 1.
  지원자는 4월 1일까지 이력서를 제출할 것을 요청합니다.

A: When is the deadline? 데드라인이 언제야?
B: They are asking applicants to submit their resumes by next
Monday. 지원자들은 담월요일까지 이력서를 제출해야 돼.

A good cover letter will help you get an interview
커버레터를 잘 쓰면 면접을 볼 수 있을거야

- Cover letters **are very important for finding a job.**
  일자리를 찾는데 커버레터는 매우 중요해.
- I need to **write a cover letter for that new job opening.**
  새로 난 일자리에 지원하려고 커버레터를 써야 돼.
- Can you **teach me** how to write a cover letter? 어떻게 커버레터를 쓰는지 알려줄테야?

A: Have you applied for that job yet? 그 일자리에 지원했어?
B: No, I need to write a cover letter tonight and I'll submit it and my
CV tomorrow. 아니. 난 오늘밤에 커버레터를 써야 되고 그것과 이력서를 내일 제출할거야.

003

I've got a job interview next Monday

난 담주 월요일에 면접이 잡혀 있어

이력서를 보냈으면 이제는 면접을 봐야 한다. 면접이 잡혔다, 즉 있다라고 하려면 have a job interview. 면접일정을 잡는다라고 할 때는 set up 혹은 arrange라는 동사를 사용하면 된다.

01 I have a job interview this afternoon
오늘 오후에 구직면접이 있어

● You'll have a good job interview. **Cheer up**. 면접을 잘 볼거야. 기운내.

● **I heard he has an interview this morning.** 그 친구 오늘 아침에 면접이 있다고 들었어.

● You'll kill your job interview! **Don't worry**. 넌 면접 죽여주게 잘 할거야! 걱정마.

A: I'm really stressed out about this job interview.
이 면접 때문에 스트레스를 엄청 받아.

B: Don't worry. You'll kill it. 걱정마. 넌 잘할거야.

02 I've got a job interview next Monday
난 담주 월요일에 면접이 잡혀 있어

● I've several job interviews **next week**. 난 담주에 면접이 여러 개 잡혀 있어.

● I have two job interviews **today: one in the morning and one in the afternoon.** 난 오늘 면접이 2개 있어. 하나는 오전에 다른 하나는 오후에.

● My job interview **went very well**. 내 면접은 잘됐어.

A: What are your plans for this week? 이번주에 무슨 계획있어?
B: I have a few job interviews lined up. 면접이 몇개 잡혀 있어.

03 I'll set up the interview times for next week
담주로 면접시간을 잡을거야

- I'll arrange the job interviews **for next month.** 난 담달로 면접일정을 잡을거야.
- I've organized the job interviews **for tomorrow.** 난 면접들을 내일로 잡아놨어.
- Are **you** setting up the job interviews? 면접일정을 잡을건가요?

A: Can you arrange the job interviews for tomorrow? 면접을 내일로 잡을까요?
B: Yes sir, I'll do that right away. 네, 그렇게 하겠습니다.

04 When are we going to schedule the interviews?
언제로 면접일정을 잡을까요?

- What time are the interviews **at?** 면접시간이 언제야?
- When did you **arrange** to hold the interviews? 면접일정을 언제로 잡았어?
- What dates are **we** scheduling the interviews? 면접일자는 어느 날로 잡을거야?

A: What time are the interviews? 면접은 몇시예요?
B: From 1 to 5pm. 오후 1시부터 5시까지요.

05 Make sure that all of the applicants are qualified for the job
모든 구직자는 일자리에 필요한 자격을 갖추고 있어야 합니다

- Are **the applicants** fully qualified? 지원자들이 완벽하게 자격을 갖추고 있나요?
- Does **he** have the right qualifications? 그는 적합한 자격요건들을 갖추고 있어요?
- What qualifications **does she have?** 그녀는 무슨 자격요건을 갖고 있나요?

A: My classmate is going to apply for the job. 반친구가 그 일자리에 지원할거야.
B: What qualifications does she have? 걔는 무슨 자격요건을 갖고 있는데?

004

He wants to get a job with a big company

걘 대기업에 취직하려고

취업하려면 먼저 공부를 해야 한다. 공무원시험은 a government employee exam, 대기업에 입사를 원하면 want to get a job with a big company라 한다. 특이한 것은 land a job with~ 하면 …에 직장을 구하다라는 뜻이 된다는 점이다.

01 I am preparing for a government employee exam
난 공무원 시험을 준비하고 있어

- **He is going to** study for the government exams. 걘 공무원시험을 준비할거야.
- **She is studying for** the Civil Service exams. 걘 공무원 시험을 준비하고 있어.
- I am studying to work for the federal government.
  난 연방정부 공무원되려고 공부하고 있어.

> A: What is she studying for these days? 걘 요즘 무슨 공부를 하고 있어?
> B: For the Civil Service exam. 공무원 시험보려고.

02 She is studying to get into law school
걘 로스쿨에 들어가려고 공부하고 있어

- **He is making preparations for** medical college. 걘 의사시험을 준비하고 있어.
- **She is going to write her LSATS and try to become a lawyer.**
  걘 앞으로 미국변호사 시험을 치르고 변호사가 되려고 해.
- He is studying to **get into a PhD program.**
  걘 박사학위프로그램에 들어가려고 공부하고 있어.

> A: What is she doing these days? 걘 요즘 뭐해?
> B: She is studying to get into law school. 로스쿨에 들어가려고 공부하고 있어.

03 He wants to get a job with a big company

걘 대기업에 취직하려고 해

- She is hoping to land a job with Google or Facebook.
  걘 구글이나 페이스북에 일자리를 얻기를 희망해.
- He hopes to find work at a big law firm. 걘 대형로펌에 일자리를 찾기를 바래.
- Do you want to get a job at a big company? 대기업에 취직하고 싶어?

A: What are your plans after you graduate? 졸업후에 계획이 뭐야?
B: I hope to land a job at Google or Facebook. 구글이나 페이스북에 취직하기를 바래.

04 I've been sitting all day in a study café

난 하루종일 스터디카페에서 공부했어

- I am spending the day at the library. 난 종일 도서관에서 시간을 보냈어.
- I am cramming for a test this afternoon at a coffee shop.
  난 오늘 오후 커피숍에서 벼락치기 시험공부를 할거야.
- I pulled an all-nighter at my friend's home studying for the test. 난 시험공부를
  하느라 친구집에서 밤을 샜어.

A: Where are you going to study for the exam? 시험공부 어디서 할거야?
B: I'm cramming all day at the library. 난 종일 도서관에서 벼락치기 할거야.

005

I landed a new job with Samsung

난 삼성에 일자리를 구했어

일자리를 구해서(get a job) 새로운 일을 시작한다(start a new job)고 한다. 정규직일 경우에는 a full-time worker, 시간제 일일 때는 work part-time, a temp worker이라고 한다.

01 I got a (new) job
나 취직했어

- **I got a new job at Apple.** 난 애플에 취직했어.

- **I landed a new job with Samsung.** 난 삼성에 일자리를 구했어.

- **She is starting a new job this week.** 걘 이번주에 새로운 일자리를 시작할거야.

A: She looks happy. 걘 즐거워보여.
B: She is. She landed a job at LG. 맞아. 걘 LG에 일자리를 구했어.

02 I'm very excited for John to start his new job
존이 새로 직장을 갖게 되어 정말 기뻐

- **I'm so happy that she** got a new job. 걔가 새로운 일자리를 갖게 되어 정말 기뻐.

- **It's really wonderful that he** landed that job. 걔가 그 일자리를 갖게 된 것은 정말 멋져.

- **It's amazing to hear you** got that job you wanted.
네가 원했던 그 일자리에 취직되었다는 소식을 듣고 정말 놀라웠어.

A: Did you hear the news about John? 존에 관한 소식 들었어?
B: Yes, I'm so happy he got that job. 어, 걔가 그 일자리에 취직되어서 정말 기뻐.

03 You're hired
귀하는 입사되셨습니다

- **We have a position** for you at our company. 우리 회사에 당신을 위한 일자리가 있습니다.

- **Apple** is hiring 100 new workers. 애플은 100명의 신입직원을 채용하고 있어.

- **Three positions have opened up** at our business.
  우리 회사에서 3개의 일자리가 났습니다.

A: What's the good news? 좋은 소식이 뭔가요?

B: A position just opened up at our company so we're going to hire
   you. 우리 회사에 일자리가 나서 당신을 고용할 예정입니다.

04 He is a full-time worker
걘 정규직이야

- **He is a regular worker** at our company. 그는 우리 회사에서 정규직으로 일하고 있어.

- **I am looking for** a full-time job. 난 정규직을 구하고 있어요.

- **She wants to** work full-time. 걘 정규직으로 일하고 싶어해.

A: I'm sorry but I'm looking for full-time work.
   죄송하지만 난 정규직을 구하고 있어요.

B: That's too bad. We only need part-time workers.
   안됐네요. 우리는 시간제 직원만 필요해서요.

05 She only wants to work part-time because she is a
student 걘 학생이어서 시간제 일자리만 원해요

- **I only work part-time** during the semester. 난 학기중에는 시간제로만 일하고 있어.

- **She is working part-time** while she goes to school. 걘 학교다닐 동안 시간제로 일하고 있어.

- **She worked** as a temp. 걘 임시직으로 일했어.

- **I am looking for** temp work. 난 임시직 일을 구하고 있어.

A: Are you looking for full-time work? 정규직 일을 구하고 계신가요?

B: No, just temp work. 아뇨, 임시직이요.

006 I work for a trading company

난 무역회사에 다녀

취직해서 다니는 직장을 언급하는 경우들. 공무원이면 a government worker, 무역회사에 다니면 work for a trading company, 건설업이면 work in construction이라고 하면 된다.

01 I'm an office worker

난 회사원이야

- I'm a government worker. 난 공무원이야.

- What kind of work do you do? 무슨 직업의 일을 하고 있어요?

- I work in finances. 재무 쪽 일을 하고 있어.

A: I'm a government worker. 난 공무원이야.
B: Really? Which department? 정말? 어느 분야야?

02 What do you do (for a living)?

직업이 뭔가요?

- What's your job? 직업이 뭐예요?

- What is your occupation? 직업이 뭔가요?

- How do you make a living? 직업이 뭔가요?

A: What's your job? 직업이 뭐예요?
B: I am a lab worker. 연구원이예요.

03 I work for a trading company
난 무역회사에 다녀

- Which company do you work for? 어느 회사에 다녀요?
- The company I work for is a travel agency 내가 다니는 회사는 여행사야.
- What's the name of your company? 다니는 회사 이름이 어떻게 돼요?

A: I'm an engineer. 난 엔지니어예요.
B: Which company do you work for? 어느 회사에 다녀요?

04 I'm working in construction
난 건설업계에서 일해요

- I work in the transportation business. 난 운송업계에서 일해요.
- She works in the biochemistry industry. 걘 생화학업계에서 일해요.
- He works in agriculture. 걘 농업에 종사하고 있어.

A: May I ask you what you do? 뭐하시는지 여쭤봐도 될까요?
B: I work in the agricultural industry. 농업에 종사하고 있어요.

05 She is a sales-clerk in a gift shop
걘 기념품점의 직원이야

- He works for a foreign-owned company. 걘 외국계 회사에서 일하고 있어.
- She works at an advertising company. 걘 광고회사에서 일해.
- They work at a general hospital. 개네들은 종합병원에서 일해.

A: What does she do? 걔 직업이 뭐야?
B: She is a bank clerk at Woori Bank. 걘 우리은행 직원이야.

007 직책

I'm in charge of the Marketing Section

난 마케팅부서 책임자입니다

···직장에서 ···직책으로 일한다고 할 때는 "work for+회사+as a+직책"으로 표현한다. 책임자라고 할 때는 전형적으로 be in charge of〜를 반드시 쓴다.

01 I'm Chris of the Export Section
수출부의 크리스입니다

- I'm Tony, the import manager. 난 토니입니다. 수입매니저입니다.
- My name is Sally Kim from **the Sales Department**. 나는 영업부의 샐리 킴입니다.
- I am John, assistant manager in **the Personnel Department**.
  난 인사부의 차장인 존이라고 합니다.

> A: I'm Tony, the import manager. 수입매니저인 토니입니다.
> B: Nice to meet you, Tony. 토니씨 만나서 반갑습니다.

02 I work in the sales department of LG
난 LG의 영업부에서 일해

- I'm working for **Hyundai** as a **planning manager**.
  난 현대에서 기획부장으로 일하고 있어.
- What department **are you in**? 어느 부서에서 일하고 있어요?
- I'm the logistics manager. 난 물류부장입니다.

> A: Which department do you work in? 어느 부서에서 일하십니까?
> B: The PR department. 홍보부서요.

03 I'm in charge of the Marketing Section
난 마케팅부서 책임자입니다

- I'm responsible for the marketing department. 난 마케팅부서를 책임지고 있습니다.
- I work under Mr. Suh, president of Mentors. 난 멘토스 서사장 밑에서 일하고 있어요.
- Who's the person in charge of this matter? 이 문제의 책임자가 누구입니까?

A: Who is in charge of sales? 영업은 누가 책임지고 있나요?
B: Mr. Johnson is. 존슨 씨요.

04 I've been in my present position for three years
난 3년간 현재 자리에서 일하고 있습니다

- I've been working for a trading company in Seoul for two years.
  난 2년간 서울의 무역회사에서 일하고 있어요.
- Please tell me what your position is. 직위가 무엇인지 말해줄래요.
- How long have you been in the marketing department?
  마케팅 부서에서는 몇 년간 일했나요?

A: Please tell me what your position is. 직책이 무엇인지 말해줄래요.
B: I'm the food services manager. 난 음식서비스 매니저입니다.

05 I've been assigned as an office manager of the company
난 회사의 실장으로 배정되었어요

- He is our executive vice president. 그는 우리회사 부사장이야.
- Our vice president just resigned. 우리 부서장이 방금 사직했어.
- He is the assistant manager of our accounting department.
  그는 우리 회계부서의 차장이야.

A: Who is the manager of the marketing department?
마케팅부서의 부장이 누구인가요?
B: I'm not sure. I'll ask. 잘모르겠는데요. 물어볼게요.

008

We mainly deal in Italian shoes

우리는 주로 이태리 구두를 취급합니다

다니는 회사의 업무 등을 소개할 때 사용하는 표현이다. 수입회사는 We import and sell+품목이라고 하면 되고 주로 …을 취급하고 있다고 하려면 We mainly deal in~이라고 쓴다. 또한 do business with는 …와 거래하다라는 뜻이다.

01 The company I work for is a trading company
내가 다니는 회사는 무역회사야

- **We make home appliances.** 우리는 가전제품을 제조해.
- **We produce computer parts.** 우리는 컴퓨터 부품을 생산합니다.
- **We manufacture office supplies.** 우리는 사무용품을 만듭니다.

A: What kind of products does your company make?
너희 회사는 무슨 종류의 제품을 만들어?

B: We make home appliances. 우리는 가전제품을 만들어.

02 We import and sell antique furniture
우리는 고가구를 수입해서 판매해

- **We import and sell cosmetics for women.** 우리는 여성용 화장품을 수입하여 판매합니다.
- **We are a small-sized importer of personal computers.**
우리는 개인용 컴퓨터를 수입하는 소기업입니다.
- **To which countries do you export?** 어느 나라에 수출을 합니까?

A: What does your company do? 너희 회사는 뭘 하는거야?
B: We import and sell cosmetics for women. 여성용 화장품을 수입해서 판매해.

03 We mainly deal in Italian shoes
우리는 주로 이태리 구두를 취급합니다

- Our company deals with importing and selling leather products.
  우리 회사는 가죽제품을 수입하여 판매합니다.

- We lease copy machines and so on. 우리는 복사기 등등을 임대합니다.

- We handle all automobile imports from Europe.
  우리는 유럽으로부터 모든 자동차수입을 취급합니다.

A: What kind of company do you work at? 너희 회사가 하는 일은 뭐야?
B: We deal with importing and selling leather products.
우리는 가죽제품을 수입하여 판매하고 있어.

04 We have about 50 people
우리는 약 50명의 종업원이 있어

- There are about 10 employees. 근로자가 약 10명이 있어.

- How many employees do you have in your company?
  너희 회사에 근로자는 몇이야?

- We employ over 1000 workers. 우리는 1000명 이상의 근로자를 고용하고 있어.

A: How many workers are at your company? 너희 회사 근로자는 몇 명이야?
B: We employ over 500 workers. 500명 이상의 근로자를 고용하고 있어.

05 We're doing business with about 30 companies
우리는 약 30개 넘는 회사와 거래를 하고 있어

- We have 10 branches in Japan. 우리는 일본에 10개의 지점이 있어.

- Our company was founded in 1990. 우리 회사는 1990년에 창립되었어.

- Our headquarters is located in Seoul. 우리 회사 본사는 서울에 위치해 있어.

A: How many branches do you have? 너희 회사 지점이 몇 개나 돼?
B: We have over 50 branches in 5 countries. 우린 5개국에 50개 넘는 지점을 갖고 있어.

It takes 20 minutes on foot from Pangyo Station
판교역에서 걸어서 20분 걸려

회사가 어디에 있는 지 말할 때는 ~ be located in~ be in~ near~ 등을 쓰고, 몇 층에 있다고 할 때는 be on the fifth floor of the~라는 패턴을 사용한다.

01 Our office is located in Pangyo
우리 회사는 판교에 위치해 있어

- It takes 20 minutes on foot from Pangyo Station. 판교역에서 걸어서 20분 걸려.

- Where's your office? 사무실이 어디에 있어?

- Our office is in Gangnam near Samsung subway station.
  우리 사무실은 강남에 있는데 삼성역 근처에 있어.

A: Where is your office? 사무실이 어디야?
B: It's in Yeouido next to the 63 Building. 여의도 63빌딩 옆에 있어.

02 My office is on the fifth floor of the Alphadom city
우리 사무실은 알파돔시티 5층에 있어

- Our office is a six-story gray building. 우리 사무실은 6층짜리 회색 건물이야.

- Our headquarters are a 30 story building in Gangnam.
  우리 회사 본사는 강남에 30층짜리 건물이야.

- The factory complex is in the countryside near Suwon.
  공장단지는 수원근처의 시골지역에 있어.

A: How big is your office building? 너희 사무실 빌딩 크기는 어때?
B: It's a six story building. 6층짜리 건물이야.

03 Do you see Burger King? Our office is just behind it 버거킹 보이지? 사무실은 바로 그 뒤에 있어

- Our office is just around the corner from the post office.
  우리 사무실은 우체국을 지나 바로 코너에 있어.

- The company is just down the road from Seoul Station.
  회사는 서울역을 지나 도로변에 있어.

- We are located right next to the Hana bank. 우리 회사는 하나은행 바로 옆에 있어.

A: I came out of the subway exit #4. Where is the office?
4번출구로 나왔는데, 사무실이 어디야?

B: It's right next to the post office. 우체국 바로 옆이야.

04 You can park in front of our office
사무실 앞에 주차할 수 있어

- There's a parking garage in the basement of the building.
  건물지하에 주차장이 있어.

- There's a parking lot on the first floor of the building. 건물 1층에 주차장이 있어.

- I'll come by car. Where can I park? 차로 왔는데 어디에 주차할 수 있어?

A: Can I park at your building? 너희 빌딩에 주차할 수 있어?
B: Yes, there is parking in the basement. 어. 지하에 주차장이 있어.

05 The Marketing Section is Room 7 on the sixth floor
마케팅 부서는 6층 7번 방에 있어

- On which floor is the Export section? 수출부는 몇 층에 있어?

- The sales department is on the ground floor. 영업부는 1층에 있어.

- You can find the accounting department on the 3rd and 4th floors.
  회계부서는 3층과 4층에 있어.

A: The marketing department is on the 7th floor? 마케팅 부서는 7층에 있나요?
B: No, it's on the 10th. 아뇨. 10층에 있습니다.

Unit 04

010 I drive to work

난 차로 출근해

출근중일 때는 be on one's way to work. 차로 출근은 drive to work. 출퇴근 시간이 왕복 2시간 걸린다고 할 때는 I have a 2 hour commute both ways라고 하면 된다.

01 I'm on my way to work
난 출근중이야

● I'm going to work **right now.** 난 지금 바로 출근할거야.

● I have to go to the office **today.** 난 오늘 사무실에 출근해야 돼.

● I usually arrive at work **before 9 am.** 난 보통 오전 9시 전에 사무실에 도착해.

A: Can you do the dishes? 설거지 할 수 있어?
B: Sorry, I'm late and I have to go to work. 미안. 나 늦었어. 출근해야 돼.

02 I use a car to commute to my job
난 차로 출퇴근해

● I drive to work. 난 차로 출근해.

● **How long is** your commute? 출퇴근 시간이 얼마나 돼?

● I have a 2 hour commute **both ways.** 난 출퇴근하는데 2시간이 걸려.

A: How long is it for you to drive to work? 너 차로 출근하는데 얼마나 걸려?
B: I have a 2 hour commute both ways. 출퇴근하는데 2시간 걸려.

03 I like to take the subway
난 지하철타는 것을 좋아해

- I don't often use the subway. 난 종종 지하철을 이용하지 않아.
- I usually take the bus to go to work. 난 보통 버스를 타고 출근해.
- I live close to my office so I can walk to work.
  난 사무실 근처에 살아서 걸어서 출근할 수 있어.

A: You walk to work? 너 걸어서 출근하니?
B: Yes, luckily I live close. 어, 운좋게도 근처에 살아.

02 I usually check my cell phone on the subway
난 보통 지하철에서 핸폰을 확인해

- What do you usually do on the train? 지하철에서는 주로 뭐를 해?
- I change trains to the Bundang line at Gangnam station.
  난 강남역에서 신분당선으로 열차를 갈아타.
- Every train is overcrowded during the rush hour.
  모든 지하철은 러시아워에 사람들이 넘쳐나.

A: I hate taking the subway during rush hour. 난 러시아워에 지하철타는 것을 싫어해.
B: Me too. The trains are always overcrowded.
   나도 그래. 지하철은 언제나 사람들로 바글바글해.

03 I'm always kept standing on the train
난 지하철에서 항상 계속 서있어

- I have to stand all the way on the train. 지하철타는 동안 계속 서있어야 해.
- I'm exhausted when I reach the office. 사무실에 도착하면 기진맥진하지.
- I often see young people crossing their legs.
  가끔 젊은이들이 다리를 꼬고 앉아 있는 것이 보여.

A: Why do you hate taking the subway? 왜 지하철 타는 것을 싫어하는거야?
B: I can never get a seat so I have to stand the entire ride.
   자리에 앉을 수가 없어서 지하철타는 동안 내내 서있어야 해서.

011

I use a scooter to get to work
난 스쿠터를 타고 출근해

출퇴근하면 교통혼잡. get caught in a bad traffic, heavy traffic 등으로 표현하고 자전거로 출근하려면 ride to work on a bicycle, 그리고 퀵보드를 타고 출근한다고 하려면 use a scooter to get to work라 하면 된다.

01 I was stuck in a traffic jam
차가 막혀서 꼼짝달싹 못했어

- I got caught in a bad traffic jam today. 오늘 차가 너무 많아서 꼼짝달싹 못했어.
- They were trapped in rush hour traffic.
  걔네들은 러시아워 체증으로 꼼짝못하고 갇혀 있었어.
- She was late because of the heavy traffic. 차가 무지 막혀서 걔는 지각을 했어.

A: Why are you so late? 왜 이렇게 늦은거야?
B: I got caught in bad traffic. 차가 너무 많아 꼼짝달싹 못했어.

02 The traffic is bumper to bumper
차가 무지 막혀

- The traffic is moving slowly. 차량들이 서서히 움직인다.
- The traffic is really crawling today. 오늘은 차량들이 정말 엉금엉금 기어가고 있어.
- In Seoul the traffic is really bad. 서울의 교통은 정말이지 안좋아.

A: I hate living in Seoul. 난 서울에 사는게 정말 싫어.
B: Because the traffic is so bad, right? 교통이 너무 안좋기 때문이지, 그지?

03 I started to ride to work on a bicycle
난 자전거로 출근하기 시작했어

- I sold my car and am using public transportation to commute to work.
  난 차를 팔고 대중교통을 이용해서 출퇴근하고 있어.

- I use the electric kickboards to get to school now.
  난 이제 전동킥보드를 이용해 학교에 가고 있어.

- I am walking to work unless it is raining. 비가 오지 않을 때면 걸어서 출근해.

A: You look like you lost weight! 너 살이 빠진 것처럼 보여!
B: Yes, I have been riding a bicycle to work. 어. 나 자전거를 타고 출근해.

04 I use a scooter to get to work
난 스쿠터를 타고 출근해

- Three of my co-workers and I carpool to get to work. 3명의 동료와 난 카풀로 출근해.

- I take the express bus to get to work. 난 직행버스를 타고 출근해.

- I use the bus and subway to commute to work. 난 버스와 지하철을 이용해 출퇴근해.

A: Do you use public transportation? 대중교통을 넌 이용하니?
B: Yes, I use the express bus to get to work. 어. 난 직행버스를 타고 출근해.

05 I am going to be late for work
난 회사에 지각하게 될거야

- I woke up early to try and beat the traffic. 교통막히는 것을 피하려고 난 일찍 일어났어.

- I found a shortcut to get to work 15 minutes earlier than normal.
  난 보통 때보다 15분 빨리 출근할 수 있는 지름길을 발견했어.

- Do you know a faster way to get to work? 출근하는데 빨리 갈 수 있는 길을 알고 있어?

A: Why are you waking up so early today? 넌 왜 오늘 일찍 일어난거야?
B: I want to try and beat the traffic this morning.
난 오늘 아침에는 차가 막히는 것을 피하고 싶어서.

012

We're on a five-day (work) week

우리는 주 5일제야

주 5일제는 be on a five-day week, 유연근무는 have flexible working hours라 한다. 교대제 근무를 말하려면 do shift work라고 하면 된다. 토요일마다 쉰다고 할 때는 We are off on Saturdays라 한다.

01 We're on a five-day (work) week
우리는 주 5일제야

- **Our company** is on a five-day week. 우리 회사는 주 5일제를 하고 있어.
- **Our company** has flexible working hours. 우리 회사는 근무시간이 유연해.
- **We have to** do shift work **at my office.** 우리는 사무실에서 교대제 근무를 해야 돼.

A: Do you have to do shift work? 넌 교대제 근무를 해야 돼?
B: Yes, this week I am working the night shift. 어, 이번주에는 밤근무야.

02 Our working hours are from nine to six
근무시간은 9시에서 6시까지야

- **What are your** working hours? 너 근무시간은 어떻게 돼?
- **I can't make personal phone calls** during business hours.
  난 근무시간 중에 개인전화를 할 수가 없어.
- **We work 8 hours a day** with a 1 hour lunch break.
  우리는 하루 8시간 근무를 하고 점심시간은 한 시간이야.

A: What are your hours like? 너희 근무시간은 어때?
B: I work from 9 to 6 with a one hour lunch break.
   9-6시간 일을 하고 점심시간은 한 시간이야.

03 I work about seven hours a day
난 하루에 약 7시간 일을 해

- I work about 30 hours **a month**. 난 한 달에 약 30시간 일을 해.
- My part-time hours **are about 10 a week**. 나의 시간제 근무시간은 일주일에 한 10시간이야.
- **She** has a 40 hour workweek. 걔의 주당 근무시간은 40시간이야.

A: How many hours do you work a week? 넌 일주일에 몇시간을 일해?
B: About 40. 약 40시간.

04 We are off on Saturdays
우리는 토요일마다 근무를 하지 않아

- I am off work **at 6pm**. 난 오후 6시에 퇴근해.
- **She's** on duty right now **so she can't talk**. 걘 지금 근무중이라 대화할 수 없어요.
- Are you off on Saturdays? 토요일은 쉬니?

A: Are you off on Saturdays? 너 토요일 쉬니?
B: Yes I am. 어 그래.

05 I'm on call today
난 오늘 대기야

- I **may** get called into work **today**. 난 오늘 일하러 오라는 전화가 올지 몰라.
- I'm off-duty but on call. 비번이지만 대기중이야.
- I'm sorry but I can't. I'm on call **all weekend**. 미안하지만 안돼. 주말내내 비상대기야.

A: Let's go to Busan this weekend. 이번주말에 부산에 가자.
B: I'm sorry but I can't. I'm on call all weekend.
미안하지만 안돼. 주말내내 비상대기야.

013

What shift are you on?
넌 무슨 근무조야?

사무실이나 회사가 시작한다고 할 때는 open이나 start를 이용해 표현하면 되고, 앞
서 나온 시프트 근무를 말할 때는 work the night[day] shift라고 말하면 된다.

01

I work by the hour
난 시간제로 근무하고 있어

- **What time does** your office open? 네 사무실은 몇 시에 열어?
- **What time do** you start work? 몇 시에 근무가 시작돼?
- **What time is your company** open for business? 네 회사는 몇 시에 영업을 시작해?

A: What time does the bank open for business? 은행은 몇 시에 영업을 시작해?
B: It opens for business at 9am but the workers arrive at 8am.
오전 9시에 영업시작이지만 근무자들은 8시까지 도착해.

02

I work the night shift a few times a month
난 한달에 몇 번 밤근무를 해

- I work the day shift for 4 days then the night shift for 4 days.
난 4일간 낮근무를 하고 4일간 밤근무를 해.
- **We rotate the shifts** every 2 weeks. 우리는 2주마다 교대제 근무를 돌아가면서 해.
- I enjoy the night shift **because it isn't as busy.** 난 바뻐 돌아가지 않아서 밤근무가 좋아.

A: Are you working the night shift next week? 넌 담주에 밤근무니?
B: No, I have the day shift for one more week. 아니, 일주일 더 낮근무야.

What shift are you on?
년 무슨 근무조야?

- I would rather work the day shift **than** the night shift.
나라면 밤근무보다는 낮근무를 하겠어.

- I prefer a 9 to 5 job **to** shift work. 난 교대제 근무보다 9-5 근무를 더 좋아해.

- **He always** works the night shift. 걘 항상 밤근무를 해.

A: What shift are you on this week? 이번 주에는 무슨 근무조야?
B: The evening shift. 저녁조.

I'm sure I will get a job with a high salary
난 고임금의 일자리에 취직될거라 확신해

- How is the salary **at your company?** 네 회사의 급여는 어때?

- The salary **is pretty good.** 급여는 꽤 괜찮아.

- She makes very good money **at her job.** 걘 자기 직장에서 꽤 많은 돈을 벌고 있어.

A: How is the salary? 급여는 어때?
B: The money at this company is very good. 이 회사의 급여는 매우 좋아.

014

I work overtime almost every day

난 거의 매일 야근해

야근하다의 전형적인 표현은 work overtime 혹은 work late이고 한 시간 추가근무를 한다고 말할 때는 work one hour extra hour이라고 말한다. 초과근무수당을 받는다는 get overtime pay라 하면 된다.

01 I don't want to work overtime every day

난 매일 야근하고 싶지 않아

- **Do you often** work overtime? 자주 야근하니?
- I work overtime **almost every day.** 난 거의 매일 야근해.
- **I usually** have 5 to 10 hours of overtime **every month.**
  난 보통 매달 5–10시간 야근을 해.

  A: Are you working overtime tonight? 너 오늘밤 야근하니?
  B: No, I did last night though. 아니. 그래도 어제는 야근했어.

02 I work one extra hour every day

난 매일 한 시간 추가근무를 해

- I **rarely** work overtime. 난 거의 야근을 하지 않아.
- **This company doesn't** pay overtime. 이 회사는 야근수당을 지급하지 않아.
- The overtime rates **are very good here.** 여기는 초과근무수당이 매우 좋아.

  A: Do you like working overtime? 넌 야근하는 것을 좋아해?
  B: Yes, the overtime rates here are very good. 어. 여기는 초과근무수당이 매우 좋아.

03 I have to work late today
난 오늘 야근해야 돼

- We are always being asked to work late. 회사는 늘상 우리에게 야근을 시켜.
- The manager needs us to stay a bit longer today.
  부장은 우리가 오늘 좀 더 연장근무를 해야 된대.
- We are going to work late tonight. 우리는 오늘밤 야근을 할거야.

A: Sorry honey, I have to work late tonight. 자기야, 미안해, 오늘밤 야근해야 돼.
B: Not again! 또야!

04 They get overtime pay if they work past 6pm
6시 지나서 근무를 하면 초과근무수당을 받아

- Fifteen extra minutes doesn't qualify as overtime pay.
  15분 초과근무했다고 초과근무수당이 나가지 않아.
- How much do you get for overtime? 초과근무로 얼마나 받아?
- I got a lot of overtime last month. 난 지난달에 초과근무수당을 많이 받았어.

A: Your paycheck is bigger than usual. 당신 급여가 보통때보다 많아.
B: Yes, I got a lot of overtime last month. 어, 지난달에 초과근무수당을 많이 받았어.

05 She requested to work overtime
걔는 초과근무 요청을 했어

- The workers are only allowed to work 10 hours overtime per week max.
  근로자는 주당 최대 10시간의 야근을 하는게 가능해.
- Can I put in a request to get more overtime? 더 많은 야근을 하도록 신청할 수 있을까요?
- We aren't allowed to work overtime here. 우리는 여기서 야근을 못하도록 되어 있어.

A: Can I put in a request to work some overtime? 좀 야근신청을 할 수 있을까요?
B: Sorry but we aren't allowed to work overtime here.
   미안하지만, 우리 회사는 야근을 못하도록 되어 있어요.

015 급여

My salary is about 5,000,000 won a month after taxes

내 급여는 세후 월 약 5백만원 정도야

시간제 급여는 be paid on an hourly basis. 시급까지 말하려면 get+돈 +an[per] hour라고 한다. 월급은 salary로 연봉은 be paid+돈+a year 혹은 My annual salary is~ 라고 하면 된다.

01 I get 9,600 won an hour
난 시급으로 9,600을 받아

- **I'm paid on an hourly basis.** 난 시급으로 지급받아.
- **How much do you get an hour?** 시간당 수당이 얼마나 돼?
- **What's your hourly salary?** 너 시급이 얼마야?

A: What's your hourly salary? 너 시급이 얼마야?
B: 12,500 won per hour. 시간당 12,500원이야.

02 My salary is about 5,000,000 won a month after taxes
내 급여는 세후 월 약 5백만원 정도야

- **I'm paid about 50 million won a year before taxes.** 난 세전 연봉이 약 5천만원 돼.
- **My annual salary is just under 100,000,000 won after taxes.**
  내 연봉은 세후 1억이 조금 안돼.
- **How much is your monthly salary?** 너 월급은 얼마나 돼?

A: She gets paid 3 million won per month. 걔는 월 3백만원을 받아.
B: That's not too bad. 나쁘지 않네.

03 I get paid extra for more than a half hour overtime
30분이상 야근 시에 야근수당을 받아

- We receive bonuses in June and December. 6월과 12월에 보너스를 받아.

- We get time and a half for working holidays. 휴무일에는 1.5배의 지급을 받아.

- Our annual bonus is paid at Christmas. 우리 연간보너스는 성탄절에 지급돼.

A: Why do you look so happy? 왜 그렇게 즐거운 표정이야?

B: I got my Christmas bonus today. 오늘 성탄절 보너스를 받았거든.

04 I can take 30 days off with pay a year
난 일년에 30일의 유급휴가를 쓸 수 있어

- I get 2 weeks paid vacation. 난 2주 유급휴가를 쓸 수 있어.

- We get 5 days of sick leave per year. 우리는 연간 5일 병가를 쓸 수 있어.

- Women get 1 month for maternity leave. 여성은 한 달간의 출산휴가를 쓸 수 있어.

A: I'm going to use 1 week of my paid vacation in August.
난 8월에 유급휴가 1주일을 쓸거야.

B: Nice. I'm going to use 2 weeks in July. 좋으네. 난 7월에 2주를 쓸건데.

05 We all had to take a pay cut this year because of the recession
올해는 경기침체로 임금삭감을 모두 감내해야 했어

- We usually get a 5% pay raise every year. 우리는 매년 5% 임금인상을 받아.

- Our salary went up again this year. 우리 급여는 올해도 다시 올라갔어.

- We all got a pay raise because the company did so well last year.
작년 회사실적이 아주 좋아서 우리는 모두 임금인상을 받았어.

A: Did you hear the good news? 좋은 소식을 들었다며?

B: About our pay raise? Yes. 우리 임금인상에 대해서? 어.

016

I have to call in sick today

오늘 아파 결근한다고 전화해야 되겠어

몸이 아파서 학교나 회사에 출근하지 못하겠다고 전화하는 것을 call in sick란 한다. 잠깐 쉬는 것은 take a (short) break, 그리고 휴가중이라고 할 때는 be on leave 라는 표현을 즐겨 쓴다.

01 I have to call in sick today
오늘 아파 결근한다고 전화해야 되겠어

- **I had to use a sick day last week.** 난 지난주에 병가를 하루 써야 했었어.

- **I am going to call in sick today.** 오늘 병가를 전화로 낼거야.

- **I need to use a sick day.** 난 병가를 써야 돼.

A: I have a horrible cold so I'm going to use one of my sick days.
감기가 심해서 병가를 하루 써야 되겠어.

B: That is a good idea. 좋은 생각이야.

02 How about a short break?
잠깐 쉬는게 어때?

- **Why don't you take a break?** 잠시 쉬는게 어때?

- **Let's take a break.** 우리 잠시 쉬자.

- **It's time for a break.** 쉬어야 할 때야.

A: I'm exhausted. 난 지쳤어.
B: Yes, let's take a break. 그래, 우리 좀 쉬자.

03 She's on leave right now
갠 지금 휴가중이야

- He is on sick leave. 갠 병가를 냈어.

- He is taking a paid vacation. 갠 유급휴가 쓰고 있어.

- He is on paternity leave **for one week**. 갠 일주일간 육아휴가를 쓰고 있어.

A: Where has Joe been? 조는 어디 있었어?
B: He had a heart attack so he's on sick leave.
갠 심장마비가 와서 병가를 쓰고 있는중야.

04 We're going to take off shortly after lunch
우리는 점심 후에 잠깐 쉴거야

- I'm off tomorrow. **It's a national holiday.** 난 내일 휴무야. 국경일이야.

- He is off sick **today**. 갠 오늘 병가를 냈어.

- She took 5 days off. 갠 5일간의 휴가를 냈어.

A: Why are you taking a week off? 넌 왜 일주일 휴가를 낸거야?
B: My mother is sick and I need to take care of her.
어머니가 아프셔서 돌봐드려야 하거든.

05 I need to skip work this morning to drop my kids off at school
애들 학교에 데려다주느라 오늘 아침 근무를 빠져야 돼

- You're skipping work **for the third time this month?** 넌 이번 달 세번째 결근이지?

- You're missing work **but you aren't sick?** 출근도 하지 않았는데 아프지도 않단말야?

- Why are you skipping out on work? 넌 왜 일을 빼먹는거야?

A: I need to skip work this morning. 난 오늘 아침 근무를 빠져야 돼.
B: Don't let the manager find out. 부장이 모르도록 해.

Unit 04

017 Do you work inside or outside?

내근직이야 아니면 외근직이야?

사무실에서 주로 일할 때는 work at one's desk, deskwork 혹은 work inside 라고 한다. 반대로 외근직은 work outside로 표현하면 된다.

01 I almost always work at my desk
난 거의 사무실에서 일해

- I don't like doing deskwork. 난 사무직으로 일하는게 싫어.

- I don't mind deskwork. 난 사무직도 괜찮아.

- I hate being stuck at my desk. 난 책상 앞에 처박혀 있는게 싫어.

A: I want to change jobs. I hate being stuck at my desk all day.
직장을 바꾸고 싶어. 종일 책상 앞에 처박혀 있는게 싫어.

B: I hate deskwork too. 나도 사무직일이 싫어.

02 I always work outside the office
난 사무실 밖에서 항상 일해

- Do you work inside or outside? 내근직이야 아니면 외근직이야?

- My work takes me out of the office often. 일 때문에 가끔 사무실 밖으로 나가야 돼.

- My job requires a lot of travel. 내 일 때문에 많이 돌아다녀야 돼.

A: You are on the road a lot. 넌 외근을 많이 하더라.

B: Yes, my job requires me to travel. 맞아, 일 때문에 출장을 가야 돼.

03 When I'm busy, I stay up all night working
바쁠 때면 밤새고 일을 해

- We're busy in the evenings. 우리는 저녁마다 바빠.

- I had to work late. 난 야근을 해야 됐어.

- I pulled an all-nighter to finish the project. 난 그 프로젝트를 끝내기 위해 밤을 샜어.

A: Why do you look so tired? 너 왜 그렇게 피곤해 보여?
B: I had to work late the past three nights. 지난 3일밤 야근을 해야 됐어.

04 I work even on a holiday
난 휴일에도 일을 해

Unit 04

- I had to postpone my holiday this year because of work.
  난 금년도에 일 때문에 휴가를 연기해야 했어.

- I was unable to take a vacation this year. 난 금년에 휴가를 쓸 수가 없었어.

- My vacation had to be canceled because of work.
  내 휴가가 일 때문에 취소되어야 했어.

A: You don't look too happy. 넌 무척 안좋아 보여.
B: Yes, I had to postpone my vacation because of work.
어, 일 때문에 내 휴가를 연기해야 했어.

05 I share a rental room with my friend
난 친구와 방을 같이 임대하고 있어

- My friend and I share an apartment together. 내 친구와 나는 함께 아파트를 쓰고 있어.

- I'm not married but I have a roommate to help share the costs of my
  apartment. 난 총각이지만 아파트 비용을 줄이기 위해 룸메이트와 함께 쓰고 있어.

- I live with my two university friends. 난 두명의 대학친구와 함께 살고 있어.

A: Do you live alone? 너 혼자 살고 있어?
B: No, I have a roommate. 아니. 룸메이트가 있어.

018

I'm working as a cashier

난 출납원으로 일을 하고 있어

구체적으로 직업을 언급하는 경우. 요즘 인기좋은 배달라이더는 a delivery man. 출납원은 a cashier라고 한다. 또한 뭔가 프리랜서로 일을 할 때는 I work freelance as a~ 라는 표현을 이용해 말하면 된다.

01 I'm a delivery man
난 배달원이야

- **I'm working as a cashier.** 난 출납원으로 일을 하고 있어.

- **She's a receptionist.** 걔는 접수담당자로 일을 해.

- **She works in the healthcare industry as an X-ray technician.**
  걘 의료업계의 엑스레이 기사로 일을 해.

A: What does your wife do? 네 아내 직업은 뭐야?
B: She's a receptionist at the Hilton Hotel. 힐튼 호텔에서 접수담당자야.

02 I'm working in a chain store for women's wear
난 여성의류 체인점에서 일하고 있어

- **I work at a famous coffee shop.** 난 유명한 커피숍에서 일을 해.

- **She has a job at a high end department store.** 걘 명품백화점에서 일을 해.

- **He works for a prestigious car company.** 걘 일류 자동차 회사에서 일을 해.

A: He works for a prestigious car company. 걘 일류 자동차 회사에서 일을 해.
B: Which one? 어느 회사인데?

I'm a freelance photographer
난 프리랜서 사진작가야

- I work freelance as a photographer. 난 사진작가로 프리랜서로 일해.
- I started freelancing two years ago. 난 2년전에 프리랜서를 시작했어.
- I've freelanced for more than five years. 난 5년이상 프리랜서로 일을 했어.
- How long have you freelanced? 얼마동안 프리랜서 일을 한거야?

A: Do you enjoy freelance work? 넌 프리랜서 일을 좋아해?
B: Yes, it gives me very flexible working hours. 어. 일하는 시간이 아주 유연하거든.

I'm in the import business by myself
난 수입업체를 운영해

- I make tables, chairs, and so on from wood. 난 목재로 테이블이나 의자 등등을 만들어.
- I make handmade crafts. 난 수공예품을 만들어.
- I run my own coffee business. 난 커피숍을 운영하고 있어.

A: You run your own business? 넌 네 사업을 하고 있어?
B: Yes, I am my own boss. 어. 내가 사장야.

I don't think I'm suited to be a salaried worker
난 급여근로자로 적합하지 않다고 생각해

- I give piano lessons at home. 난 집에서 피아노 강습을 해.
- I am a private English tutor. 난 영어개인 과외교사야.
- I prefer to do freelance work. 난 프리랜서 일을 더 좋아해.

A: You don't want a regular job? 넌 정규직을 원하지 않지?
B: No, I prefer to work independently. 맞아. 난 독립적으로 일하는 것을 더 좋아해.

019

Our shop carries[handles] sporting goods

우리 가게는 스포츠 용품을 취급해

구체적으로 자기가 하는 업무를 말하려면 My job is to+V, 혹은 좀 어렵지만 My job requires me to+V의 형태로 말하면 된다. …을 취급하다라고 할 때는 deal in 과 carry라는 동사를 기억해둔다.

01

My job is to handle complaints from customers
내 일은 고객들의 불만을 처리하는거야

- My job is to **sell our new products.** 내 일은 우리 신제품을 파는거야.

- My job is to **visit our regular clients.** 내 일은 단골고객들을 방문하는거야.

- My job is to **take reservations and help guests check-in to the hotel.**
내 일은 예약을 받고 손님들이 호텔에 체크인하는 것을 도와주는 것이야.

A: What are your job duties? 네가 해야 하는 일을 뭐야?
B: To sell our new products. 우리 신제품을 파는거야.

02

I've had more opportunities to send e-mails lately
최근에 이멜을 보낼 기회가 많았어

- I **occasionally** have to use English **at work.** 종종 난 직장에서 영어를 써야 해.

- My job requires me to **talk with foreigners.**
내 일은 외국인들과 대화를 하는 것이 필요로 해.

- Do you often write **e-mails in English?** 넌 종종 영어로 이멜을 쓰니?

A: Do you use English at your job? 넌 직장에서 영어를 쓰니?
B: Occasionally I have to use English. 종종 난 영어를 써야 돼.

03 We deal in sporting goods
우리는 스포츠 용품을 취급해

- What kind of goods do you deal in? 너희는 어떤 종류의 제품을 취급해?
- We deal in furniture. 우리는 가구를 취급해.
- He deals in diamonds and other gems. 걘 다이아몬드와 다른 보석류를 취급해.

A: What does your company deal in? 너희 회사는 뭘 취급해?
B: We deal in food products. 우리는 식료품을 취급해.

04 Our shop carries[handles] sporting goods
우리 가게는 스포츠 용품을 취급해

- Does your shop carry men's clothing? 너희 가게는 남성용 의류를 취급해?
- Their store carries home appliances. 걔네들 가게는 가전제품을 취급해.
- We handle airplane and train tickets. 우리는 항공권과 기차티켓을 취급합니다.

A: Our shop handles all kinds of sporting goods.
우리 가게는 모든 종류의 스포츠 용품을 취급합니다.
B: What about sports clothing? 스포츠 의류는요?

05 I run[manage, own] a boutique
난 양품점을 운영하고 있어

- 8 years have passed since we opened the store in Bundang.
우리는 8년전에 분당에 가게를 열었어.
- I've owned the restaurant since 2019. 난 2019년 이래로 식당을 운영하고 있어.
- I manage a small clothing boutique. 난 소규모 의류점포를 운영하고 있어.

A: What does he do? 걔 직업이 뭐야?
B: He runs a small convenience store. 걘 조그만 편의점을 운영하고 있어.

Unit 04

020

Is there a dress code at your workplace?

네 직장에서 복장규정이 있어?

가게문을 열고 문을 닫는다고 할 때는 open, close를 사용하고 유니폼을 입고 일해야 하는 경우에는 wear a uniform이라고 한다.

01 I have to wear a uniform while I'm on duty
난 근무중에 유니폼을 입어야 돼

- **Do you wear a necktie during working hours?** 너희는 근무시간에 넥타이를 매?
- **Do you have a casual Friday at your office?**
  너희 사무실에서는 금요일에 캐주얼 복장을 하니?
- **Is there a dress code at your workplace?** 네 직장에서 복장규정이 있어?

A: You're wearing jeans and a golf shirt to work?
너 청바지와 골프셔츠를 입고 출근하는거야?

B: Yes, today is casual Friday. We do it once a month.
어, 오늘은 캐주얼을 입는 금요일이어서. 한달에 한번 이렇게 해.

02 My store is open from 11:00 to 9:00 pm
내 가게는 11시부터 오후 9시까지 문을 열어

- **What time do you close?** 몇 시에 문을 닫아?
- **What time are you open till?** 몇 시까지 영업해요?
- **What are your business hours?** 영업시간이 어떻게 돼요?

A: Their business hours are from 9 to 9 Monday to Saturday and they aren't open Sundays. 거기 영업시간은 월요일부터 토요일까지 9-9이고 일요일은 문을 안열어.

B: Let's meet there at 10am tomorrow. 거기서 내일 오전 10시에 만나자.

I have a heavy[full] schedule this month
나 이번달에는 일정이 꽉 찼어

- My schedule is very full **this week.** 내 일정이 이번 주에는 꽉 찼어.
- I have a very busy schedule **this afternoon.** 오늘 오후에는 아주 일정이 바빠.
- My schedule is free **tomorrow afternoon.** 내일 오후에 내 일정은 비어.

A: When can we meet? 언제 우리 만날까?
B: My schedule is free all weekend. 주말내내 일정은 비어 있어.

We're paid according to ability
우리는 능력에 따라 급여를 받아

- My income varies **greatly every month.** 내 수입은 매달 아주 크게 변해.
- Do you have a regular income **every month?** 넌 매달 고정적인 소득을 벌어?
- I get paid by **sales commission.** 난 판매수수료에 따라 지급 받아.

A: What's your salary? 너 급여는 어떻게 돼?
B: I work on commission. I get 5% of every sale.
수수료 장사해. 모든 판매의 5%를 받아.

We have branches in five department stores
우리는 5개 백화점에 지점을 갖고 있어

- Health foods are selling well **these days.** 요즘 건강식이 잘 팔리고 있어.
- The price includes **a consumption tax.** 가격은 소비세를 포함하고 있어.
- We're very annoyed with **shoplifters.** 우리는 소매치기들 때문에 매우 화가 나.

A: Are there a lot of shoplifters these days? 요즘 소매치기들이 많아?
B: No, but we still have a security guard who watches for them.
아니, 하지만 소매치기들을 감시하는 경비원이 있어.

자기사업

I have plans to start up a coffee shop

난 커피숍을 시작할 계획이야

거의 우리말화 된 신규창업회사(start-up)를 이용해 자기 사업을 시작한다고 할 때는 start up my own business, 혹은 start a small business 등으로 표현한다. 또한 스스로 고용한 것이니 be self-employed라고도 한다.

01 I'm going to try starting up my own business
내 사업을 시작해볼까 해

- I started a small business **last year**. 난 작년에 소기업을 시작했어.

- I'm opening up a restaurant **next year**. 난 내년에 식당을 오픈할거야.

- I have plans to start up a coffee shop. 난 커피숍을 시작할 계획이야.

A: You are starting up a coffee shop? 넌 커피숍을 시작할거야?
B: No, it's a restaurant. 아니, 식당이야.

02 We want to start our own business
우리는 우리 사업을 시작하고 싶어

- They founded the company **20 years ago**. 그들은 20년 전에 회사를 설립했어.

- Who is the company's founder? 누가 회사를 창립한거야?.

- Who started this business? 누가 이 사업을 시작한거야?

A: Who is he? Why is everyone treating him with such respect?
그는 누구야? 왜 다들 예를 갖추어 대하는거야?
B: He is the founder of the company. 회사의 창립자야.

 ## Do you have enough money to start up the company? 회사를 시작할 정도로 충분한 돈을 갖고 있어?

- We need to raise some money to start the company.
  우리는 회사를 시작하기 위해서 돈을 좀 모아야 돼.

- We are getting a bank loan to start the company.
  우리는 회사를 시작하기 위해 은행대출을 받을거야.

- He is borrowing money from family and friends to start up his business.
  걘 자기 회사를 차리기 위해 가족과 친구들로부터 돈을 빌리고 있어.

A: How are they getting money to start up the company?
개네들은 회사를 설립할 돈을 어떻게 구한대?

B: They got a bank loan. 개네들은 은행대출을 받았어.

 ## I have my own importing company
난 수입회사를 운영해

- I work at a trading company. 난 무역회사에서 일을 해.

- My company exports computer chips to Europe. 내 회사는 유럽에 컴퓨터 칩을 수출해.

- We import car parts and sell them domestically. 자동차부품을 수입해서 국내에서 판매해.

A: What kind of goods does your company export?
너희 회사는 어떤 종류의 제품을 수출하니?

B: We mostly export computer chips. 우리는 대개 컴퓨터 칩을 수출해.

 ## I'm self-employed
난 자기 사업을 해

- I am my own boss. 나 자기 사업을 해.

- I have about 20 people working for me. 난 종업원이 한 20여 명이 돼.

- I own a small computer factory and have about 50 employees working for me. 난 소규모 공장을 운영하고 있는데 종업원 수는 약 50명이야.

A: How many people work for you? 종업원 수가 어떻게 돼?
B: Nine. It's a very small company. 아홉명. 아주 소기업이야.

022

That business is really cut-throat

저 사업은 정말 치열해

비즈니스, 즉 거래를 한다고 할 때는 do business with~를 사용하고 …와 거래를 하고 있다고 할 때는 deal with~ 라고 하면 된다. 회사를 확장할 때는 expand the business라고 하면 된다.

01 We do business with Japan
우리는 일본과 비즈니스를 해

- We are meeting the Chinese clothing producer to talk business.
  우리는 중국의류생산업자와 만나서 사업을 논의할거야.

- I need to discuss some important business with you today.
  난 오늘 너와 중요한 비즈니스를 논의해야 돼.

- We deal with many North American companies.
  우리의 많은 거래처는 북미의 회사들이야.

A: We do a lot of business with Canadian companies.
우리는 캐나다 기업들과 많은 거래를 해.

B: Are they easy to deal with? 그들이 거래하기 쉽니?

02 We're going to expand the business this year
우리는 금년에 사업을 확장할거야

- We are opening several new branches this year.
  우리는 금년에 몇몇 새로운 지점을 오픈할거야.

- We are closing down all of our branches in Russia.
  우리는 러시아의 모든 지점을 폐쇄할거야.

- We plan to increase the number of products we are selling next year.
  우리는 내년에 우리가 판매하는 제품의 양을 늘릴 계획이야.

A: We're going to expand into China this year. 우리는 금년에 중국으로 진입할거야.
B: How exciting! 와 흥분되네!

His business is very successful
그의 사업은 아주 성공적이야

- She is a very successful business woman. 그녀는 아주 성공한 여성 사업가야.
- That company is one of the best in Korea.
  저 회사는 한국에서 최고로 인정받는 회사 중 하나야.
- The car company is a top 3 company. 저 자동차 회사는 탑 3에 들어.

A: Is his business successful? 걔의 사업이 성공했어?
B: Yes, it's a top 5 company in Korea. 어, 한국에서 탑 5에 들어.

We would be one of the leaders in our field
우린 우리 업계에서 선두가 될 수 있을거야

- We are market leaders in the coffee import business.
  우리는 커피 수입업계에서 점유율이 높은 기업이야.
- Hyundai is the top car company in Korea. 현대는 한국에서 최고의 자동차 회사야.
- What field of business are you in? 너는 어느 분야의 사업을 하고 있어.

A: Is his company good? 걔 회사는 괜찮은 곳이야?
B: Yes, it's one of the market leaders in the fertilizer industry.
   어, 비료업계에서는 선두그룹에 속해.

That business is really cut-throat
저 사업은 정말 치열해

- Did you read that business report? 너 그 사업보고서 읽었어?
- It's a really tough business to be in. 그건 정말 살아남기 힘든 사업이야.
- The competition is very cut-throat. 경쟁이 정말 치열해.

A: Why did he quit? 걔 왜 그만둔거야?
B: The competition was too cut-throat for him.
   걔가 감당하기에 경쟁이 너무 치열해서.

023 미팅

I won't be able to attend the meeting

난 회의에 참석할 수 없을거야

회의가 있으면 have a meeting. 회의에 참석한다는 attend the meeting. 혹은 make it to~란 표현을 쓰면 된다. 또한 회의에서 일찍 나가는 것은 leave the meeting라 한다.

01 I have a meeting. I've got to run

난 회의가 있어. 빨리 가야 돼

- **I have to** cancel tomorrow's meeting. 내일 회의를 취소해야 되겠어.
- **You've got** a meeting at **three.** 3시에 회의가 있어요.
- **I have to** go for a meeting. 회의 때문에 나 가야 돼.

A: I'm late for the meeting. I've got to run! 나 회의에 늦었어. 빨리 가야 돼!
B: OK. Let me know how it goes. 좋아. 어떻게 됐는지 알려줘.

02 Excuse me but I must leave the meeting early

실례지만 회의에서 일찍 일어나야겠습니다

- **I won't be able to** attend **the meeting.** 난 회의에 참석할 수 없을거야.
- **She can't** participate in **this week's meeting.** 걘 이번주 회의에 참석할 수가 없어.
- **How was** the conference's attendance? 회의 참석자수는 어땠어?

A: Why did you leave the meeting so suddenly? 왜 그렇게 급히 회의에서 나간 거야?
B: I was frustrated with you! You talk too much!
너 땜에 진이 빠졌어! 넌 말이 너무 많아!

They are having a discussion at a meeting
걔네들은 회의에서 토의를 할거야

- Are you going to the staff meeting tonight? 오늘 밤에 있을 직원회의에 갈거니?
- We need to bring up that issue at the board meeting.
  우리는 이사회의에서 그 문제를 꺼내야 돼.
- That matter needs to be discussed at the next meeting.
  그 문제는 다음 회의에서 논의되어야 돼.

A: Did they discuss that issue at the meeting? 그들이 회의에서 그 문제를 토의했어?
B: No, they'll bring it up at the next one. 아니, 다음 회의에서 그 문제를 꺼낼거야.

Unit 04

I won't be able to make it to the presentation
프레젠테이션 제 시간에 도착할 수 없을거야

- He is going to give a presentation on last year's sales.
  걘 작년 매출에 대한 프레젠테이션을 할거야.
- I want to make the presentation at 10 am. 난 오전 10시에 발표회를 하고 싶어.
- She is giving a presentation today. 걔가 오늘 프레젠테이션을 할거야.

A: She is giving a presentation today at 2pm.
   걔는 오늘 오후 2시에 프레젠테이션을 할거야.
B: What's the topic? 주제가 뭔데?

She's presenting information about the business profits
걘 영업이익에 대한 정보를 발표할거야

- He is giving a speech. 걔가 연설을 할거야.
- He's in a meeting right now. 지금 그는 회의중이세요.
- The advertising department is meeting now. 광고부는 지금 회의중예요.

A: Where is everyone? 다들 어디갔어?
B: They are all in a meeting. 모두 다 회의중이야.

024

He is away on a business trip
걔는 출장중이야

출장이라고 말할 때는 대표적으로 be out on business, be out of town, be away on a business trip, 해외출장은 go abroad on business라고 하면 된다. 그리고 사무실에 없다고 할 때는 be out of the office라고 한다.

01 He's out on business
걘 외근중이야

- I'll be on the road most of next month. 난 다음 달 대부분 출장중일거야.
- He is away on a business trip. 걔는 출장중이야.
- I have to go to Japan for business. 난 사업차 일본에 가야 돼.

A: Can I speak to Jennifer? 제니퍼 있어요?
B: I'm sorry. She's out on business. 미안하지만 출장중이에요.

02 He's out of town now
지금 출장중이야

- I'll be out of town all next week. 난 다음 주 내내 출장갈거야.
- He's out of the office at the moment. 그는 지금 사무실에 없습니다.
- He's on his lunch break right now. 그는 지금 점심먹으러 나갔습니다.

A: May I speak to the manager please? 매니저와 통화할 수 있을까요?
B: Sorry but he's away on business until Friday.
죄송하지만 금요일까지 출장중이세요.

03 I'm afraid he's on a business trip
미안하지만 그는 출장중이신데요

- I'm sorry but he's **out of town until tomorrow.** 미안하지만 그는 내일까지 출장중이십니다.
- **She is in Japan** for a conference. 그녀는 회의차 일본에 있습니다.
- He is out **entertaining the customers tonight.**
  그는 오늘밤 고객들을 대접하느라 사무실에 안계십니다.

A: I need to see Mr. Johnson. 존슨 씨를 만나야 되는데요.
B: I'm afraid he's on a business trip right now. 죄송하지만 지금 출장중이세요.

04 I have to go to Boston on business on Thursday
목요일에 출장차 보스톤에 가야 돼

- He's away on business **for a week.** 일주일 간 출장중이세요.
- She is out of the office **this afternoon.** 그녀는 오늘 오후에 외근이세요.

A: She is out of town at the moment. 그녀는 지금 출장이세요.
B: When will she be back? 언제 돌아오실까요?

05 I go abroad on business several times a year
일년에 수차례 출장으로 해외에 가

- We have several overseas business trips **a year.** 우리는 일년에 수차례 해외출장을 가.
- There is an annual business conference in Busan every summer.
  매년 부산에서 연례 비즈니스총회가 열려.
- She is out of the office **meeting customers every Wednesday afternoon.**
  그녀는 매주 수요일 오후에 고객상담으로 외근해.

A: Do you travel a lot for work? 너는 출장을 많이 가?
B: I go abroad several times a year. 일년에 수차례 해외에 나가.

전근[승진]하다

025

I heard you've been promoted
너 승진했다며

전근가다는 transfer라는 동사를 이용해 표현하며 승진했다고 말하려면 be promoted, 혹은 get the promotion. 그리고 직업을 바꾸는 것은 change jobs 라 한다.

01 I'm being transferred
나 전근 가

- I just found out that I got transferred. 내가 전근 대상이 되었다는 걸 방금 알았어.
- I am changing departments **next month**. 나 담달에 부서를 변경해.
- They are sending me to the Jeju branch. 나를 제주도 지사로 발령냈어.

A: Why are you packing up? 왜 짐을 싸고 있는거야?
B: I'm being transferred to the PR department. 난 홍보부서로 이동해.

02 I'm getting transferred to a new office location
새로운 사무소로 전근을 가게 됐어

- We are relocating our headquarters **from Yeosu to Gwangju**.
  우리 회사 본사는 여수에서 광주로 이전해.
- They are being transferred to **the Gangneung branch**. 그들은 강릉지사로 발령났어.
- He is being moved to **the marketing department**. 그는 마케팅 부서로 옮겨.

A: Did you hear the news? We are relocating our headquarters to Seoul. 소식들었어? 본사를 서울로 옮긴대.
B: That's fantastic! 멋진 일이네!

03 I heard you've been promoted
너 승진했다며

● **Congrats! I heard you** passed your promotion test. 축하해! 승진시험 통과했다며.

● **How many workers** got promoted? 승진한 사람이 몇 명이야?

● **Her promotion** was really unexpected. 그녀의 승진은 전혀 예상못한 일이었어.

A: Her promotion surprised me. 그녀의 승진으로 놀랐어.

B: Not me. She is a really hard worker and smart.
난 아냐. 걘 열심히 일하고 똑똑하잖아.

04 I didn't get the promotion
난 승진을 못했어

● **I didn't pass** the promotion exam again. 난 승진시험에 또 떨어졌어.

● **I was overlooked** for the promotion. 난 승진에서 누락되었어.

● **I wasn't promoted.** 난 승진을 못했어.

A: Why so glum? 왜 그렇게 침울해?

B: I was overlooked for the promotion again. 난 또 승진에서 누락되었어.

05 You changed jobs?
너 직업을 바꿨어?

● **I recently** changed jobs. 최근에 직업을 바꿨어.

● **I switched** jobs. 난 업무를 바꾸었어.

● **I decided to** change my job. 난 직업을 바꾸기로 맘먹었어.

A: You look happy. 너 행복해 보여.

B: Yes, I changed jobs and love my new one.
어, 직장을 바꾸었는데 새로운 직장이 너무 좋아.

026

He was charged with sexual harassment

그는 성희롱으로 고소를 당했어

성희롱은 sexual harassment, 성적으로 집적대는 sexual advances, 수작을 거는 것은 make a pass at~ 혹은 hit on을 많이 쓴다. 그리고 언어로 폭언을 한다고 할 때는 verbally abuse sb라고 하면 된다.

01 He made sexual advances towards me
걘 내게 성적으로 집적됐어

● He slapped me on the butt. 걘 내 엉덩이를 손바닥으로 찰싹 때렸어.

● He made several inappropriate remarks to her.
걘 그녀에게 몇몇 성적으로 부적절한 말을 했어.

● He verbally abused his employees. 걘 자기 직원들에게 폭언을 했어.

A: Why was he fired? 걘 왜 잘린거야?
B: He made sexual advances towards one of his employees.
걘 직원 한명에게 성적으로 집적됐어.

02 She made a pass at her boss
그녀는 사장에게 성적으로 수작을 걸었어

● He was hitting on his secretary at the conference.
걘 총회에서 비서에게 성적으로 수작을 걸었어.

● He made moves on one of his co-workers so he was fired.
걘 자기 동료중 한명에게 성적으로 수작을 걸어서 해고됐어.

● He sexually harassed her so he was fired. 걘 그녀에게 성희롱을 해서 잘렸어.

A: Why was she fired? 걘 왜 잘린거야?
B: For sexual harassment. 성희롱으로

03 I'm filing a lawsuit against my boss for sexual harassment 성희롱으로 사장을 고소했어

- She was thinking of charging you with sexual harassment.
  그녀는 널 성희롱으로 고소할 생각였어.

- He was warned for making inappropriate sexual jokes.
  그는 부적절한 성적농담을 해서 경고를 받았어.

- She was charged with sexual harassment. 그녀는 성희롱으로 고소를 당했어.

A: Was she charged with sexual harassment? 그녀는 성희롱으로 고소당했어?
B: Yes, I was very surprised too. 어, 나도 무척이나 놀랐어.

04 She has experienced sexual harassment at their workplace 그녀는 직장에서 성희롱을 겪었어

- Sexual harassment is a big problem these days. 요즘 성희롱이 큰 문제야.

- Inappropriate sexual jokes are a form of sexual harassment.
  부적절한 성적농담은 성희롱의 한 형태야.

- People used to get away with sexual harassment but not anymore.
  과거에는 성희롱이 그냥 처벌없이 지나갔지만 요즘은 더 이상 그러지 않아.

A: Have you ever been sexually harassed? 성희롱을 당해본 적이 있어?
B: Thankfully no. 다행이게도 없어.

05 In most cases of sexual harassment, the male comes on to the female 대개의 성희롱의 경우, 남성이 여성에게 집적대지

- Some men try to secretly photograph women with short skirts.
  일부 남성들은 짧은 치마의 여성들을 몰래 사진찍으려 해.

- He touched her in an inappropriate way when they were having their picture taken. 그는 사진을 함께 찍을 때 부적절한 방법으로 그녀를 만졌어.

A: Why is she so upset? 그녀가 왜 그렇게 화가 난거야?
B: Her boss made some inappropriate jokes to her. 사장이 걔에게 부적절한 농담을 했대.

You need to get certified

너는 자격증을 따야 돼

자격을 갖추다라고 할 때는 qualify라는 단어를 활용하여 get qualified, a qualified applicant 등으로 쓰이고, 자격증을 따는 것을 말할 때는 certify란 단어를 이용하며 표현들을 만들어낸다.

01 She needs to get qualified before she applies for the job 그녀는 그 직에 지원하기 앞서 자격을 갖추어야 돼

● He is a very qualified applicant. 걘 매우 자격이 넘치는 지원자야.

● Her qualifications are very good. 그녀의 자격조건은 매우 좋아.

● He doesn't have good enough qualifications to work here.
걘 여기서 일하기에 충분한 자격을 갖추지 못하고 있어.

A: Why did you hire her? 넌 왜 그녀를 뽑았어?
B: Because her qualifications were very good. 그녀의 자격요건이 매우 좋아서.

02 He didn't qualify for the promotion
걘 승진요건을 갖추지 못했어

● I want to qualify as a lawyer. 변호사 자격증을 따고 싶어.

● She was overqualified for the job. 걘 이 일자리에 필요이상의 자격을 갖추고 있었어.

● He was underqualified so he didn't get the job.
걘 자격미달이어서 일자리를 구하지 못했어.

A: Why wasn't she hired? 그녀는 왜 채용되지 못했어?
B: She was underqualified. 자격미달이어서.

 03 You need to get certified
너는 자격증을 따야 돼

● He got his accounting certification. 걘 회계자격증을 가지고 있어.

● He is a certified teacher. 그는 교사 자격증을 지니고 있어.

● She is getting her scuba diving certification this summer.
걘 이번 여름에 스쿠버다이빙 자격증을 딸거야.

A: I am looking for a job as an accountant. 난 회계사 일자리를 구하고 있어.
B: Are you certified? 자격증은 있고?

 04 He needs to get his business license
걘 영업허가증을 취득해야 돼

● I want to get a pharmacist's license. 난 약사자격증을 따고 싶어.

● To drive the truck he needs a special driver's license.
트럭을 몰려면 걘 특수면허증이 필요해.

● To sell alcohol you need a liquor license from the government.
술을 판매하기 위해서는 정부가 발급한 주류판매허가증이 있어야 돼.

A: Do you have a liquor license? 주류판매허가증이 있어?
B: Not yet but we've applied for one. 아직은 하지만 허가증 신청을 했어.

028 Many students attend English institutes

많은 학생들이 영어학원에 다녀

학원은 institute란 단어를 사용하면 된다. 영어학원은 English institute, 일본어학원은 Japanese language institute, 그리고 TOEIC학원은 TOEIC academy. 그리고 이런 곳에 다닌다고 할 때의 동사는 attend를 쓰면 된다.

01 She is attending a private Japanese language institute 걘 사설 일본어학원에 다니고 있어

- Many students attend English institutes. 많은 학생들이 영어학원에 다녀.
- I hope to attend the TOEIC academy this summer.
  난 이번 여름에 토익학원에 다니길 바래.
- I am going to a photography academy every Thursday evening.
  난 매주 목요일저녁에 사진학원에 다녀.

A: What kind of academy are you attending. 넌 무슨 학원에 다녀?
B: A Chinese language one. 중국어학원에.

02 She is attending a private institute for government employees 걘 공무원 학원에 다녀

- There is a Civil Service Exam Academy for people who hope to work in the government. 공무원되려는 사람을 위한 공무원시험 학원이 있어.
- To prepare for the Civil Service Exam, he is attending a special institute.
  걘 공무원시험을 준비하려고 전문학원에 다녀.
- He passed the Civil Service Exam thanks to that academy.
  걘 학원의 도움을 받아 공무원 시험에 통과했어.

A: I hope to pass the Civil Service Exam. 공무원 시험에 붙기를 바래.
B: Are you attending any academies? 학원 다니는거 뭐 있어?

03 He is going to culinary school
갠 요리학원에 다녀

- She is attending a cooking school. 갠 요리학원에 다니고 있어.

- He wants to go to a baking school to learn how to make bread and cakes.
빵과 케익만드는 법을 배우기 위해 제과학원에 다니기를 원해.

- I graduated from a famous culinary school in Paris.
난 파리의 유명요리학원을 졸업했어.

A: He is going to a famous culinary school in Japan.
갠 일본의 유명한 요리학원에 갈거야.

B: Is he going to be a sushi chef? 갠 초밥요리사가 되는거야?

04 I never went to art school
난 미술학원에 다닌 적이 전혀 없어

- She attended an art academy. 갠 미술학원에 다녔어.

- He wants to go to a music school and become a conductor.
갠 음대에 가서 지휘자가 되기를 원해.

- She is going to art school and focusing on sculpting.
갠 미대에 가서 조각에 전념할거야.

A: What is she specializing in at art school? 넌 미대에서 뭐를 전공하고 있어?
B: Painting. 그림.

029

My son decided to attend law school

내 아들이 로스쿨에 가기로 했어

변호사가 되기 위해서는 attend law school(로스쿨에 들어가다)해야 되며, 의사중에 …전문의라고 말하려면 ~ specialist라고 하면 된다.

01 I need you to call my lawyer
내 변호사에게 연락 좀 해

- I'll contact my lawyer **after the meeting.** 난 회의 후에 내 변호사에게 전화할거야.
- I'll put you in touch with **my lawyer.** 네가 내 변호사와 연락이 닿도록 할게.
- My lawyer will be in touch with **you.** 내 변호사가 너에게 연락을 취할거야.

A: I am having some legal troubles. 난 좀 법적인 문제에 처했어.
B: Sorry to hear that. I'll put you in touch with my lawyer. She's very good. 안됐네. 내 변호사와 연락이 되도록 할게. 매우 유능해.

02 He's from a famous law school
걘 유명 로스쿨 출신이야

- I don't think you should go to law school. 넌 법대가지 않는게 좋다고 생각 돼.
- **That law school** is very hard to get into. 저 로스쿨은 들어가기가 너무 어려워.
- He attended law school **in America.** 걘 미국에서 로스쿨을 다녔어.

A: Where did he go to law school? 걘 어느 로스쿨에 들어갔어?
B: I think it was SNU but I'm not sure. 서울대 로스쿨인 것 같은데 확실하지 않아.

03 My son decided to attend law school
내 아들이 로스쿨에 가기로 했어

- **My daughter** wants to be a lawyer. 내 딸은 변호사가 되기를 원해.

- **He needs to** write LSAT **if he wants to** go to law school.
  걘 로스쿨에 가려면 LSAT 작문을 해야 돼.

- **Before you become a lawyer in America, you have to** pass the bar exam.
  미국에서 변호사가 되려면 변호사 자격시험을 통과해야 돼.

A: What does she want to do? 걘 뭐를 하고 싶어해?
B: She wants to be a lawyer. 걘 변호사가 되기를 원해.

Unit 04

04 I want to see a specialist
전문의와 상담하고 싶어

- **You're just a general practitioner. I want to** see a specialist.
  당신은 그저 일반의잖아요. 난 전문의와 상담하고 싶어요.

- **I need to** see an eye specialist. 난 안과전문의에 가야 돼.

- **He is going to** see a heart specialist. 걘 심장전문의에게 갈거야.

A: You can't help me doctor? 저를 치료할 수 없다구요?
B: I'm afraid not, you'll need to see a knee specialist.
네 안될 것 같아요. 무릎전문의에게 가셔야 합니다.

05 She is visiting my psychiatrist today
걘 내 정신과의사를 오늘 방문했어

- **Are you going to** see a shrink? 정신과 진찰을 받을거야?

- **That shrink** has a very good reputation. 저 정신과 의사는 아주 유명해.

- **My psychiatrist is very good.** 내 정신과의사는 매우 유능해.

A: Are you going to see a shrink? 정신과 진찰을 받을거야?
B: Yes, and he has a very good reputation. 어, 그 선생은 명망이 아주 높아.

030

He's a fast worker

개는 일을 빨리해

직원이 일을 잘 하면 be good at one's job. 능력있으면 be competent. 일을
빨리 하면 a fast worker. 그리고 일을 잘 알면 know one's job이라고 한다. 또한
일벌레는 a workaholic.

01 He's good at his job
개는 일을 잘 해

- **He's the pride of our office.** 개는 우리 사무실의 자랑거리야.
- **She is a very competent worker.** 걘 매우 유능한 직원이야.
- **My boss is highly competent.** 우리 상사는 매우 유능해.

A: Do you like working for her? 넌 걔 밑에서 일하는게 맘에 들어?
B: Yes, she is very competent and a nice person too.
어, 그녀는 매우 유능하고 또한 매우 착한 사람이야.

02 He's a fast worker
개는 일을 빨리해

- **He's a real asset.** 개는 정말 인재야.
- **The boss has high expectations of him.** 사장은 걔한테 많은 기대를 하고 있어.
- **That company is lucky to** have her as a manager.
그녀가 부장인게 저 회사에게는 운이지.

A: That company is lucky to have him as a manager.
저 회사에게 운좋게도 그는 부장으로 일하고 있어.
B: Yes, he's a real asset for them. 맞아. 그는 정말 회사의 인재야.

03 She really knows her job
개는 일을 잘 해

- **They have a high opinion of her.** 그들은 걔를 아주 높게 평가해.
- **She knows her job inside and out.** 걘 안팎으로 자기 일을 잘 처리해.
- **He is one of the best at his job.** 자기 일을 처리하는데 있어 최고중의 한명이야.

> A: They have a high opinion of her. 걔 평판이 아주 좋아.
> B: So do I. She's very good at her job.
> 나도 그렇게 생각해. 걘 자기 일을 처리하는데 아주 잘해.

04 He's a real workaholic
개는 정말 일벌레야

- **He's a smooth operator.** 걔는 일을 무리없이 잘 처리해.
- **His ideas are unique.** 걔의 생각은 매우 독창적이야
- **She's a real workhorse.** 걘 정말 열심히 일을 해.

> A: This is going to be a very tough assignment. 이건 매우 어려운 과제가 될거야.
> B: Ask her to help. She's a real workhorse.
> 걔에게 도움을 청해. 걘 정말 열심히 일을 하거든.

031

직장 사람들 2

You're pathetic

너 참 한심하다

일 잘하는 사람만 있으면 세상이 아닐게다. 부정적인 단어들로는 lazy, a loser, a nerd, pathetic, 그리고 an asshole, a jerk 등이 있다. 뒷담화하면서 스트레스 풀 때 필요한 단어들이다.

01 I feel so lazy today
오늘 좀 몸이 안 움직이네

- I think you're lazy. **You'd better work harder.** 넌 게을러. 더 열심히 일을 해야 돼.

- **When are you going to fire that lazy secretary?** 저 게을러 빠진 비서를 언제 자를거야?

- He is one of the laziest workers I know. 걘 내가 아는 가장 게으른 직원 중 하나야.

A: Don't ask him for help. 걔에게 도움을 청하지마.
B: Yeah, he's one of the laziest workers I know.
그래, 걘 내가 아는 가장 게으른 직원 중 하나야.

02 You're a loser!
넌 한심한 놈이야!

- He's such a nerd. 걘 정말 멍청해.

- He is very anti-social. 걘 정말이지 비사교적이야.

- She is a socially awkward person. 걘 같이 지내기에 불편한 사람이야.

A: Why doesn't he have any friends? 왜 걘 친구가 하나도 없는거야?
B: He's very anti-social. 걘 매우 비사교적이야.

03 You're pathetic
너 참 한심하다

- He is a pathetic loser. 걘 정말이지 한심한 놈이야.

- Why is she so pathetic? 걘 왜 그렇게 한심해?

- Don't be so pathetic. 그렇게 한심하게 굴지마.

A: Why don't you like him? 넌 왜 걔를 좋아하지 않아?
B: Because he is such a pathetic loser. 걘 정말이지 한심한 놈이기 때문이야.

04 He is such an asshole
걘 정말이지 멍청해

- Don't be an asshole. 멍청하게 굴지마.

- Why is he being an asshole? 왜 걘 그렇게 멍청해?

- He is acting like a complete asshole. 걘 완전 멍충이처럼 행동해.

A: Why is he being such an asshole? 왜 걘 그렇게 멍청하게 구는거야?
B: He was born an asshole. 걘 타고난 멍청이야.

05 He is a big jerk
걘 정말이지 얼간이야

- Don't be a jerk. 얼간이처럼 행동하지마.

- Is he always a jerk? 걘 늘상 얼간이처럼 굴어?

- She treats me like a jerk. 걘 나를 얼간이로 대해.

A: Why did you break up with her? 넌 왜 걔와 헤어졌어?
B: She treated me like a jerk. 나를 얼간이처럼 대했어.

032

He fired the manager

걘 부장을 해고 했어

해고를 뜻하는 가장 기본적인 단어는 fire란 동사. fire sb. 혹은 get[be] fired 등의
표현을 만들어낸다. 또한 get axed란 동의표현도 함께 알아둔다. lay off는 경기침체
로 일시적으로 해고하는 것을 말한다.

01 I got fired today
난 오늘 잘렸어

- What if you get fired for calling in sick too much?
  너무 자주 병가를 내서 잘리면 어떻게 할거니?

- He fired the manager. 걘 부장을 해고 했어.

- I got axed because I was always late for work. 난 늘상 지각하다가 잘렸어.

A: Did he get fired? 걔 잘렸어?
B: Yes, he called in sick too often. 어, 병가를 너무 자주 내서.

02 The company laid off over 100 workers
회사는 100명 넘게 해고 했어

- We got laid off because of the bad economy. 경기가 안좋아서 우리는 잘렸어.

- Business was bad so we had to let him go. 경기가 너무 안좋아서 우리는 걔를 해고했어.

- Many companies are laying off workers because of the pandemic.
  많은 회사들이 전염병 때문에 직원들을 해고하고 있어.

A: Was he fired? 걘 잘렸어?
B: No, he was a very good worker but he got laid off because business
has been bad this year. 아니, 걘 매우 유능한 직원이었지만 금년도 경기가 나빠서 일시해고됐어.

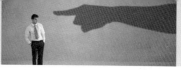

03 I left the company to start my own business
난 내 사업을 시작하려고 퇴사했어

- She quit her job. 걘 그만뒀어.
- She decided to stop working there. 걘 거기서 그만 일하기로 맘먹었어.
- He is going to leave his job next year and move overseas.
  걘 내년에 회사를 그만두고 해외로 이주할거야.

A: Was he fired or laid off? 걘 잘린거야 일시해고 된거야?
B: No, he quit. 아니, 걘 스스로 그만뒀어.

04 He was unhappy with his job so he resigned
걘 자기 일에 만족을 못해서 그만뒀어

- I'm handing in my resignation tomorrow. 난 내일 사직서를 제출할거야.
- I came by to tell you that I need to resign. 그만둬야겠다는 말을 하려고 들렸어요.
- I want to resign but I'll wait a few more weeks before I decide.
  난 그만두고 싶지만 결정하기 전에 몇주 더 기다릴거야.

A: I'm handing in my resignation. 난 사직서를 낼거야.
B: I'm very sorry to hear that. 너무 안됐다.

05 I plan on retiring when I'm 55
난 55세에 회사를 퇴직할거야

- I just heard that our law professor retired.
  우리 로스쿨 교수가 퇴임할거라는 얘기를 들었어.
- We need to organize a retirement party for John.
  우리는 존을 위한 퇴직파티를 준비해야 돼.
- Can you find a replacement for him? 걔를 대신할 사람을 찾을 수 있어?

A: John is retiring next year. 존은 내년에 퇴직할거야.
B: Yes, we need to start looking for his replacement.
   그래, 우리는 그를 대체할 사람을 찾기 시작해야 돼.

취미생활

001

His main interest is in K-pop music

걔의 주된 관심사는 K-pop 음악이야

자신의 관심사나 흥미는 interest나 enjoy ~ing의 단어들로 표현할 수 있다. 특히 뭔가 아주 좋아할 때는 be crazy about~, be into~ 그리고 be a big fan of~ 라고 하면 된다.

01 I enjoy playing sports when I have free time
난 여유시간에는 운동을 즐겨 해

- When I'm not busy I like going to the park. 바쁘지 않을 때는 난 공원에 가는 걸 좋아해.
- I love going window shopping when I'm not working.
  일하지 않을 땐 윈도쇼핑가는 걸 좋아해.
- I watch a lot of TV when I'm home alone. 난 집에 혼자 있을 때 TV를 많이 봐.

A: What do you do when you have some free time? 여유시간이 있을 때 넌 뭐해?
B: I really enjoy playing computer games. 난 컴퓨터 게임을 아주 즐겨해.

02 I have a lot of interests
난 관심사항이 많아

- I have a wide range of hobbies. 난 취미가 아주 많아.
- I enjoy a few different leisure activities. 난 몇몇 다른 여가활동을 즐기고 있어.
- I enjoy a variety of different physical activities. 난 여러가지 다양한 신체활동을 즐겨.

A: Do you like working out? 넌 운동하는 것을 좋아해?
B: Yes, it's one of my many interests. 어. 내가 관심있어 하는 여러가지 중 하나야.

03 I'm crazy about crossword puzzles
난 크로스워드 퍼즐 맞추는걸 정말 좋아해

- **She** is very passionate about art. 걘 미술에 매우 열정적이야.
- **I** am really into music. 난 정말이지 음악에 푹 빠져 있어.
- **They** are both big fans of comic books. 걔네들은 둘 다 만화책을 무척 좋아해.

A: Does she like movies? 걘 음악을 좋아해?
B: Yes, she is crazy about movies, especially action movies.
어, 걘 영화, 특히 액션영화를 무척 좋아해.

04 I'm very interested in recycling
난 재활용하는데 관심이 많아

- **We** are interested in **volunteer work**. 우리는 자원봉사하는 일에 관심이 있어.
- **She** is interested in **working overseas**. 걘 해외에서 일하는데 관심이 있어.
- **He** is interested in **Chinese politics**. 걘 중국정치에 대해 관심이 있어.

A: Why is she always watching Japanese movies? 걘 왜 늘상 일본영화를 보는거야?
B: She is interested in Japanese pop culture. 걘 일본대중문화에 관심이 있어.

05 I have great interest in volunteer work
난 자원봉사하는데 관심이 아주 많아

- **His** main interest is in **K-pop music**. 걔의 주된 관심사는 K-pop 음악이야.
- **She** is extremely interested in **Korean history**. 걘 한국역사에 대한 관심이 무척 커.
- **They** have a deep interest in **philosophy**. 걔네들은 철학에 깊은 관심을 갖고 있어.

A: He is always listening to jazz. 걘 항상 재즈를 듣고 있어.
B: Yeah, his main interest is jazz music. 그래, 걔의 주된 관심사는 재즈음악이야.

002

I'd like to try it if I have time

시간있으면 그것을 해보고 싶어

뭔가 재미있다고 하려면 be a lot of fun. 그래서 한번 해보다라고 하려면 give it a try. take crack at~ 혹은 give it a go 등의 표현을 사용하면 된다.

01

I'm into working out

난 운동하는데 빠져 있어

- **She's into fashion.** 걔는 패션에 빠져 있어.

- **He's into training his dogs.** 걘 자기 개들을 훈련시키는데 빠져 있어.

- **They are really into rock climbing.** 걔네들은 암벽등반하는데 빠져 있어.

A: Why is she always reading fashion magazines? 걘 항상 패션잡지를 왜 읽는거야?
B: She's really into fashion. 걘 정말이지 패션에 몰입되어 있어.

02

It's a lot of fun, but I'm making slow progress in it

재미는 많지만 난 천천히 나아가고 있어

- **It's really interesting.** 그거 정말 재미있겠다.

- **It's a real challenge so it is taking more time than I thought.**
  그건 정말 어려운 일이어서 내 생각보다 더 많은 시간이 필요로 해.

- **It's difficult but still a lot of fun.** 그건 어렵지만 그래도 무척 재미있어.

A: How is the project coming along? 그 프로젝트는 어떻게 돼 가?
B: It's a lot of fun but still a challenge. 무척 재미있지만 그래도 만만치 않은 일이야.

03 I'm learning as I go along, but I enjoy it
일을 해나가면서 배우고 있지만 즐겁게 하고 있어

- She's learning on the fly but having fun. 걘 즉석에서 배우고 있는데 재미있어 해.
- He is learning on the job and having a tough time.
  걘 일을 배우고 있는데 어려움을 겪고 있어.
- I am learning while I work but it's not too bad. 일하면서 배우고 있지만 그리 나쁘지 않아.

A: Is the new job hard? 새로운 일이 힘들어?
B: I'm learning on the fly but it's fun. 즉석에서 배우고 있지만 재미있어.

04 I'd like to try it if I have time
시간있으면 그것을 해보고 싶어

- I'll give it a go if you let me. 네가 허락한다면 한번 해보고 싶어.
- Let me take a crack at it. 내가 그거 한번 해볼게 .
- She wants to give it a try. 걘 한번 해보고 싶어해.

A: This is really hard work. 이건 정말 어려운 일이야.
B: I'll take a crack at it if you let me. 네가 허락한다면 내가 한번 해볼게.

003 Let's go to a movie tonight

오늘밤 영화보러 가자

영화를 보러 가다는 go to a movie 혹은 go to the movies를 많이 쓴다. 영화자체를 본다라고 할 때는 see a movie, catch a movie를 사용하면 된다. 영화평을 물어볼 때는 What did you think of the movie?라 한다.

01 Let's go to a movie tonight

오늘밤 영화보러 가자

- **We're about to take off and** see a movie. 우리는 바로 나가서 영화보려고 해.
- **Do you want to** catch the late movie **tonight?** 오늘밤 심야 영화 볼래?
- **Why don't we** go to the movies **tonight?** 오늘밤 영화보러가는게 어때?

A: Want to catch a movie tonight? 오늘밤 영화볼래?
B: Sure. Which one do you have in mind? 물론. 생각해둔거 있어?

02 Would you like to go to the movies tonight?

오늘밤 영화보러갈래?

- **Would you like to** see a movie or a play? 영화나 연극을 볼래?
- **Do you want to** go to a movie? 영화보러갈래?
- **Have** you seen any movies **recently?** 최근에 뭐 영화본거 있어?

A: Have you seen any movies recently? 최근에 뭐 영화본거 있어?
B: No, I've been too busy with work. 아니. 일로 너무 바빴어.

03
What kind of movies do you like?
어떤 종류의 영화를 좋아해?

- **I prefer to** see action movies. 난 액션영화보는걸 더 좋아해.
- **I love all the genres.** 난 장르구분없이 다 좋아해.
- **He is really into cult movies.** 걘 컬트무비에 푹 빠져 있어.

A: What kind of movies do you like? 넌 어떤 종류의 영화를 좋아해?
B: I love all movies. 모든 종류의 영화를 좋아해.

04
Would you like to go and see the new Eva Green movie? 에바 그린 나오는 신작영화 보러 갈래?

- **I really want to see his new movie.** 난 걔의 신작영화를 정말 보고 싶어.
- **Brad Pitt has a new movie out.** 브래드 피트의 신작영화가 나왔어.
- **The Bong Junho movie is coming out tomorrow.** 봉준호 영화가 내일 개봉해.

A: The new superhero movie is coming out tomorrow.
새로운 수퍼히어로 영화가 내일 나와.
B: Let's go see it. 가서 보자.

05
What did you think of the movie last night?
지난밤에 본 영화 어떻게 생각해?

- **What do you think was** the best part of the movie?
그 영화의 가장 좋았던 부분이 어디였어?
- **How was the movie last night?** 어젯밤에 영화는 어땠어?
- **What was your favorite scene from the movie?** 영화에서 어떤 장면이 가장 좋았어?

A: My favorite scene from the movie was when they kissed.
그 영화에서 가장 좋아하는 장면은 걔네들이 키스할 때였어.
B: Mine too! 나도 그랬어!

004

I like watching good movies on TV

TV에서 좋은 영화 보는 걸 좋아해

영화가 개봉되는 것은 come out이나 release를 쓰고 예고편은 trailer라 한다. 영화를 좋아하는 사람은 moviegoer나 a film buff[nerd]라고 하면 된다.

01

When is that movie going to come out?

그 영화 언제 나오는거야?

- I hope you'll enjoy the movie. 네가 그 영화를 좋아하길 바래.
- The trailer for that new movie looks really good. 신작영화의 예고편은 정말 좋아 보여.
- The movie's release date is July 3. 영화개봉일은 7월 3일이야.

A: When is that movie coming out? 저 영화 언제 나오는거야?
B: Its release date is October 24. 개봉일은 10월 24일이야.

02

I heard that he's a real moviegoer

걘 정말 영화팬이라고 들었어

- He is a real film buff. 걘 지독한 영화광이야.
- He is a film nerd. 걘 골수 영화팬이야.
- She is crazy about movies. 걘 영화를 무척 좋아해.

A: She knows so much about that actress. 걘 저 여배우에 대해 모르는게 없어.
B: Yes, she's a big film buff. 그래. 걘 골수 영화광이야.

03 The movie starts in 20 minutes
영화가 20분 후에 시작해

- We'd better go. The movie starts in 20 minutes.
  우린 가야 돼. 영화가 20분 후에 시작해.
- The movie is about to start. Turn off your phone please.
  영화가 시작합니다. 핸드폰을 꺼주세요.
- The theater lights are dimming. That means it's about to start.
  극장불빛이 희미해지네. 영화가 시작하려나 봐.

A: The movie is about to start. 영화가 시작하려해.
B: Let's turn off our phones. 핸드폰을 끄자.

04 I like watching good movies on TV
TV에서 좋은 영화 보는 걸 좋아해

- I watch a lot of movies on TV. 난 TV에서 많은 영화를 봐.
- There are a lot of good streaming services you can watch movies on.
  영화를 볼 수 있는 많은 스트리밍 서비스가 있어.
- OCN is a good movie channel. OCN은 좋은 영화채널이야.

A: Which streaming service is your favorite to watch movies on?
   네가 영화를 보는 좋아하는 스트리밍서비스는 뭐야?
B: I like Netflix and HBO Max. 넷플릭스와 HBO 맥스를 좋아해.

05 What's your favorite TV show?
네가 좋아하는 TV프로그램은 뭐야?

- What kind of TV programs do you like? 어떤 TV프로그램을 좋아해?
- Do you watch much TV? 넌 TV를 많이 보니?
- How often do you watch TV? 얼마나 자주 TV를 봐?

A: How often do you watch TV? 얼마나 자주 TV를 봐?
B: Probably 2 hours a day. 하루에 약 2시간 정도.

005

We can see movies on Netflix at home

우린 집에서 넷플릭스로 영화를 볼 수 있어

OTT의 최고봉은 역시 넷플릭스다. 넷플릭스에서 영화를 보다는 see movies on Netflix 혹은 단순히 watch Netfilx라고 한다. 계속해서 신작들을 올린다고 할 때는 add란 단어를 이용한다.

01 We can see movies on Netflix at home
우린 집에서 넷플릭스로 영화를 볼 수 있어

● **Netflix** is one of the most popular streaming services **in the world.**
넷플릭스는 세계에서 가장 인기있는 스트리밍서버스 중의 하나야.

● **Netflix** has a lot of very good content. 넷플릭스에는 정말 많은 내용들이 있어.

● **Netflix** is very popular **in Korea.** 넷플릭스는 한국에서 매우 인기있어.

A: Which streaming service is the most popular in Korea?
한국에서 가장 인기있는 스트리밍서비스는 뭐야?

B: Probably Netflix. 아마도 넷플릭스일거야.

02 Netflix gives us access to TV shows, movies, and documentaries 넷플릭스로 우리는 TV쇼나 영화 그리고 다큐멘터리 등을 볼 수 있어

● It's kind of like VOD. We can pick any movie on the menu.
그건 주문형비디오와 같은 종류야. 우리는 메뉴에서 아무 영화나 고를 수 있어.

● **Netflix** produces a lot of its own content. 넷플릭스는 자체 컨텐츠를 많이 제작하고 있어.

● **Squid Game was** one of the most popular shows **on Netflix last year.**
오징어 게임은 작년도 가장 히트한 넷플릭스 프로 중 하나였어.

A: Why do you like Netflix so much? 왜 그렇게 넷플릭스를 많이 좋아해?
B: It gives me access to a lot of TV shows and movies for a cheap price. 넷플릭스로 우리는 TV쇼나 영화 그리고 다큐멘터리 등을 저렴한 가격에 볼 수 있어서.

With one account, we can watch Netflix through up to 5 devices 하나의 계정으로 5개의 기기에서 넷플릭스를 시청할 수 있어

- I usually watch Netflix on a big screen TV at home. 집에서 TV 대화면을 통해 넷플릭스를 봐.
- Sometimes I'll watch Netflix on my smart phone. 때론 폰으로 넷플릭스를 보고 있어.
- I share my Netflix account with my sister. 난 넷플릭스 계정을 내 누이와 함께 공유하고 있어.

A: Who do you share your Netflix account with?
넌 넷플릭스 계정을 누구와 공유하고 있어?

B: I share it with my parents and my older brother.
부모님과 형과 함께 공유하고 있어.

Netflix adds TV shows and movies to their menu all the time 넷플릭스는 TV쇼나 영화를 계속해서 신규로 올리고 있어

- A few new movies were added to Netflix's menu today.
오늘 넷플릭스 메뉴에 신작영화가 몇 편이 추가됐어.
- My favorite movie is no longer on Netflix. 좋아하는 영화가 더 이상 넷플릭스에서 볼 수없어.

A: Why are you smiling? 왜 너는 웃고 있는거야?
B: My favorite TV series just got added to Netflix's menu.
내가 좋아하는 TV드라마가 넷플릭스에 올라와서.

I like to chill out by watching Netflix
난 넷플릭스를 보면서 머리식히는 것을 좋아해

- I relax at home by watching Netflix. 난 집에서 넷플릭스를 보면서 쉬어.
- When I feel stressed I chill out by watching my favorite Netflix series.
스트레스를 받을 때는 난 내가 좋아하는 넷플릭스 시리즈를 보면서 머리를 식혀.
- I unwind after work by watching action movies on Netflix.
난 넷플릭스에서 퇴근후 액션영화를 보면서 긴장을 풀어.

A: How do you relax when you are stressed? 스트레스를 받을 때 어떻게 긴장을 풀어?
B: I watch action movies on Netflix. 난 넷플릭스에서 액션영화를 봐.

TV 예능, 드라마

I don't like watching TV entertainment shows

난 TV 예능프로 보는 것을 좋아하지 않아

난립하는 TV예능은 TV entertainment shows라 하고, 오디션 프로그램은 singing contest programs 혹은 Talent contest TV shows, 그리고 리얼리티 쇼는 그대로 Reality TV shows라 한다.

01 I don't like watching TV entertainment shows
난 TV 예능프로 보는 것을 좋아하지 않아

- I hate watching the news. It depresses me.
  난 뉴스보는 것을 싫어해. 사람 기운빠지게 해.
- My mother loves watching Korean soap operas. 엄마는 한국 드라마 보는 것을 좋아해.
- My father doesn't enjoy watching sports on TV.
  아버지는 TV로 스포츠 보는 것을 즐겨하지 않으셔.

A: Do you like watching sports on TV? TV로 스포츠 보는 것을 좋아해?
B: No, I prefer to go watch sports live. 아니. 난 현장에 가서 직접 보는 것을 더 좋아해.

02 Many people watch entertainment shows and dramas on TV 많은 사람들이 TV에서 예능이나 드라마를 봐

- These days, reality shows are very popular on TV.
  요즘에는 리얼리티 쇼가 TV에서 인기야.
- Koreans love watching cooking shows. 한국인들은 요리프로를 보는 것을 좋아해.
- Watching ice hockey on TV is very popular in Canada.
  TV로 아이스하키를 보는게 캐나다에서는 아주 인기있어.

A: What do Canadians love watching on TV?
   캐나다 사람들은 TV로 뭐를 보는 걸 좋아해?
B: Lots of different shows but especially ice hockey.
   많은 TV쇼들, 하지만 아이스하키를 특히 좋아해.

Some dramas have become popular worldwide
일부 드라마들은 전세계적으로 유명해졌어

- Squid Game was popular all around the world. 오징어게임은 전세계적으로 인기였어.

- Netflix is watched in many different countries. 넷플릭스는 많은 나라에서 시청되고 있어.

- Korean dramas have taken off in popularity around the world.
  K-드라마는 전세계적으로 급격히 인기를 얻었어.

A: Do you enjoy watching Korean dramas? 넌 K-드라마보는 것을 즐겨해?

B: Yes, they've really taken off in popularity these days.
어, 요즘 K-드라마 인기가 부쩍 올랐어.

We enjoy many kinds of singing contest programs
우린 많은 종류의 노래경연프로를 즐겨봐

- Talent contest TV shows have become super popular.
  장기(노래)경연 TV쇼가 엄청 인기를 얻었어.

- Reality TV shows are much more common than before.
  리얼리티 TV쇼가 어느 때보다 유행해.

- I really enjoy watching sports on TV. 난 TV로 스포츠보는 것을 정말 좋아해.

A: What do you usually watch on TV? 넌 보통 TV로 뭐를 봐?

B: I enjoy talent contest shows. 난 장기(노래)경연쇼를 즐겨봐.

People are crazy to know who will win the contest
사람들은 누가 경연에서 우승할지 엄청 알고 싶어해

- People get hooked because they want to find out who will win in the end.
  사람들은 결국 누가 우승하게 될지 알고 싶어하기 때문에 깊이 빠져들고 있어.

- People love to cheer for the underdog to win. 약자가 이기기를 응원하는 것을 좋아해.

A: Did you see the final show of the talent contest?
넌 노래경연대회의 최종회를 봤어?

B: Yes, it was so unexpected. I didn't think she was going to win, did you? 어, 전혀 예상밖이었어. 난 그녀가 우승하리라고는 생각못했어. 그지?

007

I watch TV series without any subtitles

자막없이 미드를 봐

영화가 아니라 미드나 영드처럼 TV 시리즈를 본다고 할 때의 표현들로 가장 기본적인 형태는 watch+특정미드라고 하면 된다. 영어배우기에 도움이 된다고 하려면 ~a helpful way to learn real life English라고 한다.

01

TV viewers are increasing every year

TV시청하는 사람들이 매년 점점 늘어나고 있어

- **More and more people are watching TV.** 더욱 더 많은 사람들이 TV를 시청하고 있어.
- The ratings for that show **are very good.** 그 쇼의 시청률은 아주 좋아.
- That show has poor ratings. 그 쇼는 시청률이 아주 저조해.

A: What is the most popular show on TV? TV에서 가장 인기있는 프로가 뭐야?
B: I'm not sure. I'll check the ratings. 잘 모르겠어. 시청률을 확인해볼게.

02

Game of Thrones was so popular that the producers decided to make a prequel

왕좌의 게임은 너무 인기가 많아서 제작자들은 그 앞 이야기를 다룬 속편을 만들기로 결정했어

- Have you watched Game of Thrones yet? 너 왕좌의 게임 봤어?
- Game of Thrones was the most popular show on TV for a long time.
  왕좌의 게임은 오랫동안 TV에서 가장 인기있는 TV쇼였어.
- I can't wait for the Game of Thrones prequel to come out.
  난 어서 빨리 왕좌의 게임 속편이 나오기를 바라고 있어.

A: Have you ever seen Game of Thrones? 왕좌의 게임 본 적 있니?
B: Of course. I can't wait for its prequel to come out.
물론. 빨리 속편이 나오기를 기다리고 있어.

Famous TV shows include Friends, Big Bang Theory, Walking Dead, and Breaking Bad

03

유명한 미드로는 프렌즈, 빅뱅이론, 워킹데드 그리고 브레이킹배드 등이야

- **One of the most famous sitcoms is Friends.** 가장 유명한 시트콤 중의 하나는 프렌즈야.
- **There are** too many good TV shows **on these days.** 요즘 좋은 드라마가 아주 많아.
- **What are** some classic TV shows? 오래된 드라마로는 뭐가 있어?

A: X-files is my favorite TV show of all time. 엑스파일은 내가 역대 가장 좋아하는 미드야.
B: Mine too. It's a classic. 나도 그래. 오래된 드라마지.

Watching TV Dramas is a helpful way to learn real life English

03

미드를 보면 진짜 영어를 배우는데 도움이 돼

- **I like to watch TV shows to help me study English expressions.**
  난 드라마를 보는 것을 좋아하는데 영어표현들을 배우는데 도움이 돼.
- **She watches Big Bang Theory to learn useful slang.** 걔는 슬랭 배우려고 빅뱅이론을 봐.
- **Watching TV shows is good listening practice.** TV 드라마를 보면 좋은 리스닝 훈련이 돼.

A: I like watching TV shows for listening practice. 미드를 즐겨 보면서 청취훈련을 해.
B: Me too. I also watch them to learn slang. 나도 그래. 난 또한 보면서 슬랭도 배워.

Sometimes, I watch TV series without any subtitles

04

때로는 자막없이 미드를 봐

- **I often watch TV shows with subtitles to help me follow the English being used.** 난 가끔 영어가 쓰이는 것을 따라가는데 도움이 되도록 자막켜놓고 미드를 봐.
- **I first watch a show without subtitles but then I'll watch it again with subtitles.** 첨에는 자막없이 미드를 보다가 나중에 자막을 틀어놓고 다시 봐.

A: How do you learn English from watching TV shows?
넌 미드를 보면서 어떻게 영어실력을 늘리니?

B: I rewatch scenes several times to improve my listening.
리스닝을 늘리기 위해 여러 차례 장면들을 반복 시청해.

Unit 05

008

E-books are very easy to carry and read

이북은 갖고 다니면서 읽기가 아주 편해

시간이 날 때는 in one's free time, in one's spare time이라고 하면 된다. …에 관한 책을 독서하다는 read (a lot) on~, read books about~ 이라고 표현하면 된다.

01 What do you like to do in your free time?

여가 시간에는 뭐하는 것을 좋아해?

- **How do you like to spend your free time?** 여가 시간에 뭐하면서 보내는 것을 좋아해?
- **She doesn't have much free time.** 걘 여가 시간이 그리 많지 않아.
- **I need to kill some time.** 난 잠깐 동안 시간을 때워야 돼.

A: I need to kill some time while I'm waiting for my friend to write the test. 내 친구가 시험을 치루는 걸 기다리는 동안 시간을 좀 때워야 돼.
B: Let's go to a PC room! PC방으로 가자!

02 I like to read in my spare time

난 여가 시간에 독서하는 것을 좋아해

- **I've read extensively about the Korean War.**
  난 한국전쟁에 대해 광범위하게 책을 읽었어.
- **He reads a lot on American Politics.** 걘 미국정치에 관해 많은 책을 읽어.
- **She loves reading biographies.** 걘 자서전 읽는 것을 좋아해.

A: He knows so much about the Korean War. 걘 한국전쟁에 관해 박식해.
B: Yes, he's read extensively about it. 맞아. 걘 한국전쟁에 관해 많은 책을 읽었어.

03 I'm fond of reading novels
난 소설 읽는 걸 좋아해

- I read an article in the Economist about it.
  난 그에 관한 이코노미스트 지의 기사 하나를 읽었어.

- I read mysteries as a pastime. 난 여가 시간에 미스터리물을 읽어.

- I read poetry for fun. 난 재미삼아 시를 읽어.

A: I'm really fond of reading poetry. 난 정말 시읽는 것을 좋아해.
B: So am I. 나도 그래.

04 I like to read books about the art of living
난 처세술에 관한 책을 읽는 것을 좋아해

- I usually buy 2-3 books a month. 난 한 달에 2권내지는 3권의 책을 사.

- I enjoy reading self-help books. 난 자기계발서 책읽는 것은 즐겨해.

- She is always reading books on how to get rich quick.
  걘 항상 빠르게 부자가 되는 법에 관한 책을 읽어.

A: How much do you read? 책을 얼마나 읽어?
B: Usually 3-4 books a month. 보통 한 달에 3~4권 정도.

05 E-books are very easy to carry and read
이북은 갖고 다니면서 읽기가 아주 편해

- E-readers are very practical. 이북 독자들은 아주 실용적이야.

- Bookstores aren't as popular these days because of e-books.
  서점들은 이북 때문에 요즘 많이 없어.

- Do you buy many e-books? 넌 이북을 많이 사니?

A: E-books are very practical. 이북은 매우 실용적이야.
B: Yes, they don't take up any space. 맞아. 공간을 차지하지 않잖아.

009

I'll have a white wine, please
백포도주 한 잔 주세요

와인에 대해서 더 알다, 배우다는 know more about wine, learn more about wine이라고 한다. 저녁먹을 때 와인을 마신다고 하려면 I drink a glass of ~ wine이라고 하면 된다. 자기 술잔에 술을 따르는 것은 pour oneself~ 이라고 한다.

01 I want to know more about wine
난 와인에 대해 더 많이 알고 싶어

● I'm interested in learning about wine. 난 와인에 대해 배우는데 관심이 있어.

● I'd like to learn more about computers. 난 컴퓨터에 관한 더 많은 것을 배우고 싶어.

● I find making beer a fascinating topic. 난 맥주 만드는게 흥미있다고 생각해.

A: I'm interested in learning more about wine.
난 와인에 대해 더 많은 것을 배우는데 관심이 있어.

B: Let's take a class. 우리 강좌를 듣자.

02 I drink a glass of red wine when having dinner
난 저녁을 먹을 때 적포도주 한 잔을 마셔

● I enjoy a glass of wine with my dinner. 난 저녁할 때 와인 한 잔을 즐겨 마셔.

● Most French people drink wine at least once a day.
대부분의 프랑스 사람들은 적어도 하루 한 번 와인을 마셔.

● A glass of wine a day is supposed to be good for you.
하루에 와인 한 잔은 너에게 좋을거야.

A: I hear a glass of wine a day is good for you. 하루에 와인 한 잔은 몸에 좋다는데.
B: I've heard that too. 나도 그렇게 들었어.

03 I'll have a white wine, please
백포주 한 잔 주세요

● Would you like to choose a wine to go with your meal?
저녁식사에 같이 할 와인을 고르시겠어요?

● I'll have a glass of house red. 식당에서 나오는 적포도주 주세요.

● Do you have any sparkling wine here? 여기 스파클링 와인이 있나요?

A: Would you like some wine with your dinner? 저녁식사에 와인을 곁들이시겠어요?
B: Yes, we'll take a bottle of the house red. 네, 식당에서 나오는 적포도주 한 병 주세요.

04 I joined a wine club
난 와인클럽에 가입했어

● We have a small wine cellar in our home. 우리 집에는 자그마한 와인저장고가 있어.

● I am a wine connoisseur. 난 와인 전문가야.

A: I heard you joined a wine club. 너 와인클럽에 가입했다며.
B: Yes and I even made a small wine cellar in my home.
어, 그리고 집에는 자그마한 와인저장고도 있어.

05 I poured myself a glass of wine
난 와인 한 잔을 잔에 딸았어

● He was a collector of vintage wines. 걘 고급포도주를 수집하는 사람였어.

● He was a lover of fine wines and good food.
걘 고급포도주와 고급식사를 좋아하는 사람였어.

● He did a wine tour in Italy. 걘 이태리로 와인여행을 했어.

A: He is a real lover of fine wines. 걘 고급포도주를 정말 좋아하는 사람이야.
B: Yeah, he is always doing wine tours. 그래, 항상 와인여행을 하더라.

Unit 05

010 Kongbang is a workshop for making something

공방은 뭔가 만들기 위한 작업장야

뭔가 만드는 작업장인 공방은 workshop이라고 생각하면 되고, 혹은 용도에 따라서 atelier나 studio로 표현하면 된다.

01 Kongbang is a workshop for making something
공방은 뭔가 만들기 위한 작업장야

- **He enjoys** spending time in the workshop. 걘 공방에서 시간 보내는 것을 즐겨해.
- **He built that doghouse** in his workshop. 걘 공방에서 저 강아지 집을 만들었어.
- **He is teaching me** how to use a saw in the workshop.
  걘 공방에서 톱이용법을 내게 가르쳐줬어.

A: What are you doing in the workshop? 넌 공방에서 뭐하고 있는거야?
B: I'm fixing the door. 문을 고치고 있어.

02 It's also called an atelier or a studio
공방은 아틀리에 혹은 스튜디오라고도 해

- **The artist spends a lot of time** in her atelier. 그 미술가는 아틀리에에서 많은 시간을 보내.
- **I'm in the studio** working on a painting. 난 스튜디오에서 그림을 그리고 있어.
- **She bought a studio** so she can teach art. 걘 미술을 가르치려고 스튜디오를 구했어.

A: Where did you paint this? 이거 어디서 그린거야?
B: At my studio. 내 스튜디오에서.

I'd like to open a workshop for making scented candles and soap

향기나는 초와 비누를 만드는 공방을 열고 싶어

- I started golfing **last summer.** 난 지난 여름에 골프를 시작했어.

- I tried fishing **for the first time last week.** 난 지난 주에 처음으로 낚시를 해봤어.

- She is trying her hand at skiing **for the first time.** 걘 처음으로 스키를 시도해볼거야.

A: I'd like to open a workshop for making scented candles and soap.
향기나는 초와 비누를 만드는 공방을 열고 싶어.

B: Yes, it's great way to sell the products while also teaching people how to make candles, etc. 그래. 초만드는 방법을 사람들에게 알려주면서 동시에 제품을 판매하는 아주 좋은 방법이지.

011

Have you ever tried making bread?

빵을 만들어본 적 있어?

빵을 만든다는 make bread. bake the bread. 케익을 만들다 역시 bake cakes라 한다. 또한 쿠키를 만들다도 make cookies라고 하면 된다.

01 I enjoy making cookies at home
난 집에서 쿠키만드는 것을 즐겨해

- **My mother** is an excellent baker. 엄마는 아주 능숙하게 빵을 만드셔.
- **He loves** baking cakes and pies. 걘 케익과 파이 굽는 것을 좋아해.
- **She can** bake anything! 걘 뭐든지 다 구울 수 있어!

A: Can you make muffins? 너 머핀을 만들 수 있어?
B: I can bake anything. 난 뭐든 다 구울 수 있어.

02 I joined and learned how to bake the bread
난 가입해서 빵만드는 법을 배웠어

- **I enjoy** baking cakes **during my holidays.** 난 휴일마다 케익 굽는 걸 좋아해.
- **Baking cakes is harder than I imagined.** 케익을 굽는 건 생각보다 어려워.

A: I learned how to bake bread last year. 난 작년에 빵만드는 법을 배웠어.
B: Could you teach me? 나 좀 가르쳐줄 수 있어?

Have you ever tried making bread?
빵을 만들어본 적 있어?

- **Have you ever** made your own beer? 마실 맥주를 스스로 만들어본 적 있어?
- **Can you** make an omelet? 너 오믈렛 만들 수 있어?
- **My mother** makes the best French toast. 엄마는 최고의 프렌치 토스트를 만드셔.

A: Do you like French toast? 너 프렌치 토스트 좋아해?
B: Yes! My mother makes the best French toast. You have to try it.
어! 엄마는 최고의 프렌치 토스트를 만드셔. 너 한번 먹어봐야 돼.

I cut bread into slices to eat it
난 빵을 먹기 위해 얇게 썰었어

- **I prefer** thick sliced bread. 난 두껍게 썬 빵을 더 좋아해.
- **Please** cut off the bread crusts **for my sandwich.**
  샌드위치에 들어가는 빵껍데기를 걷어내 주세요.
- **I baked** 12 loaves of bread. 난 12개의 덩어리빵을 구웠어.

A: How do you want your bread sliced? 빵을 어떻게 썰어드릴까요?
B: Thin slices please. 얇게 부탁드려요.

A preservative is added to the bread to keep it
fresher longer 방부제는 빵을 더 오래 신선하게 보존하기 위해서 첨가돼

- **Food companies** use too many preservatives **in food these days.**
  요즘 식품회사들은 음식에 너무 많은 방부제를 사용해.
- **This candy** has artificial flavoring. 이 사탕에는 인공향 냄새가 나.
- **The flour** has been refined. 이 밀가루는 정제된거야.

A: I prefer unrefined flour. 난 정제되지 않은 밀가루를 더 좋아해.
B: Yes, the refined flour isn't as healthy for you.
맞아, 정제된 밀가루는 건강에 그리 좋지 않아.

012 요리 1

You're such a great cook
너 참 훌륭한 요리사야

요리학원에 등록하다는 register for a cooking class. 요리학원에 다니다는 go to a cooking class라 하면 된다. 요리학원은 cooking class 대신에 cooking school이라고도 한다. 위 문장에서 cook 대신에 cooker라고 하면 큰일남.

01 I go to a cooking class five times a month
한 달에 다섯번 요리강좌에 가

- I am learning cooking **from a private tutor.** 난 개인교사로부터 요리하는 법을 배우고 있어.
- My cooking teacher **comes to my house twice a week.**
  내 요리강사는 일주일에 두 번 집에 와.
- I registered for a cooking class. 난 요리강좌에 등록했어.

A: What are you doing on the computer? 넌 컴퓨터로 뭘 하는거야?
B: I am registering for a cooking class. 난 요리강좌에 등록하고 있어.

02 I haven't learned to cook Korean food
한국 음식 요리하는 법을 배우지 못했어

- I am going to a French cooking school. 난 프랑스 요리학교에 갈거야.
- She is teaching me how to **make Thai food.**
  걘 나에게 태국음식 만드는 법을 가르쳐주고 있어.
- I am going to India to learn how to **make curry.**
  카레만드는 법을 배우기 위해 인도에 갈거야.

A: Why are you going to Bangkok? 넌 왜 방콕에 가는거야?
B: I am going to learn how to make Thai food.
태국음식 만드는 법을 배우려고 가는거야.

03 He cooks Italian food pretty well
걘 이태리 음식요리를 잘해

- **He is** an expert bbq chef. 걘 바비큐 전문 요리사야.
- **She is really good at** cooking poultry. 걘 닭이나 오리 등의 요리를 아주 잘해.
- **He is good at** making pastas. 걘 파스타를 아주 잘 만들어.

A: What kind of food is she good at cooking? 걘 무슨 종류의 요리에 능숙한거야?
B: She is good at most kinds of food but especially Korean.
걘 모든 종류의 음식을 잘 만들지만 특히 한국음식을 잘 만들어.

04 How would you like your steak cooked?
고기를 어떻게 구워드릴까요?

- **Would you** like your meat rare? 고기를 레어로 드릴까요?
- **Do you prefer your steak** rare, medium, or well-done?
고기를 레어, 미디엄 아니면 웰던으로 해드릴까요?
- **She likes her steak** bloody rare. 걘 고기를 피가 흐르는 레어로 먹는걸 좋아해.

A: Would you like your steak rare? 고기를 레어로 해드릴까요?
B: No. Medium-rare please. 아뇨, 살짝 덥혀주세요.

05 How do you like my cooking?
내가 한 요리 괜찮아?

- **You're such a** great cook. 너 참 훌륭한 요리사야.
- **Your cooking is** terrible. 네 요리솜씨 끔찍하다.
- **I'm an** average cook. 난 평범한 요리사야.

A: How's your cooking? 네 요리솜씨는 어때?
B: It's OK. 괜찮아.

013

I like to read recipe books
난 요리책 읽는 것을 좋아해

요리를 잘한다고 하려면 be good at cooking 혹은 a gook cook이라 한다. 특별히 잘하는 음식을 말하려면 specialty란 단어를 사용하고 read recipe books는 요리책을 읽다라는 의미가 된다.

01 I'm good at cooking
난 요리를 잘 해

- **I'm a good cook.** 난 요리를 잘 해.

- **I'm good at** cooking fish. 난 생선요리를 잘 해.

- **She's really good at** cooking vegetarian dishes. 걘 특히 채식주의자 음식요리를 잘 해.

A: I'm a great cook. 난 요리를 아주 잘 해.

B: Really? That's perfect because I'm a great eater!
정말? 난 대식가인데 아주 완벽하네!

02 One of my specialties is Mexican-style food
내 전문분야 중 하나는 멕시코 식의 음식야

- **My mother's specialty is desserts.** 엄마의 전문은 디저트야.

- **What is this restaurant's specialty?** 이 식당이 잘하는 음식은 뭐예요?

- **Do you have any specialties you could cook for her birthday?**
넌 걔 생일에 맞춰 요리할 수 있는 특별한게 있어?

A: One of my mother's specialties is spaghetti.
엄마의 전문요리 중 하나는 스파게티야.

B: I've eaten your mom's spaghetti. It was fantastic.
네 엄마 스파게티 먹어봤어. 환상적이었어.

03

I like to read recipe books
난 요리책 읽는 것을 좋아해

● You can find many recipes **on the Internet.** 넌 인터넷에서 많은 요리책을 찾을 수 있어.

● **It's easy to** learn to cook **from watching YouTube videos.**
유튜브 동영상으로 요리하는 법을 쉽게 배울 수 있어.

● I found a good recipe **for fish tacos on the Internet.**
난 인터넷에서 생선타코 요리법을 찾았어.

A: Where did you learn to make this? It's delicious.
이거 만드는거 어디서 배웠어? 맛있다.

B: I got it from a YouTube cooking channel. 유튜브 요리채널에서 배운거야.

You can enjoy many kinds of foreign foods in Seoul
넌 서울에서 여러 종류의 외국음식을 즐길 수 있어

● **Seoul has a lot of** different international restaurants.
서울에는 다양한 많은 외국식당이 있어.

● **Seoul has** a very diverse restaurant scene. 서울에서는 다양한 식당의 풍경을 볼 수 있어.

● **Itaewon is** the best place to go **in Seoul for foreign foods.**
이태원은 서울에서 외국음식을 먹기 가장 좋은 곳이야.

A: What's the restaurant scene like in Seoul? 서울의 식당풍경은 어때?
B: It's very good. Lots of different ethnic restaurants are there.
아주 좋아. 많은 다양한 민족의 식당이 있어.

014 I don't feel like making dinner tonight

오늘밤은 저녁식사준비를 하기 싫어

…을 위해 저녁식사를 만들다는 make dinner for sb. 준비하다는 prepare dinner라고 한다. 요리하기 싫으면 외식을 하게 되는데 이때는 eat out. 혹은 take sb out to dinner라고 하면 된다.

01 What's for dinner tonight?
오늘 저녁은 뭐야?

- Got to make dinner **for the kids.** 아이들을 위해 저녁을 만들어야 돼.
- I am preparing dinner **now.** 난 지금 저녁식사를 준비하고 있어.
- What would you like **for dinner tonight?** 오늘 저녁에는 뭐를 먹고 싶어?

A: What are you doing? 뭐해?
B: I'm preparing dinner. 저녁식사 준비하고 있어.

02 I don't feel like making dinner tonight
오늘밤은 저녁식사준비를 하기 싫어

- Can you pick up dinner **on the way home?** 집에 오는 길에 저녁 먹을거 사올 수 있어?
- I'm tired so shall we go **out to eat tonight?** 나 힘든데 오늘밤 외식할래?
- Let's eat out **tonight.** 오늘밤은 나가서 먹자.

A: You look exhausted. Would you like to eat out tonight?
너 지쳐보인다. 오늘밤 외식하고 싶어?
B: That sounds good to me. 난 좋지.

03   I think I'm going to take you out to dinner
널 데리고 나가 저녁먹을까 하는데

- Let's go out to dinner **tonight**. 오늘밤은 나가서 저녁먹자.

- **Would you like to** go out to dinner with **me tonight?**
오늘밤 나와 함께 나가서 저녁먹을래?

- I want to take you to **my favorite restaurant.** 내가 좋아하는 식당에 널 데리고 가고 싶어.

A: Would you like to go out for dinner with me tonight?
오늘밤 나와 함께 나가서 저녁먹을래?

B: I'd love to but I'm afraid I already have plans.
그러고 싶지만 미안하지만 선약이 있어서.

04   Would you like to come for dinner?
저녁 먹으러 올래?

- **Please** come to my house for dinner **on Thursday.** 목요일에 우리집에 저녁 먹으러 와.

- **Do you want to** join me for dinner? 나와 함께 저녁 먹을래?

- **Would you like to** join me for dinner? 나와 함께 저녁 먹을래?

A: Would you like to join me for dinner? 나와 함께 저녁 먹을래?

B: I'd love to. Where are we going? 그럼 좋지. 어디로 가는데?

05   What should I order for dinner?
저녁식사로 뭐를 주문할까?

- We **should** come here **more often.** 우리는 더 자주 여기에 와야겠다.

- I go out to a sushi bar **once in a while.** 난 가끔 초밥집에 가.

- I am a **regular customer here.** 난 여기 단골이야.

A: All the waiters and waitresses know you. 모든 종업원이 너를 알고 있네.

B: Yes, I'm a regular customer here. 어. 난 여기 단골야.

015

Nothing can be delivered these days

요즘에는 배달이 안되는게 없어

포장은 take-out, get sth to go 등으로 표현하고 …을 배달시키다라고 하려면 have sth delivered라고 쓰면 된다. 배달어플 쓰는 것을 말하려면 I use the app named ~라고 한다.

01

I like to order some take-out foods on apps
어플로 포장음식을 주문하는걸 좋아해

● **Can I get it to go, or do I have to eat here?** 포장할까 아니면 여기서 먹어야 될까?

● **Do you have take out service?** 포장도 되나요?

● **I have a really great restaurant app on my phone.**
내 폰에 아주 멋진 식당 어플이 깔려 있어.

A: How do you know so many good restaurants?
넌 어떻게 그렇게 많은 좋은 식당을 알고 있는거야?

B: I have a really good restaurant app on my phone.
내 폰에 아주 멋진 식당 어플이 깔려 있어.

02

Nothing can be delivered these days
요즘에는 배달이 안되는게 없어

● **I'm having trouble finding a good delivery service.**
괜찮은 배달 서비스를 찾는데 어려움을 겪고 있어.

● **Do you know any good delivery service?** 괜찮은 배달 서비스 알고 있는데 있어?

● **I am looking for a delivery service these days.** 난 요즘 배달 서비스를 찾고 있어.

A: I'm having trouble finding a good delivery service these days.
요즘 괜찮은 배달 서비스를 찾는데 어려움을 겪고 있어.

B: Yes, nothing can be delivered it seems. 맞아, 배달 안되는게 없는 것 같아.

03 I can buy the groceries and have them delivered to my house 난 식료품을 사서 집으로 배달시킬 수 있어

- Coupang delivers a wide variety of goods to people's homes.
  쿠팡은 사람들 집으로 아주 다양한 물품을 배달해.

- There are several good delivery services you can use.
  네가 이용할 수 있는 배달 서비스 업체가 여러 개 있어.

- What's the best delivery service? 가장 좋은 배달 서비스는 뭐야?

A: I can buy groceries and have them delivered to my home.
난 식료품을 사서 집으로 배달시킬 수 있어

B: Really? What do they charge you? 정말? 배달비는 어떻게 되는데?

04 I use the app named "Baedal ui Minjok" 난 배달의 민족이라는 어플을 이용해

- I use Coupang. 난 쿠팡을 이용해.

- Which app do you use? 어느 어플을 이용해?

- Which app do you recommend? 어느 어플을 추천해?

A: Which delivery app do you recommend? 어느 배달 어플을 추천하는거야?
B: I use the app named "Baedal ui Minjok." 난 배달의 민족이라는 어플을 이용해.

05 If I order a coffee, it only takes 20 minutes to get to my home 커피를 주문하면 20분만에 집에 와

- The delivery took longer than I expected. 배달이 내 생각보다 더 오래 걸렸어.

- It took over one hour for the delivery. 배달하는데 한 시간 걸렸어.

- The delivery took less than 20 minutes. 배달은 20분도 안 걸렸어.

A: How did you like their delivery service? 걔네들 배달 서비스가 어땠어?
B: It was great. It took less than 20 minutes. 아주 좋았어. 20분도 안 걸렸어.

016 배달 2

Delivery men are expected to deliver goods ASAP

배달원은 물품을 가능한 빨리 배달해야 돼

배달원은 the delivery man, 피자를 주문하다는 order pizza to be delivered to+장소명사라고 써주면 된다. 하지만 신속배달을 경쟁적으로 다투는 바람에 많은 사고(be injured in traffic accidents)도 당하는게 현실이다.

01 The delivery man is at my door with a package
배달원이 포장물을 들고 문 앞에 왔어

- Get the door. I think I hear the delivery man. 나가봐. 배달원이 온 것 같아.
- The delivery service is here. Answer the door please.
  배달 서비스가 도착했어. 문을 열어봐.
- Why is the delivery service here? We didn't order anything.
  왜 배달 서비스가 온거지? 아무것도 주문하지 않았는데.

A: The delivery man is here with a package. 배달원이 포장물을 들고 여기 왔어.
B: Why? We didn't order anything, did we?
  왜? 우리 아무것도 주문하지 않았잖아, 그지?

02 I ordered pizza to be delivered to my apartment
난 아파트로 피자배달을 주문했어

- I ordered some fruit and vegetables from a delivery app.
  난 배달앱으로 과일과 채소를 좀 주문했어.
- I bought some clothes from Coupang and they are being delivered today.
  난 쿠팡에서 옷을 좀 샀고 오늘 배달될 예정이야.
- I ordered a sushi lunch from a delivery service and it should be here
  soon. 난 배달 서비스를 통해 점심으로 초밥을 주문했는데 곧 도착할거야.

A: What are you having for lunch? 점심으로 뭘 먹을거야?
B: I ordered pizza and it should arrive soon. 피자를 주문했고 곧 도착할거야.

03 The big increase in deliveries is causing many problems 배달이 크게 증가해서 많은 문제를 야기하고 있어

- Small businesses don't like the delivery services.
  소상공인은 배달 서비스를 좋아하지 않아.

- Delivery drivers are under too much pressure to deliver goods quickly.
  배달 라이더는 빨리 배달해야 된다는 압력을 많이 받고 있어.

A: I hear small businesses don't like the delivery services.
소상공인은 배달 서비스를 좋아하지 않는다며.

B: Yes, delivery services are hurting taking away customers from them. 맞아. 배달 서비스는 소상공인의 고객들을 빼앗아가 피해를 주고 있어.

04 Delivery men are expected to deliver goods ASAP 배달원은 물품을 가능한 빨리 배달해야 돼

- The pressure delivery drivers are under is enormous. 배달원들이 받는 압력은 엄청나.

- Delivery men work under a great deal of pressure to deliver goods on time. 배달원은 제 시간에 물품을 배달해야 되는 엄청난 압력을 받고 일하고 있어.

A: Why does he hate his job so much? 걘 자기 일을 그렇게 싫어하는거야?
B: Because delivery men are under so much pressure to deliver their goods quickly. 배달 라이더는 빨리 배달해야 된다는 압력을 많이 받고 있어서.

05 Many delivery men are injured in traffic accidents 많은 배달원들은 교통사고로 상처를 입고 있어

- Traffic accidents occur frequently for delivery companies.
  교통사고는 배달회사 때문에 종종 일어나.

- Being a delivery man is a more dangerous job than most because of the high rates of traffic accidents. 배달원이 되는 것은 높은 교통사고율 때문에 대개의 일보다 더 위험해.

A: Traffic accidents occur very frequently for delivery drivers.
교통사고가 배달 라이더에게 아주 빈번히 일어나.

B: Yes, it's a high risk job. 맞아. 그건 고위험의 일이야.

Unit 05

017

I enjoy going for an evening walk after dinner

난 저녁먹고 산보나가는 것을 좋아해

산보하다는 take a walk[stroll], go for a walk. 그리고 거리를 산책하다는 walk the street라고 하면 된다. walk me home은 집까지 걸어서 데려다주다라는 표현이다.

01 What do you say we go take a walk?
가서 산책하면 어때?

- Is it safe to walk the street **at night?** 밤에 거리를 걷는게 안전해?

- I enjoy going for an evening walk **after dinner.** 난 저녁먹고 산보나가는 것을 좋아해.

- Let's take a stroll in the park **after lunch.** 점심먹고 나서 공원을 산책하자.

A: Shall we go for a walk tonight? 오늘밤에 산책을 갈까?
B: That's a great idea. I could use the exercise. 좋은 생각이야. 나 운동 좀 해야 돼.

02 I like to take a walk
난 산책하는 걸 좋아해

- I don't want to go for a walk **in the rain.** 비맞으며 산책하고 싶지 않아.

- I'd like to go for a walk. **Do you mind?** 산책하고 싶은데, 괜찮겠어?

- Would you mind going for a walk **in the park?** 공원에 산책하러 갈래?

A: I'd like to go for a walk. Do you mind? 산책하고 싶은데, 괜찮겠어?
B: No, that sounds like a lovely idea. 물론, 아주 좋은 생각 같은데.

03 I found a four leaf clover today walking in the park!
오늘 공원에서 산책하다 네잎 클로버를 발견했어!

● I was walking through the park and I slipped and fell down.
난 공원을 산책하다가 미끄러져 넘어졌어.

● We were walking along the footpath and we saw a deer.
우리는 오솔길을 따라 걷다가 사슴을 봤어.

● We found a 10,000 won bank note while hiking at the mountain.
우리는 하이킹을 하다가 만원짜리 지폐를 발견했어.

A: I found a four leaf clover today while walking in the park.
오늘 공원에서 산책하다 네잎 클로버를 발견했어.

B: How lucky. 운이 좋으네.

04 You don't have to walk me home
집까지 안 데려다 줘도 되는데

● May I walk you to your home? 집까지 같이 걸어가 줄까요?

● I'd like to take a walk with you. 난 너와 산책을 하고 싶어.

● Would you like to take a walk with me? 나와 함께 산책을 하고 싶어?

A: You don't have to walk me home. 집까지 같이 걸어다주지 않아도 돼.
B: It's no trouble at all. 전혀 문제되지 않아.

05 Is it within walking distance?
걸어서 가도 돼?

● It's a ten minute walk from here. 여기서 걸어서 10분 거리에 있어.

● The hospital is a five minute walk from the bus stop. 병원은 정거장에서 걸어서 5분 걸려.

● There are places to enjoy walking. 산책을 즐길 곳들이 있어.

● Tell me your favorite walking course. 네가 좋아하는 산책코스를 말해봐.

A: It takes me 10 minutes to get home on foot. 걸어서 집에 오는데 10분 걸려.
B: That's an easy walk. 얼마 안 걸리네.

018

I like to go to museums on my day off

난 쉬는 날에 박물관에 가는 것을 좋아해

유화를 그리다는 paint in oils, 수채화를 그리다는 paint in watercolors, 박물관에 가다는 go to museum 또한 미술전시관에 가다는 visit art galleries로 표현하면 된다.

01 I paint in oils for fun
난 재미삼아 유화를 그려

- I paint in watercolors. 난 수채화를 그려.
- I sketch landscapes. 난 풍경을 스케치해.
- I enjoy painting still lifes. 난 정물화 그리는 것을 좋아해.

A: What kind of painting do you do? 어떤 종류의 그림을 그려?
B: I love painting still lifes. 난 정물화 그리는 것을 좋아해.

02 I like to go to art exhibitions while traveling
난 여행중에 미술관에 가는 것을 좋아해

- I like to go to museums **on my day off**. 난 쉬는 날에 박물관에 가는 것을 좋아해.
- I often visit art galleries **in my free time**. 난 여가시간에 미술전시관을 종종 가.
- I saw the Van Gough exhibition **last weekend**. 난 지난 주말에 반 고흐 전시회를 봤어.

A: Do you often go to art galleries. 넌 미술전시관에 자주 가?
B: Yes, I saw the Picasso exhibit last weekend. 어. 지난 주말에 피카소 전시회를 봤어.

03 My favorite painter is Chagall
내가 좋아하는 화가는 샤갈이야

- There's a print by Van Gogh on the wall in my office.
  내 사무실 벽에 반 고흐의 그림이 걸려있어.
- I am a big fan of Dali's work. 난 달리의 작품을 무척 좋아해.
- I really enjoy the impressionist movement. 난 인상파운동을 정말 좋아해.

A: Who are your favorite painters? 네가 좋아하는 미술가는 누구야?
B: I am a big fan of Picasso's work. 난 피카소의 작품을 무척 좋아해.

04 I enjoy learning how to write calligraphy
난 손글씨로 작품을 쓰는 법을 즐겨 배워

- Calligraphy is a beautiful art. 캘리그래피는 아름다운 미술이야.
- How long have you been learning calligraphy? 얼마동안 캘리그래피를 배웠어?
- She is taking a calligraphy course. 걘 캘리그래피 수강을 듣고 있어.

A: Calligraphy is so beautiful to look at. 캘리그래피는 보기에 참 아름다워.
B: Yes, but it's very difficult to learn. 그래, 하지만 배우기에 아주 어려워.

05 I don't draw pictures, but I like to look at them very much
난 그림을 그리지 않지만 감상하는 것을 무척 좋아해

- I have zero artistic ability. 난 미술에는 젬병이야.
- I don't have an aptitude for art. 난 미술에는 소질이 없어.
- I can't even draw stick figures. 난 졸라맨 조차 그리지 못해.

A: Are you artistic at all? 너 그림에 소질이 있어?
B: No, I have zero artistic ability. 아니. 난 미술에는 젬병이야.

019 사진

I usually photoshop the picture I took

난 찍은 사진을 보통 포토샵을 해

요즘은 보통 스마트폰을 이용해 사진을 찍고(use a smartphone to take pictures), 사진이 좋으면 ~ be impressive 혹은 ~capture the beauty of~ 라 하면 된다.

01 I use a smartphone to take pictures
난 스마트폰을 이용해 사진을 찍어

- My smartphone camera takes amazing photos.
  내 스마트폰 카메라는 멋진 사진을 찍어.

- I never use a regular camera anymore, just my smartphone.
  난 전혀 일반 카메라를 더 이상 사용하지 않아. 그냥 스마트폰을 사용해.

- I take tons of pictures every day using my smartphone.
  난 스마트폰을 이용해서 매일 많은 사진을 찍어.

A: Do you take a lot of pictures with your smartphone?
넌 스마트폰으로 사진을 많이 찍니?

B: Yes, I take tons of pictures every day with it. 어. 매일 폰으로 많은 사진을 찍어.

02 These are the pictures I took in Seoul
이건 내가 서울에서 찍은 사진들이야

- Here are the pictures from my last trip to Jeju.
  여기 이거는 내가 지난 제주여행에서 찍은 사진들이야.

- Do you have the photos from my birthday party? 내 생일파티 사진을 갖고 있어?

- These pictures were taken from the top of Lotte Tower.
  이 사진들은 롯데타워 위에서 찍은 사진들이야.

A: These pictures are fantastic. Where were they taken from?
이 사진들 아주 멋지다. 어디서 찍은 것들이야?

B: From Namsan Tower. 남산타워에서.

03   I was impressed to see the view from Namhansanseong Mountain 남한산성 산에서 본 전망이 인상적이었어

- The pictures are very impressive. 이 사진들은 매우 인상적이야.
- The pictures of the scenery around Gyungju are very beautiful.
  경주 풍경사진들은 너무 아름다워.
- Your pictures capture the beauty of Korea. 너의 사진들은 한국의 미를 포착하고 있어.

A: I was impressed to see the temple pictures.
사찰들의 사진을 보고 깊은 인상을 받았어.

B: Yes, you really captured the beauty of Korean temples.
그래, 넌 한국 사찰의 아름다움을 정말 잘 포착했어.

04   Whose pictures do you like best?
누구의 사진을 가장 좋아해?

- Who has the most skill at photography? 누가 사진에 가장 재능이 많아?
- He has an eye for taking pictures. 걘 사진 찍는데 안목이 있어.
- She has a photographer's eye. 걘 사진사의 재능이 있어.

A: Whose pictures do you like the most? 누구의 사진을 가장 좋아해?
B: My mom's. She has a real eye for photography.
엄마꺼. 엄마는 사진 찍는데 안목이 높아.

05   I usually photoshop the picture I took
난 찍은 사진을 보통 포토샵을 해

- That photo looks photoshopped. 저 사진은 포토샵을 한 것처럼 보여.
- She is very good at using photoshop. 걘 포토샵을 사용하는데 아주 능숙해.
- Your photoshop skills are very good. 너의 포토샵 기술은 정말 좋아.

A: Can you photoshop this to make me look better?
내가 더 잘 나오도록 이거 포토샵할 수 있어?

B: Sure. I have some photoshop skills. 물론. 난 포토샵을 좀 잘 다루거든.

020

My favorite composer is Schubert

내가 가장 좋아하는 작곡가는 슈베르트야

특정 작곡가의 음악을 즐겨 듣는다고 할 때는 I like listening to+작곡자라 쓰면 된다. 아니면 위에서처럼 My favorite composter is+작곡가라고 하면 된다.

01 I like listening to classical music
난 고전음악을 즐겨 들어

- I like listening to Cello music. 난 첼로 연주듣는 것을 좋아해.

- I like listening to Schubert. 난 슈베르트의 음악을 듣기 좋아해.

- I like most classical composers. 난 대부분의 고전음악가들의 음악을 좋아해.

  A: Who is your favorite classical composer? 가장 좋아하는 고전음악가는 누구야?
  B: I really love Mozart. 난 모짜르트를 정말로 좋아해.

02 My favorite composer is Schubert
내가 가장 좋아하는 작곡가는 슈베르트야

- Vivaldi is one of my favorite composers.
  비발디는 내가 가장 좋아하는 작곡자 중의 한 명이야.

- Do you enjoy listening to Beethoven? 넌 베토벤 음악 듣는 것을 좋아해?

- I enjoy modern composers like Bernstein. 난 번슈타인 같은 현대 작곡자를 좋아해.

  A: My favorite composer is Beethoven. 내가 좋아하는 작곡가는 베토벤이야.
  B: Me too. 나도 그래.

03 I heard Mozart's Requiem the other day
요전날 모짜르트의 장송곡을 들어봤어

- Chopin was just on the radio a few minutes ago.
  쇼팽음악이 몇분 전에 라디오에서 나왔어.

- I was listening to Beethoven's 9th before I went to bed last night.
  난 지난밤 잠들기 전 베토스의 9번 교향곡을 들었어.

- Listening to Mozart helps relax me. 모짜르트의 음악을 듣고 있으면 긴장이 풀려.

A: I was listening to Beethoven's 5th symphony this morning.
난 오늘 아침에 베토벤의 5번 교향곡을 들었어.

B: Yes, listening to classical music is really relaxing.
그래. 고전음악을 들으면 정말로 긴장이 풀려.

021

Andrew Lloyd Weber is a genius of our times

앤드류 로이드 웨버는 우리 시대의 천재야

우리시대의 뮤지컬을 얘기하면서 앤드류 로이드 웨버를 빼면 얘기를 할 수가 없다. 유튜브에서 …을 본다고 할 때는 I like watching~ on YouTube라고 한다. 뭔가 감동받았을 때는 I was so impressed by~라 한다.

01 I like watching The Phantom of the Opera on YouTube 난 유튜브로 오페라의 유령 보는 것을 좋아해

- Have you ever seen the musical, the Phantom of the Opera before?
  전에 뮤지컬 오페라의 유령을 본 적이 있어?

- I loved the Phantom of the Opera. 난 오페라의 유령을 좋아했었어.

- I bought the soundtrack for the Phantom of the Opera musical.
  난 뮤지컬 오페라의 유령의 사운드 트랙을 구입했어.

A: Have you ever seen the musical, the Phantom of the Opera?
뮤지컬 오페라의 유령을 본 적이 있어?

B: Yes, I even bought the soundtrack. 그럼. 난 사운드 트랙을 사기조차 했는걸.

02 I have seen The Phantom of the Opera, Les Miserable and Cats in New York 난 뉴욕에서 오페라의 유령, 레미제라블 그리고 캣츠를 봤어

- Every time I get a chance, I see a musical. 기회있을 때마다 뮤지컬을 봐.

- I really enjoy the musicals of Broadway. 난 브로드웨이의 뮤지컬을 정말 즐겨 봐.

- I have been to five different Westend musicals so far this year.
  금년에 지금까지 5편의 뮤지컬을 영국에서 봤어.

A: You're really crazy about musical theater, aren't you?
너 뮤지컬이라면 미쳐 죽지, 그렇지 않아?

B: Yes, I've seen six Broadway musicals so far this year.
어, 금년에 지금까지 브로드웨이 뮤지컬 6편을 봤어.

03
My favorite singer is Sarah Brightman
내가 좋아하는 가수는 사라 브라이트맨이야

- Who is your favorite musical star? 가장 좋아하는 뮤지컬 배우는 누구야?
- My mother's favorite musical singer **was Julie Andrews.**
  엄마가 좋아하는 뮤지컬 가수는 줄리 앤드류스야.
- I am a big fan of Broadway musical singers.
  난 브로드웨이의 뮤지컬 가수들을 아주 좋아해.

A: Who is your favorite musical star? 가장 좋아하는 뮤지컬 스타는 누구야?
B: Probably Sierra Boggess. 아마도 시에라 보게스야.

04
Andrew Lloyd Weber is a genius of our times
앤드류 로이드 웨버는 우리 시대의 천재야

- Weber is one of the greatest musical composers **ever.**
  웨버는 역사상 최고의 뮤지컬 작곡자 중의 하나야.
- What is your favorite Weber musical? 웨버의 뮤지컬 중에서 가장 좋아하는 것은 뭐야?

A: My favorite Weber Musical is Cats. How about you?
  내가 좋아하는 웨버의 뮤지컬은 캣츠야. 너는?
B: I love the Phantom of the Opera. 난 오페라의 유령을 좋아해.

05
I was so impressed by Ted Nelly's "Gethamane"
난 테드 넬리의 "게세마네"에 감명받았어

- I was deeply moved by Miranda's Hamilton.
  난 미란다의 뮤지컬 해밀턴에 깊이 감동받았어.
- The funniest musical I've ever seen was The Book of Mormon.
  본 뮤지컬 중에 가장 재미있던 것은 북 오브 몰몬였어.

A: Have you ever seen The Book of Mormon. 너 뮤지컬, 북 오브 몰몬 본 적 있어?
B: Yes, it was the funniest musical I've ever seen.
  어, 그렇게 재미있는 뮤지컬은 처음였어.

I like Na Hoon Ha's songs, in particular, "Brother, Tess"

난 나훈아, 특히 "테스형"이란 노래를 좋아해

악기를 직접 연주할 수 있을 때는 I can play the+악기명을, 특정 음악을 들어봤냐고 물어볼 때는 Did you listen to sb' song, 노래명?이라고 하면 된다. 콘서트에 직접 갈 때는 go to concerts라고 한다.

01 I play the guitar
난 기타를 쳐

- I can play the clarinet a little bit. 난 클라리넷을 조금 불 수 있어.
- I wish I could play a musical instrument. 악기를 다룰 수 있으면 좋을텐데.
- I am a good drummer. 난 드럼을 잘 쳐.

A: Can you play any musical instruments? 뭐 악기 다룰 수 있는게 있어?
B: Yes, I'm a pretty good guitarist. 어, 나 기타를 꽤 잘 쳐.

02 I like listening to Helene Fischer's songs
난 헬렌 피셔의 노래듣는 것을 좋아해

- Did you listen to Caro Emerald's song, "A Night like this?"
  카로 에메랄드의 "A Night like this"를 들어본 적 있어?
- I love to listen to Lara Fabian's Adagio. 난 라라 파비앙의 아다지오를 아주 즐겨 들어.
- I am a big fan of jazz music. 난 재즈음악을 아주 좋아해.

A: I am a big fan of K-pop. 난 K팝을 아주 좋아해.
B: Really? I don't care for it that much. 정말? 난 그렇게까지는 좋아하지 않는데.

03 The Animals' "House of the Rising Sun" is my favorite song 애니몰즈가 부른 "해뜨는 집"이 내가 좋아하는 노래야

● The song I listen to most often is probably "Stairway to Heaven."
내가 가장 자주 듣는 노래는 아마도 "Stairway to Heaven"일거야.

● These days I'm always listening to Michael Jackson's Thriller album.
요즘 난 마이클 잭슨의 스릴러 앨범을 계속 들어.

A: What's your favorite song? 가장 좋아하는 노래는 뭐야?
B: These days I'd say it's Sting's "Shape of My Heart."
요즘에는 난 스팅의 "Shape of My Heart"일거야.

04 I sometimes go to concerts
난 종종 콘서트에 가

● I go to concerts every chance I get. 난 기회가 있을 때마다 콘서트에 가.

● I see about a dozen concerts a year. 난 일년에 한 12개 정도의 콘서트에 가.

● After having kids I hardly ever see concerts. 아이 생긴 이후에는 콘서트에 가질 못하네.

A: You love going to concerts, don't you? 넌 콘서트에 가는 것을 좋아하지. 안그래?
B: Yes but after having kids I hardly ever see any.
어. 하지만 애들이 생긴 후에는 거의 못가네.

05 Folk music is not my thing
포크음악은 내 스타일이 아냐

● I like Na Hoon Ha's songs, in particular, "Brother, Tess."
난 나훈아, 특히 "테스형"이란 노래를 좋아해.

● I like drinking and singing at karaoke bars. 노래방에서 노래부르고 술마시는 것을 좋아해.

● I'm poor at singing songs. 난 노래를 잘 못불러.

A: I enjoy going to karaoke bars. 난 노래방에 가는 것을 즐겨해.
B: Me too. I usually go once a week. 나도 그래. 난 보통 일주일에 한번은 가.

023

I prefer traveling on my own to package tours

난 패키지 여행보다 혼자서 여행하는 것을 더 좋아해

패키지 여행은 package[group] tours. 혼자 여행을 할 때는 travel alone 또는 travel on my own이라고 한다. 국내여행은 domestic trips. 해외여행은 go overseas라 하면 된다.

01 I like traveling very much
난 여행다니는 것을 좋아해

- **I like visiting historic sites.** 난 역사적인 명소에 가는 것을 좋아해.
- **I really like package tours.** 난 패키지 여행을 정말 좋아해.
- **I enjoy backpacking holidays.** 난 배낭여행 휴일을 즐겨.

A: You travel a lot, don't you? 너 여행 많이 하지, 그렇지 않아?
B: Yes but only backpacking holidays. 어, 하지만 배낭여행 휴일에만.

02 We're traveling to London next week
우리는 다음주에 런던으로 여행을 가

- **I traveled to the US last month.** 난 지난달에 미국에 여행갔었어.
- **I am planning a trip to Southeast-Asia next winter.** 난 다음 겨울에 동남아로 여행을 갈 계획이야.
- **I went to South America for a trip after I graduated from university.**
  난 대학졸업 후에 남미여행을 했어.

A: You look very tan. 너 피부가 매우 타 보인다.
B: Yes, I just got back from a trip to Hawaii yesterday.
어, 어제 하와이 여행에서 돌아왔어.

I prefer traveling in Korea to traveling abroad
난 해외여행보다 국내여행을 더 좋아해

- I enjoy domestic trips **more than** going overseas.
  내 해외여행 가는 것보다 국내여행을 즐겨해.
- Traveling in Korea **is very underrated.** 한국여행은 많이 과소평가되어 있어.
- **There is a lot to see and do in Korea.** 한국에서는 볼 것도 할 것도 많아.

A: Are you taking a trip overseas this year? 금년에 해외여행할 생각이야?
B: No, I'm driving around Korea. It's very underrated.
  아니, 차로 국내일주하려고. 국내여행은 매우 과소평가되어 있어.

I prefer traveling alone to group tours
난 단체여행보다 혼자 여행하는 것을 더 좋아해

- I **prefer** traveling on my own **to** package tours.
  난 패키지 여행보다 혼자서 여행하는 것을 더 좋아해.
- Traveling by myself **is much more comfortable than** with others.
  혼자서 여행하는 것은 다른 사람들과 함께 하는 것보다 훨씬 편해.
- I enjoy traveling on my own. 난 혼자서 여행하는 것을 즐겨.

A: I enjoy traveling on my own. 난 혼자 여행하는 것을 즐겨.
B: Me too. You can do and see whatever you want.
  나도 그래. 원하는 것이 뭐든지 할 수도 있고 볼 수도 있잖아.

I prefer staying home to traveling
난 여행하는 것보다 집에 있는 것을 더 좋아해

- I **enjoy** spending my vacation at home. 난 집에서 휴가보내는 것을 좋아해.
- I'd **rather** relax at home **than** take a trip somewhere.
  어딘가로 여행가는 것보다 집에서 쉬는게 나아.

A: Are you going anywhere for your vacation? 휴가 때 어디 가?
B: No, I'm a homebody. I'll just relax at home and get some rest.
  아니, 난 집돌이야. 방콕하면서 쉴거야.

024

She's been to Europe a few times

갠 유럽을 몇차례 갔다 온 적 있어

…에 여행을 다ㅕ온 적이 있다고 표현할 때는 현재완료를 써서 I've been to+장소명사로 나타내면 된다. 아니면 I visited[went to]+장소명사 혹은 took a trip to+장소명사로 한다.

I've been to Japan once
난 일본에 한번 갔다 온 적 있어

- I've visited Vietnam once. 난 한번 베트남에 갔다 온 적 있어.

- She's been to Europe a few times. 걘 유럽을 몇차례 갔다 온 적 있어.

- I've only been to Jeju once when I was in high school.
  난 고등학교 때 딱 한번 제주도에 가본 적이 있어.

  A: What's Jeju like? 제주도는 어때?
  B: Sorry. I can't really say. I've only been there once and it was when I was 5 years old. 미안. 잘몰라서. 5살 때 딱 한번 가본 적이 있을 뿐이야.

I visited Bali with my family in June
난 6월에 가족과 함께 발리에 갔었어

- I went to Sapporo on a ski holiday last January.
  난 지난 1월에 삿포로에 스키휴가를 갔었어.

- My family took a trip to France last Christmas.
  우리 가족은 지난 성탄절에 프랑스에 여행갔었어.

- She is going to take a trip to China this year. 걘 금년에 중국여행을 갈거야.

  A: How was your summer? 여름 어땠어?
  B: Great. My family and I took a trip to Italy.
  아주 좋았어. 가족들과 함께 이태리를 여행했어.

03 I haven't been overseas yet
난 아직 해외에 나가본 적이 없어

- I've never been abroad. 난 해외에 가본 적이 없어.
- I've only traveled domestically. 난 국내여행만을 했어.
- I am still waiting to take my first trip abroad. 난 아직 첫 해외여행하기를 기다리고 있어.

A: Have you ever been to Europe? 유럽에 가본 적이 있어?
B: No, I've never been abroad before. 아니. 난 아직 해외에 나가본 적이 없어.

04 I hope to see Rio de Janeiro's Carnival someday
난 언젠가 리오데자네이로의 카니발을 보길 바래

- I like going to spas. 난 스파에 가는 것을 좋아해.
- I want to go on a trip to Spain. 난 스페인 여행을 하고 싶어.
- She is doing a tour of Japan. 걘 일본여행을 하고 있어.

A: I hope to see the Eiffel Tower someday. 난 언젠가 에펠탑을 보기를 바래.
B: Why don't you go this year? 금년에 가보는게 어때?

05 Are you all set for your trip?
여행 갈 준비됐어?

- I'm itching to go traveling again. 난 다시 여행을 하고 싶어 안달이 나.
- I can't wait to get to Thailand. 난 어서 빨리 태국에 가고 싶어.
- I'm dying to go on a trip. 난 여행을 하고 싶어 죽겠어.

A: Six more weeks until vacation. 휴가 때까지 6주가 더 남았네.
B: I know! I'm itching to take a trip. 알아! 여행하고 싶어 죽겠는데.

What did you enjoy most about Tokyo?

도쿄여행에서 가장 좋았던게 뭐였어?

여행이나 휴가계획을 짤 때는 plan a trip to~. organize a vacation to~라 하고, 즐거운 여행을 보냈다고 하려면 My trip to+장소명사+was so fascinating[went very well]이라고 표현해주면 된다.

01 Our family is planning a trip to the Caribbean
우리 가족은 캐리비언으로 여행을 계획하고 있어

● We are talking about taking a trip to Australia. 우리는 호주여행에 대해 얘기하고 있어.

● We are thinking about a holiday in England. 우리는 영국에서 휴가를 보낼 생각이야.

● We are organizing a vacation to Spain. 우리는 스페인에서의 휴가계획을 짜고 있어.

A: We are thinking about taking a trip to Australia.
우리는 호주로 여행을 갈까 생각 중이야.

B: I've never been there but it sounds beautiful. 난 가본 적이 없지만 멋질 것 같아.

02 Will you be attending the trip to Mexico this spring? 이번 봄에 멕시코 여행에 같이 갈거야?

● I heard you are going to Cuba this summer. 이번 여름에 쿠바에 갈거라며.

● Are you taking a trip to Kenya? 케냐여행을 할거야?

● Where are you thinking of going for your summer break?
여름휴가 때 어디로 갈 생각이야?

A: Are you taking a trip to Kenya? 케냐여행을 할거야?
B: Yes, I am doing a safari tour. 어, 사파리여행을 할거야.

03 My trip to London was so fascinating
런던여행은 너무 환상적이었어

- My trip to **Africa went very well.** 아프리카여행은 아주 잘 됐어.
- I had a fantastic time in **New York.** 난 뉴욕에서 멋진 시간을 보냈어.
- Their trip to Jeju **was amazing.** 걔네들 제주여행은 아주 멋졌어.

A: How was Africa? 아프리카는 어땠어?
B: It was amazing. 환상적이었어.

04 I can't afford to go on the ski trip next month
난 담달에 스키여행을 갈 여력이 안돼

- I don't have enough money saved for a vacation trip this year.
난 금년휴가에 여행갈 돈을 충분히 마련하지 못했어.
- I want to travel **but airfares are too expensive at the moment.**
여행을 하고 싶지만 항공료가 현재 너무 비싸.
- I would love to go to **Paris with you but I'm broke at the moment.**
난 너와 함께 파리에 가고 싶지만 지금 빈털터리야.

A: Let's go to London this year. 금년에 런던에 가자.
B: I'd love to but I'm broke at the moment. 그러고 싶지만 지금 빈털터리야.

05 What was the highlight of your trip?
여행에서 가장 좋았던게 뭐였어?

- What did you enjoy most **about Tokyo?** 도쿄여행에서 가장 좋았던게 뭐였어?
- What was your favorite part of being in Spain?
스페인에 있으면서 가장 좋았던 부분이 뭐였어?
- What was the best thing **about Barcelona?** 바르셀로나에서 가장 좋았던 것은 뭐였어?

A: What did you enjoy most about Rome? 로마에서 가장 좋았던 것은 뭐였어?
B: The old buildings were so beautiful. 오래된 빌딩들이 아주 아름다웠어.

꽃키우기

I enjoy seeing autumn leaves in November

난 11월에 단풍보는 것을 아주 좋아해

꽃을 가꾸거나 정원을 가꾸는(gardening) 사람, 즉 원예에 재능이 있는 사람은 a green thumb이라고 한다. 정원에서 채소를 재배하는 것은 grow vegetables in the garden이라고 하면 된다.

01 My favorite pastime is gardening
난 여가시간에 정원가꾸는 것을 좋아해

● **My father loves** working in his garden. 아버지는 정원에서 일하는 것을 좋아하셔.

● **My mother has a real green thumb.** 엄마는 원예에 정말 재능이 있어.

● **I really** enjoy growing vegetables and plants. 난 채소나 식물 기르는 것을 정말 좋아해.

A: My father loves working in the garden. 아버지는 정원에서 일하는 것을 좋아하셔.
B: He has a green thumb I guess? 원예에 재주가 많으신가보군?

02 I grow vegetables in the garden
난 정원에 채소를 길러

● **I planted roses in the garden the other day.** 요전날 난 정원에 장미를 심었어.

● **I am growing sweet potatoes this year.** 난 금년에 고구마를 재배하고 있어.

● **My father is trying to** grow sunflowers for the first time.
아버지는 처음으로 해바라기를 기르시려고 해.

A: What are you planting in your garden this year? 금년에 정원에 뭘 심을거야?
B: Lettuce, tomatoes, and carrots. 상추, 토마토 그리고 당근.

03 I enjoy seeing autumn leaves in November
난 11월에 단풍보는 것을 아주 좋아해

● The changing colors of the leaves in Autumn is one of my favorite things.
단풍잎의 색변화는 내가 아주 좋아하는 것 중의 하나야.

● I love the colors of autumn. 난 가을색을 아주 좋아해.

● The cherry blossoms in spring **are beautiful.** 봄의 벚꽃은 아름다워.

A: Why do you love autumn so much? 넌 왜 가을을 그렇게 좋아해?

B: The colors of the autumn leaves are so beautiful. 단풍색은 정말이지 아름다워.

04 I like roses best and then lilies
난 장미를 가장 좋아하고 다음에는 백합을 좋아해

Unit 05

● **What are** your favorite flowers? 좋아하는 꽃은 뭐야?

● **I always** buy my mother lilacs for parent's day.
난 부모님의 날에 엄마에게 라일락을 사드려.

● I love daisies. 난 데이지 꽃을 아주 좋아해.

A: I love daisies. 난 데이지 꽃을 아주 좋아해.

B: I do too, but my favorite are yellow roses.
나도 그래 하지만 내가 좋아하는 건 노란 장미야.

05 Watering the plants is my job at home
식물에 물을 주는게 집에서의 내가 맡은 일이야

● **The yard** is overgrown with weeds. 마당에 잡초가 너무 무성하게 자랐어.

● I really feel comfortable in a botanical garden. 난 식물원에서 정말 맘이 편해져.

● **I need to** weed the garden. 난 정원의 잡초를 뽑아야 돼.

A: The garden is overgrown with weeds. 정원에 잡초가 무성하게 자랐어.

B: Yes, I'll weed it today. 그래. 내가 오늘 정원의 잡초를 뽑을게.

027

I like to buy things on the Internet

난 인터넷으로 물건사는 것을 좋아해

쇼핑하러가다는 go shopping. 인터넷으로 물건을 사는 것은 buy things on the Internet이라고 한다. 물건을 안사고 눈으로만 쇼핑하는 것은 window shopping 이란 단어를 사용하면 된다.

01 I'm going shopping today
오늘 나 쇼핑하러 간다

- I enjoy window-shopping **on weekends.** 난 주말마다 윈도우쇼핑을 즐겨해.
- **I'm going to** enjoy shopping in New York. 난 뉴욕에서 쇼핑을 즐길거야.
- **I'd like to** go shopping for **my kids.** 애들한테 줄 것을 좀 사러 가고 싶어.

A: How often do you go shopping in Seoul? 서울에서 얼마나 자주 쇼핑을 해?
B: A few times a week. 일주일에 두세번.

02 I like to buy things on the Internet
난 인터넷으로 물건사는 것을 좋아해

- **I like to** get things at a flea market. 난 벼룩시장에서 물건들을 사는 것을 좋아해.
- **I have a tendency to** buy things on impulse. 난 충동적으로 물품을 사는 경향이 있어.
- **Shopping is** one of my stress reducers. 쇼핑은 스트레스를 완화시켜주는 것 중의 하나야.

A: You seem like an impulse shopper. 넌 충동적으로 쇼핑하는 사람같아.
B: Yes, because shopping is one of my stress reducers.
맞아. 쇼핑하면 스트레스가 완화되거든.

03 I bought this chair for 300,000 won
난 이 의자를 30만원에 샀어

- Why don't we head over to the mall and do some shopping?
  쇼핑센터에 가서 쇼핑이나 하자.

- I'll buy you something at the duty free shop, if you want.
  필요하면 면세점에서 뭐 좀 사올게.

- I got a really good deal on this sofa. 난 이 소파를 정말 좋은 가격에 샀어.

A: Why don't we head over to the department store and do some shopping? 쇼핑센터에 가서 쇼핑이나 하자.

B: Sure. I hear there are some good deals on clothing this week.
그래. 이번주에 의류를 싸게 판다며.

04 The thing I want most now is my own car
내가 지금 가장 원하는 것은 내 소유의 자동차야

- Nothing in this shop attracts me. 이 가게엔 마음에 드는게 없네.

- Nothing is catching my eye today. 오늘은 눈에 들어오는게 아무것도 없네.

- I really need some new pants. 난 좀 새로운 바지가 필요해.

A: Nothing in this shop attracts me. 이 가게엔 마음에 드는게 없네.

B: Yes, nothing is catching my eye either. 그래. 내 눈에도 확 들어오는게 아무것도 없어.

05 Almost all of my clothes were selected by my wife
내 옷의 거의 모든 것은 다 아내가 고른거야

- I'm not very good at shopping. 난 쇼핑하는데 서툴러.

- My wife has a good eye for clothes shopping. 내 아내는 옷을 사는데 안목이 있어.

- My brother is good at bargain hunting. 내 형은 싼 물건 찾는 것을 잘해.

A: That only cost you 20,000 won? That's so cheap!
저걸 겨우 2만원에 샀다구? 거저네!

B: Yes, I am a good bargain hunter. 어, 난 싼 물건을 찾는 것을 잘해.

028

Have you ever collected anything before?

전에 뭐 수집해본 적 있어?

뭔가 수집한다고 할 때는 전형적으로 collect, collection이란 단어를 사용한다. 수집한 것을 보여준다고 할 때는 show my collection이라고 하고 골동품 수집가는 an antique collector라 하면 된다.

01 I collect different kinds of buttons
난 다양한 종류의 버튼을 수집해

- I like to buy things I can get cheap. 난 싸게 구할 수 있는 물건을 사는 것을 좋아해.

- I like to collect things I can get for free.
  난 공짜로 얻을 수 있는 물건들을 수집하는 걸 좋아해.

- I'm good at finding cheap and inexpensive things.
  난 싸고 저렴한 물건 찾는 것을 잘해.

A: My wife is good at finding things for cheap. 아내는 싼 물건들을 찾는 것을 잘해.
B: I like to buy things I can get cheap too.
   나도 역시 싸게 구할 수 있는 물건을 사는 것을 좋아해.

02 I'm going to continue collecting
난 계속해서 수집을 할거야

- My wife tolerates my hobby of collecting stamps.
  아내는 내가 우표수집하는 취미를 참고 있어.

- Have you ever collected anything before? 전에 뭐 수집해본 적 있어?

- My sister collects teddy bears. 내 여동생은 테디곰인형을 수집해.

A: My sister has been collecting teddy bears since she was a child.
   내 여동생은 어렸을 때부터 테디곰인형을 수집해왔어.

B: How many does she have in her collection now?
   지금까지 수집한게 몇 개야?

Do you collect anything interesting?
넌 뭐 좀 흥미로운 것을 수집하니?

- I like to collect coins from different countries.
  난 다양한 여러나라의 동전을 수집하는 것을 좋아해.

- Do you have any collections of anything? 너 뭔가 수집해온게 있어?

- Are you an antique collector? 넌 골동품을 수집하니?

A: That's a beautiful bronze statue. 저건 아름다운 동상이야.
B: Yes, I am a collector of bronzes. 그래. 난 동상을 수집하고 있어.

I'll show you my collection any time
언제 한번 내 수집한 것을 보여줄게

- Would you like to see my stamp collection? 내 우표수집한 것을 볼래?

- Has she ever showed you her doll collection?
  걔가 인형수집한 것을 너에게 보여준 적 있어?

- He has a small collection of classic movie posters.
  걘 많지 않지만 고전영화포스터 수집물이 있어.

A: Would you like to see my stamp collection? 내 우표수집한 것을 볼래?
B: Yes please! 어 어서!

I'm going to sell part of my collection
내 수집물의 일부를 팔거야

- He has a big comic book collection. 걘 만화책을 엄청 수집했어.

- Her antique collection is worth a lot of money.
  그녀의 골동품 수집물은 고액의 가치가 있어.

- She collects toy cars. 그녀는 장난감 차를 수집해.

A: She likes collecting toy cars. 그녀는 장난감 차를 수집하는 것을 좋아해.
B: That's unusual for a girl. 여자애로는 드문 일이네.

029

I sold my shares in that company's stock

저 회사 주식을 팔았어

주식을 하다는 play the stock market이라고 하고 stock은 전체 주식을, share 는 개별 주식을 말한다는 점을 구분해야 한다. 사고 팔 때는 기본단어인 buy와 sell이 란 동사를 사용하면 된다.

01

I should start buying stock in the company now
이제 그 회사 주식을 사두기 시작해야겠네

- The stock price **has gone up a lot these days**. 요즘 주가가 많이 올랐어.
- I sold my shares **in that company's stock**. 저 회사 주식을 팔았어.
- I am thinking of **investing in that company**. 난 저 회사에 투자할 생각이야.

A: I should start buying stock in that company now.
이제 그 회사 주식을 사두기 시작해야겠네.

B: Yes, I hear it is going to go up soon. 그래, 곧 상승할거라던데.

02

I wish I had bought some stock in their company
그 회사 주식을 좀 사두는건데

- I should have sold my stock **last week**. 난 지난 주에 주식을 팔아야 했는데.
- I wish I **hadn't bought that stock**. 내가 그 주식을 사지 않았더라면 좋았을텐데.
- I shouldn't have waited so long to **sell my stock**.
  내 주식을 파는데 그렇게 오래 기다리는게 아니었는데.

A: You look sad. 너 슬퍼보인다.

B: Yes, I wish I had bought some stock in their company. I would be rich now if I had done that.
그 회사 주식을 좀 사두는건데. 그랬더라면 지금쯤 부자가 되어있을텐데.

03 Make sure you keep an eye on that stock
그 주식을 확실하게 잘 지켜보도록 해

- Did you ever look into that stock I told you about?
  내가 너한테 말했던 그 주식 잘 살펴봤니?

- That stock was recommended to me by a smart investor.
  영리한 한 투자자로부터 저 주식을 추천받았어.

- I strongly suggest you buy some of that company's stock.
  저 회사의 주식 좀 사라고 네게 강력히 추천해.

A: Did you ever look into that stock I told you about?
내가 너한테 말했던 그 주식 잘 살펴봤니?

B: I'm keeping an eye on it but haven't decided yet.
지켜보고는 있지만 아직 결정을 하지 못했어.

04 I invested a lot of money in the market
난 주식에 돈을 엄청 투자했어

- The stock market has dropped by 30 points since it opened this morning.
  주식 시장이 오늘 아침 개장한 이래 30포인트 떨어졌어.

- Do you think the stock will bounce back? 주식이 반등할 것 같아?

- I lost everything I invested in that company. 저 회사에 투자한 모든 것을 잃었어.

A: Do you think the stock will bounce back? 주식이 반등할 것 같아?
B: I hope so or I am going to lose a lot of money. 그래야지 아님 많은 돈을 잃게 될거야.

05 Did they go public with their stock?
걔네들 회사 상장했니?

- That company is going public next month. 저 회사는 담달에 주식을 상장할거야.

- He is going to take his company public soon. 걘 자기 회사를 곧 상장할거야.

- They aren't going public yet. 걔네들은 아직 비상장이야.

A: They are going public with their stock soon. 걔네들은 곧 주식 상장할거야.
B: As soon as they do, I'll buy some shares. 상장하면 바로 난 주식 조금을 살거야.

주식투자 2

030

Do you use e-trade?

넌 전자거래를 하니?

시대가 바뀌어서 객장에서 하는 사람들도 있지만, 핸드폰 등을 통해 전자거래 (e-trade)를 하는 사람들이 많아졌다. 그리고 play the stock market을 하다가 돈을 잃었다고 할 때는 lose를 사용한다.

01

I'm now using e-trade

지금은 전자거래를 하고 있어

● How do you buy and sell stock? 주식을 어떻게 사고 팔아?

● What app are you using to play the stock market? 주식을 할 때 어떤 어플을 사용해?

● Do you use e-trade? 넌 전자거래를 하니?

A: How do you buy and sell stocks? 주식을 어떻게 사고 팔아?
B: I use e-trade. 전자거래를 하고 있어.

02

That stock is a sure thing

저 주식은 확실해

● You can't miss with that stock. 저 주식이라면 손해보지 않을거야.

● That stock is foolproof. 저 주식은 실패할 염려가 없어.

● I guarantee you that stock will go up. 내 장담하는데 저 주식은 올라갈거야.

A: You really think I should buy that stock? 내가 저 주식을 사야 된다고 정말 생각해?
B: Yes, it's foolproof. 어. 실패할 염려가 없어.

03 Are you sure about that stock?
저 주식에 관해서 확신해?

- Are you certain the price will go up? 주가가 올라갈거라 확신해?
- How sure are you about the stock? 저 주식에 대해 어떻게 확신해?
- How confident are you in that stock? 어떻게 저 주식에 대해 확신하는거야?

A: You need to buy that stock today! 너 오늘 저 주식 사야 돼!
B: Really? How certain are you the price will go up?
정말? 저 주식이 오를거라는 것을 어떻게 확신해?

04 He put all of his money in the stock market
걔는 주식에 갖은 돈을 다 투자했어

- I put everything I had into that stock. 난 그 주식에 갖고 있던 모든 것을 몰빵했어.
- She put all of her savings into the stock market. 걘 주식에 저축한 돈 모두를 투자했어.
- All of his money is in the stock market. 걔 돈의 전부가 주식에 들어있어.

A: Did you hear the news about Joe? 너 조에 대한 뉴스를 들었어?
B: Yes, he put everything he had in the stock market. That's so risky.
어, 걘 주식에 갖고 있던 모든 것을 몰빵했어. 아주 위험하지.

05 I put my money on the line with that stock and I lost it all
그 주식에 무리하게 투자해서 돈을 다 날려버렸어

- I lost everything I had in the stock market. 주식하다 갖고 있던 모든 것을 잃었어.
- He lost all his money when the stock market crashed.
걘 주식시장이 폭락했을 때 모든 돈을 잃었어.
- Everything I had was lost when the price of the stock dropped.
주가가 떨어졌을 때 난 갖고 있던 모든 것을 잃었어.

A: He lost everything he had in the stock market.
걘 주식하다 갖고 있던 모든 것을 잃었어.
B: Yes, you should never put all your eggs in one basket.
어, 절대로 몰빵을 해서는 안돼.

031

We sent relief goods to the flooded region

우리는 수해지역에 구호품을 보냈어

자원봉사활동은 volunteer activities. 자원봉사를 하다는 volunteer를 동사로 사용하면 된다. 참고로 수화는 sign language, 좀 어렵지만 점자는 braille이라고 한다는 점도 알아둔다.

01 I'm interested in volunteer activities
난 자원봉사활동에 관심을 갖고 있어

- I do volunteer work at an elementary school.
  난 한 초등학교에서 자원봉사일을 하고 있어.

- I am a member of a volunteer group in my city.
  난 내가 살고 있는 도시의 자원봉사단체 회원이야.

- I am a volunteer at the Senior Home. 난 양로원에서 자원봉사하고 있어.

A: I hear you do a lot of volunteer work. 너 자원봉사 일을 많이 한다며.
B: Yes, I do volunteer work at an elementary school and at the children's hospital. 어, 초등학교와 어린이 병원에서 자원봉사일을 하고 있어.

02 I help children from abroad study Korean
난 외국아이들이 한국어를 배우는데 도움을 줘

- I help walk dogs at the animal rescue shelter.
  난 동물보호소에서 강아지들 산보시키는 일을 도와.

- I volunteer as a Sunday School teacher at my church.
  난 내가 다니는 교회에서 주일학교교사 봉사활동을 해.

- She volunteers every weekend at an orphanage.
  갠 고아원에서 매 주말 자원봉사를 해.

A: What are you doing this weekend? 이번 주말에 뭐할거야?
B: I volunteer every Saturday at the animal rescue shelter.
난 매주 토요일마다 동물보호소에게 자원봉사해.

I can talk by sign language
난 수화로 얘기를 할 수 있어

- **I teach sign language as a volunteer.** 난 자원봉사자로 수화를 가르치고 있어.
- **Can you use sign language?** 수화를 할 수 있어?
- **I can read braille.** 난 점자를 읽을 수 있어.

A: You know sign language? 넌 수화알아?
B: Yes, I learned it so I could be a volunteer. 어, 배웠고 자원봉사자가 될 수 있어.

I take care of elderly people
난 어르신들을 돌보고 있어

- **I visit old peoples' homes.** 난 어르신 집에 방문해.
- **We serve meals for the homeless.** 우리는 집없는 분들을 위해 식사를 제공해.
- **I do volunteer work at a nursing home.** 요양원에서 자원봉사일을 하고 있어.

A: Let's meet this Sunday. 이번 일요일에 만나자.
B: Sorry, I do volunteer work at a nursing home every Sunday.
미안, 나 매주 일요일마다 요양원에서 자원봉사일을 해.

We sent relief goods to the flooded region
우리는 수해지역에 구호품을 보냈어

- **We raised money for the physically handicapped.**
우리는 장애인들을 위해 쓸 돈을 모았어.
- **We started a GoFundMe page to help raise money for the earthquake victims.**
우리는 지진 피해자들을 위해 모금하기 위해 클라우드 소싱 자선단체인 GoFundMe 페이지를 시작했어.
- **I am going to Cambodia to help build a hospital.**
난 캄보디아에 가서 병원짓는 일을 도울거야.

A: We sent relief goods to the earthquake region.
우리는 지진이 난 지역에 구호품을 보냈어.

B: That's so wonderful of you. Can I donate some money to help?
참 훌륭하구나. 도움이 되도록 돈 좀 기부할까?

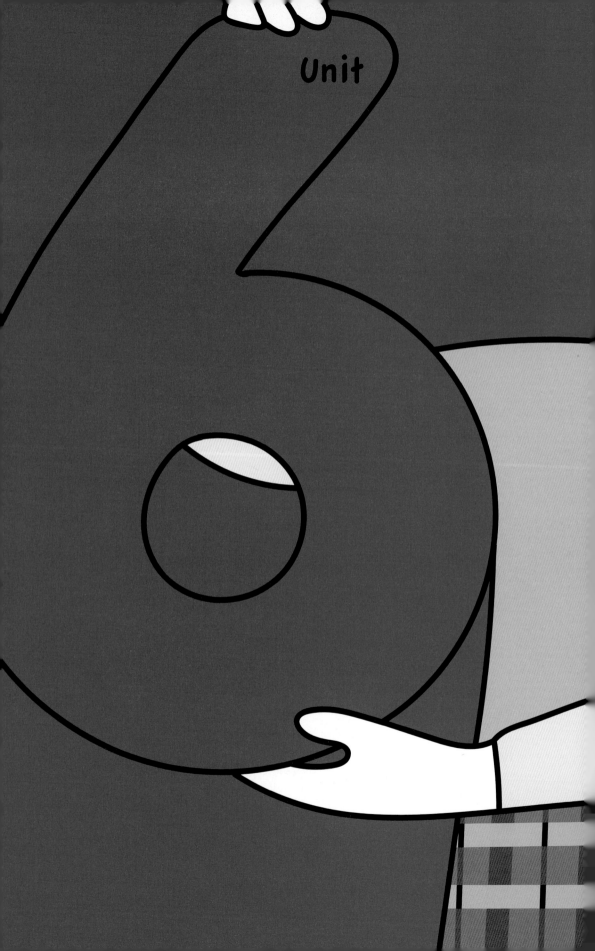

Unit

6

인터넷/ SNS

001

You need to log on to our home page

넌 우리 홈페이지에 접속해야 돼

로그인으로 거의 우리말화된 log를 사용하여 log on하게 되면 접속하다라는 의미로 have access to~의 의미가 된다. 인터넷에 연결되었다고 할 때는 be connected to the Internet이라고 한다.

01 You need to log on to our home page
넌 우리 홈페이지에 접속해야 돼

- I'm often unable to log on to the system. 난 가끔 시스템에 연결이 안돼.
- I am having trouble logging on. 컴퓨터를 연결하여 사용하는데 어려움을 겪어.
- She got logged on without any problems. 걘 아무 문제없이 연결됐어.

A: I am having trouble logging on to the system.
난 시스템에 연결하는데 어려움을 겪어.

B: Are you sure the password is correct? 비번이 맞는지 확인했어?

02 What time did you log in?
몇시에 로그인한거야?

- Please log in after 9am. 오전 9시 이후에 로그인 하세요.
- Are you logged in yet? 벌써 로그인 했어?
- I logged in at 10am. 난 오전 10시에 로그인했어.

A: What time did you log in? 몇시에 로그인 한거야?
B: Just before 9am. 오전 9시 바로 전에.

My computer is now connected to the Internet
내 컴퓨터가 이제 인터넷에 연결됐어

● My internet connection isn't very good. 내 인터넷 연결이 그리 썩 좋지 않아.

● How did you get connected to the internet in this area?
이 지역에서 어떻게 인터넷에 연결했어?

● The internet connection is very good here. 인터넷 연결이 여기는 아주 좋아.

A: Why didn't you email me? 왜 내게 이멜을 보내지 않은거야?
B: I tried but my internet connection was very poor.
보낼려고 했는데 인터넷 연결이 잘 안되었어.

He is going online this morning
걘 오늘 아침에 온라인에 접속할거야

● I'm going to go back online in one hour. 난 한 시간후에 다시 온라인 접속할거야.

● We went back online a few minutes ago. 우리 몇분 전에 다시 온라인으로 접속됐어.

● What time are you going online? 몇시에 온라인 접속할거야?

A: He is going to go back online soon. 걘 곧 다시 온라인에 접속할거야.
B: What time exactly? 정확히 몇시에?

I have to have access to a computer before dinner
난 저녁먹기 전에 컴퓨터에 접속해야 돼

● Do you have access to Wi-Fi at your school? 너는 학교에서 와이파이에 접속하니?

● I have access to a laptop for my job. 난 일을 하려고 노트북으로 접속했어.

● He didn't have access to the Internet when he was in Africa.
걘 아프리카에 있을 때 인터넷에 접속을 하지 못했어.

A: I have to have access to the Internet. 난 인터넷에 접속해야 돼.
B: Don't worry. The hotel I booked has Internet access.
걱정마. 내가 예약한 호텔에서는 인터넷 사용이 가능해.

Unit 06

002

The kids spend a lot of time surfing the Internet
아이들은 인터넷을 검색하면서 많은 시간을 보내

인터넷 검색하다는 browse, surf the Internet을 사용하며, 검색하면서 뭔가 찾고 있을 때는 do some research on the Internet이라고 한다. '사전에서 찾다'라는 의미인 look up을 쓰기도 한다.

01

I usually spend time browsing the Internet
난 보통 인터넷을 검색하면서 시간을 보내

- The kids spend a lot of time surfing the Internet.
  아이들은 인터넷을 검색하면서 많은 시간을 보내.

- I spent a few hours surfing YouTube while waiting at the airport.
  난 공항에서 기다리는 동안 몇시간 유튜브를 검색하면서 시간을 보냈어.

- I was channel surfing on my TV but nothing good was on.
  난 TV에서 채널을 이리저리 돌려봤는데 좋은거 하는데가 없었어.

A: I was browsing different websites looking for hotels.
난 호텔을 찾으면서 여러 사이트를 검색했어.

B: Did you find any good ones? 뭐 좀 좋은 호텔 찾았어?

02

He's doing some research on the Internet
걘 인터넷으로 뭔가 찾고 있어

- She's doing research on the Internet. 걘 인터넷으로 검색하고 있어.

- I was searching the Internet looking for cheap shoes.
  난 싼 구두를 찾느라 인터넷을 뒤졌어.

- I googled "discount hotels in Tokyo" and found a few good ones.
  난 "도쿄의 호텔할인"을 구글검색해서 몇몇 좋은 호텔을 찾았어.

A: What is she doing right now? 걔 지금 뭐하고 있어?
B: She's doing research on the Internet. 인터넷으로 뭔가 찾고 있어.

03 I found it on the Internet
인터넷으로 그걸 찾았어

- Is it on the internet? 그게 인터넷에 있어?

- He said he found out how to do it on the internet.
  걘 그거 어떻게 하는지 인터넷에서 알아냈다고 말했어.

- I learned how to cook using the Internet. 인터넷으로 요리하는 법을 배웠어.

A: How did you get the address? 이 주소는 어떻게 구한거야?
B: I found it on the Internet. 인터넷에서 찾았어.

04 You should just look it up on the Internet
인터넷으로 그것을 찾아보면 돼

- I didn't know that word so I looked it up in a dictionary.
  난 그 단어를 몰라서 사전에서 찾아봤어.

- I looked up the story in Google News. 난 구글뉴스에서 그 기사를 찾았어.

- I tried to look him up on Facebook but couldn't find him.
  난 페이스북으로 걔를 찾으려고 했지만 찾을 수가 없었어.

A: If you can't find it in the training manual, just look up how to do it
   on the Internet. 훈련매뉴얼에서 그것을 찾을 수 없으면, 인터넷으로 어떻게 그걸 하는지 찾아봐.
B: I'll do that. 그렇게 할게.

05 He is looking at a site on the internet
걘 인터넷으로 한 사이트를 보고 있어

- I was looking at the restaurant's website but it was a bit confusing.
  난 그 식당의 사이트를 보고 있는데 좀 헷갈렸어.

- I checked out your website today. 오늘 귀사의 사이트를 확인했습니다.

- Your company's website looks great. 네 회사의 사이트는 아주 좋아.

A: Did you take a look at my company's website today?
   오늘 내 회사의 사이트를 둘러보셨나요?

B: Yes, I checked it out and it looks great. 예. 확인했는데 아주 좋아보였습니다.

My computer shut down this evening

내 컴퓨터가 오늘 저녁 고장났어

컴퓨터가 고장났을 때는 be down, shut down 혹은 isn't working 등의 표현을 쓴다. 또한 crash란 표현을 사용해도 되고 컴퓨터가 정지되어서 커서가 먹지 않을 때는 freeze up, be frozen을 사용하면 된다.

01 He shut down his computer
걔 컴퓨터를 껐어

- **My computer shut down this evening.** 내 컴퓨터가 오늘 저녁 고장났어.
- **My computer is down.** 내 컴퓨터가 고장났어.
- **My computer isn't working for some reason.** 내 컴퓨터가 무슨 이유로 작동하지 않아.

A: Call the tech people. My computer shut down again.
컴퓨터 기사 불러. 내 컴퓨터가 다시 다운됐어.

B: I'll let them know ASAP. 가능한 빨리 연락할게.

02 My computer crashed this morning
컴퓨터가 오늘 아침 고장났어

- **Every time I turn on the computer, it crashes.** 내가 컴퓨터를 켤 때마다 망가지더라고.
- **My computer is always freezing up.** 내 컴퓨터는 항상 고장나 멈추더라.
- **Her computer crashed today.** 걔 컴퓨터가 오늘 고장났어.

A: Why didn't you finish your project today? 오늘 네 프로젝트를 끝내지 못한거야?
B: My computer crashed again. 내 컴퓨터가 또 고장났어.

03 The system stopped working
시스템이 작동을 멈추었어

- My mouse doesn't work properly. 마우스가 제대로 작동하지 않아.

- My keyboard had a problem. 내 키보드에 뭔가 문제가 생겼어.

- The monitor isn't working. 모니터가 고장났어.

A: Is your mouse still having problems? 네 마우스 아직도 문제가 있어?

B: No, but my monitor isn't working now. 아니, 하지만 이제는 모니터가 고장났어.

04 My computer is frozen
내 컴퓨터가 멈추었어

- My computer has a virus. 내 컴퓨터가 바이러스에 감염됐어.

- My computer files suddenly vanished and I can't find them.
내 컴에 있던 파일들이 갑자기 사라져서 찾을 수가 없어.

- I think someone hacked into my computer system.
누군가가 내 컴퓨터를 해킹한 것 같아.

A: I think someone hacked my computer files.
누가 내 컴퓨터 파일들을 해킹한 것 같아.

B: What makes you think that? 왜 그렇게 생각하는거야?

Please save the file after you receive it

그 파일을 받으면 저장해

....

파일을 업로드, 다운로드는 글자 그대로 upload, download를 쓴다. 프로그램을 설치할 때는 install, 그리고 압축된 파일을 풀 때는 unzip이란 동사를 사용하면 된다.

---

01 You need to upload the file

넌 그 파일을 업로드해야 돼

- Can you copy the files and send them to me? 그 파일들 복사해서 내게 보내줄래?

- Put those files on a USB. 그 파일들을 USB에 담아.

- I saved the files and emailed them to you.
  난 그 파일들을 저장하고 너에게 이멜로 보냈어.

A: Can you please put these files on a USB? 그 파일들을 USB에 담아줄래요?
B: Right away, sir. 바로 하겠습니다.

---

02 I just need to download a file

난 파일을 다운로드해야 돼

- I downloaded the file but can't find it. 파일을 다운로드했는데 찾을 수가 없어.

- I tried to download it but it failed. 난 그걸 다운로드하려고 했는데 안됐어.

- I don't have enough space on my computer to download it. The file is too big. 난 그걸 다운로드할 충분한 공간이 내 컴퓨터에 없어. 그 파일용량이 너무 커.

A: Did you download the files? 그 파일들 다운로드했어?
B: I tried but they are too big. 하려고 했는데 용량이 너무 커.

03 You need to install this program today
넌 오늘 이 프로그램을 설치해야 돼

◉ **After you install it**, run the program. 그걸 설치한 후에 프로그램을 돌려봐.

◉ **The program** is being installed **right now**. 그 프로그램이 지금 설치되고 있어.

◉ **You need to uninstall it** then reinstall it. 넌 그걸 삭제한 후에 다시 설치해야 돼.

A: Did you install it yet? 그거 설치했어?
B: I did. I'm running it right now. 어. 지금 돌려보고 있어.

04 I unzipped the file
난 그 파일의 압축을 풀었어

◉ **After unzipping the file** you can open it.
그 파일의 압축을 푼 후에 그 파일을 열어볼 수 있어.

◉ **The file won't open until you** unzip it. 그 파일은 압축을 풀기 전에 열리지 않을거야.

◉ **I sent you a file but it** needs to be unzipped.
너에게 파일을 하나 보냈는데 압축을 풀어야 돼.

A: Did you get the file? 그 파일 받았어?
B: Yes, I just unzipped it and am looking at it now.
어. 압축을 풀고 지금 보고 있는 중이야.

05 Please save the file after you receive it
그 파일을 받으면 저장해

◉ **I was able to** recover the lost data. 난 잃어버린 데이터를 다시 살릴 수 있었어.

◉ **I always** back up my documents. 난 항상 서류들을 백업해.

◉ **Did you** make back up files? 백업파일을 만들어놨어?

A: I accidentally deleted the files. 난 파일들을 실수로 삭제했어.
B: You need to try and recover them. 다시 그 파일들을 살리도록 해야 돼.

005

Try calling his cell phone

걔 핸드폰으로 전화를 걸어봐

핸드폰으로 통화중이다라고 말하려면 be on one's cell phone. 걔의 핸드폰으로 전화를 해보라고 할 때는 call one's cell phone이라고 한다. 'on'이 있고 없음에 뜻이 달라지지 잘 구분해야 한다.

 She's on her cell phone at the moment
걘 지금 핸드폰으로 통화중이야

- **May I please** use the phone? 전화를 사용해도 될까요?
- **She's talking on the phone right now.** 걘 지금 전화로 얘기하고 있어.
- **I need to** use the phone. 전화기를 사용해야 돼.

A: May I please use the phone? 전화를 사용해도 될까요?
B: Sorry, the manager is using it right now. 미안하지만, 매니저가 지금 사용하고 있어요.

 Try calling his cell phone
걔 핸드폰으로 전화를 걸어봐

- **I've been trying to reach him on his cell phone all day.**
난 온종일 걔 핸드폰으로 통화를 해보려고 시도했어.
- **Have you tried calling his landline?** 걔 일반전화로 통화를 해봤어?
- **I tried reaching her on her smart phone, office phone, and home landline.**
난 핸드폰, 사무실폰, 그리고 집전화로 연결을 해보려고 시도했어.

A: Martin isn't in the office and I need to talk to him.
마틴은 사무실에 없는데 그와 얘기를 해야 되는데요.

B: Have you tried calling him on his smart phone?
스마트폰으로 연락을 해보셨나요?

03 I'm waiting for the company to call me about the job interview 난 회사가 면접건으로 내게 전화주기를 기다리고 있어

● I'm expecting a call **from my customer.** 난 내 고객으로부터 전화를 기다리고 있어.

● Are you expecting a call **from her?** 넌 걔로부터 전화오기를 기다리고 있는거야?

● I can't talk right now. I'm expecting a very important call **any moment.**
지금 얘기 못해. 중요한 전화가 언제라도 올거야.

A: Are you expecting a call from the manager?
매니저로부터 전화가 올걸 기다리는거야?

B: Yes, she is going to call me at any moment now. 하시라도 내게 전화를 할거야.

04 Please turn off the cell phone before the meeting begins 회의 시작전에 핸드폰을 꺼두세요

● All cell phones must **be turned off during class.** 모든 핸드폰은 수업 중에 꺼야 된다.

● Make sure your phone is turned off **during the meeting.**
회의중에 핸드폰을 꺼두었는지 확실히 해.

● I always turn off my phone **when I am driving.** 난 운전중에 항상 핸드폰을 꺼둬.

A: Don't forget to turn off your phone during the meeting.
회의중에 핸드폰 꺼두는 것을 잊지마.

B: Of course. I hate it when a meeting is interrupted by a ringing
phone. 물론. 회의하는데 핸드폰 울리는 소리에 방해될 때 정말 싫어.

05 I have my phone on vibrate
난 핸드폰을 진동으로 해두었어

● Can you put your phone **on vibration mode, please?** 폰을 진동모드로 해두시겠어요?

● Instead of turning it off, I usually put **my phone on vibrate.** 폰끄는 대신 진동으로 해놔.

● I can hear **your phone vibrating.** 네 폰 진동이 울린다.

A: What's that noise? 저건 무슨 소리야?
B: My phone is vibrating. It's on vibration mode. 폰 진동소리야. 진동모드로 해놨거든.

006

I made a call to the office

난 사무실에 전화를 했어

call back과 call again은 의미가 다르지만 거의 구분없이 쓰는 경향이 있으며, 전화를 하다는 make a call, 전화를 받다는 take the call이라고 하는 점을 꼭 기억해둔다.

01 Please call security right away

당장 경비를 불러줘

- Call the manager **at 5pm.** 오후 5시에 매니저에게 전화해.
- **Call 911 right now!** 당장 911에 전화해!
- Call the store **between 10 and 11am.** 오전 10시에서 11시 사이에 가게에 전화해.

A: There's been a bad accident! 안좋은 사고가 있었어!
B: I'll call 911 right now. 지금 당장 911로 전화할게.

02 I'll ask him to call you back

걔보고 전화하라고 할게

- I'm returning a call **from the CEO.** 회장님 전화에 답신전화를 하는거예요.
- I called back **but the salesman wasn't in.** 난 답신전화를 했지만 영업사원은 외근중이었어.
- You need to call me back **before lunchtime.** 점심시간전에 내게 답신전화를 해야 돼.

A: I'll ask him to call you back. 걔보고 전화하라고 할게.
B: Thank you. Please tell him to call me back before 5pm.
고마워. 오후 5시 이전에 전화달라고 말해줘.

03 Would you call again later?
나중에 전화할래?

- I'll call again **next Monday.** 담주 월요일에 내가 전화 다시 할게.
- Could you call again **in a few minutes?** 조금 후에 전화 다시 할래?
- I called again **but she still wasn't in.** 내가 전화를 다시 했는데 걘 아직 들어오지 않았어.

A: Is Mr. Jones there? 존스 씨 계신가요?

B: Could you call again in a few minutes? He just stepped out for a moment. 조금 후에 전화 다시 주시겠어요? 지금 잠깐 나가셨는데요.

04 I have to make some calls
난 몇군데 전화를 돌려봐야 돼

- I made a call to **the office.** 난 사무실에 전화를 했어.
- She made a long distance call to **the UK.** 걘 영국으로 장거리 전화를 했어.
- Do you have to make any calls **this afternoon?**
넌 오늘 오후에 전화를 할 데가 있는거야?

A: I can't talk right now. I have to make a few calls.
지금 얘기 못해. 전화 몇군데 돌려야 돼.

B: No problem. Let me know when you're done. 그래. 다하고 나면 알려줘.

05 I gotta take this call
난 이 전화를 받아야 돼

- I had to take the call **from the CEO.** 회장 전화를 받아야 했어.
- She's gotta take the call **from the customer.** 걘 고객전화를 받아야 했어.
- I have to take a call **in a few minutes.** 난 조금 후에 전화를 받아야 돼.

A: I can't go to lunch. I gotta take a call in a few minutes.
난 점심먹으러 못가. 조금 후에 전화를 받아야 돼.

B: OK. Let's have lunch together tomorrow. 그래. 내일 함께 점심먹자.

007

I'm calling for an appointment
약속을 잡으러 전화했습니다

전화한 이유를 말하려면 I'm calling to+V 혹은 I'm calling for+N의 형태로 써준다. …로부터 전화를 받았다고 할 때는 I got a call from~, 전화를 끊다는 get off the phone이라고 한다.

01

I'm calling to ask about the accounting records
회계장부에 대해 물어보려고 전화했어

- I'm calling for **an appointment**. 약속을 잡으러 전화했습니다.
- She called to **make a reservation**. 그녀는 예약을 하려고 전화했어.
- He called to **order some computer monitors**. 걘 컴퓨터 모니터를 주문하려고 전화했어.

A: What did he call us for? 걘 뭐 때문에 전화했어?
B: To order some car parts. 차 부품 좀 주문하려고.

02

I got a call from a customer saying that she was very happy with our service
우리 서비스에 무척 만족하다고 말하는 고객의 전화를 받았어

- There was a call from **the head office** asking **about this month's sales records**. 이번달 매출액을 알려 달라는 본사의 전화가 있었어.
- I received a call from **the accounting department** asking **you to send your tax records to them**. 너의 세무기록을 보내달라는 회계부서의 전화를 받았어.
- A customer called to complain **about the service she received**.
  한 고객이 서비스불만을 하기 위해 전화했어.

A: Were there any calls while I was out? 내가 나가 있던 사이에 뭐 전화온거 있어?
B: Yes, I received a call from the personnel department to talk about the new recruits. 어, 신입채용에 관해 인사부로부터 전화를 받았어.

03 Can you get the phone, please?
전화 좀 받을테야?

- I answered the phone but nobody was on the other line.
  난 전화를 받았는데 아무도 다른 전화를 받지 않았어.

- Could you answer this call? I think it's the manager and he wants to talk with you. 이 전화 좀 받을테야? 매니저 같은데 너와 얘기하고 싶어해.

- Get that phone. It's probably for you. 저 전화 받아. 너한테 걸려온 전화일거야.

A: The phone is ringing! 전화가 울린다!

B: Yes, can you answer it please? I'm in the middle of something.
어, 좀 받아줄테야. 나 뭐 좀 하는 중이거든.

04 I have got another call on line 2
2번 라인으로 다른 전화를 받고 있어

- I have a customer on hold so I'll have to call you back.
  고객이 전화를 대기중이야 그러니 내가 다시 전화걸게.

- I have got another call coming through so I need to put you on hold.
  다른 전화가 들어오니 너를 통화중 대기로 해놓을게.

- Can you take the call on line 3 please? 3번 라인 전화 좀 받아줄테야?

A: I have got another call on line 2. 2번 라인으로 다른 전화를 받고 있어

B: I'll take it. 내가 받을게.

Unit 06

05 Please get off the phone!
전화 좀 끊어!

- The manager got angry and hung up on me.
  매니저는 화가 나서 도중에 내 전화를 끊어버렸어.

- Can you please get off the phone? 전화 좀 끊을테야?

A: You've been on the phone for the last 40 minutes. 넌 40분간 통화를 하고 있어.

B: Sorry, I'll get off right away. 미안, 바로 끊을게.

008

You have a call from the head office

너 본사에서 전화가 왔어

전화가 왔다고 말할 때는 There is a phone call for sb 혹은 간단히 Phone call for sb라고 한다. 또한 통화연결을 바란다고 할 때는 좀 어렵지만 get through to sb라고 한다는 점을 기억해둔다.

01 There is a phone call for Mr. McCarthy
매카시 씨를 찾는 전화가 왔어

- I have a phone call for **Mr. Park**. 박 씨를 찾는 전화가 왔어.
- Is there a phone call for me? 내게 걸려온 전화 있어?
- I heard there was a phone call for me. 나한테 전화온게 있다면서?

A: There is a phone call for Mr. Kim. 김 씨를 찾는 전화가 왔어.
B: He's out of the office at the moment. Take a message.
지금 외출중이야. 메시지 받아놔.

02 You have a call from the head office
너 본사에서 전화가 왔어

- Head office called you. 본사가 너에게 전화를 했어.
- She got a call from **her boss**. 걘 사장으로부터 전화를 받았어.
- Did he get a call from **that customer**? 걘 그 고객으로부터 전화를 받았어?

A: She got a call from her boss. 걘 사장으로부터 전화를 받았어.
B: What did he want? 뭐라고 했는데?

03 I'm available for a call all afternoon
오후내내 전화 받을 수 있어

- When are you available for a call? 언제 통화할 수 있어?

- She won't be available for a call today. 오늘 걘 통화할 시간이 없을거야.

- Are you available for a call before noon? 너 오전 중에 통화할 수 있어?

A: When are you going to be available for a call? 언제 통화할 수 있는거야?
B: Anytime this morning. 오늘 오전 아무때나.

04 I'm trying to get through to Mr. Olson
올슨 씨와 통화하려고 하는데요

- I've been trying to get through to the manager all day.
난 종일 매니저와 통화하려고 했어.

- I finally got through to him this morning. 마침내 오늘 아침 그와 통화가 연결됐어.

- I can't get through to the head office. 본사와 통화가 안돼.

A: Did you get through to the sales team? 영업팀과 통화됐어?
B: Yes, I talked to them this afternoon. 어, 오늘 오후에 그들에게 말했어.

Unit 06

05 I'm on line 3 with the customer
라인 3번으로 고객과 통화중이야

- Who is on line 2? 2번 라인에 누구야?

- Can you connect me with the customer on line 4?
4번 라인으로 고객과 연결시켜줄테야?

- She is talking with him on line 1. 그녀는 1번 라인으로 그와 얘기하고 있어.

A: Is somebody talking with the manager now?
지금 누구 매니저와 얘기하는 사람있어?

B: Yes, I'm on line 2 with him right now.
어, 내가 2번 라인으로 매니저와 통화중이야.

009

She's on the phone right now
걘 지금 통화중이야

통화중일 때는 be on the phone. 그래서 기다리라고 할 때는 hold[hang] on, hold the line이라고 하면 된다. 메시지를 줘서 남기는 것은 give a message for sb, 메시지를 받아 남기는 것은 take a message for sb라 한다.

01 She's on the phone right now
걘 지금 통화중이야

● **Is someone** on the phone? 누가 지금 통화중이야?

● **I can't help you right now because I'm** on the phone **with headquarters.**
본사와 통화중이어서 짐 너를 도울 수가 없어.

● **She's** on the phone **with her co-worker.** 걘 동료와 통화중이야.

> A: Where is she? 걔는 어디 있어?
> B: She's on the phone with headquarters. She'll be here in a few
> minutes. 걘 본사와 통화중이야. 조금 후에 이리로 올거야.

02 Please hold the line and we'll be with you in a minute 좀 기다리시면 곧 연결시켜드릴게요

● **Can you** hold the line **please?** 전화 끊지 않고 기다리시겠어요?

● **You need to** hold the line **for a second.** 잠시 전화 기다리셔야 돼요.

● Hold the line **for just a moment, sir.** 잠시만 기다려주세요.

> A: May I speak to Miss Mackay, please? 매케이 양 좀 바꿔줄래요?
> B: Yes, just hold the line for a moment. 예. 잠시만 기다려주세요.

03 Please hang on for a second
잠시만 기다려주세요

- Could you hang on **for a moment?** 잠시만 기다려주시겠어요?
- Just hang on **a sec.** 잠시만 기다리세요.
- You'll need to hang on **for a minute.** 잠시만 기다려주셔야 돼요.

A: I need to speak with your boss. 사장님과 통화를 해야 돼요.
B: Just hang on a sec. I'll get her. 잠시만 기다려주세요. 바꿔드릴게요.

04 Can I give you a message for him?
그에게 메시지를 남길 수 있을까요?

- Can I take a message **for you?** 메시지 남겨드릴까요?
- Would you like to **give him a message?** 그에게 메시지를 남겨드릴까요?
- I gave her the message. 걔에게 메시지를 남겼어.

A: I didn't know you called. 네가 전화한 줄 몰랐는데.
B: Really? That's strange. I gave her a message to let you know.
정말? 이상하다. 그녀에게 내가 전화했다고 알려주라는 메시지를 남겼는데.

Unit 06

05 Could you have him call me, please?
걔보고 내게 전화달라고 해줘요?

- Please tell her to call me **as soon as you see her.**
그녀를 보면 바로 내게 전화달라고 해줘요.
- Can you have him give me a call ASAP? 걔보고 가능한 빨리 내게 전화달라고 해줄래요?
- I told her to give you a call. 걔보고 너에게 전화하라고 말했어.

A: Can you have him give me a call ASAP?
걔보고 가능한 빨리 내게 전화달라고 해줄래요?
B: Of course! 물론이죠!

010

Put him on the phone, please

그 사람 좀 바꿔주세요

전화를 바꿔줄 때는 put A through B, 혹은 put A on the phone이라고 한다. 또한 get을 써서 get sb on the phone, give를 써서 give me sb라고 하면 된다.

01 I'll put you through to the Accounting Department

회계부서로 전화 연결시켜드릴게요

● I put her through to my team leader. 그녀의 전화를 팀장에게 돌려줬어.

● They put me through to headquarters. 그들은 내 전화를 본사로 연결시켜줬어.

● Can you put me through to the sales department? 영업부서로 전화를 바꿔주실래요?

A: Could you put me through to the Marketing Department?
마케팅 부서로 전화를 돌려줄래요?

B: Yes, sir. 예. 알겠습니다.

02 Put him on the phone, please

그 사람 좀 바꿔주세요

● I need you to put the manager on the phone. 매니저 좀 바꿔주세요.

● I put her on the phone because he asked to speak to her.
통화하고 싶다고 해서 그녀를 바꿔줬어.

● Could you please put the customer on the phone? 그 고객 좀 바꿔주시겠어요?

A: I need you to put the sales assistant on the phone please.
영업차장을 좀 바꿔주세요.

B: I'm sorry but he's out at the moment. Can I take a message?
죄송하지만 외근중입니다. 메시지 남겨드릴까요?

03 Could you get Mr. Kim on the phone for the customer please? 고객전화인데 김 씨 바꿔줄래요?

- I need you to get her on the phone to talk with the manager.
  매니저와 얘기해야 되니 그녀를 바꿔주세요.

- Get her on the phone ASAP for the customer please.
  고객 때문에 그러는데 그녀를 빨리 바꿔주세요.

- I need you to get the manager on the phone right away.
  매니저 좀 바로 연결해주세요.

A: Why are you looking for James? 제임스를 왜 찾으시나요?
B: I need you to get him on the phone for the sales assistant right away. 영업차장을 당장 바꿔주세요.

04 Can you give me Mr. O'Connor please?
오코너 씨를 바꿔주시겠어요?

- I need you to give me the manager ASAP. 빨리 매니저 좀 바꿔주세요.
- Can you give me the Research and Development Department please?
  연구개발부서 좀 바꿔주세요.
- Give me the manager please. 매니저 좀 바꿔주세요.

A: I need you to give me the manager ASAP. 빨리 매니저 좀 바꿔주세요.
B: This is the manager speaking. How can I help you?
  제가 매니저입니다. 뭘 도와드릴까요?

05 I'm trying to reach the PR Department at 748-0264
748-0264로 홍보부서와 통화하려고 합니다

- I was unable to reach him at his office. 난 사무실로 그와 통화연결을 할 수가 없었어.
- Were you able to reach her at the hotel? 호텔로 걔와 통화연결 할 수 있었어?

A: I was unable to reach him at his office. 난 사무실로 그와 통화연결을 할 수가 없었어.
B: Do you have his smartphone number? 걔 핸드폰 번호 갖고 있어?

011

You're breaking up a bit

네 소리가 조금씩 끊겨

통화상태가 안좋으면 get a bad reception. 혹은 break up이란 표현을 사용한다.
그러다 전화가 끊겼을 때는 be cut off나 be dead를 쓰면 된다.

01

I am getting a bad reception in this area
이 지역에서는 수신상태가 안좋아

- I'm having trouble hearing you. 네 목소리가 잘 안들려.

- The reception in the basement isn't very good. 지하실에서는 수신상태가 썩 좋지 않아.

- Outside the city the phone reception is very poor.
  시내를 벗어나면 전화수신도가 형편없어.

A: I can't hear you very well. 네 목소리 잘 안들려.
B: Yes, the phone reception where I'm at isn't very good.
　　어, 내가 있는 곳의 전화수신도가 썩 좋지 않아.

02

You're breaking up a bit
네 소리가 조금씩 끊겨

- The poor reception is causing you to break up a bit.
  수신상태가 안좋아서 네 목소리가 좀 끊겨.

- He kept breaking up so I called him back.
  걔 전화가 계속 끊겨서 내가 걔에게 전화를 다시 했어.

- You keep breaking up so can I call you back?
  너 전화 계속 끊기는데 내가 다시 전화할까?

A: I'm sorry, you keep breaking up. Can you say that again?
　　미안, 너 소리가 계속 끊겨. 다시 말해줄래?
B: I'll call you right back. 내가 바로 다시 전화할게.

03 The phone was suddenly cut off
전화가 갑자기 끊겼어

- We were in the middle of the conversation when the phone was cut off.
  우리는 얘기 도중인데 갑자기 전화가 끊겼어.
- What did she say before the phone was cut off? 전화가 끊기기 전에 걔가 뭐라고 했어?
- I was about to tell him the big news when the phone was cut off.
  난 걔에게 빅뉴스를 전하려고 할 때 전화가 끊겼어.

A: What did she say? 걔가 뭐라고 했어?
B: I don't know. The phone was suddenly cut off. 몰라. 전화가 갑자기 끊겼어.

04 The phone went dead
전화가 꺼졌어

- This phone model eats up the battery 이 전화기 기종은 배터리를 빨리 잡아먹어.
- My phone battery is dying. 내 핸드폰 배터리가 다해가고 있어.
- My phone battery is about to go dead. 내 핸드폰 배터리가 다하려고 해.

A: Hey, my phone battery is about to die. 야. 내 폰 배터리가 거의 없다.
B: OK. Call me back later. 알았어. 나중에 전화해.

05 I always try to keep my cell phone charged
난 항상 내 폰의 충전을 가득 채워놓으려고 해

- My phone is only half charged right now. 내 폰의 배터리가 지금 겨우 반 남았어.
- I forgot my phone charger at home. 충전기를 집에 깜박 두고 왔어.
- When fully charged the phone battery lasts 12 hours.
  충전을 가득했을 때 폰배터리는 12시간 가.

A: My phone needs to be charged but I forgot my charger at home.
  핸드폰 충전을 해야 되는데 충전기를 집에 두고 왔어.
B: Use this one. 이거 써.

012

Did you miss his call?

걔 전화 못받았어?

전화를 못받고 놓치는 경우에는 miss란 동사를 사용하고, 컴퓨터처럼 스마트폰에 어플을 설치할 때는 install이란 단어를 사용하면 된다. 스마트폰에 연동되는게 많은 요즘 be linked to one's smartphone이란 표현도 알아둔다.

01 I missed his call
걔 전화를 놓쳤어

● You missed a call but I took a message for you.
너가 전화를 못받았지만 내가 메시지를 받아놨어.

● Did you miss his call? 걔 전화 못받았어?

● I kept missing her call. 내가 계속해서 걔 전화를 놓치네.

A: I think I missed a call from Mrs. Sayer. 세이어 부인의 전화를 내가 못받은 것 같아.
B: You did but I took a message for you. It's on your desk.
그랬는데 내가 메시지 받아놨어. 네 책상위에 있어.

02 I installed some new applications on my phone
내 폰에다 새로운 어플을 설치했어

● I need to uninstall some of my phone apps.
난 폰에 있는 어플 일부를 설치삭제를 해야 돼.

● Have you installed the new security app on your phone yet?
네 폰에 새로 나온 보안어플을 깔았어?

● I just installed the latest banking app on my phone.
난 폰에 최신 은행어플을 방금 깔았어.

A: How many apps do you have on your phone? 네 폰에 깔린 어플이 몇 개야?
B: Too many. I need to uninstall some of them. 너무 많아. 일부는 삭제해야 돼.

03 I just downloaded that new e-book about technology from an iBookstore

아이북스토어에서 기술에 관한 새로 나온 이북을 다운로드 받았어

- **Can you please** download that security app **for your phone today?**
  오늘 네 폰에 보안어플을 다운로드 받을래?

- **I am going to** download that e-book **today.** 난 오늘 저 이북을 다운로드할거야.

- **Downloading e-books has really hurt book stores.**
  이북을 다운로드하는 것은 서점들에게 정말 피해를 입혔어.

A: Have you downloaded that new e-book I told you about yet?
내가 얘기한 새로 나온 이북을 다운로드했어?

B: Yes, I started reading it too. 어. 읽기 시작했어.

04 I heard his car is linked to his Smartphone

걔 자동차는 걔 스마트폰하고 연동된다고 들었어

- **My phone app is linked to the security cameras.**
  내 폰의 어플은 보안카메라와 연동되어 있어.

- **Can you link your phone to the drone?** 네 폰과 드론을 연동시킬 수 있어?

- **I want to link my phone to the security system.** 내 폰은 보안카메라와 연결시키고 싶어.

A: How do you know who is in the office right now?
넌 지금 사무실에 누가 있는지 어떻게 알아?

B: Because my phone app is linked to the security cameras.
내 폰의 어플이 보안카메라와 연동되어 있거든.

013

I will pay using my phone

난 폰으로 지불할거야

스마트폰으로 안되는게 없는 세상. 온라인 결제는 pay online using~, 폰으로 송금할 때는 send the money through phone banking, pay sb through Internet banking이라고 한다.

01 She is going to pay online using her credit card

갠 신용카드를 이용해 온라인결제를 할거야

- **Can I pay online with Paypal?** 페이팔로 온라인 결제 가능한가요?

- **Do you use online banking much?** 넌 온라인 뱅킹을 많이 이용해?

- **My credit card isn't working for** the online payment.
  내 신용카드는 온라인 결제가 안돼.

A: How is she going to pay, with her credit card or Paypal?
갠는 신용카드 아니면 페이팔 중 어떤 걸로 결제할거야?

B: I think she prefers Paypal. 갠 페이팔을 더 좋아하는 것 같아.

02 I will pay using my phone

난 폰으로 지불할거야

- **I paid using my phone banking app.** 난 폰뱅킹 어플을 이용해서 지불했어.

- **Can you use your phone for banking?** 폰으로 뱅킹업무를 이용할 수 있어?

- **My father doesn't know how to use his phone to** pay for online shopping yet. 아버지는 폰으로 온라인 쇼핑결제하는 법을 몰라.

A: What were you showing to your father? 네 아버지에게 뭐 보여주는 거였어?

B: I was teaching him to use his phone for online shopping.
폰을 이용해서 온라인 쇼핑결제하는 법을 가르쳐주고 있었어.

03 I will send the money through phone banking
폰을 이용해서 돈을 보낼거야

- Do you know how to transfer money through your phone banking app?
  폰에 깔린 은행어플로 돈을 이체하는 법을 알고 있어?

- I'll use my phone to transfer you the money. 난 폰을 이용해서 너에게 돈을 이체할게.

- Can you use your phone banking app to send me the money now?
  폰에 깔린 은행어플을 이용해서 내게 돈을 보낼 수 있어?

A: I will use my phone banking app to send you the money, OK?
은행어플을 이용해서 너에게 돈을 송금할게, 알았지?

B: That's fine. Just let me know when you send it. 좋아. 언제 보낼건지만 알려줘.

04 Can I pay you through Internet banking?
인터넷뱅킹으로 결제할 수 있나요?

- Have you ever used Internet banking to pay bills? 청구서결제를 인터넷으로 해봤니?

- I am going to try Internet banking for the first time today.
  오늘 처음으로 인터넷뱅킹을 해볼거야.

- My father doesn't understand how to do Internet banking.
  아버지는 인터넷뱅킹을 어떻게 하는 이해를 못하셔.

A: Can I pay you through Internet banking? 인터넷뱅킹으로 결제할 수 있나요?
B: I'd prefer cash, please. 현금이면 더 좋겠는데요.

05 I forgot my mobile phone banking PIN number
핸드폰 뱅킹 비밀번호를 잊어버렸어

- Don't ever tell anyone your banking app PIN number.
  어느 누구에게도 은행어플의 비번을 알려주지마.

- She punched in the wrong PIN number for her smartphone banking app.
  걔는 은행어플 비번을 잘못 눌렀어.

A: Why didn't you transfer the money yet? 왜 돈을 아직 이체하지 않은거야?
B: I forgot my mobile phone banking PIN number. 은행어플의 비번을 잊어버렸어.

Online education has become very popular

온라인 강의가 매우 인기가 있어

온라인 강의를 듣다는 take an online course. 온라인 교육은 online education. 원격수업은 a distance learning class. 즉 distance learning이라고 하면 된다.

01 He is studying by taking an online course through his smartphone 걘 스마트폰을 이용해 온라인강의를 들으며 공부하고 있어

- Are you in an online class right now on your smartphone?
  넌 지금 스마트폰으로 온라인 강의를 듣고 있어?

- I registered to take an online class this semester.
  난 이번 학기에 온라인 강의 들려고 등록했어.

- Online classes have good points and bad points. 온라인 강의는 장점과 단점이 있어.

A: Is he in an online class right now? 걘 지금 온라인 강의를 듣고 있어?
B: Yes, he's using his smartphone to attend it. 어. 스마트폰으로 강의를 듣고 있어.

02 Online education has become very popular

온라인 강의가 매우 인기가 있어

- Online education has become very popular, and allows students to study anywhere and at any time.
  온라인 교육은 매우 인기가 있고 그로 인해 학생들은 언제 어디서나 공부를 할 수 있게 해줘.

- Online education really took off during the pandemic.
  온라인 교육은 전염병 중에 급격하게 인기를 얻었어.

- The COVID pandemic really helped online education develop a lot of new technologies. 코로나 전염병은 정말로 온라인 교육이 새로운 기술들을 개발하는데 도움이 되었어.

A: The pandemic helped some industries develop.
전염병으로 일부 산업은 발전하는데 도움이 됐어.
B: Yes, especially online education. 그래. 특히 온라인 교육이 그래.

03 She is taking a class by remote learning
걘 원격수업을 듣고 있어

- Remote learning is good for students who live in rural areas.
  원격수업은 시골지역에 사는 학생들에게 도움이 돼.

- I took a remote learning class last year and enjoyed it a lot.
  작년에 난 원격수업을 들었고 정말 좋았어.

- The remote learning class was more fun than I imagined.
  원격수업은 내가 생각하는 것보다 더 재미있었어.

A: Did you enjoy the remote learning class you took?
네가 수강한 원격수업 재미있었어?

B: Yes, it was better than I thought it would be. 어, 내 예상보다 훨씬 좋았어.

04 She is teaching a distance learning class
걘 원격수업으로 강의하고 있어

- Distance learning is hard for students who enjoy face-to-face interactions.
  원격수업은 상호소통하는 대면수업을 좋아하는 학생들에게는 어려워.

- Distance learning allows many people a good opportunity to study.
  원격수업은 많은 사람들이 학습할 기회를 주고 있어.

A: Distance learning is hard for students who enjoy face-to-face interactions with their classmates and teachers.
원격수업은 반학생들과 선생님들과의 의사소통을 즐기는 학생들에게는 어려워.

B: Yes but it allows many students who live far from the school a good opportunity to study. 그래 하지만 학교에서 먼곳에 사는 많은 학생들에게 학습할 좋은 기회를 주잖아.

05 She signed up for the distance class
걘 원격수업강의를 등록했어

- Have you signed up for the online class yet? 온라인 강의 등록했어?

- The deadline to sign up for the program is tomorrow. 프로그램 등록마감은 내일이야.

A: Have you signed up for the class yet? 그 수업 등록했어?
B: I will do that this afternoon. 오늘 오후에 할거야.

015

I posted my resume on the job website

취업사이트에 내 이력서를 올렸어

새롭게 각광받는 단어들은 post와 comment이다. post는 글이나 게시물을 올리는 것을 말하며, comment는 write[make] a comment라는 형태로 댓글을 달다라는 표현이 된다.

01 I posted my resume on the job website
취업사이트에 내 이력서를 올렸어

- You need to post your ideas on the work website. 직장 홈피에 네 생각을 올려야 돼.

- I won't post anything about the wedding date until I know for sure.
  난 결혼날짜를 확실히 알 때까지는 그에 대한 어떤 것도 게시하지 않을거야.

- You need to be careful about what you post on the Internet.
  넌 인터넷에 올리는 글에 대해 조심해야 돼.

A: Did you see the pictures he posted on his FB page?
개가 페이스북 페이지에 올린 사진들 봤어?

B: Yes, he needs to be more careful about what he posts there.
어, 걘 거기에 올리는 것에 관해 좀 더 조심해야 돼.

02 He posted his opinion about the election on Reddit
걘 레딧에 투표에 관한 의견을 올렸어

- I posted my idea about improving the sales in our workplace chat room.
  난 직장 단톡방에 매출증가에 대한 나의 생각을 올렸어.

- Don't post anything about politics on the website please.
  사이트에는 정치에 관한 어떤 것도 올리지 마세요.

- Can I post some of my family pictures in our chatroom?
  우리 대화방에 가족사진을 올려도 될까?

A: He posted his thoughts on the election on his FB page.
걘 페이스북 페이지에 선거에 관한 자신의 생각을 올렸어.

B: I'd never do that. 나라면 절대 그러지 않을거야.

I write comments on Internet stories all the time
난 항상 인터넷 기사에 댓글을 달아

- After an interesting article, I always read the comments section.
  흥미로운 기사를 읽고 나면, 난 항상 댓글부분을 읽어.

- He wrote some very strong comments about her attitude.
  걘 그녀의 태도에 관해서 강력한 댓글을 좀 썼어.

- I hated reading her comments about my presentation.
  난 내가 한 발표에 대한 그녀의 댓글을 읽기 싫었어.

A: Reading comments is something I always do after a good article.
좋은 기사를 읽은 후에는 항상 달린 댓글을 읽어.

B: Not me. Too many dummies say dumb things.
난 아냐. 너무 가짜 사람들이 멍청한 얘기들을 해대서.

I suspect the person who made that comment was using a false name
그 댓글을 단 사람은 가명을 쓰고 있다고 생각돼

- His name is Jack Adams but when he comments on the internet he uses a nickname. 걔 이름은 잭 아담스이지만 인터넷에 댓글을 달 때는 가명을 써.

- That comment on Twitter seems like it came from a burner account.
  트위터의 그 댓글은 대포계정에서 쓴 것 같아.

- He has a pseudonym he uses instead of his real name.
  걘 진짜 자기 이름 대신에 가명을 쓰고 있어.

A: Who is the guy named John Doe who made that comment about you? 너에 대한 댓글을 단 존 도우라는 이름의 사람은 누구야?

B: It's obviously a false name. 분명히 가명이지.

016

He's trolling you

걔가 너를 악플로 괴롭히고 있어

역시 새롭게 등장하여 많이 쓰이는 단어인 troll은 명사나 동사로 인터넷상에 부정적인 악플을 다는 것, 다는 사람, 혹은 그런 글을 달다라는 의미의 단어이다. 또한 cyber bully는 사이버 폭력 혹은 그런 폭력을 가하다라는 동사로 쓰인다.

Trolls use the Internet to cyber bully people
악플러들은 인터넷을 이용해 사람들을 괴롭혀

- Trolling on the Internet can be fun if you don't take it too far.
  인터넷 악플은 너무 심각하게 받아들이지 않는다면 재미있을 수도 있어.

- He's trolling you. 걔가 너를 악플로 괴롭히고 있어.

- I can't tell if she's trolling or if she really means it.
  걘 악플로 괴롭히는건지 아니면 진심으로 그러는건지 모르겠어.

A: Your trolling is coming close to cyber bullying.
  너의 괴롭힘은 사이버폭력에 가까워지고 있어.

B: OK, I'll stop doing it. 그래. 이제 그만할게.

He is a big troll on the Internet
걘 인터넷상에서 아주 심한 악플러야

- When you reply to him you're just feeding the troll.
  걔에게 반응하면, 악플거리를 제공할 뿐이야.

- I can't stand trolls so I never respond to them.
  난 악플러들을 참을 수가 없어서 아예 절대 반응을 하지 않아.

- Responding to trolls is the worst thing you can do.
  악플러에게 반응하는 것은 네가 할 수 있는 최악의 일이야.

A: I really want to reply to his horrible post.
  난 걔의 끔찍한 게시글에 대답을 정말 하고 싶어.

B: Don't do that. You'll just be feeding the troll.
  그러지마. 악플거리를 제공할 뿐이야.

Some mean people get online just to harass and troll others 일부 비열한 사람들은 온라인에 들어와 다른 사람들을 괴롭히고 악플을 달아

- He is a real cyber bully. 걔 정말이지 사이버 폭력자이야.
- She is a total keyboard warrior. 걔 정말이지 온라인상에서 남을 헐뜯는 사람이야.
- Cyber bullies always attack in big groups. 사이버폭력은 항상 대규모로 공격을 해.

A: She is always posting bad things about other people.
걔 언제나 다른 사람들에게 관해 안좋은 것들을 게시해.

B: Yeah, she is a real keyboard warrior. 어. 걔 정말 온라인상에서 남을 헐뜯는 사람이야.

Someone has been cyber stalking and bullying her over the Internet 어떤 사람이 인터넷으로 그녀를 사이버 스토킹을 하고 사이버 폭력을 휘두르고 있어

- Be careful of Internet stalkers. 인터넷 스토커들을 조심해.
- He was creeping her Instagram and Facebook.
걔 그녀의 인스타그램과 페이스북을 살금살금 훔쳐보고 있었어.
- These days cyber bullying has become a real problem.
요즘 사이버폭력은 정말 문젯거리가 됐어.

A: He keeps liking my Facebook posts and I barely know him.
걔 내 페이스북에 좋아요를 계속 눌러주지만 난 거의 걔를 알지 못해.

B: That's horrible. Sounds like he has been creeping on your Facebook
for a long time. 끔찍하네. 걔가 오랫동안 네 페이스북을 살금살금 보고 있었나보다.

He cyber bullied the young student on the Internet
걔 인터넷상에서 젊은 학생에게 사이버폭력을 가했어

- The police are trying to protect people from cyber bullies.
경찰은 사이버폭력으로부터 사람들을 보호하려고 해.
- Have you ever been cyber bullied before? 넌 전에 사이버폭력을 당해본 적 있어?

A: Have you ever been cyber bullied before? 넌 전에 사이버폭력을 당해본 적 있어?
B: Yes, when I was in middle school. 어. 내가 중학교 다닐 때.

017

Can you contact him via Instant Messaging?

인스턴트 메시지를 해서 걔에게 연락을 할 수 있어?

카톡이나 텔레그램과 같은 메신저에서 보내는 메시지 혹은 그렇게 메시지를 보내다라는 뜻으로 쓰이는 단어는 Instant Message이다. 명사로 쓰일 경우 동사는 send를 써서 send an instant message라고 한다.

01

I instant messaged her

난 걔한테 인스턴트 메시지를 보냈어

- **Can you contact him via Instant Messaging?**
  인스턴트 메시지를 해서 걔에게 연락을 할 수 있어?

- **Sending instant messages is very convenient.**
  인스턴트 메시지를 보내는 것은 매우 편리해.

- **How many instant messages do you send a day?**
  하루에 인스턴트 메시지를 몇 개나 보내?

A: He just instant messaged me. 걔 방금 인스턴트 메시지를 보냈어.
B: What did he say? 뭐라고 했는데?

02

I need to add him to my Messenger's list

난 걔를 내 메신저 리스트에 추가해야 돼

- **Can you please add me to your Messenger list?** 나를 네 메신저 리스트에 추가해줄래?

- **I don't have you in my Messenger contact list.** 내 메신저 연락 리스트에는 네가 없어.

- **She accidentally deleted me from her Messenger list.**
  걔 실수로 나를 자기 메신저 리스트에서 지웠어.

A: You don't have me on your Messenger list? 너의 메신저 리스트에 내가 없다고?
B: I did but accidentally deleted you. 있었는데 실수로 삭제했어.

What do you use instant messenger for mostly?
대개 어떤 이유로 인스턴트 메신저를 이용해?

- I usually use Instant Messenger for keeping in touch with my family back home. 난 집에 있는 가족들과 연락을 주고 받기 위해 인스턴트 메신저를 보통 이용해.
- She uses Messenger a lot for work. 걘 일을 하는데 메신저를 많이 사용해.
- He never uses Instant Messenger for work.
  걘 업무용으로는 인스턴트 메신저를 절대로 사용하지 않아.

A: She uses her Instant Messenger a lot for her work.
걘 자기 일을 하는데 메신저를 많이 사용해.

B: Really? For chatting with customers? 정말? 고객들과 채팅하는데에?

I sent an instant message to my wife
난 아내에게 인스턴트 메시지를 보냈어

- Did you send me an Instant Message a minute ago? I accidentally deleted one. 조금 전에 내게 인스턴트 메시지를 보냈어? 내가 실수로 지워버렸거든.
- She sent her manager an Instant Message about the conference.
  걘 매니저에게 총회에 관한 인스턴트 메시지를 보냈어.

A: How did you get that information so fast? 어떻게 그렇게 빨리 그 정보를 알았어?
B: My coworker sent me an Instant Message. 내 직장동료가 인스턴트 메시지를 보냈어.

I got an instant message from her a few minutes
ago 난 조금전에 걔로부터 인스턴트 메시지를 받았어

- She got an Instant Message from her boss. 걘 사장으로부터 인스턴트 메시지를 받았어.
- Who did he get that Instant Message from? 걘 누구로부터 그 인스턴트 메시지를 받은거야?
- I have never gotten an Instant Message from any of my coworkers.
  난 내 직장동료 누구로부터도 인스턴트 메시지를 받아본 적이 없어.

A: Who did she get that Instant Message from?
걘 누구로부터 그 인스턴트 메시지를 받은거야?

B: I think it was her boss. 자기 사장으로부터 받은 것 같아.

018

I changed my email address from Naver to Gmail

난 이멜주소를 네이버에서 Gmail로 바꾸었어

이멜계정을 새로 만들 때는 set up a new email account, 새로 바꿀 때는 change one's email address, 메일링주소에 이멜 주소를 추가할 때는 add one's address to one's mailing list라고 하면 된다.

01 I had to set up a new email account for my new job 새로운 직장용으로 이멜계정을 새로 만들어야 했어

● Have you deleted your old email accounts yet? 너 옛날 이멜계정을 삭제한거야?

● Do you have a work email account? 업무용 이멜 계정이 있어?

● I had to set up a new email account for my mother.
엄마용으로 이멜계정을 새로 만들어야 했어.

A: What are you doing? 뭐해?
B: I'm setting up a new email account for my job.
업무용 이멜계정을 새로 만들고 있어.

02 Why did you change your email address?
왜 이멜주소를 바꾼거야?

● I changed my email address from Naver to Gmail.
난 이멜주소를 네이버에서 Gmail로 바꾸었어.

● Do you have Gmail? 너 Gmail 계정있어?

● What's your email address please? 네 이멜 주소가 어떻게 돼?

A: Why did you change your email address? 왜 이멜주소를 바꾼거야?
B: I was getting much spam at my old one. 내 옛 이멜주소로 너무 많은 스팸이 왔거든.

03 I'll give you my email address
너에게 내 이멜주소를 알려줄게

- I wrote down her email address but lost it. 난 걔 이멜주소를 적어놨는데 잃어버렸어.
- Did I give you my email address before? 내가 전에 내 이멜주소를 너에게 줬니?
- She refused to give me her email address. 걘 내게 자기 이멜주소를 주지 않았어.

A: Why are you so sad? 왜 슬퍼하는거야?
B: I gave him my email address a few weeks ago but I haven't heard from him yet. 몇주전 걔한데 이멜주소를 줬는데 아직까지 걔로부터 연락이 없어.

04 We exchanged email addresses after the meeting
우린 회의 후에 서로 이멜주소를 교환했어

- We gave each other our email addresses. 우리는 서로에게 이멜주소를 줬어.
- Did you exchange email addresses so you can contact each other later on? 나중에 서로 연락할 수 있게 이멜주소를 교환했어?

A: Do you know her email address? 너 걔의 이멜주소를 알고 있어?
B: Yes, we exchanged email addresses at our last meeting.
어, 지난 회의에서 서로 이멜주소를 교환했어.

05 I added his address to my mailing list
난 나의 멜리스트에 걔의 이멜주소를 추가했어

- Can you please add these addresses to the company mailing list?
회사 멜리스트에 이 주소들을 추가해줄테야?
- How do I get my email address taken off the mailing list?
멜리스트에서 어떻게 내 이멜주소를 빼?
- He put me on the company mailing list. 걘 나를 회사의 멜리스트에 추가했어.

A: I keep getting emails from that company. 난 저 회사로부터 이멜을 계속 받고 있어.
B: Someone must have put you on their mailing list.
누군가가 그들 회사의 멜리스트에 너를 넣었나보다.

019

I got an e-mail from him early this afternoon

오늘 오후 일찍 걔로부터 이멜을 받았어

이멜이 왔는지 확인할 때는 check one's email 혹은 check for emails. 이멜을 받았다고 하려면 got an email from sb라고 한다. got 대신에 received를 써도 된다.

01 He's checking for email on his phone
걘 핸드폰으로 이멜을 확인하고 있어

- I just got an email notification on my phone. 방금 핸드폰에서 이멜왔다는 알림을 받았어.
- Can I borrow your phone to check my emails please?
  내 이멜을 확인하기 위해 네 폰을 빌릴 수 있을까?
- Are you checking for emails on your phone during class?
  수업중에 폰으로 이멜을 확인하는거야?

A: Who are you texting with? 누구와 문자를 주고 받니?
B: Nobody. I'm checking my emails. 아무하고도 안해. 이멜을 확인하고 있어.

02 I got an e-mail from him early this afternoon
오늘 오후 일찍 걔로부터 이멜을 받았어

- Have you gotten an email from the company yet? 그 회사로부터 이멜을 받았어?
- I get emails from them every day. 난 매일 그들로부터 이멜을 받고 있어.
- I get my emails printed out sometimes. 난 때때로 내 이멜을 프린터 해.

A: I get emails from them every day. 난 그들로부터 매일 이멜을 받고 있어.
B: Really? I never get emails from them. 정말? 난 그들에게서 전혀 멜이 안오는데.

03 Have you received my email?
내 이멜을 받았어?

● I received an email from the school saying I'd been accepted.
내가 합격됐다고 학교로부터 멜을 받았어.

● I haven't received an email from the company yet.
난 그 회사로부터 이멜을 받지 못했어.

● She received an email from her assistant a few minutes ago.
걘 조금전에 조수로부터 메일을 받았어.

A: Have you received my email yet? 내 이멜을 받았어?
B: Yes, I just got it a few moments ago. 어, 조금전에 받았어.

04 The email finally got through to him
마침내 이멜이 걔한테 갔어

● Did my email get through to you? 내 이멜을 너한테 갔어?

● The email didn't get through to him for some reason.
무슨 이유에서인가 이멜이 걔한테 가지 않았어.

A: You didn't get my email? 내 이멜을 받지 못했어?
B: No, for some reason it didn't get through to me.
어, 무슨 이유인지 모르겠지만, 내게 오지 않았어.

05 Have you read the company's latest email?
회사의 최근 이멜을 읽었어?

● I read the email you sent me today. 네가 오늘 보낸 이멜을 읽었어.

● Did you read all of those emails? 그 이멜들 다 읽었어?

● He never reads spam emails. He just deletes them.
걘 절대로 스팸멜을 읽지 않아. 그냥 삭제해버려.

A: Did you read today's email? 오늘 온 이멜을 읽었어?
B: Yes, of course! 어, 물론이지!

020

She sent the email to the hotel

갠 그 호텔에 이멜을 보냈어

반대로 이멜을 보낼 때는 send 동사를 활용한다. 혹은 drop sb an email이라고 써도 되며 아니면 아예 email를 동사로 써서 email sb about~이라고 해도 된다.

01 She sent me a very funny e-mail
갠 내게 아주 재미있는 이멜을 보냈어

- I'll send you an email with **all the information.**
  그 모든 정보가 들어있는 이멜을 너에게 보낼게.

- She sent the email to **the hotel.** 갠 그 호텔에 이멜을 보냈어.

- I am going to send them an email about **the presentation.**
  난 발표회에 관한 이멜을 그들에게 보낼거야.

A: Do they know about the presentation? 걔네들이 발표회에 대해 알고 있어?

B: No but I'm going to send them an email about it today.
아니, 하지만 오늘 그에 대해 걔네들에게 이멜을 보낼거야.

02 He sent the pictures to my Gmail address
갠 내 Gmail 주소로 사진들을 보냈어

- He sent an email to **the wrong address** 갠 틀린 주소로 이멜을 보냈어.

- I will send the file to **Chris's Gmail address.**
  난 크리스의 Gmail 주소로 그 파일을 보낼거야.

- He sent the file to **my old email address.** 갠 내 옛 이멜주소로 파일을 보냈어.

A: Make sure you send it to Chris's Gmail address, not his old one.
크리스의 옛 멜주소가 아니라 Gmail 주소로 그걸 확실히 보내도록 해.

B: Thanks for reminding me. 알려줘서 고마워.

03

I'll drop him an email to say we're getting married
우리가 결혼한다고 하는 이멜을 걔에게 보낼거야

- You can contact her by email. 넌 이멜로 걔와 연락을 취할 수 있어.
- Can you drop me an email the next time you're going to be in town?
  네가 시내에 다음번에 올 때 내게 이멜을 보낼테야?
- She contacted me via email. 걘 이멜로 내게 연락을 해왔어.

A: I don't know her phone number. 난 걔 전화번호를 몰라.
B: Just contact her by email. 이멜로 연락을 취해봐.

04

She emailed me about the meeting tomorrow
걘 내일 회의에 관한 이멜을 내게 보냈어

- What did he email you about? 걘 너에게 무슨 내용으로 이멜을 보낸거야?
- The email was in regard to the new employee. 그 이멜은 신입사원에 대한 거였어.
- I will email you about the test. 내가 그 테스트에 관해 너에게 이멜을 보낼게.

A: What's on the test next week? 담주 테스트에 뭐가 나와?
B: I will send all of you an email about it. 그에 관해 너희들 모두에게 이멜을 보낼게.

05

I always block unwanted spam emails
원치않는 스팸메일을 난 항상 차단해

- You should never open unknown emails.
  모르는 사람에게서 온 이멜은 절대로 열어보지 마라.
- Can you forward her email to me please? 걔가 보낸 이멜을 내게 전달해줄래?
- I'll forward the message to you right now. 지금 바로 그 메시지를 너에게 전달할게.

A: What did she say in her email? 걔가 이멜에서 뭐라고 했어?
B: I'll forward you her email right now. 지금 바로 걔 이멜을 너에게 전달해줄게.

021

I attached the wrong file to the email

난 이멜에 엉뚱한 파일을 첨부했어

이멜에 첨부파일을 보내는 것은 일상화된 일. 파일을 첨부하다는 attach a[the] file, 첨부파일을 보내다는 send some attachments, 그리고 첨부파일을 열다는 get the attached file opened라고 하면 된다.

01

Make sure you attach the file before sending the email 이멜을 보내기 전에 파일을 확실히 첨부하도록 해

- **Did she attach a file to the email?** 걔가 이멜에 파일을 첨부했어?

- **I attached the wrong file to the email.** 난 이멜에 엉뚱한 파일을 첨부했어.

- **Could you please attach the hotel file to the email?** 이멜에 호텔파일을 첨부해줄래?

A: Did she attach the file to the email? 걔가 이멜에 파일을 첨부했어?
B: Of course, she did. 물론, 그랬어.

02

She sent some attachments with her Gmail
걘 자기 Gmail로 보낸 이멜에 첨부파일을 보냈어

- **What were in those attachments you sent?** 네가 보낸 그 첨부파일엔 뭐가 들어있었어?

- **I can't open up the attachments I got in the email.**
이 이멜에 달려온 첨부파일을 열 수가 없어.

- **Did you have any trouble opening those attachments?**
그 첨부파일을 여는데 무슨 어려움이라도 있었어?

A: Did you have any trouble opening those attachments in the email?
이멜에 달린 그 첨부파일들을 여는데 무슨 어려움이라도 있었어?

B: Yes, for some reason I couldn't open them.
어, 어떤 까닭인지 그 파일들을 열수가 없었어.

03 Please send this file as an attachment
이 파일을 첨부파일로 보내줘

- He sent that picture as an attachment. 걘 그 사진을 첨부파일로 보냈어.
- The file is too big to send it as an attachment.
  그 파일은 용량이 너무 커서 첨부파일로 보내지 못해.
- Will you send these files as attachments? 이 파일들을 첨부파일로 보내줄래?

A: I don't remember him sending me that picture.
걔가 내게 그 사진을 보낸게 기억안나.

B: He sent it to all of us. He sent it as an attachment.
우리 모두에게 보냈어. 첨부파일로 보냈어.

04 Please see the attached file for more detailed information 더 상세한 정보는 첨부파일을 보세요

- You need to read the attached file to understand the situation.
  상황을 이해하기 위해서는 첨부파일을 읽어야 돼.
- Please refer to the attached file. 첨부파일을 참고하세요.
- You need to open the attached file, read it, then call me.
  첨부파일을 열어서 읽고 난 후 내게 전화해야 돼.

A: I don't understand the email content. 이멜에 쓰인 내용을 이해못하겠어.
B: That's why you need to read the attached file. All the information is in it. 그래서 넌 첨부파일을 읽어야 돼. 모든 정보가 그 안에 들어있어.

05 I couldn't get the attached file opened
난 첨부파일을 열 수가 없었어

- Did she get the email with the attached file? 걘 첨부파일이 달린 이멜을 받았어?
- Why haven't they got the attached file email yet?
  왜 걔네들은 첨부파일이 달린 이멜을 받지 못한거야?

A: Did she get the email with the attached file? 걘 첨부파일이 달린 이멜을 받았어?
B: No, not yet. 아니. 아직.

Unit 06

022

The email got returned to me

이멜이 내게 다시 돌아왔어

받은 메일함은 inbox, 자동으로 스팸메일함으로 들어간다고 할 때는 get automatically put into my junk email folder라고 하면 된다. 또한 이멜이 돌아왔다고 할 때는 get returned to me라고 한다.

01 Your email just arrived in my inbox

네 이멜은 받은메일함에 방금 왔어

- **My inbox is empty today.** 오늘 내 받은메일함은 비어 있어.

- **I need to reorganize my inbox.** 난 받은메일함을 재정리해야 돼.

- **She was deleting unnecessary emails from her inbox.**
  걘 받은메일함에서 불필요한 이멜들을 삭제하고 있었어.

A: Wow. Your inbox is completely empty. 와우. 네 받은메일함은 완전히 비어 있네.

B: Yes, I deleted all the emails in it today.
어. 난 오늘 받은메일함의 모든 이멜을 삭제했어.

02 Unknown emails get automatically put into my junk email folder 모르는 사람에게서 오는 이멜은 자동으로 스팸메일함에 들어가

- **Your email may have gotten put into my junk email folder.**
  네 이멜이 내 스팸메일함으로 들어갈 수도 있었을거야.

- **Spam gets automatically put into my junk folder.**
  스팸메일을 자동적으로 내 스팸메일함으로 들어가.

- **I'm not sure how but your email was in my junk folder.**
  어떻게 그렇게 된지 모르겠지만, 네 이멜은 내 스팸메일함으로 들어갔어.

A: How did my email get put into your junk folder?
어떻게 내 이멜이 네 스팸메일함으로 들어간거야?

B: I'm not really sure. 정말 잘 모르겠어.

Were you able to get the file open?
그 파일을 열 수 있었어?

- Don't open the attached file. 첨부파일은 열지마.
- I opened the file **without any trouble**. 난 어려움없이 그 파일을 열었어.
- He told me **not to open the file**. 걘 내게 그 파일을 열지 말라고 했어.

A: Why didn't you open the attached file? 넌 왜 첨부파일을 열지 않은거야?
B: I was told not to open unknown files.
모르는 사람에게서 온 이멜을 열지말라는 얘기를 들었어.

The email got returned to me
이멜이 내게 다시 돌아왔어

- My email **got rejected** for some reason. 내가 보낸 이멜이 어떤 까닭인지 거절당했어.
- The email address I sent it to **was rejected**. 그 이멜을 보낸 이멜주소는 거절당했어.
- The email **was returned** automatically. 이멜이 자동으로 되돌아왔어.

A: The email didn't get accepted? 이멜이 가지 않은거야?
B: Right. It was returned to me automatically. 어. 자동으로 되돌아왔어.

It was returned to my inbox
그건 내 받은메일함으로 되돌아왔어

- You'll know if it was rejected because it will **get returned to your inbox**.
네 받은메일함으로 되돌아올거기 때문에 거절당했다는 것을 알게 될거야.
- She told me the email she sent **was returned to her inbox**.
걘 자기가 보낸 이멜이 자기 받은메일함으로 돌아왔다고 했어.

A: Did you get her email? 걔 이멜을 받았어?
B: No, she told me it was returned to her inbox automatically. I'm not
sure why. 아니. 걘 자동으로 자기 받은메일함으로 되돌아왔다고 했어. 이유를 확실히 모르겠어.

Unit 06 인터넷/SNS | 369 |

023

Please answer my email ASAP

내 이멜에 가능한 빨리 답을 줘

이멜에 답하는 것은 answer one's email, 답장을 하다는 respond to one's email이라고 하거나 혹은 send a reply, reply to sb를 사용해도 된다. 그렇게 답장을 받다는 receive a response라고 한다.

I need to answer their emails by today
난 오늘까지 그들의 이멜에 답을 해야 돼

- **Please answer my email ASAP.** 내 이멜에 가능한 빨리 답을 줘.
- **I didn't answer any of his emails.** 난 걔 이멜 어떤 거에도 답을 하지 않았어.
- **Not answering emails is a bit rude.** 이멜에 답을 하지 않는 것은 좀 무례해.

A: I didn't answer any of his emails. 난 걔 이멜 어떤 거에도 답을 하지 않았어.
B: Why not? Isn't that a bit rude? 왜 안했어? 좀 무례한 것 아냐?

I responded to her email yesterday
난 어제 걔의 이멜에 답을 했어

- **She responded to my email earlier today.** 걘 오늘 일찍 내 이멜에 답을 했어.
- **I need to respond to this email right now.** 난 지금 바로 이 이멜에 답을 해야 돼.
- **Can I respond to your email later on?** 내가 나중에 네 이멜에 답을 해도 될까?

A: You need to respond to their email right now.
   넌 지금 바로 그들의 이멜에 답을 해야 돼.
B: I can't. I have a meeting until 4pm. 안돼. 난 오후 4시까지 회의가 있어.

03 Have you received a response yet?
넌 이멜답장을 받았어?

- I received his response **this morning**. 난 오늘 아침 걔의 답장을 받았어.
- His response to my email **was positive**. 내 이멜에 대한 그의 답장은 긍정적이었어.
- Why hasn't he responded yet? 왜 걘 답장을 쓰지 않았던거야?

A: Why hasn't he responded yet? It's been one week.
왜 걘 답장을 쓰지 않았던거야? 일주일이 지났는데.

B: Maybe he didn't receive your email? 네 이멜을 혹 받지 못한게 아닐까?

04 You need to send a reply to him immediately
넌 즉시 걔에게 답장을 보내야 돼

- I sent him my reply **one month ago but haven't heard back from him**.
난 한달전에 걔에게 답장을 보냈는데 그로부터 답장을 받지 못했어.
- Did you reply to his offer? 넌 걔의 제안에 답장을 했어?
- Why hasn't he replied? 왜 걘 답장을 하지 않은거야?

A: Did you reply to his offer? 넌 걔의 제안에 답장을 했어?
B: Yes, I accepted it. 어. 제안을 받아들였어.

05 I need to reply to her soon
난 곧 걔에게 답장을 해야 돼

- How soon do you need a reply? 얼마나 빨리 답장을 보내야 돼?
- When do you need a reply? 언제 답장이 필요한거야?
- I have to reply by today. 난 오늘까지 답장을 해야 돼.

A: How soon does she need a reply? 걘 얼마나 빨리 답장을 해야 돼?
B: By tomorrow. 내일까지.

024

I texted her back a few minutes ago

난 조금전에 걔에게 답장문자를 보냈어

역시 새롭게 인기를 얻고 있는 단어는 text일게다. 명사나 동사로 쓰이며 또한 좀 더 자세히 말하려면 text message라고도 하는데 이때도 역시 명사뿐만 아니라 동사로도 쓰인다는 점을 유념해둔다.

01 He's texting his friend at work

걘 직장동료에게 문자를 보내고 있어

- I texted her back a few minutes ago. 난 조금전에 걔에게 답장문자를 보냈어.
- He always texts me when I'm eating. 걘 내게 먹고 있을 때 항상 문자를 보내.
- Can you text me when you arrive? 네가 도착하면 문자를 보낼테야?

A: Can you text me when you arrive? 네가 도착하면 문자를 보낼테야?
B: Of course. 물론.

02 People send text messages from their mobile phones

사람들은 자신의 핸드폰으로 문자메시지를 보내

- I sometimes send text messages from my computer. 난 종종 컴퓨터로 문자를 보내.
- Remember when text messages didn't exist? 문자메시지가 없던 때를 기억해?
- I hate it when I meet people and they start texting.
  사람들 만나고 있는데 그들이 문자를 하기 시작하면 정말 싫더라.

A: Remember when text messages didn't exist? 문자메시지가 없던 때를 기억해?
B: No, it seems like they've always existed. 아니, 없었던 적이 없었던 것 같아.

She receives text messages all day long
걘 하루내내 문자메시지를 받아

- I get text messages often. 난 종종 문자메시지를 받아.
- She never gets any text messages. 걘 문자메시지를 전혀 받지 않아.
- Did you receive a text message a few minutes ago? 너 조금전에 문자메시지 받았어?

A: How often do you receive text messages? 얼마나 자주 문자메시지를 받아?
B: All day long! 하루내내!

Do you use emoticons in your text messages?
문자메시지에 이모티콘을 사용해? ·

- I hate it when people overuse emojis when texting.
  문자할 때 이모티콘을 너무 많이 사용하는 사람들 정말 싫더라.
- What's your favorite emoji for texting? 문자할 때 좋아하는 이모티콘은 뭐야?
- She overuses emoticons when she texts. 걘 문자할 때 이모티콘을 너무 많이 사용해.

A: Do you use emojis in your text messages? 넌 문자메시지할 때 이모티콘을 사용해?
B: Yes, I usually use the "Thumbs up" or "Thumbs down" emojis.
   어, 난 보통 "아주 좋아" 혹은 "거절"이라는 이모티콘을 사용해.

I was able to delete the text message before they
saw it 난 보낸 문자를 상대방이 보기 전에 삭제할 수 있었어

- I sent the text message to the wrong chat room. 난 엉뚱한 채팅방에 문자를 보냈어.
- I am in several different chat rooms that I use regularly.
  난 정기적으로 사용하는 채팅방이 여러 개가 있어.
- I sometimes mix up the chat rooms and send messages to the wrong
  rooms. 난 종종 채팅방을 혼동해서 엉뚱한 채팅방에 메시지를 보내.

A: What's wrong? 왜 그래.
B: I sent an embarrassing message to the wrong chat room and didn't
   delete it before they all saw it.
   엉뚱한 채팅방에 난처한 메시지를 보냈는데 그들이 읽기 전에 삭제하지 못했어.

Unit 06

Unit 06 인터넷/SNS | 373 |

025

I did a video chat with my brother

난 형과 화상채팅을 했어

화상통화의 대명사가 된 skype가 동사로도 쓰인다. 그리고 화상채팅을 하다는 do a video chat, 화상통화를 하다는 make[do] a video call이라고 하면 된다.

01

I used to skype a lot

난 스카이프를 많이 사용하곤 했어

● My skype family lives in four different countries: Canada, South Korea, Japan and Germany. 내 스카이프 패밀리는 4개국에서 살고 있어. 캐나다, 한국, 일본 그리고 독일.

● Skype is great for grandparents who want to regularly see their grandchildren in faraway places.
스카이프는 멀리 떨어진 곳에 사는 손자손녀들을 정기적으로 보기 원하는 조부모에게는 아주 좋아.

● I have a really big skype family all over the world.
나는 정말 전세계에 걸쳐 있는 스카이프 대가족이야.

A: I heard you have a really big skype family. 너 스카이프 대가족이라며.
B: Yes, they are all over the world. 어, 전세계에 걸쳐 있어.

02

My text service has a voice talk feature

내 문자서비스는 보이스톡 기능도 돼

● The voice talk feature is very convenient for when I'm driving.
보이스톡 기능은 운전할 때 매우 편리해.

● Sometimes the voice talk makes spelling mistakes.
때때로 보이스톡할 때 철자가 잘못될 때가 많아.

● You need to speak clearly for the voice talk feature to work correctly.
보이스톡 기능이 제대로 되기 위해서는 말을 명확하게 해야 돼.

A: Why don't you like using the voice talk feature?
보이스톡 기능을 왜 이용하지 않아?

B: It makes a lot of spelling mistakes. 철자가 너무 많이 틀리게 나와서.

03 I did a video chat with my brother
난 형과 화상채팅을 했어

- Do you prefer video chats to texting? 문자보다 화상채팅을 더 좋아해?
- I video chat with my family back home once a week.
  일주일에 한번 집에 있는 가족과 함께 화상채팅을 해.
- When did you last do a video chat? 언제 마지막으로 화상채팅을 했어?

A: I did a video chat with my sister who lives in Germany yesterday.
난 어제 독일에 사는 누이와 화상채팅을 했어.

B: Do you prefer video chats to texting? 문자보다 화상채팅을 더 좋아해?

04 I'm going to make a video call to my friend in America tonight 오늘밤에 미국에 있는 내 친구에게 화상통화를 할거야

- I make video calls with my parents once a week.
  난 일주일에 한번 부모님과 화상통화를 해.
- Did you make a video call last night? 지난밤에 화상통화를 했어?
- Have you ever made a video call before? 전에 화상통화를 해본 적이 있어?

A: Why can't you meet tonight? 왜 오늘밤에 만날 수 없어?

B: I'm going to make a video call to my parents. We do it every
Thursday night. 부모님에게 화상통화를 걸거야. 매주 목요일 저녁에 하거든.

05 I did a video call with my girlfriend
내 여친과 화상통화를 했어

- She does video calls with her customers every week. 걘 매주 고객들과 화상통화를 해.
- Have you ever done a video call? 화상통화를 해본 적이 있어?
- I didn't do a video call last night. 난 지난밤에 화상통화를 하지 않았어.

A: How does she have such good relationships with her customers?
어떻게 걘 고객들과 그렇게 좋은 관계를 유지하는거야?

B: She does video calls with them regularly. 걘 정기적으로 고객들과 화상통화를 해.

Unit 06

026

I do a lot of chatting on the Internet

난 인터넷으로 채팅을 많이 해

chat 역시 명사나 동사로 사용되는 거의 우리말화 된 단어이다. 온라인으로 만나는 것은 meet sb online. …와 채팅하다는 chat with sb라고 말하면 된다.

01 They met each other online

걔네들은 온라인으로 서로 만났어

- Meeting online is very common these days. 온라인 만남은 요즘 아주 흔한 일이야.
- She met her boyfriend through an online dating site.
  걘 남친을 온라인 데이트 사이트를 통해서 만났어.
- Have you ever met anyone online? 온라인으로 누구 만나본 적 있어?

A: How did you meet your husband? 네 남편을 어떻게 만났어?
B: We met online. 우리는 온라인으로 만났어.

02 I first met him in a chat room

처음 난 걔를 채팅방에서 만났어

- I've met a few girlfriends in chat rooms. 난 몇몇 여친들을 채팅방에서 만났어.
- Meeting people in chat rooms is a good way to get to know them.
  채팅방에서 사람을 만나는 것은 서로를 알아가는 아주 좋은 방법이야.
- I prefer meeting in chat rooms before deciding whether to meet them face-to-face. 난 직접 만나기를 결정하기에 앞서 채팅방에서 만나는 것을 더 좋아해.

A: I heard you met each other at work. 너희들 직장에서 서로 만났다며.
B: No, we first met in a chat room then we became coworkers afterwards. 아니. 우린 채팅방에서 먼저 만났고 그런 다음 나중에 동료가 된거야.

03 I can live chat with people from around the world
난 전세계에 있는 사람들과 라이브채팅을 할 수 있어

- I love chat rooms for keeping up with friends who live far away.
  난 멀리 사는 친구들과 연락하고 지내기 위해 채팅방을 아주 좋아해.

- My favorite way to stay in touch with friends is via chat rooms.
  내가 좋아하는 친구들과 소통하기 좋아하는 방법은 채팅방을 통해서야.

A: How do you stay in touch with so many people?
넌 어떻게 그렇게 많은 사람들과 연락하고 지내는거야?

B: I use chat rooms. 난 채팅방을 이용해.

04 I do a lot of chatting on the Internet
난 인터넷으로 채팅을 많이 해

- Chatting with strangers on the Internet can be dangerous.
  인터넷으로 모르는 사람과 채팅하는 것은 위험할 수도 있어.

- I kill time by chatting with my friends on the Internet.
  난 인터넷으로 친구들과 채팅하면서 시간을 보내.

A: You should be careful about chatting with strangers on the Internet.
인터넷으로 모르는 사람과 채팅할 때는 조심해야 돼.

B: I know and I am. 알고 있어 그리고 조심하고 있어.

05 Do you chat online often?
너 자주 온라인 채팅을 하니?

- How much time a day do you spend chatting online?
  하루에 얼마동안 온라인 채팅을 하면서 보내?

- She is always chatting online. 걘 늘상 온라인 채팅을 하고 있어.

- He wastes a lot of time chatting online. 걘 온라인 채팅을 하면 많은 시간을 보내.

A: Do you chat online often? 너 자주 온라인 채팅을 하니?

B: About an hour a day or so. 하루에 한 한시간 정도.

027

I use Kakao Talk for messaging

난 메시지를 주고 받는데 카카오톡을 이용해

메신저하면 카톡이나 라인 그리고 비밀대화방으로 유명한 텔레그램이다. 카톡의 많은 기능들은 features라고 하고, 카톡메시지 확인하는 것은 check one's Kakao Talk, 카톡으로 메시지를 보내다는 send sb a message on Kakao라고 한다.

 01

I got a Kakao Talk message
난 카톡 메시지가 왔어

- I use Kakao Talk for messaging. 난 메시지를 주고 받는데 카카오톡을 이용해.
- Kakao Talk is the most popular messaging service in Korea.
  카카오톡은 한국에서 가장 많이 쓰이는 메시지 서비스야.
- Kakao Talk has many useful features. 카카오톡에는 많은 유용한 기능들이 있어.

A: Why do you like Kakao Talk? 넌 왜 카카오톡을 좋아하는거야?
B: It has many useful features. 많은 유용한 기능들이 있어서.

 02

Please check your Kakao Talk right now
지금 바로 네 카카오톡을 확인해봐

- Mom says she just sent you a message on Kakao. 엄마가 그러는데 방금 카카오톡으로 메시지 보냈대.
- You are always checking your Kakao Talk. 넌 늘상 카카오톡을 확인하는구나.
- I forgot to check my Kakao so I missed your message.
  카카오톡 확인하는 것을 깜박해서 네 메시지를 놓쳤어.

A: What bothers you about me? 내가 뭐 걸리는게 있어?
B: Well, you are always looking at your Kakao.
  음, 넌 늘상 네 카카오톡을 보고 있잖아.

03 The Kakao messenger is an application that allows Korean speakers to use the Internet to chat and communicate with each other

카카오톡 메신저는 한국사람들이 인터넷으로 채팅하고 서로 의사소통할 수 있게 해주는 어플이야

- Kakao Talk has made communication much more convenient for all of its users. 카카오톡은 그 모든 사용자들에게 의사소통을 훨씬 쉽게 만들어줬어.

A: Kakao Talk has made communication much more convenient for everyone. 카카오톡은 사용자들 모두에게 의사소통을 훨씬 쉽게 만들어줬어.
B: I agree. 맞는 말이야.

04 It's a great way to keep in touch with friends and family members 그건 친구와 가족들과 연락하고 지내는 아주 좋은 방법이야

- I use Kakao to stay in touch with all my friends and family.
난 친구, 가족들 모두와 연락하고 지내기 위해 카카오톡을 이용해.

- He stays in contact with his high school friends with Kakao Talk.
걘 카카오톡으로 고등학교 친구들과 연락을 하고 지내.

- Do you use Kakao to remain in touch with your old friends?
넌 옛 친구들과 연락하고 지내기 위해 카카오톡을 사용해?

A: I love Kakao Talk. 난 카카오톡이 좋더라.
B: Me too. It's a great way to stay in touch with friends and family.
나도 그래. 그건 친구와 가족들과 연락하고 지내는 아주 좋은 방법이야.

05 Telegram got popular for its "secret chat" function
텔레그램은 비밀채팅 기능으로 유명해졌어

- Snapchat is super popular for following your friends and famous celebrities. 스냅챗은 친구들과 셀렙들을 팔로우하는데 최고의 인기야.

- Which social media platform do you like the most? 가장 좋아하는 소셜미디어플랫폼은 뭐야?

A: Do you use Facebook? 넌 페이스북을 사용해?
B: No, that's for old people. I use Instagram. 아니. 그건 노땅들거구. 난 인스타 해.

Unit 06

028

You people are really into taking selfies
너희들 정말 셀카찍는데 빠졌구만

스마트폰으로 사진을 찍다는 take pictures through[with] smartphones이고 셀카를 찍다는 take a selfie라고 한다. 이때 사용되기도 하는 셀카봉은 a selfie stick이라고 하면 된다.

01 I love to take pictures through smartphones
난 스마트폰으로 사진찍는 것을 좋아해

- Most people don't own cameras anymore because they all use their smartphone cameras.
  대부분의 사람들은 스마트폰으로 사진을 찍기 때문에 더 이상 카메라를 갖고 있지 않아.

- I take about 500 pictures a week with my smartphone camera.
  난 스마트폰으로 일주일에 한 500장의 사진을 찍어.

- The newest iPhone camera takes amazing pictures.
  신형 아이폰 카메라로 아주 뛰어난 사진을 찍을 수 있어.

A: How many pictures do you take a week with your camera?
카메라로 일주일에 몇 장 정도의 사진을 찍어?

B: I can't count that high! 그렇게 많이 찍지 않아!

02 I took a selfie with my wife in front of the Eiffel Tower
난 에펠탑 앞에서 아내와 함께 셀카를 찍었어

- I finally bought a selfie-stick this week. 마침내 이번주에 셀카봉을 샀어.

- You people are really into taking selfies. 너희들 정말 셀카찍는데 빠졌구만.

- She is always posting her selfie pictures on Instagram.
  걘 항상 인스타그램에 셀카사진을 올려.

A: When did people get into taking selfies? 언제 사람들이 셀카찍는거에 빠진거야?

B: When smartphone cameras became a regular feature. 일반적으로 스마트폰에 카메라가 달린 때에.

Have you ever used a selfie stick?
셀카봉을 사용해본 적이 있어?

- He has a selfie wrist from taking so many selfies.
  걘 너무 많은 셀카를 찍어서 손목이 뻤어.

- I can't move my hand because I have selfie-wrist.
  셀카찍다가 손이 삐어서 손을 움직일 수가 없어.

- Selfie-wrist has become a common ailment these days.
  셀카찍다가 손이 삐는 것은 요즘 흔한 병이 되었어.

A: What's wrong with your hand? 너 손이 왜그래?
B: I have selfie-wrist. 셀카찍다가 손이 삐었어.

I have stored over 20 phone albums
난 20개가 넘는 폰앨범을 저장해놨어

- How many albums have you stored on your phone?
  네 폰에 몇 개의 앨범을 저장했어?

- She was showing me some of her phone albums this afternoon.
  걘 오늘 오후에 자신의 폰앨범 중 몇 개를 보여줬어.

- I am putting together a phone album of our trip. 난 우리 여행 폰앨범을 정리하고 있어.

A: What are you doing on your phone? 네 폰으로 뭘하고 있는거야?
B: I'm putting together a phone album of your birthday party.
네 생일파티 폰앨범을 정리하고 있어.

029
She really enjoys playing computer games

갠 정말 컴퓨터 게임하는 것을 좋아해

컴퓨터 게임을 하다는 play video games on a computer. 혹은 간단히 play computer games라 한다. 그리고 스마트폰으로 한다고 할 때는 play games on one's smartphone이라고 한다.

He is playing video games on a computer
갠 컴퓨터로 게임을 하고 있어

- **She really enjoys** playing computer games. 갠 정말 컴퓨터 게임하는 것을 좋아해.
- **I waste too much time** playing games on my computer.
  난 컴퓨터로 게임하는데 시간을 많이 허비해.
- **My friends and I all love to** play interactive computer games.
  내 친구들과 나는 모두 대화형 컴퓨터 게임을 아주 좋아해.

A: What are your plans tonight? 오늘밤에 뭐할거야?
B: My friends and I are going to play some computer games.
   친구들과 난 컴퓨터 게임들을 좀 할거야.

She loves to play games on her smartphones
갠 스마트폰으로 게임하는 것을 아주 좋아해

- **Smartphone games** have become extremely popular.
  스마트폰 게임은 아주 인기가 엄청 있어.
- **Do you ever** play games on your smartphone? 스마트폰으로 게임을 해?
- **What's the most popular smartphone game** these days?
  요즘 가장 인기있는 스마트폰 게임이 뭐야?

A: She is always on her smartphone playing games.
   갠 항상 스마트폰으로 게임을 하고 있어.
B: Yes, she's a game addict. 맞아. 갠 게임중독자야.

03 I'm so into smartphone games
난 스마트폰 게임에 아주 빠졌어

● She's crazy about smartphone games. 걘 스마트폰 게임을 엄청 좋아해.

● How much do you enjoy playing games on your phone?
폰으로 얼마나 게임을 즐기는거야?

● How many hours a day does she play smartphone games?
걘 하루에 얼마나 스마트폰 게임을 하는거야?

A: How often do you play smartphone games?
얼마나 자주 스마트폰 게임을 하는거야?

B: About 4 or 5 hours a day. 하루에 4–5시간 정도.

04 Angry Birds was a popular smartphone game
앵그리 버즈는 인기있는 스마트폰 게임였어

● These days, which smartphone games are popular? 요즘, 어떤 스마트폰이 인기야?

● Odin has been a very popular smartphone game the past few years.
오딘은 지난 몇 년간 매우 인기있는 게임였어.

● She only likes the popular smartphone games. 걘 인기있는 스마트폰 게임만을 좋아해.

A: These days which smartphone games are popular?
요즘, 어떤 스마트폰이 인기야?

B: A lot of people really like Odin. 많은 사람들인 오딘을 아주 좋아해.

His tweet was very shocking
걔의 트윗은 매우 충격적이었어

짧은 메시지 플랫폼으로 유명한 Twitter. 트위터에서 너를 팔로우한다는 follow you on Twitter라고 하고 이렇게 트위터에 올린 메시지는 tweet라고 하는데 동사로도 쓰여, '트윗을 올리다'라는 뜻이 되기도 한다.

01 Do you use Twitter?
너 트위터 하니?

- **Many young people** use Twitter. 많은 젊은이들이 트위터를 해.
- **I am following you** on Twitter. 난 트위터에서 널 팔로우 해.
- **Did you read his tweets today?** 너 오늘 걔의 트윗 읽었니?

A: Did you read his latest tweets? 걔의 최근 트윗을 봤어?
B: No, I'm not following him on Twitter. 아니, 난 트위터에서 걔를 팔로우하지 않아.

02 It's on Twitter
그게 트위터에 올라왔어

- **I found out about it** on Twitter. 난 트위터에서 그거에 관해 알아냈어.
- **He has over 100,000 followers** on Twitter. 걘 트위터 팔로워가 10만이 넘었어.
- **His tweet** was very shocking. 걔의 트윗은 매우 충격적이었어.

A: He has a lot of followers on Twitter. 걘 트위터에서 많은 팔로워가 있어.
B: Over 1 million I heard. 듣기로는 백만명이 넘는데.

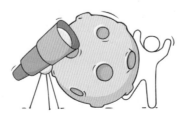

03

Twitter on the move
이동중에 트위터 해

- I am going to sign up for Twitter. 난 트위터에 가입할거야.
- Can you deactivate your Twitter account? 넌 트위터 계정을 비활성화할 수 있어?
- Why did she deactivate her Twitter account? 왜 걘 트위터 계정을 비활성화시켰어?

A: I thought his Twitter account was deactivated.
걔의 트위터 계정은 비활성화된 것으로 생각했었는데.

B: Well I just saw some of his Tweets today so he must have reactivated it. 오늘 걔의 트윗을 좀 봤으니 걔가 계정을 다시 활성화시킨 것 같아.

04

She tweeted a funny reply to her friend's tweet
걘 친구의 트윗에 재미난 답을 트윗했어

- Are you going to tweet about your wedding? 네 결혼식에 대해 트윗을 할거야?
- She sent out a series of tweets about the election.
걘 선거에 관한 일련의 트윗을 올렸어.
- He tweeted throughout the baseball game. 걘 야구경기 내내 트윗을 올렸어.

A: What are you laughing about? 뭐 때문에 웃고 있는거야?

B: His tweets about the election are really funny.
선거에 관한 걔의 트윗이 정말 재미나서.

05

I learned about the accident through Twitter
난 그 사고에 관한 것을 트위터를 통해 알게 됐어

- Did you find out the news through Twitter? 트위터를 통해 그 소식을 알게 된거야?
- She learned she had been fired on Twitter. 걘 해고소식을 트위터를 통해서 알게 됐어.
- I learned my girlfriend dumped me on Twitter.
난 여친이 트위터로 날 차버린 것을 알게 됐어.

A: My girlfriend dumped me on Twitter! 내 여친이 트위터로 날 차버렸어!

B: That's a terrible way to learn you've been dumped.
끔찍한 방법으로 차인 것을 알게 됐네.

031

He friended me on Facebook last week

갠 지난주에 페이스북에서 날 친추했어

이번에는 friend가 친구추천하다라는 동사로 쓰이는 페이스북. 페이스북을 비활성화하는 것은 deactivate, 아예 삭제하는 것은 delete란 동사를 사용하면 된다.

I joined Facebook over 10 years ago
난 지난 10년 넘게 페이스북을 사용하고 있어

- How can you delete your Facebook account? 어떻게 페이스북 계정을 삭제할 수 있어?

- I found my best friend in elementary school on Facebook a few days ago.
  며칠 전에 페이스북에서 초등학교 때의 베프를 찾았어.

- I am thinking of deactivating my Facebook account for a few months.
  몇 달동안 페이스북 계정을 비활성화 할까 생각중이야.

A: How can you delete your Facebook account?
어떻게 페이스북 계정을 삭제할 수 있어?

B: I'm not sure. Why? Are you thinking of doing that?
잘 모르겠어. 왜? 그럴 생각이야?

He friended me on Facebook last week
갠 지난주에 페이스북에서 날 친추했어

- I hate it when I get friended by people I don't know well on Facebook.
  페이스북에서 잘 모르는 사람들이 친구로 추가할 때 정말 싫더라.

- I got invited to a FB group for people who love chess.
  난 체스를 좋아하는 페이스북 그룹에 초대됐어.

- How many Facebook friends do you have? 페이스북 친구가 몇 명이나 돼?

A: I got friended by that guy I barely know today.
난 오늘 거의 알지 못하는 사람이 날 친구로 추가했어.

B: I hate it when I get friended by people I don't know well.
잘 모르는 사람이 날 친구로 추가할 때 정말 싫더라.

Let's get together via Facebook Messenger
페이스북 메신저를 통해 함께 만나자

- I'll start a private Facebook group for our high school reunion.
  난 고등학교 사적인 동창회 페이스북 그룹을 시작할거야.

- How many different Facebook groups do you belong to?
  너가 속한 페이스북 그룹이 몇 개나 돼?

- I have reconnected with many old friends on Facebook.
  난 페이스북으로 많은 옛친구들과 다시 연결됐어

A: We need to start planning the party. 우리는 파티를 준비하기 시작해야 돼.

B: I'll start a private Facebook group and invite everyone who is coming to help organize it.
난 개인적인 페이스북 그룹을 만들어서 와서 조직구성을 도와주는 모든 사람들을 초대할거야.

She updated her Facebook profile
걘 페이스북 프로필을 업데이트 했어

- I need to update my Facebook profile photo. 페이스북 프사를 업데이트 해야 돼.

- She hasn't updated her Facebook profile in years.
  걘 오랫동안 페이스북 프로필을 업데이트 하지 않았어.

A: She just updated her Facebook profile picture.
걘 방금 페이스북 프로필 사진을 업데이트 했어.

B: Yes, it looks great. 어. 아주 좋아 보여.

I will send him a message on Facebook today
난 오늘 페이스북에 걔에게 메시지를 보낼거야

- I messaged him via Facebook yesterday. 난 어제 페이스북을 통해 메시지를 보냈어.

- I'll post a message for him on his Facebook wall.
  난 걔의 페이스북 페이지에 걔에게 메시지를 올렸어.

A: Did you hear about her new job? 걔의 새로운 일자리에 대해 들었어?

B: Yes, she posted a message on my Facebook wall about it.
어. 걘 내 페이스북 페이지에 그에 관해 메시지를 올렸어.

Unit 06

032

He posts a ton of pictures on Instagram

걘 인스타그램에 많은 사진들을 올려

사진올리는 것으로 많은 유저들을 사로잡은 인스타그램. 좋아요를 누르다는 touch the love icon. 사진 등을 올리다는 post. 그리고 regram은 다른 사람의 피드를 다시 올리다, grammable은 인스타에 올릴 만하다라는 뜻이다.

---

01 He's touching the 'love' icon
걘 좋아요 아이콘을 누르고 있어

- He commented on her Instagram post.
  걘 그녀의 인스타그램 포스트에 댓글을 달았어.

- He is following her on Instagram. 걘 인스타그램에서 그녀를 팔로우하고 있어.

- Who do you follow on Instagram? 인스타그램에서 누구를 팔로우하고 있어?

A: My last Instagram post got a lot of hearts.
내가 지난번에 올린 인스타그램에는 좋아요가 많았어.

B: My posts never get any. 내가 올린 글에는 하나도 없는데.

---

02 She plans to post the photo on Instagram
걘 인스타그램에 사진을 올릴 생각이야

- He posts a ton of pictures on Instagram. 걘 인스타그램에 많은 사진들을 올려.

- I put up my wedding pictures on Instagram. 난 인스타그램에 결혼사진들을 올렸어.

- He is taking a photo of it before he eats it. He plans to post the photo on Instagram so his friends will see it.
  걘 먹기 전에 사진을 찍을거야. 그래서 친구들이 볼 수 있도록 인스타그램에 그 사진을 올릴 계획이야.

A: She spends a lot of time posting her selfies on Instagram.
걘 인스타그램에 셀카를 올리는데 많은 시간을 보내.

B: That's why I stopped following her. 그래서 난 걔를 언팔로우를 했어.

03 It's grammable
그건 사진찍어서 인스타에 올릴 만해

- He regrammed that post. 다른 사람의 사진의 출처를 밝히고 다시 올렸어.

- The birthday pictures he took weren't grammable.
  걔가 찍은 생일사진은 인스타에 올릴 만하지 못해.

- She always takes grammable pictures. 걘 항상 인스타에 올릴 만한 사진들을 찍어.

A: She is an amazing photographer. 걘 사진을 아주 뛰어나게 찍어.

B: Yes, her pictures are always grammable.
   맞아. 걔 사진들은 언제나 인스타에 올릴만해.

04 I will follow him
난 그 사람을 팔로워할거야

- I unfollowed him when I saw he liked Trump.
  그 사람이 트럼프를 좋아하는 것보고 언팔했어.

- How many people do you follow on Instagram?
  넌 인스타에서 몇 명이나 팔로우하고 있어?

- My Instagram account has a lot of followers. 내 인스타계정은 팔로워가 많아.

A: Did you see his Instagram feed what he posted?
   걔가 올린 인스타 게시물을 봤어?

B: Yes and I immediately stopped following him. 어. 난 바로 언팔로우했어.

05 It's on Instagram. Look for it on Instagram
인스타그램에 있어. 인스타에서 그걸 찾아봐

- You can check it out on my Instagram. 내 인스타에서 그걸 확인할 수 있어.

- I was watching for her newest Instagram feed.
  걔가 새로 올린 인스타 게시물들을 보고 있었어.

- Have you ever checked out her Instagram? 걔의 인스타 게시물을 확인해본 적 있어?

A: I just checked out your Instagram. 네 인스타그램을 확인했어.

B: Nice! What did you think? 좋아! 어때?

033

I don't check my DMs
난 DM을 확인하지 않아

페이스북이나 인스타에서 메시지를 직접 보내는 경우를 말한다. DM을 확인하다는 check my DM. 보내다는 send sb a DM. 그리고 동사로도 쓰여서 DMed하면 DM를 보냈다라는 뜻이 된다.

01 He DMed me about the party
걘 파티에 관해 내게 쪽지를 보냈어

- If anyone is interested in buying this laptop, please send me a DM.
  이 노트북을 사고 싶은 사람은 누구나 내게 쪽지를 보내세요.

- Drop me a DM if you want to have dinner. 저녁을 먹고 싶으면 내게 쪽지를 보내.

- She DMed me about the job interview. 걘 면접에 관한 쪽지를 내게 보냈어.

A: I'd like to meet you again. 널 다시 만나고 싶어.
B: Sure. Drop me a DM anytime you want to meet up.
  그래. 다시 만나고 싶을 때 언제든 쪽지를 보내.

02 DM me for dates
DM으로 날짜를 알려줘

- Please DM me if you want more information about the job.
  일에 관해 더 많은 정보를 알고 싶으면 쪽지를 보내세요.

- Can you send me a DM with your flight information ASAP?
  가능한 빨리 너의 비행정보를 쪽지로 보낼래?

- He DMed me asking for a date. 걘 쪽지로 데이트를 신청했어.

A: Please DM me if you want more information about the house.
  그 집에 대해 더 많은 정보를 알고 싶으면 쪽지를 보내세요.
B: I'll do that. 그렇게 할게요.

Let's talk on DM
DM으로 얘기하자

- This conversation needs to go to DMs. 이 대화는 DM으로 가서 해야겠어.
- Instead of chatting in the group chat, let's DM each other.
  단체방에서 얘기하는 대신에 둘만의 쪽지를 하자.
- I'd prefer it if you DM me. 네가 내게 쪽지를 보내면 더 좋겠어.

A: This conversation is getting too personal. Let's DM each other.
이 대화는 너무 사적이네. 둘만의 쪽지를 하자.

B: Sounds good. 좋아.

I sent a DM to night_sea_alone
난 night-sea-alone에게 쪽지를 보냈어

- She hasn't DMed me yet. 걘 아직 내게 쪽지를 보내지 않았어.
- He received a DM from his coworker. 걘 직장동료로부터 쪽지를 받았어.
- Have you ever sent a DM to your boss? 상사에게 쪽지를 보내 본 적이 있어?

A: She hasn't DMed me yet. I'm so disappointed.
걘 아직 내게 쪽지를 보내지 않았어. 실망이 커.

B: Have you sent her a DM yet? 넌 걔에게 쪽지를 보내지 않았어?

I don't check my DMs
난 DM을 확인하지 않아

- Please check the DM I sent you. 내가 보낸 쪽지를 확인해봐.
- I forgot to look at my DMs. 난 나에게 온 쪽지를 확인하는 것을 깜박했어.
- I sent a DM to the wrong person. 난 엉뚱한 사람에게 쪽지를 보냈어.

A: Why didn't you reply to my DM? 왜 내 DM에 답을 하지 않는거야?
B: I haven't checked them yet. 아직 확인을 하지 못했어.

유튜브

034
I have my YouTube channel
난 내 유튜브 채널이 있어

요즘 핫한 없는게 없는 YouTube. 유튜브를 둘러보다는 browse YouTube. 유튜브에서 …에 관한 영상을 보다는 watch videos about sth from YouTube라고 한다.

01 He's browsing YouTube
걘 유튜브를 둘러보고 있어

- I like to surf YouTube channels. 난 유튜브 채널들을 둘러보는 것을 좋아해.
- I got lost in a YouTube rabbit hole last night. 지난밤에 시간가는 줄 모르고 유튜브를 봤어.
- I usually watch gaming live streams on YouTube. 난 보통 유튜브로 실시간 게임을 봐.

A: Why do you look so tired this morning? 너 오늘 아침 왜 그렇게 피곤해보여?
B: I got lost in a YouTube rabbit hole last night.
지난밤에 시간가는 줄 모르고 유튜브에 빠졌어.

02 YouTube has many videos
유튜브에는 많은 영상이 있어

- YouTube has a huge variety of different channels.
유튜브에는 다양한 여러 채널들이 엄청 많아.
- I use YouTube cooking channels instead of cook books.
난 요리책 대신에 유튜브 요리채널을 이용해.
- I've learned so much from watching YouTube instructional videos.
난 유튜브의 교육용 영상들을 보면서 많은 것들을 배웠어.

A: I love YouTube. 난 유튜브를 아주 좋아해.
B: Me too. It has such a huge variety of different channels.
나도 그래. 유튜브에는 다양한 여러 채널들이 엄청 많아.

03 I'm watching videos about Yoga from YouTube
난 유튜브에서 요가에 관한 영상을 보고 있어

- I watched a YouTube video on how to do push ups correctly.
난 푸시업을 제대로 하는 방법에 관한 유튜브 영상을 봤어.

- I love watching sports highlights on YouTube.
난 유튜브로 스포츠 하이라이트 보는 것을 좋아해.

A: What were you watching on YouTube last night? 지난밤에 유튜브로 뭐를 봤어?

B: Sports highlights and some concert videos.
스포츠 하이라이트하고 콘서트 영상들을 좀 봤어.

04 I have my YouTube channel
난 내 유튜브 채널이 있어

- She started a really good Korean cooking YouTube channel.
걘 정말 좋은 한국요리 유튜브 채널을 시작했어.

- Her YouTube channel has a lot of subscribers. 걔 유튜브 채널 구독자수는 정말 많아.

- Please subscribe to my channel. 내 채널을 구독해주세요.

A: I started a new YouTube channel for guitar lessons.
난 기타배우는 새로운 유튜브 채널을 시작했어.

B: I'll subscribe to it tonight. 오늘밤에 구독할게.

Unit 06

05 There is a lot of fake news on YouTube
유튜브에는 가짜 뉴스가 아주 많아

- You can't trust all the news on YouTube. 유튜브에 있는 뉴스를 모두 믿으면 안돼.

- YouTube channels can have a negative influence on how people see the world. 유튜브 채널들은 사람들이 세상을 보는데 부정적인 영향을 끼칠 수도 있어.

A: Why are people so angry at each other about politics these days?
요즘 사람들이 정치에 대해 왜 서로 화가 나 있는거야?

B: Because there is so much fake news on YouTube that gets people angry. 사람들을 열받게 만드는 유튜브의 가짜 뉴스가 너무 많아서 그래.

035 I'm always posting on my blog

내 블로그에 항상 글을 올려

상대적으로 영향력이 줄어든 블로그. 블로그를 시작하다는 start a ~ blog라고 하고, 블로그에 …에 관한 글을 쓰다는 write about sth on one's blog라고 하면 된다.

01 I visited her cooking blog
난 걔의 요리블로그를 방문했어

● He started a travel blog. 걘 여행 블로그를 시작했어.

● She is blogging about her job. 걘 자기 일에 대한 블로그를 하고 있어.

● I want to be a famous blogger. 난 유명한 블로거가 되고 싶어.

A: He never comes out anymore. 걘 더 이상 외출을 전혀 하지 않아.
B: He is busy starting a movie blog. 걘 영화에 관한 블로그를 시작하느라 바빠.

02 He wrote about the restaurant on his blog
걘 자기 블로그에 식당에 관한 글을 썼어

● Every day he writes about a new movie on his blog.
매일 그는 자기 블로그에 신작영화에 대해 글을 써.

● She blogs about politics. 걘 정치에 관한 블로그를 운영하고 있어.

● What does he blog about? 걘 무엇에 관한 블로그를 하고 있어?

A: What does he blog about? 걘 무엇에 관한 블로그를 하고 있어?
B: He mostly blogs about real estate information.
걘 대개 부동산 정보에 관한 블로그를 하고 있어.

03 I read about the new beer in your blog
네 블로그에서 새로 나온 맥주에 관한 글을 읽었어

- She read the story **on her classmate's blog**. 걘 같은 반 친구의 블로그의 글을 읽었어.
- Whose blog **did you read that on**? 그건 누구 블로그에서 읽은거야?
- **I heard he** read that on your blog. 걘 그걸 네 블로그에서 읽었다는데.

A: Whose blog did you read that on? 그건 누구 블로그에서 읽은거야?
B: I read about it on my friend's blog. 내 친구의 블로그에서 읽었어.

04 I'm always posting on my blog
내 블로그에 항상 글을 올려

- She **is always writing stuff** on her blog. 걘 항상 자기 블로그에 글들을 올려.
- He blogs **every day**. 걘 매일 블로그를 해.
- **What is** he posting on his blog **these days**? 걔 요즘에는 블로그에 어떤 것들을 올려?

A: What is he up to these days? 요즘 걔 뭐하고 지내?
B: He is always posting stuff on his blog. 걘 늘상 자기 블로그에 글들을 올리고 있어.

My smartphone was infected with a virus

내 스마트폰은 바이러스에 감염됐어

바이러스에 감염되다는 get a virus나 be infected with a virus라고 한다. 이를 방지하기 위해 돌리는(check for viruses) 보안프로그램은 a security program 이라고 한다.

01 My computer got a virus from a website

내 컴퓨터는 어떤 사이트로부터 바이러스에 감염됐어

- **My smartphone was infected with a virus.** 내 스마트폰은 바이러스에 감염됐어.
- **I opened the file and suddenly my computer** got a virus.
  난 파일을 열었는데 갑자기 내 컴퓨터가 바이러스에 감염됐어.
- **There is a computer virus going around these days.**
  요즘 컴퓨터 바이러스가 유행이야.

A: Be careful. There is a computer virus going around these days.
조심해. 요즘 컴퓨터 바이러스가 유행이야.

B: I won't open any emails from people I don't know.
모르는 사람에게서 오는 멜은 열어보지 않을거야.

02 My computer security program checks for viruses

내 컴의 백신프로그램이 바이러스를 확인하고 있어

- **I have a program that will** clean out the virus.
  난 바이러스를 제거하는 프로그램을 갖고 있어.
- **The file is being scanned for viruses.** 그 파일은 바이러스 감염여부 스캔받고 있어.
- **I've never had a computer virus before.** 컴퓨터 바이러스에 걸려본 적이 없어.

A: How do you prevent your computer from getting viruses?
네 컴퓨터가 바이러스에 걸리지 않도록 어떻게 하고 있어?

B: My security program scans new files for viruses.
내 백신프로그램이 바이러스에 걸렸는지 새로운 파일들을 스캔해.

03   He is hacking other computers
갠 다른 컴퓨터들을 해킹하고 있어

● Hacking is illegal and often used to steal the personal information of others. 해킹은 불법이고 종종 다른 사람들의 개인정보를 훔치는데 사용돼.

● Some hackers can even access money in the bank accounts of their victims. 일부 해커들은 피해자의 은행계좌에서 돈을 인출할 수도 있어.

A: They hacked into the bank's computer system.
그들은 은행의 컴퓨터 시스템을 해킹했어.

B: Did they do much damage? 많은 피해를 끼쳤어?

04   The hackers were phishing for personal information
해커들은 피싱을 해서 개인정보를 훔쳐가

● The emails were part of a major phishing scam.
이멜들은 주요한 피싱사기의 일부분이야.

● Have you ever experienced any phishing attempts.
피싱하려는 시도를 경험해본 적이 있어?

A: Did you hear about the email phishing attempt? 이멜피싱시도에 대해 들어봤어?
B: Yes, you have to be very careful about replying to emails you aren't sure about. 어, 확실하지 않는 이멜에 대한 답장을 하는데 매우 조심해야 돼.

Unit 06

05   Special phone recordings are used for voice phishing
특수한 폰 녹음된 것들이 보이스피싱에 사용되고 있어

● I was a victim of voice phishing. 난 보이스피싱을 당했어.

● There are many different types of phishing attacks. 많은 종류의 피싱공격들이 있어.

A: My email was used in a spear phishing attack so I hope you didn't open any emails from me.
내 이멜은 스피어 피싱공격에 이용됐으니까 나로부터 오는 이멜은 어떤 것이든 열어보지 않았기를 바래.

B: I heard about it so was careful not to. 얘기 들었어 그러지 않으려고 조심했어.

Unit

자동차 등

001

I was in my thirties when I first got my license

난 처음 면허를 땄을 때 30대였어

driver's license라고 하면 「운전면허」. 「면허 소지자」는 license-holder라고 하고, 요즘 운전면허 딸 때 주행시험을 남기고 받는 「가(假)면허증」은 temporary license, 모두 합격하고 받는 「본(本)면허증」은 full license라고 한다.

01 I just got my (driver's) license today
난 오늘 운전면허증을 땄어

- I took lessons at **a driving school.** 난 운전교습학원에서 수업을 들었어.
- **Do you have your** driver's license **yet?** 운전면허증이 있어?
- **How long is your** driver's license **valid for?** 운전면허증 유효기간이 얼마나 돼?

> A: I just got my driver's license today. 오늘 운전면허증 땄어.
> B: Congrats! How long is it valid for? 축하해! 유효기간이 얼마나 돼?

02 I passed the test and got my license!
시험에 붙어서 면허증을 땄어!

- I **failed to pass the** driving test. 난 주행시험에서 떨어졌어.
- **An instructor** is giving **his student** a driving test.
  한 강사가 학생에게 주행시험을 치루고 있어.
- I am doing my driver's test **today.** 난 오늘 주행시험을 볼거야.

> A: Did you pass your driver's test? 운전면허 테스트를 통과했어?
> B: Yes, I did. Just barely though. 어, 통과했어. 하지만 아슬아슬하게.

03 I was in my thirties when I first got my license
난 처음 면허를 땄을 때 30대였어

- I got my driver's license when I was 19 years old. 난 19살에 운전면허를 땄어.

- What is the age limit for getting your driver's license in Korea?
  한국에서 면허증 따는데 나이제한이 어떻게 돼?

- She got her license when she was 20 but didn't start driving until she was 28. 20살에 면허증을 땄지만 28살 돼서야 운전을 하기 시작했어.

A: What is the age limit for getting your license in Canada?
캐나다에서 면허증 따는데 나이제한이 어떻게 돼?

B: You can get your license when you are 16 years old.
16세가 되면 면허증을 딸 수 있어.

04 I need to see your license
면허증 좀 보여주세요

- Please show me your license and vehicle registration papers.
  면허증과 차량등록증을 보여주세요.

- I got my international license so I can drive when I go to Japan next month. 난 국제면허증을 따서 담달 일본에 가서 운전을 할 수가 있어.

- I had to show the police officer my driver's license.
  난 경찰관에게 내 면허증을 보여줘야 했어.

A: Could you please show me your driver's license and vehicle registration please? 면허증과 차량등록증을 보여주시겠어요?

B: Here you are, officer. Was I driving too fast?
여기있습니다, 경찰관님. 내가 과속했나요?

Unit 07

002 면허증을 취소당하다

My license was taken away

내 면허증은 취소됐어

take away one's license라고 하면 「면허를 취소하다」는 뜻으로 일정 기간이 지나 기회를 다시 준다는 의미를 포함하고 있다. 면허가 일시 정지됐다고 할 때는 get my license suspended라고 한다.

01 My license was taken away
내 면허증은 취소됐어

- They will take away your license if you don't pay those parking tickets.
  그 주차 위반 딱지들에 대한 벌금을 내지 않으면 너의 면허는 취소될거야.
- He lost his license because of drinking and driving. 걘 음주운전으로 면허가 취소됐어.
- My grandmother had her license revoked because of her poor eyesight.
  할머니는 시력이 나빠서 면허증이 취소됐어.

A: Did you hear about Jim losing his license? 짐의 면허증이 취소됐다는 소식 들었어?
B: Yes, he got into an accident after drinking and driving.
    어, 걘 음주운전사고를 냈어.

02 He renewed his driver's license
걘 운전면허를 갱신했어

- My license needs to be renewed this year. 내 면허증은 금년에 갱신해야 돼.
- How long before you need to get your license renewed?
  네 면허증 얼마나 있다 갱신해야 돼?
- I don't need to renew my license for another 5 years.
  난 다음 5년간 면허증을 갱신할 필요가 없어.

A: Do you have to get your license renewed soon? 면허증을 곧 갱신해야 돼?
B: No. I just got it renewed last year. 아니. 작년에 갱신했는걸.

03 I got my license suspended
면허증이 정지됐어

- His license was suspended for one year after he got caught drinking and driving. 걘 음주운전으로 걸려서 일년간 면허가 정지됐어.
- How long will the suspension be for? 정지기간이 얼마나 될까?
- Her license was suspended for 6 months because of her speeding tickets. 걘 과속으로 6개월간 면허가 정지됐어.

A: How long will the suspension be for? 정지기간이 얼마나 될까?
B: For 6 months. 6개월간.

04 I had my license suspended
내 면허증이 정지됐어

- Have you ever had your license suspended before? 전에 면허증 정지된 적 있어?
- The judge suspended her license for 3 months.
  판사는 걔의 면허증을 3개월간 정지시켰어.

A: I heard the doctor had her license suspended for medical reasons.
   의사가 의학적 이유로 걔의 면허증을 정지시켰다며.

B: Yes, her eyesight has gotten a lot worse so she can't drive for now.
   어, 시력이 아주 나빠져서 이제는 운전을 할 수가 없어.

05 I had my license revoked
난 면허가 취소됐어

- Her license was revoked for not paying her car insurance.
  걔의 면허증은 자동차보험료를 내지 않아 취소가 됐어.
- Why was your license revoked? 왜 너의 면허증이 취소된거야?

A: I had my license revoked for driving a stolen car.
   도난차량을 운전한 이유로 면허가 취소됐어.

B: That was stupid of you. 너 참 멍청했네.

Unit 07

003

차를 사다

I have a BMW 540i xDrive car

내 차는 BMW 540i xDrive야

차를 사다는 buy a new car. 차를 사려고 생각할 때는 look at buying a new car라 한다. 반면 지금 갖고 있는 차를 말할 때는 I have~ 혹은 I own~이라고 하면 된다.

01 I need to buy a new car
난 새 차를 뽑아야 돼

- My car is too old to drive. 내 차는 운전하기에 너무 낡았어.
- My car is a 2007 Honda Legend model. 내 차는 2007년형 혼다 레전드야.
- I am looking at buying a used car. 난 중고차를 사려고 해.

A: Have you ever bought a new car? 새 차를 사본 적이 있어.
B: No, only used ones. 아니. 중고차만 사봤어.

02 I need a car to go shopping at the mall
쇼핑몰에 쇼핑가려고 차가 필요해

- I need a car to get around. 돌아다닐 때 쓸 자동차가 필요해.
- I need a car to go out with my girlfriend. 여친과 데이트할 자동차가 필요해.
- I'd like a car for weekend trips. 주말여행할 자동차를 원해.

A: Why do you need a car? You live near the subway.
왜 차가 필요한거야? 지하철에서 가까운 곳에 살잖아.
B: I'd like one for weekend trips. 주말여행할 때 쓸 자동차를 원해.

03   I have a BMW 540i xDrive car
내 차는 BMW 540i xDrive야

- I have a used van. 난 중고 밴을 몰아.

- I have a new 2021 model. 내 차는 2021년형 신차야.

- I own a Hyundai IONIQ 6. 난 현대차 아이오닉 6을 몰아.

A: What kind of car do you have? 어떤 자동차를 갖고 있어?
B: I'm the proud owner of a BMW. 난 BMW를 자랑스러워하는 주인야.

04   I live in the country, so I can't do without a car
난 시골에서 살아서 차없이는 못살아

- I live downtown and near my office so I don't really need a car.
시내 회사근처에 살아서 실은 차가 필요없어.

- My job is downtown where parking is expensive so I don't really want to
buy a car. 내 직장은 주차비가 비싼 시내에 있어서 정말 차를 사고 싶지 않아.

- I live in a suburb without a subway line so a car is really convenient.
난 전철이 없는 교외에서 살아서 차는 정말 편리해.

A: Why don't you own a car? 왜 차가 없어?
B: Because I live downtown and can walk to work in 5 minutes.
시내에 살고 걸어서 5분안에 출근할 수 있어서.

05   Driving around in a Mercedes is my dream
벤츠차로 드라이브하는게 내 꿈이야

- My other car is a Porsche. 내 다른 차는 포르쉐이야.

- She owns 3 cars. 걘 차가 3대야.

- He has an SUV for the family and a sports car for fun.
걘 가족용으로 SUV, 재미로는 스포츠카를 갖고 있어.

A: Did I see her in a Tesla the other day? 요전날 걔가 테슬라 타는 것을 내가 본거 맞아?
B: Yes, she owns 3 different cars. 어, 걘 3대의 다른 차를 갖고 있어.

004

She usually drives to work
갠 보통 차로 출근해

차의 용도를 말하는 것으로 차로 출근하다는 drive to work. 아이들을 데려다주고 데려오는 것은 drive one's child to and from~이라고 표현하면 된다.

01 I almost always drive to work
난 거의 항상 차로 출근해

- **She usually** drives to work. 갠 보통 차로 출근해.

- **I never** use public transportation. 난 대중교통을 절대로 이용하지 않아.

- **Driving to work** is much more comfortable than taking public transportation because of where I live.
  내가 사는 곳 때문에 대중교통을 이용하기보다 차로 출근하는게 훨씬 더 편해.

  A: Do you always drive to work? 넌 항상 차로 출근하니?
  B: Yes, I never use public transportation. 어, 난 절대로 대중교통을 이용하지 않아.

02 I drive my child to and from the kindergarten
난 아이를 차로 유치원에 데려다 줬다 데려와

- **He drops his kids off at** school every day. 갠 매일 아이들은 차로 학교에 데려다 줘.

- **Can I catch a lift with** you to the subway station? 지하철역까지 네 차 좀 타도 돼?

- **I have to pick up my wife** on the way home from work. 퇴근 길에 아내를 픽업해야 돼.

  A: Do you want to have dinner after work? 퇴근 후에 저녁을 먹을래?
  B: Sorry, I have to pick up my kids tonight. 미안. 오늘밤에 아이들을 픽업해야 돼.

03 I often go for a drive on my days off
난 종종 쉬는 날에 드라이브를 해

- She enjoys going for drives in the countryside on weekends.
  걘 주말마다 시골길을 드라이브하는 것을 즐겨해.

- They love taking road trips every summer.
  걔네들은 매 여름마다 장거리 자동차여행을 아주 좋아해.

- He really loves driving fast. 걘 정말로 빨리 달리는 것을 좋아해.

A: What do you do on weekends? 주말마다 뭐해?

B: My husband and I are really into taking long drives in the countryside. 남편과 난 시골길을 따라 장거리 자동차여행을 하는데 빠져 있어.

04 I drive to visit customers every day
난 매일 고객을 차로 방문해

- He drives a lot for his job. 걘 일로 해서 운전을 많이 해.

- She has to drive to Busan for work once or twice a month.
  걘 한달에 한 두번 일로 부산에 차로 가야 해.

- She drives for her work so much that they gave her a company car.
  걘 업무로 운전을 많이 해서 회사업무용차를 받았어.

A: Does she have a company car? 걘 업무용 차가 있어?

B: Yes, because she has to do a lot of driving for her job.
어, 걘 일로 해서 운전을 아주 많이 해야 해서.

I went for a drive
난 드라이브갔어

드라이브가다는 take a drive to+장소, …을 드라이브 시켜주다는 take sb for a drive라고 말하면 된다. 또한 많이 쓰이는 표현으로는 go for a drive with sb가 있다.

01 I took a drive and got some fresh air
난 드라이브해서 신선한 공기를 마셨어

● I took a drive to the east coast last weekend to see the sunrise.
난 지난 주말에 해돋이를 보려고 동해안으로 드라이브갔어.

● We took a drive to the mountains 2 weeks ago. 우리는 2주전에 산으로 드라이브갔어.

● Have you ever taken a drive to the south coast? 남해안으로 드라이브간 적 있어?

A: Have you ever taken a drive to Jeju Island? 제주도에서 드라이브해본 적 있어?
B: Yes, last year. I drove to Mokpo and then took the ferry to Jeju.
어, 작년에. 목포까지 차로 간 다음 카페리를 타고 제주도에 갔었어.

02 I had a nice drive in the countryside
전원지역으로 멋진 드라이브를 갔었어

● I will have a long drive to Busan. 난 부산까지 멀리 드라이브갈거야.

● I am going to have a nice drive with my boyfriend this weekend.
난 이번 주말에 남친과 함께 멋진 드라이브를 할거야.

● Has she ever had a drive to Gwangju? 걘 광주까지 드라이브해본 적 있어?

A: What are your plans this weekend? 이번 주말에 뭐할거야?
B: I will have a nice drive down to Busan. 부산으로 멋진 드라이브할거야.

03 I took her for a drive
난 걔를 드라이브 시켜줬어

- She took me for a ride to **school**. 걘 나를 학교까지 차로 데려다줬어.

- **Has he ever** given you a lift **in his new car**? 걔가 자기 새 차로 널 태워준 적 있어?

- I took my mom for a ride to **the new shopping center.**
  난 엄마를 차로 모시고 새로운 쇼핑센터로 갔어.

A: He is my classmate. Nice guy. 걘 내 반친구야. 좋은 친구야.
B: I know. Has he ever given you a ride in his car?
알아. 자기 차로 널 태워준 적 있어?

04 I went for a drive
난 드라이브갔어

- She is going for a drive **with her family tonight**. 걘 오늘밤 가족과 함께 드라이브할거야.

- Who are you going for a drive with? 넌 누구하고 드라이브할거야?

- How often do you go for drives? 얼마나 자주 드라이브해?

A: How often do you go for drives? 얼마나 자주 드라이브해?
B: Usually once or twice a month. 보통 한달에 한 두번.

05 He drives very fast
걘 차를 아주 빨리 몰아

- I drove very fast to **get home early.** 난 집에 일찍 도착하려고 차를 빨리 몰았어.

- He drives fast and recklessly. 걘 차를 빨리 함부로 몰아.

- She always goes over the speed limit. 걘 항상 제한속도 이상으로 차를 몰아.

A: I hate driving with her. 난 걔 차 타는게 싫어.
B: Yes, she always drives over the speed limit.
그래. 걘 항상 제한속도 이상으로 차를 몰아.

Unit 07

006

I'll give you a ride
내가 차 태워줄게

차를 태워주다는 give sb a ride to+장소명사로, 집까지 태워줄 때는 give sb a ride home이라고 한다. 반대로 차를 얻어탈 때는 need a ride나 get a ride to~라고 하면 된다.

01 I'll give you a ride
내가 차 태워줄게

- Would you like a lift to the subway station? 지하철까지 차 태워줄래?

- Can I give you a ride home? 집까지 차로 데려다줄까?

- He offered me a ride but I told him I'd prefer to walk.
  걘 차 태워주겠다고 했는데 내가 걸어가겠다고 했어.

A: Would you like a ride to school today? 오늘 학교까지 차로 데려다줄까?
B: No thanks. My friend is picking me up. 고맙지만 됐어. 친구가 데리러 올거야.

02 Let me give you a ride home
집까지 차로 데려다줄게

- Allow me to give you a lift to work. 내가 직장까지 차로 데려다줄게.

- If you want, my mom can give us a ride to school.
  원한다면, 우리 엄마가 우리를 학교까지 차로 데려다주실거야.

- How often do you get rides from your parents? 얼마나 자주 부모님 차를 얻어 타?

A: Let me give you a ride home. 집까지 차로 데려다줄게.
B: Thanks so much. 정말 고마워.

Can you give me a ride to the office?
사무실까지 나 좀 차로 데려다줄래?

- Could you give my sister a ride to the bus stop?
  내 여동생을 버스 정거장까지 차로 데려다줄래?

- I told him I could give him a lift but he said he wanted to take the subway.
  걔한테 차 태워준다고 했는데 걘 지하철을 타겠다고 했어.

- I asked if he wanted a ride and he said yes.
  난 걔에게 차태워줄까라고 물었는데 개는 예스라고 말했어.

A: Could you give him a ride home? 걔를 집까지 차로 데려다줄 수 있어?
B: Sorry but I'm going to a movie after work.
미안하지만 난 퇴근 후에 영화보러 가기로 했어.

I need a ride
나 차 좀 얻어 타야 돼

- I hitched a ride back to my hometown. 난 지나가는 차를 얻어 타고 고향으로 왔어.

- Hitchhiking is dangerous for women. 히치하이킹은 여성들에게는 위험해.

- I hitchhiked all over Europe when I was in university.
  난 대학다닐 때 히치하이크하면서 유럽 전 지역을 여행했어.

A: How did you get home? 어떻게 집에 온거야?
B: I hitched a ride with a trucker. 지나가는 트럭을 얻어 타고 왔어.

Can I get a ride with you?
너 나 좀 차 태워줄래?

- Let me drive you home. 내가 차로 집까지 태워줄게.

- Can I catch a ride with you? 너 차 좀 얻어 타도 될까?

- She offered to give him a ride to work. 걘 그에게 직장까지 태워다주겠다고 제안했어.

A: Can I catch a ride with you after work? 퇴근 후에 너 차 좀 얻어 타도 될까?
B: Where are you going? 어디 갈건데?

007

He pulled over to park the car

갠 차를 주차시키기 위해 차를 세웠어

차를 세우다는 pull up이나 pull over라 한다. 위 예문처럼 길옆에 차를 대는 것은 pull over라 하고 신호등이나 집앞에 차를 댈 때는 pull up을 쓴다. 안전벨트를 매다는 fasten your seatbelt 혹은 buckle up이라고 한다.

01 Pull up a little further
좀 더 가서 차를 세워

● I pulled up to **Mr. Green's house.** 그린 씨의 집에 차를 세웠어.

● I pulled up at **the traffic light.** 난 교통신호등에 차를 세웠어.

● **Why are you pulling up?** 왜 차를 세우는거야?

A: Why are you pulling up? 왜 차를 세우는거야?
B: Because the traffic light has turned red. 신호등이 빨강으로 바뀌어서.

02 I had to pull over for a bathroom break
화장실가려고 차를 도로변에 세워야했어

● He pulled over to **park the car.** 갠 차를 주차시키기 위해 차를 세웠어.

● I pulled over to **let the truck pass me.** 트럭이 앞지를 수 있도록 차를 옆으로 댔어.

● We pulled over to **the side of the road so the ambulance could pass us.**
앰뷸런스가 지나갈 수 있도록 차를 도로변에 세웠어.

A: I pulled over and parked when the police car turned its lights on.
경찰차가 경고등을 켜서 차를 옆에 대고 주차했어.

B: Were you speeding? 과속였어?

03 I put on the brakes too quickly
난 너무 빨리 브레이크를 밟았어

- She slammed on the brakes. 걘 브레이크를 아주 세게 밟았어.
- I had to brake suddenly. 난 갑자기 브레이크를 밟아야 했어.
- He is really soft with the brakes. 걘 브레이크를 정말 부드럽게 밟아.

A: Why did you slam on the brakes? 왜 브레이크를 세게 밟은거야?
B: A dog ran onto the road and I didn't want to hit it.
   개가 길로 뛰어들었고 난 치지 않으려고 했기 때문에.

04 Why don't you slow down a bit?
좀 속도 좀 줄이자

- You're driving way too fast. 넌 너무 빨리 차를 몰아.
- You are 20km over the speed limit. 너 제한속도보다 20킬로 이상으로 달리고 있어.
- Can you please slow down? 속도 좀 줄일래?

A: Can you please slow down? You're making me nervous.
   속도 좀 줄일래? 너 때문에 긴장된다.
B: I'm going the speed limit. 제한속도로 달리고 있어.

05 Please buckle up
안전벨트 매

- You need to wear your seatbelt in my car. 내 차 탈 때는 안전벨트를 매야 돼.
- Please fasten your seatbelt before we leave. 떠나기 전에 안전벨트를 매.
- If you don't buckle up, we aren't leaving. 너 안전벨트 매지 않으면 출발안한다.

A: Does your country have seatbelt laws? 너희 나라에는 안전벨트법이 있어?
B: Yes, everyone has to buckle up. 어. 모두 다 안전벨트를 매야 돼.

008

Don't tailgate

앞차 바싹 뒤따르지마

운전을 잘하면 a good driver. be good at driving이라고 하고, 차선변경은 change lanes 그리고 앞차의 뒤를 바싹 뒤따르는 것은 tailgate라 한다.

01

I'm a good driver

난 운전을 잘 해

● You're such a good driver. 너 운전 정말 잘 한다.

● I'm a bad driver. 난 차를 형편없이 몰아.

● I'm not good at driving. 난 운전에 서툴러.

A: She's not a bad driver, is she? 걔 괜찮게 차 몰지 않아, 그렇지?
B: No, in fact, she's a very good one. 어, 사실, 걔 차 아주 잘 몰아.

02

You have to take this exit

이번 출구를 타야 돼

● I missed the exit. 출구를 지나쳤어.

● I should take this exit on the highway. 고속도로에서 이번 출구로 나가야 돼.

● Don't miss the exit or we'll be late. 출구 지나치지마 그러면 우리는 늦을거야.

A: Damn! I missed the exit. 젠장! 출구를 놓쳤네.
B: That's alright. Just take the next one. 괜찮아. 다음 출구를 타.

03 I need to change lanes
난 차선변경을 해야 돼

- I want to get into the slow lane. 저속 차선으로 들어가고 싶어.
- You're driving in the bus lane. 너 버스차선으로 달리고 있어.
- Get into the left lane. 왼쪽 차선으로 변경해.

A: Get into the right lane. We have to turn at the next intersection.
오른쪽 차선으로 바꿔. 담 교차로에서 우회전해야 돼.

B: I'm trying to do that but there's too much traffic.
그러려고 하는데 차들이 너무 많아.

04 Don't tailgate
앞차 바싹 뒤따르지마

- Please try to observe the proper distance between cars.
적정한 차간 거리를 유지하도록 해.
- I hate tailgaters. 바싹 뒤따르는 차들 정말 싫어.
- Try to keep a good distance between the car in front of us.
앞차와의 간격을 상당히 두도록 해.

A: Please try not to tailgate. 앞차에 바싹 붙이지마.
B: I know. It's a little dangerous. 알아. 좀 위험하지.

05 Don't suddenly stop, please
급정거하지마

- Try to be soft with the brakes. 브레이크는 부드럽게 밟도록 해.
- Don't be so heavy with the brakes. 브레이크를 너무 세게 밟지 않도록 해.
- She has a very soft foot on the brakes. 걘 브레이크를 아주 살살 밟아.

A: I like how she drives. 걔 운전하는게 좋아.
B: Yes, she has a very soft foot on the brakes. 어. 걘 브레이크를 아주 살살 밟아.

Unit 07

009

My car has all the latest features

내 차에는 모든 최신의 기능들이 달려 있어

후방모니터는 have a rear video monitor. 차선이탈경고시스템은 a lane departure warning system이라고 한다. 그리고 구글에 말해서(talk to Google) 음성으로 지시를 내리는 것은 get things done with your voice라고 하면 된다.

01 My car has a car navigation system
내 차에는 네비가 달려 있어

● Does your car have a GPS? 네 차에는 GPS가 달려 있어?

● Her car has a rear video monitor for parking.
개의 차에는 주차용 후방모니터가 달려 있어.

● My car has sensors, so I know when I am going to hit something.
내 차에는 센스가 달려 있어서 내가 뭔가 부딪히려고 할 때 알게 돼.

A: Does your car have a GPS? 네 차에는 GPS가 달려 있어?
B: No, it's very old. I have to use my smartphone GPS.
아니, 오래된 차야. 난 스마트폰 GPS를 이용해야 돼.

02 This car has a lane departure warning system
이 차는 차선이탈경고 시스템이 달려 있어

● My car has all the latest features. 내 차에는 모든 최신의 기능들이 달려 있어.

● He has an electric car. 걘 전기차를 갖고 있어.

● My car is a hybrid. 내 차는 하이브리드야.

A: Wow! Is that an electric car? 왜! 저기 전기차지?
B: Yes. It's a Tesla. 어. 테슬라야.

03
Android Auto brings your favorite smartphone apps to your car, making it easier to access your favorite navigation, media, and communication apps on the road

안드로이드 오토는 좋아하는 스마트폰 어플을 차로 가져와, 운전 중에 네비, 미디어, 그리고 통신어플들을 이용하기 쉽게 해줘

● Modern cars have a lot of great features, don't they?
현대의 자동차들은 멋진 기능들이 많아, 그렇지 않아?

● Can you talk to your car? 네 자동차에 말을 걸 수 있어?

A: Can you talk to your car? 네 자동차에 말을 걸 수 있어?
B: Yes, it talks to me too. 어, 자동차가 나에게 말을 하기도 해.

04
You can talk to Google and get things done with your voice 구글로 말을 걸어 목소리로 지시사항을 하도록 할 수 있어

● "Hey Google, text Mom 'I'll be late'" "안녕, 구글, 엄마에게 '나 늦어'라고 문자보내줘"

● "Google, what's the weather today?" "구글, 오늘 날씨는 어때?"

● "Morning Google. Who won the election?" "안녕, 구글, 선거에서 누가 이겼어?"

A: "Hey Google, what's the weather forecast today?" "안녕 구글, 오늘기상예보는 어때?"
B: "Today's forecast is sunny with a high of 25 degrees Celsius."
"오늘 날씨는 최고온도가 섭씨 25도로 맑겠습니다."

05
Many cars has ADAS(Advanced Driver Assistance Systems) but it still is not reliable 많은 차들이 첨단 운전자보조시스템을 달고 있지만 아직 믿을 수는 없어

● The new electric cars have improved a lot but the batteries still have some problems. 신형 전기차들은 많이 발전했지만 배터리 문제가 아직도 좀 있어.

● Self-driving cars are still a few years away. 자율주행차는 아직 몇 년 더 기다려야 돼.

A: His car is always breaking down. 걔 차는 늘상 퍼지더라.
B: It's very unreliable. 정말 미덥지 않다니까.

010

A dashcam films what's happening on the road

블랙박스는 운전 중에 일어나는 일을 찍어

우리는 블랙박스라고 부르지만 영어로는 dashcam이라고 한다는 점에 유의한다. 보통 전후방을 녹화하는 two-way가 일반적이고 사고시에는 유용하지만 사생활에 잘못 이용될 수도 있다는 단점이 있다.

01 My car has a new dashcam
내 차에는 신형 블랙박스가 달려 있어

- The car camera helped a lot when I got into an accident.
  자동차의 카메라는 사고났을 때 많은 도움이 돼.

- The dashcam is very useful for car insurance companies.
  블랙박스는 자동차보험 회사에게 매우 유용해.

- The police asked me to look at the dashcam. 경찰은 블랙박스를 보라고 내게 요청했어.

A: What happened after the accident? 사고가 난 후에 어떻게 됐어?
B: The car dashcam showed the other driver was at fault.
블랙박스를 보니까 다른 운전자가 잘못인게 드러났어.

02 A dashcam films what's happening on the road
블랙박스는 운전 중에 일어나는 일을 찍어

- My dashcam recorded everything after I started up my car.
  내 블랙박스는 내가 시동을 건 후의 모든 일을 녹화했어.

- Could you send the insurance company the dashcam footage from the accident? 블랙박스의 사고장면을 보험회사에 보낼 수 있어?

- The dashcam recordings get automatically deleted after a certain period of time. 블랙박스 녹화는 일정시간이 지나면 자동적으로 삭제 돼.

A: Did you send your dashcam footage to the insurance company today? 너 오늘 보험회사에 블랙박스 영상을 보냈어?
B: No, I'll send it to them as soon as I get home. 아니. 집에 가서 바로 보낼거야.

My dashcam is two-way, recording the front and
back 블랙박스는 쌍방향으로 앞면과 뒷면을 녹화해

- Does a dashcam have any blindspots? 블랙박스에 사각지대가 있어?
- I only needed the rear footage from the dashcam. 블박의 후방촬영분만 필요했어.
- We were able to use the dashcam recordings. 블박의 녹화된 것을 이용할 수 있었어.

A: Did your dashcam recordings help the insurance company?
네 블랙박스 녹화한게 보험회사에 도움이 됐어?

B: Yes, they were able to use them. 어, 보험회사가 그것들을 사용할 수 있었어.

The dashcam is very useful during accidents
블랙박스는 사고가 난 경우 매우 유용해

- Dashcams have changed how people behave after accidents happen.
블랙박스는 사고가 난 후 사람들의 행태를 변화시켰어.
- If I didn't have my dashcam, I may have had to pay a lot more for that
accident. 블랙박스가 없었다면, 그 사고로 돈을 더 많이 지불했었을거야.
- Before dashcams, insurance companies had to rely on witnesses.
블랙박스가 있기 전에는 보험회사는 사고 증인들 말에 의존해야 했어.

A: What do insurance companies do if the cars in the accidents don't
have dashcams? 사고차에 블랙박스가 없으면 보험회사는 어떻게 해?

B: They have to rely on eye witnesses. 그들은 증인들 말에 의존해야 돼.

But the dashcam can be misused for privacy
하지만 블랙박스는 사생활에 오용될 수도 있어

- She caught her husband cheating on her with a dashcam recording.
걘 남편이 바람피는 것을 블랙박스 녹화로 잡았어.
- Dashcams can be used for the wrong reasons. 블박은 엉뚱한 이유로 오용될 수도 있어.

A: Dashcams are sometimes misused. 블랙박스는 때때로 오용되기도 해.

B: Yeah, a woman tried to blackmail her boss using her dashcam.
맞아, 한 여성은 자신의 블랙박스를 이용해서 상사를 협박하려고 했어.

Unit 07

011

Teslas are more popular than ever

테슬라 자동차는 어느 때보다도 인기가 있어

공기오염을 피하기(avoid air pollution) 위해서는 환경친화적인 전기차(electric cars), 즉 비가솔린 자동차(non-gasoline cars) 등을 사용해야 한다. 전기차 중의 대표주자인 Tesla의 인기가 높다.

01 I can see more Tesla electric cars on the road
난 도로에서 테슬라 전기차를 많이 볼 수 있어

- **Teslas are more popular than ever.** 테슬라 자동차는 어느 때보다도 인기가 있어.
- **Many car companies are following Tesla's footsteps.**
  많은 자동차 회사가 테슬라의 전철을 따르고 있어.
- **Teslas are more environmentally friendly than regular cars.**
  테슬라 자동차는 일반 자동차보다 더 환경친화적이야.

A: Why are Tesla's so popular these days? 요즘 왜 그렇게 테슬라의 차가 인기야?
B: They are environmentally friendly. 환경친화적이잖아.

02 Tesla is the most famous electric car in the world
테슬라는 세상에서 가장 유명한 전기차야

- **When did Tesla start becoming famous?** 언제 테슬라가 유명해지기 시작했어?
- **How did Tesla become so famous?** 어떻게 테슬라가 유명해진거야?
- **It's a good thing for the environment that Tesla is so famous.**
  테슬라가 유명해지는 것은 환경에 좋은 일이야.

A: When did Tesla start becoming famous? 언제 테슬라가 유명해지기 시작했어?
B: It was a while ago. I remember it was big news when the company
   started. 꽤 됐어. 회사가 창업했을 때 빅뉴스였다는게 기억나.

We'll have to use electric cars more to avoid air pollution 공기오염을 피하기 위해 우리는 더 전기차를 이용해야 돼

● Electric cars are very important for lowering carbon emissions.
전기차는 탄소배출을 낮추는데 아주 중요해.

● If we don't all switch to electric cars soon, climate change will become irreversible. 곧 모두 전기차로 바꾸지 못한다면, 환경변화는 돌이킬 수 없을거야.

● How many more years before everyone is driving electric cars?
얼마나 더 있어야 모든 사람들이 전기차를 몰게 될까?

A: Electric cars are very important for helping our environment.
전기차는 환경을 돕는데 매우 중요해.

B: I agree. If we don't all switch to electric cars soon, the world will be in deep trouble.
맞아. 우리 모두가 전기차로 곧 바꾸지 않으면, 세상은 커다란 곤경에 처하게 될거야.

The world is struggling to produce non-gasoline cars 세상은 비가솔린 자동차를 생산하는데 열을 올리고 있어

● Convincing car companies to switch to environmentally friendly cars has been a challenge. 자동차 회사를 설득하여 환경친화적인 차로 전환시키는 것은 어려운 일이었어.

● It is vital for car companies to make cheap electric powered cars.
자동차 회사가 저렴한 전기자동차를 만드는 것이 결정적인 문제야.

● Hydro or Electric powered cars are the future. 수소나 전기자동차가 미래야.

A: The world is struggling to produce cheap environmentally friendly cars. 세상은 친환경적인 저렴한 자동차를 생산해내려고 노력하고 있어.

B: Yes, but those cars are the future. 맞아. 그 차들이 미래지.

012 I'd like a hand wash

손세차를 하고 싶어요

손세차는 a hand wash, 기계식 세차는 an automatic car wash라 하면 된다. 주유소에서 가득 채워달라고 할 때는 fill it up, 셀프 주유소는 a self-serve station이라고 하면 된다.

01 I'm going to wash my car tomorrow

내일 세차를 할거야

- I got my car washed **a moment ago**. 난 조금전에 자동차를 세차했어.
- **My car really** needs a wash. 내 자동차는 정말 세차해야 돼.
- **How often do you wash your car?** 얼마나 자주 세차해?

A: My car really needs a wash. 내 자동차는 정말 세차해야 돼.
B: I just got mine washed yesterday. 난 어제 세차했는데.

02 I'd like a hand wash

손세차를 하고 싶어요

- **We'll** hand wash your car. 손세차 해드릴게요.
- **I went to** an automatic car wash. 난 자동세차장에 갔어.
- **I usually** wash my own car at home. 난 보통 집에서 자동차를 세차해.

A: Do you prefer the automatic or a hand car wash?
자동세차장과 손세차 중 어떤 것을 좋아해?

B: The hand wash is better but more expensive and takes longer.
손세차가 나은데 더 비싸고 시간도 더 오래 걸려.

03 I ran out of gas
기름이 떨어졌어

- **We're going to run out of gas soon.** 우리는 곧 기름이 바닥날거야.

- **The car is running on fumes.** 자동차 기름이 다 되어 가네.

- **My gas gauge is broken so I have to be careful not to run out of gas.**
  연료계가 고장나서 난 기름이 떨어지지 않도록 조심해야 돼.

A: The car is running on fumes. 자동차 기름이 다 되어 가네.

B: There is a gas station up ahead. Pull in there.
저 앞에 주유소가 있어. 그리로 들어가 차 세워.

04 Fill it up with regular unleaded
무연가솔린으로 가득 채워주세요

- **Fill it up with premium.** 고급휘발유로 가득 채워주세요.

- **Give me 30,000 won worth of regular unleaded please.** 무연가솔린 3만원치 주세요.

- **Give me 20 liters of premium.** 고급휘발유 20리터 주세요.

A: Fill it up please. 가득 채워주세요.

B: Regular unleaded or premium, sir? 무연가솔린인가요 아니면 고급유인가요?

05 We need to put some gas in the car
우리는 자동차에 기름을 좀 넣어야 돼

- I couldn't find a gas station **anywhere.** 어디에도 주유소를 찾을 수가 없네.

- It's a self-serve station. 여기는 셀프주유소야.

- I like going to full-service gas stations. 난 주유를 해주는 주유소에 가는 것을 좋아해.

A: I like going to full-service gas stations. 주유를 해주는 주유소에 가는 것을 좋아해.

B: They are getting harder to find. 점점 찾아보기가 힘들어.

013

I got held up by a traffic jam

차가 많아 교통이 막혔어

교통체증에 막힌다고 할 때는 traffic jam, a lot of traffic으로 쓴다. 또한 get를 이용하여 get held up~, get stuck in traffic, 그리고 get caught in traffic의 표현들을 사용하면 된다.

01 I got held up behind a traffic accident
교통사고로 차가 막혔어

- I got held up by **a traffic jam.** 차가 많아 교통이 막혔어.
- I got held up in **town.** 시내에서 차가 막혔어.
- I got held up at **work.** 난 일로 늦어졌어.

A: Why are you so late today? 오늘 왜 그렇게 늦은거야?
B: Sorry. I got held up at work. 미안. 일로 늦어졌어.

02 I got stuck in traffic
차가 막혔어

- The traffic was bumper to bumper. 차가 많이 막혔어.
- The traffic was moving very slowly. 차가 아주 천천히 흘러가고 있었어.
- I got caught in **rush hour traffic.** 러시아워 교통ㅁ체증에 차가 막혔어.
- I got stuck in **heavy traffic.** 차가 엄청 막혔어.

A: Why do you look so annoyed? 왜 그렇게 화가 난 표정이야?
B: It took me over 2 hours to get here because the traffic was bumper to bumper the whole way. 오는 길 내내 차가 많이 막혀서 여기 오는데 2시간 이상 걸렸어.

03 I got caught in traffic
차가 막혔어

- I got caught in a traffic jam. 교통체증에 차가 막혔어.
- We got stuck in **slow moving traffic**. 차가 막혀서 천천히 움직였어.

A: I got caught in bad rush hour traffic. 러시아워 교통체증에 차가 엄청 막혔어.
B: Next time you should take the subway. 다음 번에는 지하철을 타.

04 The traffic is backed up all the way to the river
강까지 가는 길 내내 차가 막혔어

- We were late because of a traffic jam. 교통체증 때문에 우리는 늦었어.
- The traffic is always bad **on this road**. 이 길은 언제나 차가 많이 막혀.
- Traffic on the expressway was backed up **because of the accident**.
  고속도로 교통은 사고로 막혔어.

A: Why was traffic so bad today? 오늘 왜 이렇게 차가 많이 막힌거야?
B: It was backed up because of the marathon. 마라톤 때문에 막혔어.

Unit 07

05 There was a lot of traffic
차들이 매우 혼잡했어

- Let's leave early and **beat the rush hour traffic**. 일찍 출발해서 러시아워를 피하자.
- Traffic is bad **in Shanghai**. 상하이의 교통은 아주 나빠.
- I beat the traffic **by using the new road**. 난 새로 난 도로를 이용해 교통체증을 피했어.

A: How did you get here so fast? 어떻게 그렇게 빨리 여기에 온거야?
B: I beat the traffic using a new road. 난 새로 난 도로를 이용해 교통체증을 피했어.

014

She was drunk driving last night

갠 지난밤에 음주운전을 했어

음주운전하다는 drink and drive로 과거형은 was drunk driving이라고 하면 된다. 많이 쓰이는 DUI을 이용하여 get a DUI해도 음주운전을 하다라는 의미가 된다. 또한 혈중알콜농도는 blood alcohol level이라 한다.

01 Never drink and drive

절대 음주운전 하지마

- She was drunk driving last night. 갠 지난밤에 음주운전을 했어.
- Drunk drivers kill many people every year. 음주운전자들은 매년 많은 사람들을 죽여.
- Drinking and driving isn't worth the risk. 음주운전은 위험을 감수할 가치도 없어.

A: She was drunk driving last night. 갠 지난밤에 음주운전을 했어.
B: So stupid. It's not worth the risk. 정말 한심하다. 위험을 감수할 가치도 없는데.

02 He was arrested for driving under the influence(DUI) 갠 음주운전으로 체포됐어

- He has 2 DUIs on his record. 갠 2번의 음주운전 기록이 있어.
- You don't want to get a DUI. 너 음주운전을 하지 마라.
- After his 3rd DUI he had his license revoked.
  3번째 음주운전 후에 걔 면허증은 취소됐어.

A: Just have one drink. You won't get in any trouble.
딱 한 잔만 마셔. 아무 문제 없을거야.

B: I can't take that chance. I already have 2 DUIs on my record. One more and I'll go to jail.
그렇게는 못해. 이미 음주운전 2번 걸렸거든. 한 번 더 걸리면 난 감옥에 갈거야.

03 He registered a blood alcohol content of 0.09
걔의 혈중알콜농도는 0.09로 기록됐어

- Your blood alcohol level **is over the limit.** 당신의 혈중알콜농도는 제한수치를 넘었습니다.
- His blood alcohol level **was over the legal limit.**
  걔의 혈중알콜농도는 법적허용수치를 넘었습니다.
- **What is the blood alcohol limit here?** 여기는 혈중알콜농도 제한이 어떻게 돼?

A: In Canada the blood alcohol limit is 0.05. 캐나다에서 혈중알콜농도 제한은 0.05야.
B: That's about one beer. 맥주 한 잔 정도 되는거네.

04 A license will be taken away if the blood alcohol level is over 0.08% 혈중알콜농도가 0.08% 넘으면 면허증이 취소될거야

- He had to take a breathalyzer and he blew over the limit.
  그는 음주측정기 테스트를 해야 했고 음주허용치를 넘게 불었어.
- Have you ever gotten stopped at a police checkstop?
  경찰 검문하는 곳에 멈춰진 적이 있어?
- **She blew under the limit.** 걘 불었지만 음주허용치 안에 들어왔어.

A: You got stopped at a checkstop last night?
넌 지난밤에 경찰 검문하는 곳에 멈춰진거야?
B: Yes, but I only had one beer all night so I blew under the limit.
어, 하지만 난 밤새 맥주 한 잔만 마셔서 불었지만 음주허용치 안에 들었어.

05 You should rest in the sleeping shelter if you fall asleep 졸리면 졸음쉼터에서 쉬어야 돼

- **Don't nod off at the wheel.** 운전하다 깜빡 졸지마.
- **Don't doze off while driving.** 운전하다가 잠이 들지마.
- **Don't fall asleep behind the wheel.** 운전하면서 졸지마.

A: He got in a terrible accident. 걘 끔찍한 사고를 당했어.
B: Yes, he fell asleep at the wheel. 그래, 걘 운전중에 졸았어.

딱지, 위반

015

I got a ticket on the way here

난 여기 오다가 딱지끊겼어

신호위반이든 과속이든 딱지를 끊기다는 get a ticket. 과속위반일 경우에는 get a speeding ticket 혹은 get a ticket for speeding이라고 하면 된다.

01 I got a ticket on the way here
난 여기 오다가 딱지끊겼어

- The police caught me in a speed trap last night.
  지난밤에 경찰의 속도위반단속장치에 내가 걸렸어.
- Have you ever gotten a speeding ticket? 과속위반딱지를 떼인 적이 있어?
- I got busted by a speed camera. 과속위반카메라에 걸렸어.

A: Look what you got in the mail! 우편물에 뭐가 왔나 봐!
B: Another speeding ticket? I hate those speed cameras.
또 과속딱지야? 과속위반카메라가 정말 싫어.

02 I'm giving you a ticket for speeding
과속위반 딱지를 발급하겠습니다

- The police officer wrote me up a parking ticket. 경찰관은 내게 주차위반 딱지를 뗐어.
- I tried to talk my way out of a speeding ticket.
  난 설득해서 과속위반딱지를 떼이지 않으려고 했어.
- The police officer was kind and gave me a warning instead of a ticket.
  경찰관은 친절해서 내게 딱지 대신에 경고만 줬어.

A: I tried to talk my way out of the parking ticket.
난 설득해서 주차위반딱지를 떼이지 않으려고 했어.
B: But the officer wrote it up anyhow. 하지만 경찰관은 그래도 딱지를 끊었어.

03 I was caught for ignoring a traffic light
난 신호위반으로 걸렸어

- I was caught for drunk driving. 난 음주운전으로 걸렸어.
- I was caught for speeding. 난 과속으로 걸렸어.
- I was once caught for illegal parking. 난 한 번은 불법주차로 걸렸어.

A: Have you ever gotten a ticket before? 전에 딱지를 떼인 적이 있어?
B: Yes, I was once caught for illegal parking. 어, 한번 불법주차로 걸렸어.

04 I got fined $100 for speeding
난 과속으로 100달러 벌금을 받았어

- I got fined $200 for **a traffic violation**. 난 신호위반으로 200달러 벌금을 받았어.
- I got a fine for **driving without my lights on**. 전조등을 켜지 않고 운전하다 벌금을 받았어.
- The police officer fined me for **making an illegal U-turn**.
  경찰관은 내가 불법유턴을 했다고 벌금을 매겼어.

A: Why are you broke these days? 요즘 왜 돈이 달리는거야?
B: I got fined $200 for a traffic violation. 신호위반으로 200달러 벌금을 내서.

Unit 07

05 We lowered the speed limit from 60km to 50km in town
시내에서 속도제한을 60킬로에서 50킬로로 낮추었어

- The speed limit in school zones is 30km/h. 스쿨존에서의 속도제한은 30킬로야.
- The speed limit on motorways is usually 100km/h.
  자동차 전용도로에서의 속도제한은 100킬로야.
- The freeway in Germany has no speed limit. 독일의 프리웨이에서는 속도제한이 없어.

A: What is the speed limit on city roads? 도심 도로에서의 속도제한은 얼마야?
B: Usually it is between 60 to 70km/h. 보통 60에서 70킬로 사이야.

016

I parked in a parking lot

난 주차장에 주차를 했어

주차할 때는 동사로 park 또는 park one's car라고 하면 된다. 주차장은 parking lot 혹은 parking zone이라고 한다. 특히 장애인 전용주차라고 할 때는 It's handicapped parking only라고 하면 된다.

01 You can park your car here

여기에 주차해도 돼

- **He** parked his car **on the street.** 갠 노상주차를 했어.
- **This is** a no parking zone. 여기는 주차금지구역이야.
- **This is** a handicapped parking space. 여기는 장애인주차구역이야.

A: You can't park here. It's handicapped parking only.
여기에 주차하면 안돼. 장애인 전용이야.

B: Sorry! I didn't see that sign. 미안! 저 사인을 보지 못했어.

02 I parked in a parking lot

난 주차장에 주차를 했어

- **I used** the underground parking lot. 난 지하주차장을 이용했어.
- **There is** street parking **in front of the store.** 그 가게 앞에 노상주차장이 있어.
- **You have to** use the parking meters. 넌 주차요금징수기를 이용해야 돼.

A: Is there parking at the store? 가게에 주차할 곳이 있어?

B: Yes. They have underground parking or meter parking on the street.
어. 지하에 주차하거나 노상에 주차요금징수기가 있어.

03 Be careful when you pull out of the parking lot
주차장에서 나올 때 조심해

- Pull into this parking lot. 이 주차장에 세워.
- He parked in my parking space. 걘 내 주차공간에 주차를 했어.
- He took up 2 parking spots. 걘 주차공간 두자리를 차지했어.

A: Look at that jerk! 저 멍청이 좀 봐!
B: He took up 2 parking spots. 2대가 댈 주차공간을 차지했네.

04 There are only a few parking spaces around here
주변에 주차공간은 겨우 몇 개뿐이야

- There are no parking spaces here. 여기는 주차공간이 없어.
- It's very hard to find parking near my place. 우리집 근처에 주차할 공간을 찾는게 어려워.
- Parking is very expensive in the city. 도시에서의 주차는 매우 비싸.

A: Why don't you drive to work? 차로 출근하지 그래?
B: Parking is very expensive in the city so I'd rather take the subway.
도시에서 주차가 매우 비싸서 차라리 지하철을 타.

05 The valet will bring up your car
주차요원이 네 차를 가져올거야

- She handed the valet a ticket to get her car.
주차요원에게 차가져다 달라고 주차권을 줬어.
- I gave the valet my car keys. 난 주차요원에게 자동차 키를 줬어.
- They have valet parking at the hotel. 호텔은 발레파킹을 해줘.

A: The valet parking is a nice service. 발레파킹은 좋은 서비스야.
B: Yes, but I hate tipping them. 그래, 하지만 팁주는 건 싫어.

Unit 07

017

The brakes don't work

브레이크가 작동을 하지 않아

시동이 걸리지 않을 때는 ~won't start 혹은 ~won't turn over라는 표현을 쓴다. 경고등이 뜨는 계기판은 dashboard라고 하고 차에 문제가 있다고 할 때는 have car trouble이라고 하면 된다.

01 My car won't start this morning
오늘 아침 차 시동이 걸리지 않으려고 해

- The car engine won't turn over **when I try to start it.**
  차 시동을 걸려고 하는데 엔진이 돌아가지 않으려고 해.

- **I left my lights on last night and now** my car battery is completely dead.
  지난밤에 전조등을 켜놓아서 배터리가 완전히 방전됐어.

- Her car radiator is leaking. 걔 자동차의 라디에이터가 새고 있어.

> A: I left my lights on last night and now my car battery is dead.
> 지난밤에 전조등을 켜놓아서 배터리가 방전됐어.
>
> B: I can help give you a boost. 부스트해주는 것으로 도와줄 수 있어.

02 The brakes don't work
브레이크가 작동을 하지 않아

- The power windows aren't working. 전동 창문이 작동을 하지 않아.

- **I need to** get the oil changed. 난 엔진오일을 교체해야 돼.

- The car needs a tune-up. 자동차는 정비가 필요해.

> A: Why did you take the car to the car center? 왜 정비소에 차를 가져간거야?
> B: The brakes weren't working. 브레이크가 작동하지 않아서.

03 A warning light is on my dashboard
계기판에 경고등이 켜졌어

- The engine sounds funny. 엔진소리가 이상해.
- I can smell something burning when I am running the engine.
  엔진을 작동할 때 뭔가 타는 냄새가 나.
- The oil light is flashing **on my dashboard.** 오일점검등이 계기판에 깜박거리고 있어.

A: Uh-oh! A warning light is flashing on my dashboard.
어! 경고등이 계기판에 깜박거리고 있어.

B: Better go to the car center to get it checked out.
정비소에 가서 점검받는게 좋겠어.

04 I had car trouble on my way home
집에 오는 길에 차에 문제가 있었어

- I had big trouble with my car. 내 차에 커다란 문제가 있었어.
- He got a flat tire **on the way to work.** 걘 출근 길에 타이어가 펑크났어.
- His car broke down **on the way to the store.** 걔 차는 가게로 오는 길에 퍼졌어.

A: What happened to her? Why isn't she here yet?
걔 무슨 일이야? 왜 아직도 도착하지 않은거야?

B: Her car broke down on the way here. 여기 오는 길에 차가 퍼졌어.

05 I think we have a flat tire
타이어가 펑크난 것 같아

- A tire blew out. 타이어가 펑크났어.
- A tire is low. 타이어에 바람이 빠졌어.
- The air pressure in the tire **is too low.** 자동차 공기압이 너무 낮아.

A: Your tire looks a bit flat. 네 타이어 좀 펑크난 것처럼 보여.

B: Yes, the air pressure is too low. I'll stop by the gas station and put some air in it. 어. 공기압이 너무 낮아. 주유소에 들러서 공기 좀 넣으려고.

018 I got into a car accident

난 차사고가 났어

가벼운 사고는 a fender-bender. 차사고가 나다는 get into a car accident 혹은 be involved in a car accident라고 한다. 자동차에 치였을 때는 got hit[was run over] by a car라고 하면 된다.

01 I had a fender-bender on the way here

여기 오는 길에 가벼운 사고가 났어

- She had a small accident **on the way to work.** 걘 출근길에 가벼운 사고를 당했어.
- I had an accident **on the way here.** 난 여기 오는 길에 사고가 났어.
- We had a minor accident **while parking the car.** 주차를 하다가 사소한 사고를 냈어.

A: Have you ever gotten into a car accident? 차사고 난 적 있어?
B: Yes, but it was just a small fender-bender. 어, 하지만 가벼운 사고였어.

02 I got into a car accident

난 차사고가 났어

- I was in a car accident **a few days ago.** 며칠 전에 난 교통사고가 났어.
- He was in a head on collision **this morning.** 걘 오늘 아침에 정면 충돌사고가 났어.
- She got into a serious accident **last weekend.** 걘 지난 주말에 심각한 교통사고가 났어.

A: He was in a head on collision this morning. 걘 오늘 아침에 정면 충돌사고가 났어.
B: I heard he almost died. 거의 죽을 뻔 했다고 들었어.

03 | I was involved in a car accident
난 교통사고가 났어

- She was involved in **a 5 car crash**. 걘 5중 충돌사고를 당했어.
- He caused the accident **by texting while driving**.
  운전 중에 문자하다가 교통사고를 냈어.
- She was involved in **a terrible car crash**. 걘 끔찍한 충돌사고를 당했어.

A: She was involved in a terrible car accident. 걘 끔찍한 충돌사고를 당했어.
B: I heard it was caused by texting and driving. 운전 중에 문자하다가 난 사고라며.

04 | I caused a traffic accident
내가 교통사고를 유발했어

- I brought about a traffic accident. 내가 교통사고를 초래했어.
- Who caused the accident? 누가 사고를 낸거야?
- He was at fault for the accident. 그 교통사고는 걔 책임였어.

A: Who caused the accident? 누가 사고를 낸거야?
B: The insurance company said the other driver was at fault for the
   accident. 보험회사에 따르면 다른 운전자가 사고에 책임이 있대.

05 | I got hit by a car
난 자동차에 치였어

- I was run over by a car. 난 자동차에 치였어.
- I try to avoid accidents **by driving very carefully**.
  난 교통사고를 피하려고 조심스럽게 운전해.
- He was injured in a hit and run accident. 걘 뺑소니 교통사고로 부상당했어.

A: He was injured in a hit and run accident. 걘 뺑소니 교통사고로 부상당했어.
B: Did the police ever catch the driver? 경찰이 그 뺑소니범을 잡았어?

Unit 07

019

My car was wrecked in the accident

내 차가 사고로 심하게 부서졌어

차를 박았을 때는 crash one's car. 사고로 심하게 부서졌을 때는 be wrecked in the accident. 누군가의 차를 훼손했을 때는 ~damage one's car라고 하고, 사람이 다쳤을 때는 be injured in a car accident라고 한다.

I crashed my car
내 차를 박았어

- She smashed her car into a tree. 걔 차를 나무에 박았어.
- He scraped the paint on his car door while parking.
  걔 주차하다가 차문의 페인트가 벗겨졌어.
- He blew out a tire while going to work. 걔 출근하다가 타이어가 펑크났어.

A: What happened to your car door? 네 차문 어떻게 된거야?
B: I scratched it while parking. 주차하면서 긁혔어.

I think someone damaged my car
누가 내 차를 훼손한 것 같아

- The car got a small dent in the door from the accident.
  차가 사고로 문이 조금 파들어갔어.
- Someone slashed my front tire last night. 누군가가 지난밤에 내 앞 타이어를 칼로 그었어.
- It looks like someone keyed my car. 누군가가 내 자동차에 열쇠로 긁어 흠을 낸 것 같아.

A: Look at that long scratch on your car paint. 네 자동차 페인트에 길게 긁힌 것을 봐.
B: It looks like someone keyed it. 누군가가 열쇠로 긁은 것 같네.

03　My car was wrecked in the accident
내 차가 사고로 심하게 부서졌어

- The car was a write-off after the accident.
  자동차는 사고 후에는 폐차하는게 나을 정도가 됐어.

- His car wasn't worth repairing after that crash.
  걔의 차는 충돌 후에 수리할 값어치가 없었어.

- She decided to sell her car for scrap metal after the accident.
  걘 사고 후에 차를 고철로 팔기로 결정했어.

A: The car was completely wrecked? 자동차가 완전히 부서졌어?

B: Yes, the mechanic said it wasn't worth fixing it.
어. 수리기사가 그러는데 고칠 가치가 없다고 하네.

04　He was injured in a car accident
걘 교통사고로 부상당했어

- My friend died in a car accident. 내 친구가 교통사고로 죽었어.

- He lost his life in a traffic accident. 걘 교통사고로 목숨을 잃었어.

- She was killed in the car accident. 걘 교통사고로 죽었어.

A: She lost her life in that car accident. 걘 그 교통사고로 목숨을 잃었어.

B: It was really tragic. 정말 비극적이었어.

05　I've never had an accident
난 교통사고가 난 적이 없어

- I've never gotten into an accident. 난 한번도 교통사고가 난 적이 없어.

- Have you ever had an accident? 교통사고 난 적이 있어?

- She has a perfect driving record. 걘 무사고 운전기록을 갖고 있어.

A: She's never had an accident? 걘 교통사고가 난 적이 한번도 없어?

B: That's right. She has a perfect driving record.
맞아. 걘 무사고 운전기록을 갖고 있어.

020

My car needs a tune up
내 차는 정비가 필요해

차를 수리하다는 get the car fixed, get repaired라 하고 정비는 tune up이라는 동사구를 사용한다. 카센터로 견인하다는 tow the car to the garage라고 한다.

01 Can you fix this car?
이 차를 수리할 수 있나요?

- **I have to** get the car fixed. 난 이 차를 고쳐야 하는데요.
- **The car has to be taken in to** get repaired. 그 차는 수리하기 위해 입고해야 돼.
- **Is this car worth fixing?** 이 차는 수리할 가치가 있을까?

A: I have to get this car fixed soon. 난 곧 이 차를 수리해야 돼.
B: Is it even worth fixing? You need to think about buying a new car.
수리할 가치가 있을까? 새 차를 뽑는 것을 생각해봐야 돼.

02 My car needs a tune up
내 차는 정비가 필요해

- **Could you** change the oil? 엔진오일을 바꿔줄래요?
- **I had new tires put on today.** 난 오늘 타이어를 새로 교체했어.
- **The windshield crack** can be repaired. 전면 유리창의 금간 것은 고칠 수 있어.

A: It's almost time to get the oil changed. 엔진오일을 교체할 때가 거의 됐어.
B: You might want to get the tires changed as well.
함께 타이어도 교체하면 좋을 것 같아.

03 I got my car repaired yesterday
난 어제 차를 수리했어

- My car engine was repaired **this week**. 이번주에 내 차의 엔진은 수리됐어.
- I'm taking the car in to get it fixed. 난 차를 수리하기 위해 입고하는 중이야.
- The mechanic fixed the wheel alignment **this afternoon**.
  수리기사가 오늘 오후에 휠얼라이먼트를 수리했어.

A: Did you get your car repaired yet? 네 차 수리했어?
B: I got it repaired yesterday. 어제 수리했어.

04 He made repairs to the car
걘 자동차 수리를 했어

- I made some repairs to **the brakes**. 난 브레이크 수리를 좀 했어.
- **Have you** made any repairs to the car lately? 최근에 자동차 수리한 적 있어?
- What repairs have you made to the car **this year**? 금년에 차 어디 수리했어?

A: This car is so old. 이 차는 너무 오래됐어.
B: You are always making repairs to it. 넌 항상 차수리를 하더라.

05 I had to tow the car to the garage
난 차를 카센터로 견인해야 했어

- Don't park in tow-away zones. 견인지역에 차를 세우지마.
- Her car got towed **while she was shopping**. 걘 쇼핑하는 도중에 자동차가 견인됐어.
- Did her car get towed? 걔 차가 견인됐어?

A: Where is my car? 내 차가 어디 있지?
B: It must have gotten towed away. This is a no parking zone.
견인된게 틀림없네. 여기는 주차구역이 아니잖아.

021

Why don't you take a taxi with me?

나와 함께 택시를 타는게 어때?

택시를 손으로 불러 잡는 것은 hail a cab, 일반적으로 택시를 잡는다 catch a cab 이라고 한다. 물론 cab 대신에 taxi라고 해도 된다. 또한 택시를 부르는 것은 call a taxi, 택시를 타는 take a taxi라고 하면 된다.

01 Please get me a taxi
택시 좀 불러줘

- **Can you call me a taxi?** 택시 불러줄 수 있어?
- **I hailed a cab in front of the store.** 난 가게 앞에서 손을 흔들어 택시를 잡았어.
- **I caught a cab to the airport.** 난 택시를 잡아타고 공항까지 갔어.

> A: How did you get here so fast? 어떻게 여기에 그리 빨리 온거야?
> B: I caught a cab. 택시를 잡아탔거든.

02 Why don't you take a taxi with me?
나와 함께 택시를 타는게 어때?

- **Would you like to share a cab with me?** 나와 함께 택시를 같이 탈래?
- **Let's take a taxi instead of the subway.** 지하철 대신에 택시를 타자.
- **I took a taxi home.** 택시타고 집에 왔어.

> A: You've been drinking a lot. 넌 술을 너무 많이 마셨어.
> B: Yes, let's take a taxi home instead of driving.
> 맞아. 운전하는 대신에 택시타고 집에 가자.

03 I will grab a taxi to the office
택시를 잡아타고 사무실에 갈거야

- Can you grab a taxi tonight? 오늘밤에 택시를 잡을 수 있어?
- She says she'll catch a cab home after work.
  걘 퇴근 후에 택시를 잡아타고 집에 올거라고 해.
- Trying to grab a cab after the subway closes is almost impossible.
  지하철이 끊긴 후에 택시를 잡으려하는 것은 거의 불가능해.

A: Can you grab a cab tonight? I forgot I made dinner plans.
오늘밤 택시 잡을 수 있어? 저녁식사 약속이 있는 것을 깜박했어.

B: Sure I can. Have a nice evening. 물론 할 수 있어. 좋은 저녁 돼.

04 I called a taxi
난 택시를 불렀어

- I used the hotel's taxi service. 난 호텔의 택시 서비스를 이용했어.
- I had him call me a cab. 걔보고 내가 탈 택시를 부르게 했어.
- Could you please call me a cab for a 7pm pick up?
  오후 7시 타는 걸로 택시를 불러 줄래?

A: I used the hotel's taxi service to get to the airport.
난 호텔 택시 서비스를 이용해 공항에 갔어.

B: That was smart of you. 너 참 스마트하구나.

05 I caught a taxi to get here
여기 오려고 택시를 잡아탔어

- She came here by taxi. 걘 여기로 택시를 타고 왔어.
- Did you come here by taxi? 여기 택시타고 왔니?
- She said she caught a cab to get here. 걘 택시타고 여기에 왔다고 했어.

A: How did she get here? 걘 여기에 어떻게 왔어?
B: She said she caught a cab. 택시타고 왔다고 했어.

022

I get off at the next stop

난 다음 정거장에서 내려

택시안에 들어가고 나올 때는 동일평면으로 봐서 get in, get out를 쓰지만, 버스나 기차 등 좀 높은 계단을 타고 올라가거나 내려오는 경우에는 get on, get off라는 표현을 쓴다는 점 유의한다.

01 I caught a bus going to New York
뉴욕행 버스를 탔어

- **You need to** catch a bus **bound for Gangnam.** 강남으로 가는 버스를 타야 돼.
- **I** got the express bus **to Jamsil.** 난 잠실로 가는 광역버스를 탔어.
- **Is this the bus going to Busan?** 이 버스가 부산가는 버스인가요?

A: I caught the bus to Busan at 3pm. 난 오후 3시에 부산가는 버스를 탔어.
B: How long did it take you? 얼마나 걸렸어?

02 I get off at the next stop
난 다음 정거장에서 내려

- **Press the button if you want to** get off at the next stop.
  다음 정거장에서 내리려면 버튼을 눌러.
- **What stop are you** getting off at? 어느 정거장에서 내릴거야?
- **This is the final stop so everyone** is getting off here.
  여기가 종점이니까 다들 내릴거야.

A: I need to get off at the next stop. 난 다음 정거장에서 내려야 돼.
B: You have to press the button then. 그럼 버튼을 눌러야 돼.

03 I got on the bus near my house
집 근처에서 버스를 탔어

- Fortunately my home is on a bus route. 운좋게도 우리 집은 버스가는 길에 위치해 있어.
- Is there a bus stop near your apartment? 네 아파트 근처에 버스 정거장이 있어?
- How far is it from your place to the nearest bus stop?
  네 집에서 가장 가까운 정거장이 얼마나 멀어?

A: How far is the bus stop from your home? 네 집에서 버스 정거장까지 얼마나 멀어?
B: It's a 5 minute walk. 걸어서 5분.

04 Let's take a bus to the subway
지하철까지 버스를 타자

- Take a bus to your office. 버스를 타고 사무실에 가.
- Take bus number 8100. 8100번 버스를 타.
- I had to transfer buses. 난 버스를 갈아타야 했어.

A: I had to transfer buses 3 times to get here. 여기오는데 버스를 3번 갈아타야 했어.
B: That doesn't sound fun. 힘들었겠네.

05 I have to take a bus going to Seoul
난 서울로 가는 버스를 타야 해

- I got a bus to the airport. 난 공항까지 버스를 탔어.
- The bus from the airport to the city was very quick and convenient.
  공항에서 시내로 가는 버스는 아주 빠르고 편리했어.
- How much is the standard bus fare? 일반버스 요금이 얼마야?

A: How much is the standard bus fare in your city?
   네가 사는 도시에서 일반버스 요금이 얼마나 돼?
B: $2 for zone 1 and $4 for zone 2. 1구역 내에서는 2달러고 2구역을 가는데는 4달러야.

023

I had to ride the bus to work today

오늘 버스를 타고 출근해야 했어

버스를 타고 …에 가다는 ride the bus to~가 많이 쓰이며, 또한 동사 board를 이용할 수도 있는데 be lined up to board the bus하게 되면 버스타려고 줄서 있다라는 뜻이 된다. 버스로는 by bus라는 것도 잊지 않는다.

---

01 She rides a bus to school every day

걘 매일 학교가는데 버스를 타

- I had to ride the bus to **work today.** 오늘 버스를 타고 출근해야 했어.
- He never rides the bus to school. 걘 절대로 버스타고 등교하지 않아.
- I've ridden the bus **a few times.** 난 버스를 몇 번 타봤어.

A: How does she get to school? 걘 어떻게 학교에 온대?
B: She usually rides the bus. 걘 보통 버스를 타.

---

02 The passengers lined up to board the bus

승객들이 버스를 타려고 줄을 섰어

- It's time to board the bus **to Daejeon.** 대전행 버스 승차할 때이야.
- I think I dropped my wallet while I was boarding the bus.
  버스에 올라탈 때 지갑을 떨어트린 것 같아.
- The driver wouldn't let me board the bus because I wasn't wearing a
  mask. 운전기사는 내가 마스크를 안썼다고 버스에 타지 못하게 했어.

A: It's almost 1pm. 거의 오후 1시이다.
B: Time to board the bus. 버스를 탈 시간이야.

03 She was late because she missed the bus
갠 버스를 놓쳐서 늦었어

- I missed the bus **by 1 minute.** 난 1분 차이로 버스를 놓쳤어.

- He almost missed the bus **but the driver stopped and waited for him.**
갠 거의 버스를 놓칠 뻔했는데 기사가 정차해서 갸가 타기를 기다렸어.

- I've **never** missed an airplane but I've missed the bus **many times.**
난 비행기를 놓친 적은 없지만 버스는 많이 놓쳤어.

A: Why were you late for school today? 오늘 학교에 왜 지각한거야?
B: I just missed the bus and had to wait 20 minutes for the next one.
버스를 놓쳐서 다음 차 올 때까지 20분을 기다려야 했어.

04 I went there by bus
난 버스를 타고 거기에 갔어

- Let's go by bus. 버스타고 가자.

- She usually goes to work by bus. 갠 보통 버스타고 출근해.

- I haven't gone to school by bus **in a long time.**
난 오랫동안 버스타고 학교에 가지 않았어.

A: How did you get there? 거기에 어떻게 간거야?
B: I went by bus. 버스타고 갔어.

05 It's a 30-minute bus ride into town
시내로 30분 정도 버스타고 가야 돼

- How long was the bus ride to Suwon? 수원까지는 버스로 얼마나 걸려?

- The bus ride **took over an hour.** 버스를 한 시간 넘게 탔어.

- During rush hour the bus ride **is much longer.**
러시아워 때에는 버스타는 시간이 훨씬 더 걸려.

A: How long was the bus ride today? 오늘 버스를 얼마동안 탄거야?
B: It took over an hour because of heavy traffic.
차가 많이 막혀서 한 시간 넘게 걸렸어.

Unit 07

024

I have to catch the train at 7pm

난 오후 7시에 기차를 타야 돼

기차를 타다라고 할 때는 the train 앞에 take나 catch를 쓰면 된다. 지하철 역시 take the subway라고 한다. 지하철을 갈아탈 때는 transfer, 내릴 때는 역시 get off를 쓰면 된다.

01 I took the train to Paris
기차를 타고 파리에 갔어

- I have to catch the train at 7pm. 난 오후 7시에 기차를 타야 돼.
- What time are you catching the train this morning? 오늘 아침 몇 시에 기차를 탈거야?
- She took the train back to her hometown last weekend.
  걘 지난 주말 기차를 타고 고향으로 돌아갔어.

A: What time are you catching the train today? 오늘 몇 시에 기차를 탈거야?
B: Let me check. At 2:15. 확인해보고, 2시 15분에.

02 I will take the train to Busan
난 기차를 타고 부산에 갈거야

- I took the train from Busan. 기차타고 부산에서 올라왔어.
- She took the bullet train from Tokyo to Osaka.
  걘 도쿄 출발해서 오사카로 가는 고속열차를 탔어.
- Have you ever taken the KTX before? KTX를 전에 타본 적이 있어?

A: I took the KTX to Busan. 난 KTX를 타고 부산에 갔어.
B: Was it a comfortable ride? 타기에 편안했어?

03 I usually take the subway to work
난 보통 지하철로 출근해

- Taking the subway **during rush hour sucks.** 러시아워에 지하철타는 건 정말 으악이야.
- **I hate** taking the subway **in the morning.** 난 아침에 지하철타는 것을 싫어해.
- **Do you usually take the subway?** 넌 보통 지하철을 타니?

A: I hear you usually take the subway to work. 보통 지하철타고 출근한다며.
B: Yes, it's very convenient for me. 맞아, 아주 편리해.

04 You take the orange line and get off at the next stop
노란색 라인을 타고 담 정거장에서 내리세요

- **You need to transfer at Shindorim and then take the** number 2 line to Hongdae. 신도림역에서 갈아타는데 홍대까지 2호선을 타야 돼요.
- **You have 4 stops before you get off.** 네 정거장 후에 내리세요.

A: How many stops before we get off? 몇 정거장 후에 내려야 돼요?
B: We have to transfer at the next stop then it's 5 more stops from there. 다음 정거장에서 갈아탄 다음 거기서 5정거장 더 가야 돼요.

05 Using the subway is very convenient
지하철을 이용하는 것은 매우 편리해

- **I enjoy** taking the subway. 난 지하철을 즐겨 타.
- Riding the subway **is better for the environment.** 지하철을 타는게 환경에 더 좋아.
- **More and more people** are using the subway **these days.**
  요즘에는 더욱 더 많은 사람들이 지하철을 타.

A: Do you enjoy taking the subway? 지하철 타는 것을 즐겨해?
B: Yes and it's also better for the environment. 어, 그리고 또 환경에도 좋잖아.

지하철, 기차 2

I use my smartphone on the subway to kill time

난 시간을 보내기 위해 전철에서 스마트폰을 해

버스에서 지하철로 환승할 때도 역시 transfer를 사용해 transfer the ~ bus to the subway라고 하면 된다. 그리고 지하철에서 스마트폰을 한다고 할 때는 use my smartphone on the subway라 한다.

01 I had to change trains for Busan at Daejeon
난 대전에서 부산행 기차로 갈아타야 했어

- I transferred trains in Frankfurt to get to Berlin.
  난 베를린으로 가기 위해 프랑크푸르트에서 기차를 갈아탔어.

- Where did you change trains to get to Paris?
  파리에 가기 위해서 어디서 기차를 갈아탄거야?

- How many times did you have to change trains? 몇 번이나 기차를 갈아타야 했어?

A: I traveled by train from Paris to Berlin. 난 파리에서 베를린까지 기차로 이동했어.
B: How many times did you have to change trains on your journey?
여행중 몇 번이나 기차를 갈아타야 했어?

02 I need to transfer from the 255 bus to the subway at Gangnam station 강남역에서 255번 버스에서 지하철로 갈아타야 해

- Can you let me know where I need to get off to transfer to the Hongdae subway station? 홍대 전철역에 가려면 어디서 내려 갈아타야 하는지 알려줄래요?

- I get off the subway at Shinchon station to transfer to my bus.
  난 버스로 갈아타기 위해 신촌 역에서 지하철을 내려.

- How many times do you need to transfer to get from your home to your school? 집에서 학교가는데 몇 번이나 갈아타야 돼?

A: Can you let me know where I need to get off to transfer to the Hongdae subway station? 홍대 전철역에 가려면 어디서 내려 갈아타야 하는지 알려줄래요?
B: It's two stops away. 앞으로 2정거장 남았어요.

03 I fell asleep while riding the subway last Saturday night 지난 토요일 밤에 지하철타다 잠들었어

- I often listen to my iPad while riding the subway.
  전철타는 중에 난 종종 아이패드를 들어.

- You aren't supposed to talk on your phone while riding the subway.
  지하철타는 중에 핸드폰 통화를 해서는 안돼.

A: It takes you an hour and thirty minutes to get here by subway? That's a long commute! 여기까지 지하철로 오는데 한시간 30분이 걸린단말야? 통근시간이 많이 걸리네!

B: It's OK. I usually listen to my iPad while riding it and the time goes by pretty fast. 괜찮아. 보통 지하철타고는 아이패드를 들으면 시간이 아주 빨리 지나가거든.

04 It's a long subway ride to my house 집까지 지하철을 오래 타야 돼

- It's very hard to get a seat on the subway train during rush hour.
  러시아워에 지하철에서 앉아 타는 것은 아주 어려워.

- I often give up my seat to older people when the subway is busy.
  지하철에 사람이 많을 때 난 어르신들에게 종종 자리를 양보해.

A: It's a super long subway ride to my home. 집까지 지하철로 가는데 아주 오래 타야 돼.

B: Is it hard to get a seat? I hate standing the entire ride.
자리에 앉는게 어려워? 타는 내내 서서가는건 질색야.

05 I use my smartphone on the subway to kill time 난 시간을 보내기 위해 전철에서 스마트폰을 해

- I often fall asleep while riding the subway. 난 종종 지하철을 타다 잠이 들어.

- How do you kill time while riding the subway? 지하철을 타는 동안 뭐하면서 시간보내?

- I usually read a book while taking the subway. 난 지하철을 타는 동안 보통 책을 읽어.

A: How do you kill time on your long subway ride home?
집까지 오래 지하철을 타면서 어떻게 시간을 보내?

B: I usually read a book or listen to music. 난 보통 책을 읽거나 음악을 들어.

026
I'm flying to New York this weekend

난 이번 주말에 비행기로 뉴욕에 가

비행기를 탄다고 할 때 알아두어야 하는 단어는 flight와 take 혹은 catch이다. 비행기에 타는 것은 board the plane, 비행기를 놓치다는 miss one's flight라고 하면 된다.

01 I caught the flight to Seoul
난 서울행 비행편을 탔어

- He had to catch the two-twenty flight. 걘 220 비행편을 타야 했어.
- I had to catch the connecting flight in Tokyo. 난 도쿄에서 연결비행편을 타야 했어.
- Don't you have to catch the flight soon? 곧 비행기를 타야 하지 않아?

A: Let's have one more coffee before I leave. 떠나기 전에 커피 한 잔 마시자.
B: Don't you have to catch your flight in 3 hours? Maybe you should go to the airport now. 3시간 안에 비행기를 타야 하지 않아? 지금 공항에 가는게 나을 것 같아.

02 I am going to take a flight to Bangkok
난 방콕행 비행기를 탈거야

- He has to take a long airplane flight to Brazil. 걘 브라질까지 긴 비행을 해야 돼.
- Her flight is a long one. 걔의 비행편은 길어.
- She took a flight to Jeju this morning. 걘 오늘 아침 제주도행 비행기를 탔어.

A: I need to speak with your manager. 난 매니저와 얘기해야 돼요.
B: I'm sorry but he took a flight to Jeju this afternoon. Can I take a message? 죄송하지만 오늘 오후에 제주도에 가셨는데요. 메시지 남겨드릴까요?

I have to board the plane in 10 minutes
난 10분 후에 비행기에 탑승해야 돼

- **The flight is boarding now.** 그 비행편은 지금 탑승하고 있어.
- **Business class passengers** get to board the plane **first.**
  비즈니스석 승객들이 먼저 비행기에 탑승하게 돼.
- **We can** line up to board the plane **now.** 우리는 지금 줄서서 비행기에 탑승할 수 있어.

A: Do we have time to do some duty-free shopping?
면세점에서 좀 쇼핑할 시간이 될까?

B: We do. We don't have to board the plane for another hour.
어. 한 시간내에 비행기를 탈 필요는 없어.

I'm flying to New York this weekend
난 이번 주말에 비행기로 뉴욕에 가

- **She is** flying into Seoul **today.** 걘 비행편으로 오늘 서울에 와.
- **I have to** fly to Osaka **next Tuesday for a business meeting.**
  난 비즈니스 회의차 담주 화요일에 오사카에 비행편으로 가야 돼.
- **Where are you** flying to? 넌 비행기타고 어디로 가?

A: She is flying into Seoul today for a conference.
걘 총회차 오늘 비행편으로 서울에 와.

B: What time does she arrive? 몇 시에 도착해?

Don't miss your flight
비행편을 놓치지마

- **I** slept late and almost missed my flight. 늦잠을 자서 내 비행편을 거의 놓칠 뻔했어.
- **Have you ever** missed a flight **before?** 전에도 비행편을 놓친 적이 있어?
- **How did she** miss her flight? 걘 어떻다 비행기를 놓친거야?

A: Did you hear? She missed her flight and won't arrive until
tomorrow. 너 들었어? 걔가 비행기를 놓쳐서 내일이나 돼야 도착할거래.

B: What happened? Did she sleep late again? 무슨 일인데? 또 늦잠 잔거야?

비행기 2

027

The line up to clear customs was very long

세관을 통관하려는 줄이 엄청 길었어

수화물은 check in을 해야 하며 비행기에 들고 타는 휴대용 짐은 carry-on (bag) 이라고 한다. 세관을 통관하는 것은 clear customs. 세관신고할 것을 갖고 있다는 have anything to declare이라고 한다.

01 Do you have any check in baggage?
수화물 붙일게 있습니까?

- I have some luggage to check in. 체크인 할 수화물이 좀 있어요.
- You are allowed one piece of check in luggage for free.
  하나의 수화물은 무료로 붙일 수 있어요.
- The check in baggage mustn't weigh more than 23kgs.
  붙이는 수화물은 23킬로를 넘으면 안됩니다.

A: I have some luggage to check in. 붙일 수화물이 좀 있어요.
B: Please put in here, sir. 여기에 올려놓으세요.

02 Are you taking any carry-on bags with you?
휴대용 가방을 가지고 계신가요?

- This is my carry-on bag. 이건 휴대용 가방입니다.
- Is this too big for a carry-on? 휴대하기에는 너무 크지 않나요?
- Do you have any carry-on luggage? 휴대용 짐이 뭐 있나요?

A: This is my carry-on bag. 이건 내가 휴대하는 가방인데요.
B: That's fine, ma'am. 괜찮습니다. 부인.

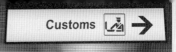

03 The line up to clear customs was very long
세관을 통관하려는 줄이 엄청 길었어

- I hate going through customs **when it's busy.** 바쁠 때 세관을 통관하는게 정말 싫어.

- The customs officers looked through **my luggage.** 세관원이 내 짐을 빠르게 훑어봤어.

- **I was randomly picked by customs to** have my bags searched.
  난 무작위로 선택되어 세관원들이 내 가방들을 뒤졌어.

A: Did you have any troubles getting through customs?
통관하는데 뭐 어려움 없었어?

B: Yes, they randomly picked me and searched through my bags.
있어서. 무작위로 나를 선택해서 내 가방들을 뒤졌어.

04 Do you have anything to declare?
뭐 신고할게 있습니까?

- **All passengers must** fill out the customs declaration form.
  모든 승객은 세관신고서를 작성해야 합니다.

- **Did you have to declare** those cigarettes? 이 담배들은 신고하셨나요?

- **I don't have anything to declare.** 난 신고할게 아무것도 없어요.

A: Did you have to declare that whisky? 저 위스키 신고했어?
B: No, you are allowed one bottle. 아니. 한 병은 허용되잖아.

05 Do you have any jet lag?
시차를 겪어?

- **She is suffering from jet lag.** 걘 시차문제로 고생하고 있어.

- **I am still recovering from jet lag.** 난 아직 시차를 극복하고 있는 중이야.

- **How long does it take you to** get over your jet lag? 시차를 극복하는데 얼마나 걸려?

A: You look tired. 너 피곤해 보여.
B: I'm still suffering from jet lag. 난 아직 시차로 고생하고 있어.

Unit 07

028

How often do you ride your bike?

자전거는 얼마나 자주 타?

자전거를 타다는 ride a bike. 올라타다라는 느낌을 주려면 get on a bike나 jump on a bike라고 하면 된다. 자전거에서 내릴 때는 아무래도 높이가 있으니 get off라 한다. 퀵보드는 scooter라고 한다는 점에 유의한다.

01 How often do you ride your bike?
자전거는 얼마나 자주 타?

- **Do you know how to ride a bike?** 너 자전거 탈 수 있어?

- **Learning to ride a bicycle is part of most childhoods.**
  자전거 타는 것을 배우는 건 대부분 어린시절의 일부야.

- **She never learned how to ride a bike.** 걘 자전거 타는 법을 전혀 배우지 못했어.

A: Does she know how to ride a bike? 걘 자전거 탈 줄 알아?
B: Yes, she cycles to work every day. 어. 걘 매일 자전거로 출근해

02 I got on my bike and cycled over to school
난 자전거에 올라타고 학교로 갔어

- **She jumped on her bike and rode home.** 걘 자전거에 올라타서 집으로 향했어.

- **She got off her bike and locked it to the bike rack.**
  걘 자전거에서 내려서 자전거 고정대에 열쇠로 걸어놨어.

- **Two of them were on the bike riding to school.** 그들 중 2명은 자전거를 타고 학교에 갔어.

A: Where is he? 걔 어디 있어?
B: He jumped on his bike and rode home 1 hour ago.
한 시간 전에 자전거타고 집에 갔어.

03 He rides to work on a bicycle
갠 자전거를 타고 출근해

- She usually rides her bike to work. 갠 보통 자전거를 타고 출근해.
- Did he ride to work on a bike today? 갠 오늘 자전거를 타고 출근했어?
- I didn't ride on my bike today because of the rain.
  오늘은 비가 와서 자전거를 타지 않았어.

A: Did he ride to work on a bike today? 갠 오늘 자전거를 타고 출근했어?
B: He usually does but not today. 보통은 그러는데 오늘은 아냐.

04 He was pushing his bicycle up the hill
갠 언덕 위로 자전거를 밀고 갔어

- He had to get off his bike and push it. 갠 자전거에서 내려서 밀고 가야 했어.
- She carried her bike onto the subway. 갠 지하철로 자전거를 끌고 갔어.
- Her bike folds up so she can put it in her car easily.
  걔 자전거는 폴더로 접혀져서 차안에 쉽게 넣을 수가 있어.

A: She took her bike to Busan? 갠 자전거를 가지고 부산에 갔어?
B: Yes, it folds up so she could put it on the KTX.
   어, 폴더로 접혀져서 KTX에 놓을 수가 있어.

05 He uses a scooter to go to work
갠 스쿠터를 이용해 출근해

- Can you drive a scooter? 스쿠터를 탈 수 있어?
- He drives a motorcycle to work. 갠 오토바이 타고 출근해.
- He comes to work by motorbike. 갠 오토바이로 출근해.

A: Does he drive a scooter? 갠 스쿠터를 탈 수 있어?
B: Yes, he drives it to work almost every day. 어, 거의 매일 그거 타고 출근해.

Unit

스포츠

001

Do you work out much these days?

넌 요즘 운동을 많이 해?

운동하면 exercise로 명사나 동사로 두루두루 쓰인다. 이에 못지 않게 쓰이는 운동하다라는 단어는 work out으로 명사로 운동이라고 하려면 work out 혹은 붙여서 workout이라고 하면 된다.

Do you do any exercise?
뭐 운동하는거 있어?

● **What kind of exercises do you do to stay healthy?**
건강을 위해 하는 운동의 종류는 뭐야?

● **How often do you exercise?** 얼마나 자주 운동을 해?

● **She loves exercising outside.** 걘 야외에서 운동하는 것을 좋아해.

A: Do you do any exercise to stay healthy? 건강을 유지하기 위해 하는 운동 뭐 있어?
B: I try to walk 20 minutes every day. 난 매일 20분씩 걸으려고 해.

Do you work out much these days?
넌 요즘 운동을 많이 해?

● **I hope to stay in shape.** 난 건강을 유지하기를 바래.

● **How do you stay in such good shape?** 어떻게 그렇게 건강을 유지하는거야?

● **He works out at the gym every day.** 걘 매일 체육관에서 운동을 해.

A: He works out at the gym a few hours a day.
걘 하루에 몇 시간 체육관에서 운동을 해.
B: It shows. He looks great. 그런 것 같아. 아주 좋아 보여.

What sports do you usually play?
보통 무슨 운동을 해?

- What sports do you enjoy **in summer?** 여름에는 무슨 운동을 즐겨 해?
- **Do you** play soccer? 축구하는거 좋아해?
- **He** loves all kinds of sports. 걘 모든 종류의 운동을 좋아해.

A: Does he play soccer well? 걘 축구를 잘 해?
B: Yes but he loves all kinds of different sports.
어, 하지만 온갖 종류의 스포츠를 좋아해.

We practice every Friday evening
매주 금요일 저녁마다 연습을 해

- I get short of breath **easily these days.** 요즘에는 쉽게 숨이 차.
- I feel refreshed in mind and body **when doing physical exercises.**
운동을 하면 심신이 재충천되는 기분이야.
- After a good workout session **I always feel great.**
기분좋게 운동을 하고 나면 기분이 아주 좋더라.

A: Are you OK? 괜찮아?
B: I'm really out of shape. I get short of breath walking up the stairs.
몸이 안좋아. 계단을 오르면 숨이 차올라.

We have a game next Sunday
다음주 일요일에 게임이 있어

- We usually play games **on Sunday morning.** 우리는 보통 일요일 아침에 운동을 해.
- Our team plays **every Saturday afternoon.** 매주 토요일 오후마다 우리 팀은 경기를 해.
- We have a basketball game **tonight at 7pm.** 오늘 저녁 7시에 농구게임이 있어.

A: When do you usually play? 언제 보통 운동을 해?
B: Our team plays every Saturday morning. 우리 팀은 매주 토요일 아침마다 경기를 해.

Unit 08

002

I play second base for the team

난 팀에서 2루수로 뛰어

이번에는 직접 운동경기를 하는 경우이다. 조기축구회에 가입하다는 join a local morning soccer club. 그리고 거리농구를 하다는 play street basketball with sb라고 한다.

01 I play soccer every Sunday morning

난 매 일요일 아침마다 축구를 해

- I joined a local morning soccer club **last month.**
  난 지난달에 지역조기축구회에 가입했어.
- I registered for the basketball league **today.** 난 오늘 농구리그에 등록했어.
- The league starts **on May 1 and ends on July 5.**
  리그는 5월 1일에 시작해서 7월 5일에 끝나.

A: Are you going to join that new basketball league?
저 새로운 농구리그에 가입할거야?

B: Yes, I registered for it this morning. 어, 오늘 아침에 등록했는걸.

02 I play second base for the team

난 팀에서 2루수로 뛰어

- I was on the baseball team **when I was in high school.**
  난 고등학교 다닐 때 야구팀 소속였어.
- What position do you play? 어떤 포지션에서 뛰어?
- I'm a power forward **on our basketball team.** 난 농구팀에서 파워포워드로 뛰어.

A: What position do you play on your soccer team?
축구팀에서 무슨 포지션에서 뛰어?

B: I'm the goalkeeper. 난 골키퍼야.

03 I play street basketball with my friends
난 친구들과 함께 거리농구를 해

- I enjoy 3 on 3 basketball. 난 3:3 농구를 즐겨 해.
- I love shooting hoops with my high school friends.
  난 고등학교 친구들과 농구공 던져 넣기를 좋아해.
- My friend and I often play 1 on 1. 내 친구와 나는 종종 1:1일로 경기해.

A: You like shooting hoops? 공 던져 넣기를 좋아해?
B: Yes, I often play 1 on 1 with my good friend.
어, 종종 내 친한 친구와 1:1로 경기를 해.

04 It's been a year since I started playing golf
내가 골프를 시작한지 일년이 됐어

- Have you played golf recently? 최근에 골프친 적 있어?
- My golf handicap is 20. 내 골프 핸디캡은 20야.
- I finished the round at 2 under par. 나는 2언더파로 라운드를 마쳤어.
- I don't have much opportunity to play golf these days.
  요즘에는 골프칠 기회가 많지 않아.

A: How long have you been playing golf? 골프친 지는 얼마나 됐어?
B: Since I was in university. 대학다닐 때부터.

05 I'd like to go curling
난 컬링하러 가고 싶어

- I heard you are a good curler. 너 컬링 잘 한다고 들었어.
- I started curling after the last Winter Olympics. 지난 동계올림픽 후에 컬링을 시작했어.
- Have you been curling for a long time? 오랫동안 컬링을 해왔어?

A: I'd like to try curling. 컬링을 해보고 싶어.
B: I started curling after watching the last Winter Olympics. It's a lot
of fun. 지난 동계올림픽을 본 후에 컬링을 시작했는데 아주 정말 재밌어.

운동하기 2

I'm good at bowling

난 볼링을 잘 쳐

그밖의 운동경기를 직접하는 경우를 보자. 당구를 치다는 shoot some pool, 볼링장에 가다는 go to the bowling alley, 스케이트[탁구]를 좋아한다고 할 때는 love skating, love table tennis라고 한다.

 ## Which would you prefer to do, billiards or bowling?
농구와 볼링 중 뭐하는 것을 좋아해?

- How about a game of billiards **this afternoon?** 오늘 오후에 당구게임 한판 어때?
- **Let's go to the bar and** shoot some pool. 바에 가서 당구 좀 치자.
- We are going to the bowling alley **today.** 우리는 오늘 볼링장에 갈거야.

A: What are we going to do if we get to the bar before everyone else arrives? 다른 사람들이 도착하기 전에 바에 도착하면 우리 뭐하지?
B: We can shoot a game of pool. 당구 한판 하지 뭐.

 ## I'm good at bowling
난 볼링을 잘 쳐

- I'm a good bowler. 난 볼링을 잘 해.
- Are you good at bowling? 너 볼링 잘 해?
- I scored 330 points **once.** 한 번은 330점이 나왔어.
- My average score is **around 110 points.** 내 애버리지는 한 110점야.

A: Are you a good bowler? 볼링 잘 쳐?
B: I don't think so. My average is around 150. 그렇지 않아. 애버리지가 150정도야.

03 I feel great when I get a strike
스트라이크를 쳤을 때 기분 정말 좋아

- She bowled a good game today. 걘 오늘 볼링게임을 잘했어.

- She got 2 strikes in a row. 걘 연속해서 두 번 스트라이크를 쳤어.

- I split the pins with my first throw. 첫번째 던지기에서 핀을 떨어트려놨어.

A: Oh no. I split the pins with my first throw.
이런. 첫번째 던지기에서 핀을 떨어트려놨어.

B: Too bad. I got a strike. 안됐네. 난 스트라이크였는데.

04 The best moment is when I gain a point with a smash
가장 좋은 순간은 힘껏 공을 쳐서 점수를 딸 때야

- Badminton is the best sport for a rainy day.
배드민턴은 비가 오는 날에 하기 가장 좋은 운동야.

- In swimming my best stroke is the backstroke.
수영에서 내가 가장 잘하는 수영법은 배영이야.

- I love skating by myself. 난 혼자서 스케이팅 타는 것을 좋아해.

A: Are you good at badminton? 너 배드민턴 잘 해?

B: No, but I am excellent at tennis. 아니. 하지만 테니스는 잘 해.

05 I like table tennis because it's easy to play anywhere
어디서나 쉽게 할 수 있기 때문에 탁구를 좋아해

- I broke my pingpong paddle when I lost the match.
경기에서 졌을 때 난 탁구채를 부셔버렸어.

- He is an expert pingpong player. 걘 전문적인 탁구 선수야.

- She is the fastest table tennis player I've ever seen.
걘 내가 본 가장 빠른 탁구 선수야.

A: Is she good at table tennis? 걘 탁구를 잘 쳐?

B: She is the fastest player I've ever seen. 걘 내가 본 가장 빠른 선수야.

Unit 08

004

I'd like to try whitewater rafting

난 급류래프팅을 해보고 싶어

낚시를 하러가다는 go fishing. 급류래프팅을 하다는 try whitewater rafting. 수영을 하다는 go swimming이라고 한다. 스쿠버 다이빙이 재미있다고 할 때는 Scuba diving is great fun이라고 하면 된다.

01 I sometimes go fishing in the bay
때때로 난 만에 가서 낚시하러 가

- **We must buy a fishing license.** 우리는 낚시 면허증을 사야 돼.
- **Do you have a fishing rod?** 넌 낚시대가 있어?
- **They go ice fishing in the winter.** 걔네들은 겨울에 얼음낚시하러 가.

A: Is your father a good fisher? 네 아버지는 낚시를 잘 하셔?
B: Yes but he needs to get a fishing license this year.
어 하지만 금년에 낚시 면허증을 사야 돼.

02 I'd like to try whitewater rafting
난 급류래프팅을 해보고 싶어

- **I love to ride big waves out in the ocean.** 난 바다에서 커다란 파도를 타는 걸 좋아해.
- **Surfing looks fun.** 서핑은 재미있어 보여.
- **Have you ever tried windsurfing?** 윈드서핑을 해본 적이 있어?

A: I'd like to try windsurfing. 난 윈드서핑을 해보고 싶어.
B: It looks very difficult. 매우 어려워 보이던데.

03 Usually, I go to Sokcho to go swimming
난 보통 속초에 가서 수영을 해

- I often go to the beach, but rarely enjoy swimming.
  난 가끔 해변가에 가지만 거의 수영을 즐기지는 않아.
- I love swimming in the ocean. 난 바다에서 수영하는 것을 좋아해.
- Do you ever go swimming in the ocean? 바다에 수영하러 가?

A: I love going to Sokcho to swim. 난 수영하러 속초에 가는 것을 좋아해.
B: I've never gone swimming in the ocean. 난 바다에 가서 수영을 해본 적이 없어.

04 I enjoy learning swimming lessons at a sports center
난 스포츠센터에서 수영강습 받는 것을 즐겨

- She started to take swimming lessons at her local sports center.
  걘 지역 스포츠센터에서 수영강습을 받기 시작했어.
- Are you a good swimmer? 너 수영 잘 해?
- He is a very fast swimmer. 걘 수영을 아주 빨리해.

A: Are you a good swimmer? 너 수영 잘 해?
B: I'm not very fast but I enjoy it. 아주 빠르지는·않지만 즐겨.

05 Scuba diving is great fun
스쿠버 다이빙은 아주 재미있어

- The beauty under the sea is beyond description.
  바다 밑의 아름다움은 말로 설명할 수가 없어.
- Scuba diving is very relaxing. 스쿠버 다이빙은 마음을 느긋하게 해줘.
- I can't scuba dive but I love to snorkel.
  난 스쿠버 다이빙을 할 수 없지만 스노클링하는 것을 좋아해.

A: Scuba diving is great fun. 스쿠버 다이빙은 아주 재미있어.
B: It looks like fun but I've only tried snorkeling.
재미있어 보이지만 난 단지 스노클링만 시도해봤어.

005

I love trekking in the countryside

난 전원지대에서 트레킹하는 것을 좋아해

트레킹을 좋아하면 love trekking, 하이킹을 하고 싶으면 would like to hike, 산을 등산하는 climb+산이라고 하면 된다. 즐긴다는 표현도 쓰는데 캠핑을 즐긴다고 할 때는 enjoy going camping이라고 하면 된다.

 01

I love trekking in the countryside

난 전원지대에서 트레킹하는 것을 좋아해

- I've been mountain climbing for the past ten years. 난 지난 10년동안 등산을 해왔어.
- I'd like to hike Mt. Jiri this summer. 난 이번 여름에 지리산을 하이킹하고 싶어.
- I heard he is a great mountain climber. 난 걔가 아주 뛰어난 등반가라고 들었어.

A: Is he a mountain climber? 걔는 등반가야?
B: Yes, he even tried to climb Mt. Everest 3 years ago.
어, 3년전에는 에베레스트 등반을 시도했어.

 02

I started mountain climbing ten years ago

난 10년전에 등산을 시작했어

- I got lost in the mountains last year. 작년에 산에서 길을 잃었어.
- I've climbed Mt. Halla three times. 난 한라산을 3번이나 올라갔어.
- We went up part of the way by cable car. 우리는 길의 일부는 케이블카로 올라갔어.

A: We took the cable car to the peak. 우리는 정상까지 케이블카를 탔어.
B: That's not mountain climbing! 그건 등산이 아니잖아!

03 I enjoy going camping with my family
난 가족과 함께 캠핑가는 것을 즐겨

- Camping **is a great family activity.** 캠핑은 아주 좋은 가족 활동이야.
- Being outdoors **is the best part of camping.**
  야외로 나왔다는게 캠핑의 가장 좋은 부분이야.
- I've been camping **my entire life.** 난 평생 캠핑을 해왔어.

A: Camping is a great family activity. 캠핑은 아주 좋은 가족 활동이야.
B: I know. I've been camping my entire life. 알아. 난 평생 캠핑을 해왔어.

04 I enjoy skiing every winter
난 매 겨울마다 스키를 즐겨

- Where did you go skiing **last winter?** 지난 겨울에 어디로 스키타러갔어?
- Are you **a good skier?** 너 스키 잘 타?
- He **is an expert skier.** 걘 아주 뛰어난 스키어야.

A: I am a pretty good skier. 난 스키를 아주 잘 타.
B: Where do you usually go skiing? 주로 어디 가서 스키타니?

05 I went skydiving for the first time last week
지난주 난 첨으로 스카이다이빙을 갔어

- She is going to **try skydiving** this weekend. 걘 이번 주말에 스카이다이빙을 해볼거야.
- He sprained his ankle **while skydiving.** 걘 스카이다이빙을 하다가 발목을 삐었어.
- She wants to **try bungee jumping.** 걘 번지점핑을 하고 싶어해.

A: I went skydiving for the first time last week.
지난주 난 처음으로 스카이다이빙을 하러 갔어.

B: You must be brave. I'm too scared of heights to try it.
용감하구나. 난 고소공포증이 있어 시도해보지를 못해.

006

I go to the fitness club once a week

난 주에 한 번 피트니스 클럽에 가

걷기 운동은 walking. 조깅은 jog, 그리고 피트니스 클럽에 가다는 go to the fitness club이라고 하면 된다. 또한 마라톤을 뛰다는 run in a marathon이라고 쓴다.

01 Walking every day reduces the risk of heart disease 매일 걷기는 심장병의 위험을 감소시켜줘

● **How long do you walk every day?** 매일 얼마나 오랫동안 걸어?

● **I try to walk 3 or 4 times a week.** 한 주에 3-4번은 걷기를 하려고 해.

● **I walk my dogs twice a day.** 난 하루에 두 번 강아지 산책을 시켜.

A: Walking is great exercise. 걷기는 아주 좋은 운동이야.

B: I know. I walk my dogs twice a day and feel great.
알아. 하루에 두 번 강아지 산책을 시키는데 기분이 아주 좋아.

02 I jog every day for my health
난 건강을 위해서 매일 조깅을 해

● **Do you enjoy jogging?** 너는 조깅을 즐겨 해?

● **I run 5 days a week.** 난 한 주에 5일 달려.

● **I try to run 50km a week.** 난 한 주에 50킬로를 달리려고 해.

A: Are you a good runner? 너는 잘 달려?

B: No but I enjoy running every day for my health.
아니, 하지만 건강을 위해 매일 달리기를 즐겨 해.

03 I go to the fitness club once a week
난 주에 한 번 피트니스 클럽에 가

- I go to a fitness club. **How about you?** 난 피트니스 클럽에 다녀. 너는?
- I usually go to the gym **after work.** 난 보통 퇴근 후에 체육관에 가.
- I bought a membership at the local fitness center.
  난 지역 피트니스 센터에 회원권을 구입했어.

A: Are you going to a gym these days? 요즘 넌 체육관에 가?
B: No but I'm planning on getting a membership at the local one this week. 아니. 하지만 이번주에 지역 체육관 회원권을 살 계획이야.

04 How long have you been lifting weights?
근력운동을 얼마동안 했어?

- **How long** have **you been riding?** 자전거를 얼마동안 탔어?
- **She's been going to the health club for over 1 year.**
  걘 일년 넘게 헬스클럽에 다니고 있어.
- I took up riding a bike **recently.** 난 최근에 자전거를 타기 시작했어.

A: How long has he been lifting weights? 걘 근력운동을 얼마동안 했어?
B: Since high school I think. 고등학교 이후인 것 같아.

05 I can run more than 10 kilometers now
난 이제 10킬로 이상을 달릴 수 있어

- I will run in a marathon **next week.** 난 담주에 마라톤 경기에 뛸거야.
- I used to be a marathon runner **when I was a schoolgirl.**
  난 학교다닐 때 마라톤 선수였어.
- I am running in my first marathon **next month.** 난 담달에 처음으로 마라톤을 뛰어.

A: I am running in my first marathon next week. 난 담주에 처음으로 마라톤을 뛰어.
B: That's great. I doubt I could run 2km. 잘됐네. 난 2킬로도 못뛸 것 같은데.

Unit 08

007

Would you like to try bungee jumping?

번지점핑을 해보고 싶어?

태권도나 쿵푸 등 무술을 한다고 할 때는 practice란 동사를 사용하면 된다. 종합격투기인 UFC를 좋아한다고 할 때는 be a big fan of UFC라고 한다.

01

I'm practicing Taekwondo for self-defense
자기방어를 위해 태권도를 배우고 있어

- **Do you** have a blackbelt in Taekwondo? 너 태권도 검은띠야?
- **She** is very good at Taekwondo. 갠 태권도를 아주 잘해.
- **He** is learning Taekwondo **to lose weight.** 갠 살을 빼려고 태권도를 배우고 있어.

A: Why is she learning Taekwondo? 왜 걔는 태권도를 배우는거야?
B: For self-defense. 자기방어를 위해서.

02

I practice kung-fu every morning
난 매일 아침 쿵푸를 연습하고 있어

- Kung-fu is the most popular martial art **in China.**
  쿵푸는 중국에서 가장 인기있는 무술이야.
- Are **you** interested in learning Kung-fu? 쿵푸를 배우는데 관심있어?
- I love watching Kung-fu movies. 난 쿵푸 영화보는 것을 좋아해.

A: Are you interested in learning Kung-fu? 쿵푸를 배우는데 관심있어?
B: No but I love watching Kung-fu movies. 아니 하지만 난 쿵푸 영화보는 것을 좋아해.

03 UFC stands for Ultimate Fighting Championship
UFC는 종합격투기대회의 약자야

- He is a big fan of UFC. 걘 UFC를 아주 좋아해.

- I watch UFC every chance I get. 난 기회있을 때마다 UFC 경기를 봐.

- I am learning MMA(mixed martial arts) because I love UFC so much.
  난 UFC를 아주 좋아하기 때문에 종합무술을 배우고 있어.

A: Why did you decide to learn MMA? 넌 왜 MMA를 배우기로 한거야?
B: Because I'm such a big fan of UFC. 난 UFC를 아주 좋아하기 때문이야.

04 She loves extreme sports
걘 익스트림 스포츠를 좋아해

- Would you like to try bungee jumping? 번지점핑을 해보고 싶어?

- Extreme sports are fun to watch but dangerous to do.
  익스트림 스포츠는 보기에 재미있지만 하기에는 위험해.

- Her son is crazy about skateboarding. 걔 아들은 스케이트보드를 광적으로 좋아해.

A: Have you ever tried any extreme sports? 익스트림 스포츠 뭐 해본 것 있어?
B: I like watching them but am too afraid to try any.
   보는 것은 좋아하는데 뭐 해보기에는 너무 겁이나.

05 My son roller-skates better than I do
내 아들은 나보다 롤러스케이트를 더 잘 타

- We sometimes ride motorcycles with our friends.
  우리는 때때로 친구들과 모터사이클을 타.

- She is very good at inline skating. 걘 인라인 스케이팅을 아주 잘 해.

- I love rollerblading with my friends. 난 친구들과 롤러블레이드 타는 것을 좋아해.

A: Is inline skating different from rollerblading?
   인라인 스케이팅은 롤러블레이딩과 달라?
B: No, they are the same thing. 아니, 같은거야.

Unit 08

008

My favorite sport is baseball
내가 좋아하는 스포츠는 야구야

이번에는 직접하는게 아니라 보는 스포츠 경기를 말해본다. 가장 좋아한다는 표현인 like the most[best]를 기억해두고, 손흥민이나 김하성 등의 해외스포츠기사를 빠지지 않고 이어서 볼 때는 like to follow~란 표현을 쓰면 된다.

01 What sport do you like the best?
어떤 스포츠를 가장 좋아해?

- What's your favorite sport? 좋아하는 스포츠는 뭐야?

- He loves all sports, but his favorite is baseball.
  걘 모든 스포츠를 좋아하지만 걔가 좋아하는 건 야구야.

- She doesn't like any sports. 걘 어떤 스포츠도 좋아하지 않아.

A: What's her favorite sport? 걔가 좋아하는 스포츠는 뭐야?
B: She doesn't like any sports. 걘 어떤 스포츠도 좋아하지 않아.

02 My favorite sport is baseball
내가 좋아하는 스포츠는 야구야

- My favorite team lost the game. 내가 좋아하는 팀이 게임에서 졌어.

- He follows pro baseball very closely. 걘 프로 야구경기를 매우 자세히 보고 있어.

- His favorite Premier League team is Arsenal.
  걔가 좋아하는 프리미어리그 팀은 아스날이야.

A: Does he follow the Premier League? 걔는 프리미어리그를 주의깊게 보고 있어?
B: Yes and his favorite team is Tottenham. 어, 그리고 걔가 좋아하는 팀은 토트넘이야.

03 I prefer watching live games
난 직접 게임보는 것을 더 좋아해

● He enjoys both watching and playing sports.
갠 스포츠 경기를 보거나 하는 것을 다 즐겨해.

● Watching sports live is much better than on TV.
직접 스포츠 경기를 보는 것은 TV로 보는 것보다 훨씬 좋아.

A: I prefer watching live games. 난 직접 게임보는 것을 더 좋아해
B: Me too. Watching games live is much better than on TV.
나도 그래. 직접 스포츠 경기를 보는 것은 TV로 보는 것보다 훨씬 좋아.

04 I enjoy reading the sports pages on the Internet
난 인터넷으로 스포츠 면을 읽는 것을 즐겨해

● I check out the sports news every day. 난 매일 스포츠 뉴스를 확인해.

● Do you follow sports closely? 스포츠 소식을 자세히 확인해?

A: Did you hear about the baseball game last night? 지난밤 야구경기소식 들었어?
B: Of course. I follow baseball very closely. 물론. 난 야구 소식을 빠짐없이 읽고 있어.

05 I'll be pleased if the Korean Major leaguers do well
한국인 메이저리거가 잘하면 기쁠거야

● Many Korean baseball players have achieved success in America.
많은 한국 야구선수가 미국에서 성공을 했어.

● I like to follow the Korean soccer players who are in Europe.
유럽에서 뛰는 한국 축구선수 소식을 빠짐없이 읽는 것을 좋아해.

● How many Koreans have gone on to play soccer in England?
영국에서 뛰는 한국 선수가 몇 명이나 돼?

A: I like to follow the Korean soccer players who play in Europe.
유럽에서 뛰는 한국 축구선수 소식을 빠짐없이 읽는 것을 좋아해.

B: So do I, especially the Premier League players.
나도 그래. 특히 영국 프리미어리그 선수들.

009

I can't believe that they jump that high

그들이 그렇게 높이 점프하는게 믿기지 않아

경기나 룰을 이해한다고 할 때는 understand를, …에 열광하다는 be crazy about~을 쓴다. 참고로 높이뛰기 등의 육상경기는 track and field라고 하는 점도 기억해둔다.

01 I don't know the rules of football very well
난 미식축구 룰은 잘 몰라

- **Does she understand baseball?** 걘 야구경기를 이해해?
- **She knows the hockey rulebook inside and out.** 걘 하키규칙을 아주 자세히 알고 있어.
- **Watching sports is much more fun if you understand the rules.**
  경기 룰을 안다면 스포츠 경기를 보는게 훨씬 더 재미있어.

A: I don't like American Football. It makes no sense to me.
난 미식축구를 좋아하지 않아. 뭐하는건지 모르겠어.

B: Watching sports is much more fun if you understand the rules.
경기 룰을 안다면 스포츠 경기를 보는게 훨씬 더 재미있어.

02 I used to be crazy about NBA basketball
난 NBA 농구를 아주 좋아했었어

- **He used to be into the KBO but now he doesn't watch it anymore.**
  걘 한국프로야구에 빠졌었지만 지금은 더 이상 경기를 보지 않아.
- **She was crazy about tennis before she got married and had children.**
  걘 결혼해서 아이들을 갖기 전까지 테니스에 열광했었어.
- **I follow the NBA very closely.** 난 NBA에 대해서는 하나도 빠짐없이 알고 있어.

A: You really love the NBA, don't you? 넌 NBA 정말 좋아하지, 그렇지 않아?

B: I used to before I got married and had children. I don't have time to watch it anymore. 결혼해서 아이를 갖기 전에는 그랬었지. 이제는 더 이상 볼 시간이 없어.

03 I like to watch UFC matches on TV
난 TV로 UFC 경기보는 것을 좋아해

- I don't have much interest in martial arts. 난 무술에는 별로 관심이 없어.
- What kind of martial arts do you like? 어떤 종류의 무술을 좋아해?
- I'm a big fan of boxing. 난 복싱을 아주 좋아해.

A: Do you like watching boxing? 복싱보는 것을 좋아해?
B: No but I follow UFC very closely. 아니. 하지만 UFC 소식을 빠짐없이 보고 있어.

04 I like Ssireum the best of all combat sports
모든 격투기 중에서 씨름을 가장 좋아해

- Do you know what Ssireum wrestling is? 너 씨름이 어떤 건지 알아?
- Have you ever watched a Sumo match? 스모경기를 본 적이 있어?
- I think wrestling is a boring spectator sport. 레슬링은 지겨운 관람스포츠인 것 같아.

A: Have you ever watched a Sumo match? 스모경기를 본 적이 있어?
B: No but I love watching Ssireum. 아니. 하지만 난 씨름경기보는 것을 좋아해.

05 I can't believe that they jump that high
그들이 그렇게 높이 점프하는게 믿기지 않아

- He loves watching track and field during the Olympics.
  걘 올림픽 기간 중 육상경기보는 것을 좋아해.
- The long jump was my best track and field event in high school.
  고등학교 때 넓이뛰기가 내가 가장 잘하는 육상경기였어.
- I don't understand how the high jumpers get so high.
  높이뛰기 선수들이 얼마나 높이 뛰는지 이해가 안돼.

A: Do you like track and field? 육상경기를 좋아해?
B: Yes, especially the 100 meter dash. 어. 특히 100미터 달리기.

010

I went to the Gocheok Dome last weekend

난 지난 주말에 고척돔에 갔어

직접 경기를 볼 때는 신경을 곤두 세우고 보기 때문에 see보다는 watch를 주로 쓴다. like to watch~ 혹은 enjoy watching~의 형태를 주로 볼 수 있다. 응원하다는 root for, …에 갔다는 went to~를 쓰면 된다.

01 I like both watching and playing sports
난 스포츠 경기를 보는 것도 하는 것도 다 좋아해

- I don't take part in sports, but I like to watch them very much.
  난 운동경기를 직접 하지는 않지만 보는 것을 매우 좋아해.

- I'm not athletic at all but I enjoy watching most sports.
  난 운동을 전혀 잘하지 못하지만 대부분의 스포츠 경기를 보는 것을 즐겨해.

- I love to play and do sports but I'm not a big fan of watching them.
  난 스포츠 경기를 하는 것을 좋아하지만 보는 것은 그리 좋아하지 않아.

A: I like both watching and playing sports.
난 스포츠 경기를 보는 것도 하는 것도 다 좋아해.

B: Not me. I'm not athletic at all so I only enjoy watching them.
난 아냐. 난 운동을 전혀 잘하지 못해서 그냥 보는 것만을 즐겨해.

02 I go to see baseball games three or four times a year
난 일년에 3~4번 야구경기를 보러 가

- I often enjoy tennis matches on TV. 난 종종 TV로 테니스 경기를 즐겨 봐.

- She watches golf on TV all the time. 걘 내내 TV로 골프를 봐.

- Have you ever been to a PGA event before? 전에 PGA 경기를 직접 본 적이 있어?

A: I love watching golf on TV. 난 TV로 골프보는 것을 좋아해.
B: Have you ever been to a PGA event before? 전에 PGA 경기를 직접 본 적이 있어?

03 I went to the Gocheok Dome last weekend
난 지난 주말에 고척돔에 갔어

- I watched the baseball game at Jamsil yesterday.
  난 어제 잠실에서 야구경기를 봤어.

- I watched Korea play a soccer game at the World Cup Stadium.
  난 월드컵경기장에서 한국이 축구경기를 하는 것을 봤어.

A: I love watching baseball games at the Jamsil Sports Complex.
난 잠실운동장에서 야구경기 보는 것을 좋아해.

B: Me too. The environment there. 나도 그래. 그곳의 환경이 좋아.

04 I rooted for the LA Dodgers yesterday
난 어제 LA 다저스를 응원했어

- Which team were you cheering for in the World Cup?
  넌 월드컵에서 어느 팀을 응원했어?

- I always cheer against the Doosan Bears. 난 항상 두산베어스를 응원하지 않아.

A: I am a big supporter of Manchester United. 난 맨유의 열렬한 팬이야.

B: I hate them so I always cheer against them. I cheer for Man City.
난 싫어서 응원을 하지 않아. 난 맨시티를 응원해.

05 I've got two tickets so how about going to see the game with me? 표 두장있는데 나와 함께 보러가는게 어때?

- I was so excited to go to the British Open this year.
  난 금년에 브리티시 오픈에 갈 생각에 아주 들떴어.

- We got tickets for the KBO finals last season.
  우리는 지난 시즌 한국시리즈의 티켓이 있었어.

- He gave us some free tickets to the basketball game.
  갠 우리에게 야구경기 무료입장권을 줬어.

A: What are you doing tonight? 오늘 저녁에 뭐해?

B: I got 2 free tickets to the soccer game. You wanna come watch it with me? 축구경기 무료입장권이 2장 있어. 나와 함께 보러 갈래?

Unit 08

011

I'm a big fan of soccer
난 축구를 아주 좋아해

---

support 또한 거의 우리말화 된 단어이다. 어떤 팀을 응원하냐고 할 때 support~ 또는 cheer for~ 혹은 …을 아주 좋아한다고 할 때 쓰는 표현인 be a big fan of~라고 하면 된다.

01 Which soccer team do you support?
어느 축구팀을 응원해?

- Some team's supporters are fanatics. 일부 팀의 서포터즈는 광적이야.

- I used to cheer for Liverpool but now I like Leeds United.
  난 리버풀을 응원했었는데 지금 리즈유나이티드를 좋아해.

- I don't really support any team. 응원하는 팀이 없어.

A: Which team do you support? 어느 팀을 응원해.
B: I don't really have a team. I just love watching good football.
    응원하는 팀이 없어. 그냥 멋진 미식축구를 보는 것을 좋아해.

02 I'm a big fan of soccer
난 축구를 아주 좋아해

- I heard she is really into watching baseball. 걔가 야구경기보는데 빠져 있다며.

- Is it true you are a hockey fanatic? 네가 하키에 광적이라는게 사실야?

- He can't watch enough sports. 걘 스포츠 경기를 아무리 봐도 부족해.

A: I heard he is crazy about watching sports. 걘 스포츠 경기 보는데 광적이라며.
B: That's right. He can't watch enough. 맞아. 걘 아무리 봐도 부족해.

03 I support Liverpool
난 리버풀을 응원해

- I'm an Aston Villa supporter. 난 아스톤 빌라를 응원해.
- She is an LG fan. 걘 LG 팬이야.
- He supports the Yankees. 걘 양키스를 응원해.

A: He is always wearing Red Sox apparel. 걘 항상 레드삭스 의상을 입어.
B: He is a huge Red Sox fan. 걘 레드삭스의 열렬한 팬이야.

04 My sister is a cheerleader
내 여동생은 치어리더야

- The cheerleading team is traveling with the football team to support them.
  치어리더들이 응원하기 위해 미식축구팀을 따라 이동하고 있어.
- Cheerleading practice is every night from 6 to 9pm.
  치어리딩 연습은 매일밤 6시부터 9시까지야.
- Cheerleaders have to be good dancers and in great shape.
  치어리더들은 춤도 잘추고 몸매도 좋아야 돼.

A: I heard you are a cheerleader. 너 치어리더라며.
B: I used to be but not anymore. 그랬는데 지금은 아냐.

05 I have some autographs of women volleyball players
여자배구 선수들의 사인을 갖고 있어

- The number of young male fans is increasing every year.
  젊은 남자팬들의 수가 매년 늘어나고 있어.
- I am an autograph hound. 난 사인 수집광이야.
- She got his autograph after the game. 걘 경기후에 그의 사인을 받았어.

A: You look so happy. Did you win the lottery? 기뻐 보이네. 로또에 당첨된거야?
B: No, I got Son Heungmin's autograph a few minutes ago! He was shopping at the same store I was at.
아니. 난 조금전 손흥민의 사인을 받았어! 내가 있던 같은 가게에서 쇼핑을 하고 있었어.

012

What makes him such a great player?

그는 무엇 때문에 위대한 선수가 된거야?

…가 최고다라고 말하려면 be second to none이나 be the best player in the world 같은 표현을 쓰면 된다. 참고로 GOAT는 스포츠에서 '역대 가장 뛰어난' 이라는 약어이다.

01 I like Lionel Messi because he is so skilled
난 기술이 아주 뛰어나기 때문에 리오넬 메시를 좋아해

- I love Messi because of the way he plays the game.
  난 메시의 게임플레이 때문에 좋아해.
- His shooting technique is second to none. 그의 슈팅기술은 독보적이야.
- He is the best footballer in the world. 그는 세계에서 가장 뛰어난 축구선수야.

A: Why do you like Messi so much? 왜 그렇게 메시를 좋아해?
B: Because of the way he plays the game. His passing skills are second to none. 그가 하는 플레이 때문에. 그의 패싱기술은 세계 최고야.

02 Michael Jordan was my favorite player because he was the ultimate competitor
난 따라올 경쟁자가 없었기 때문에 마이클 조던을 가장 좋아했어

- I loved Jordan for the way he constantly improved his game.
  난 끊임없이 경기에서 발전했기 때문에 조던을 좋아했어.
- There will never be another player like Michael Jordan.
  마이클 조던 같은 선수는 절대 없을거야.

A: Why do you like Michael Jordan so much? 넌 왜 그렇게 마이클 조던을 좋아해?
B: He was the ultimate competitor and the ultimate winner.
걘 따라올 경쟁자가 없는 최후의 승자였기 때문이야.

03

Pele is the GOAT (Greatest of all time)
펠레는 역대 최고의 선수야

- Lebron James is arguably the basketball GOAT.
  르브론 제임스는 아마 틀림없이 최고의 농구선수야.

- In your opinion, who is the soccer GOAT? 네 생각에, 누가 역대 최고의 축구선수야?

A: I think Jordan is the GOAT. 난 조던이 역대 최고의 선수인 것 같아.

B: I disagree. I say it's Lebron James. 난 아냐. 난 르브론 제임스인 것 같아.

Who is the greatest tennis player in the world right now? 지금 최고의 테니스 선수는 누구야?

- Nadal is one of the greatest tennis players in the world at the moment.
  나달은 현재 최고의 선수 중 한명이야.

- Federer used to be the greatest but now his game is in decline.
  페더러는 최고였지만 지금 그의 경기력은 쇠락하고 있어.

A: Nadal is one of the greatest players in the world at the moment.
나달은 현재 최고의 선수 중 한명이야.

B: At the moment? He is one of the greatest players ever.
현재라고? 그는 역대 최고 선수 중의 한명이야.

05

His skill and his work ethic make him a great champion 그의 기술과 성실함으로 그는 위대한 챔피언이 된거야

- What makes him such a great player? 그는 무엇 때문에 위대한 선수가 된거야?

- How did she become such an amazing athlete?
  걘 어떻게 그렇게 놀랄만한 선수가 되었어?

- His ability to overcome obstacles makes him a great champion.
  역경을 이겨내는 그의 능력은 그를 최고의 챔피언으로 만들어.

A: What is it about her that makes her such a great player?
그녀의 무엇 때문에 그렇게 위대한 선수가 된거야?

B: Her ability to overcome obstacles. 역경을 이겨내는 능력으로.

Unit 08

013

Who is winning?

누가 이기고 있어?

스포츠 경기 결과를 물어볼 때는 Who's winning?이나 Who won the game? 등을 사용하며, 좀 더 구체적으로 점수까지 말하려면 ~won 3 to 2 등으로 말하면 된다.

01 Who won the game?

누가 이겼어?

- I heard they lost the match. 그들이 게임에서 졌다며.
- We won the game easily. 우리는 쉽게 경기에서 이겼어.
- It was a very tightly fought game. 그건 정말 치열하게 싸운 게임이었어.

A: I heard the game was great and the final score was 3-2.
게임이 대단했고 최종결과는 3:2라고 들었어.

B: That's right. It was a very tightly fought match.
맞아. 그건 정말 치열하게 싸운 게임이었어.

02 What's the score?

점수는?

- Who is winning? 누가 이기고 있어?
- Chelsea is up by 2 goals in the 2nd half. 첼시는 후반전에 2골차로 앞서고 있어.
- They are losing by 1 goal with 4 minutes left.
그들은 4분 남겨진 상황에서 1골차고 지고 있어.

A: What's the score? 점수는?

B: Liverpool is up by 1 with 30 minutes left in the 2nd half.
리버풀이 후반전 30분 남겨놓고 1점차로 앞서고 있어.

03 We're winning by one goal
우리가 한 골차로 이기고 있어

- It's a tie game **at the moment.** 현재 무승부야.
- The game ended in a 1-1 draw. 그 게임은 1:1 무승부로 끝났어.
- They lost the game by **ten points.** 그들은 10점차로 졌어.

A: They lost the game by 10 points. 그들은 10점차로 게임에서 졌어.
B: So, it wasn't a very good game then. 그럼 그렇게 좋은 게임은 아니었겠네.

04 Tottenham Hotspur won three to one
토트넘이 3대 1로 이겼어

- Arsenal lost the match five to four. 아스날이 5대 4로 졌어.
- They won by four points. 그들이 4점차로 이겼어.
- They scored a golden goal to win it. 그들이 연장전에서 결승골을 넣고 경기에 이겼어.

A: Who won? 누가 이겼어?
B: Arsenal scored a golden goal to win it. 아스널이 결승골로 경기에 이겼어.

05 Can you believe San Diego Padres crushed the Yankees by a score of nine to zero
샌디에고 파드레스가 양키스를 9대 0으로 완승했다는 것이 믿기지 않아

- They blew the other team out 10-0. 그들은 10:0으로 상대팀을 크게 물리쳤어.
- We stomped on the other team and won 7 to 1. 우리는 7:1로 상대팀을 짓밟았어.
- Was it a good game or a blow out? 그건 멋진 게임였어 아니면 싱거운 게임였어?

A: Was it a good game or a blow out? 그건 멋진 게임였어 아니면 싱거운 게임였어?
B: We crushed them 6 to 2. 우리는 6:2로 상대팀을 뭉게버렸어.

스포츠결과 말하기 2

014

The Giants won by three
자이언츠가 3점차로 이겼어

이기고 있을 때는 be leading by+숫자, be up by+숫자라 표현한다. 남은 시간이 5분이라면 with 5 minutes to go라고 말하면 된다. 무승부는 draw라고 말한다.

01 The LA Dodgers are leading by two points
다저스가 2점차로 이기고 있어

● **The Blue Jays are winning by one run in the bottom of the 9th with 2 outs.**
블루 제이스가 9회말 투아웃상태에서 한 점차로 이기고 있어.

● **Arsenal is winning 1-0 at the end of the first half.**
아스널이 전반전 끝나가는데 1:0으로 이기고 있어.

● **The hockey team is losing 1-0 at the end of the 2nd period.**
그 하키 팀은 두번째 피어리드 끝나는 시점에 1:0으로 지고 있어.

A: What's the score right now? 지금 점수가 어떻게 돼?
B: The Blue Jays are winning by 2 runs in the top of the 8th.
블루 제이스가 8회초에 2점차로 이기고 있어.

02 The Giants won by three
자이언츠가 3점차로 이겼어

● **We were up by one with 2 minutes to go.** 2분 남았는데 우리가 1점차로 이기고 있었어.

● **They lost by 5 points.** 그들은 5점차로 졌어.

● **How much did your team win by?** 너의 팀은 몇 점차로 이겼어?

A: How much did you win by? 너희는 몇 점차로 이겼어?
B: We didn't win. We lost by 1 point. 졌어. 1점차로 졌어.

03 It's 2-1[two to one] with 10 minutes to go

10분 남겨놓고 2대 1로 이기고 있어

- What's the score and what inning is it in? 점수가 어떻게 돼 그리고 몇 이닝이야?
- What's the score and how much time is left? 점수가 어떻게 돼 그리고 몇 분 남았어?
- It's 1-1 and the game is in extra time. 1:1이어서 연장전을 치르고 있어.

A: What inning is it? 몇 이닝이야?
B: It's the top of the 5th. 5회초야.

04 It ended in a one-one draw

1:1로 끝났어

- We won the game 2-1. 우리는 2:1로 승리했어.
- The game ended in a 4-1 victory for the home team. 경기는 홈팀이 4:1로 승리했어.
- The game ended in a 2-1 loss for the visiting team. 경기는 방문팀이 2:1로 졌어.

A: How did the game end? 경기 결과는 어떻게 됐어?
B: The home team lost 3-0. 홈팀이 3:0으로 졌어.

05 They were ahead at halftime

그들이 전반전에 이기고 있었어

- We were winning with 2 minutes to go. 2분 남겨놓고 우리가 이기고 있었어.
- LG was losing by one run with 2 innings left in the game.
  LG가 경기 2이닝을 남겨두고 1점차로 지고 있었어.
- Man City is up by 2 goals with 10 minutes to go in the game.
  맨시티는 경기가 10분 남았는데 2골차로 이기고 있어.

A: What's the score right now? 지금 점수가 어떻게 돼?
B: The Lakers are up by 10 points with 3 minutes to go in the 4th
   quarter. 레이커스가 4쿼터 3분 남겨놓고 10점차로 이기고 있어.

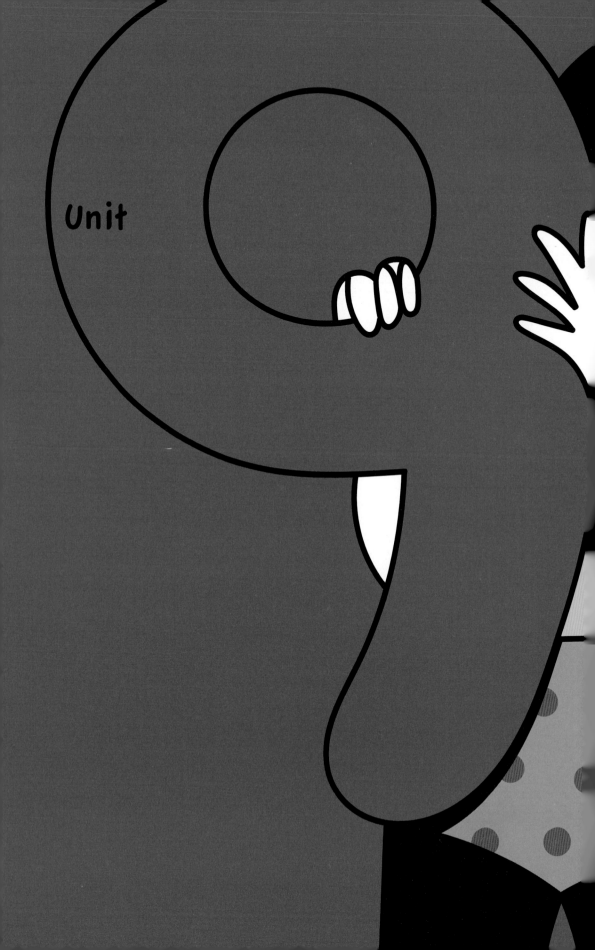

퇴직

001

I'm thinking early retirement

난 조기퇴직할까 생각 중이야

회사를 그만두는 것은 quit, 또는 resign이고 정년을 채워서 그만두는 것을 retire라고 한다. 퇴직 후의 계획은 retirement plan, 조기퇴직은 early retirement라고 하면 된다.

01 I plan to retire next month
난 다음달에 퇴직할 계획이야

- I'm thinking early retirement. 난 조기퇴직할까 생각 중이야.
- We are planning to retire **when we turn 65.** 우리가 65세가 될 때 퇴직할 생각이야.
- Do you have any plans to retire soon? 곧 퇴직할 계획이 있어?

A: I plan to retire in 2 years. 난 2년 후에 퇴직할 계획이야.
B: Sounds great. What will you do? 좋네. 뭐할건데?

02 Do you have any retirement plans?
퇴직계획이 뭐 있어?

- Are you paying into **a pension for retirement?** 퇴직연금에 돈을 넣고 있어?
- Do you have a nest egg for retirement? 넌 퇴직할 밑천이 있어?
- What are your plans for retirement? 퇴직계획이 어떻게 돼?

A: What are your plans for retirement? 퇴직계획이 어떻게 돼?
B: We have a small nest egg and we plan to buy a small place on the coast and live there. 밑천이 좀 있는데 해변가에 조그마한 집을 사서 거기서 살 계획이야.

03 I think the retirement age should be extended
정년나이가 연장되어야 된다고 생각해

● He had to put off retirement because he lost a lot of money in the stock market. 걘 주식하다 많은 돈을 잃어서 퇴직을 연기해야 했어.

● I want to postpone my retirement by one more year.
난 일년 더 퇴직을 연기하고 싶어.

● She will retire early. 걘 조기 퇴직할거야.

A: I want to postpone my retirement a few years to save a bit more money. 난 좀 더 많은 돈을 저축하기 위해 퇴직을 연기하고 싶어.

B: Not me. I want to retire early. 난 아냐. 빨리 퇴직하고 싶어.

04 I still want to work but I have to retire
난 아직 일하고 싶지만 퇴직을 해야 돼

● At our company retirement is mandatory at age 65. 우리 회사 정년은 무조건 65세야.

● They are forcing the workers to retire early. 근로자들을 조기 퇴직시키고 있어.

● I'm not looking forward to retirement. 난 퇴직을 기다리고 있지 않아.

A: Does your company have a mandatory retirement policy?
너희 회사는 강제적인 퇴직정책이 있어?

B: Yes, you have to retire at 65. 어. 65세에 퇴직해야 돼.

05 After retirement, I have nothing to do
퇴직 후에, 난 아무것도 할게 없어

● I'm worried I'll be bored when I retire. 난 퇴직하면 심심할 것 같아 걱정야.

● I am going to miss work when I'm retired. 내가 퇴직하면 일하는게 그리워질거야.

● My wife is worried I'm going to drive her crazy after I retire.
내가 퇴직하면 아내를 달달 볶을까봐 걱정하고 있어.

A: Are you looking forward to retirement? 퇴직을 기다리고 있어?

B: No, I'm worried that I'll be bored out of my mind.
아니, 무척 심심할까봐 걱정돼.

Unit 09

002

I have got to try to read my wife's mind

난 아내의 맘을 읽도록 해야 해

퇴직 후 가장 많이 변화는 건 집안의 풍속도. 집안에 죽치고(be stuck at home) 삼식이가 되어 밥달라고(Get me a meal)하면 삶이 고달파질 수 있다. start some new hobbies를 갖는게 신상에 좋을 듯하다.

01 I can't stay home all day long after retirement

난 퇴직 후에 하루종일 집에 있을 수가 없어

- I'm not really a homebody and will want to get out of the house when I'm retired. 난 방돌이가 아니어서 퇴직한 후에는 집밖으로 나가고 싶어할거야.

- I plan on starting some new hobbies so I'm not stuck at home during my retirement. 난 새로운 취미생활을 시작할 계획이어서 퇴직한 동안에 집에 쳐박혀 있지 않아.

- My wife wants me to find something to do outside the house after I retire. 내 아내는 내가 퇴직 후 집밖에서 뭔가 할 일을 찾기를 바래.

A: You don't look happy about your upcoming retirement. 다가오는 퇴직으로 행복해 보이지가 않아.

B: I'm not a homebody so I guess I'll need to find some new hobbies so I'm not stuck at home. 난 방돌이가 아니어서 난 새로운 취미를 찾아 집에 있지 않을 것 같아.

02 I have got to try to read my wife's mind

난 아내의 맘을 읽도록 해야 해

- I have a hard time knowing what my wife is thinking sometimes. 때로는 아내가 뭐를 생각하는지 알기 힘들어.

- My wife and I think alike. 아내와 나는 생각이 같아.

- My husband and I know each other so well we can finish each other's sentences. 남편과 난 서로 잘 알아서 이심전심이 돼.

A: Retirement will be easy because I love spending time with my wife. 난 아내와 시간보내는 것을 좋아하기 때문에 퇴직은 어렵지 않을거야.

B: Yes, you really read each other's minds well. 그래, 너희는 정말 죽이 잘 맞는구나.

Especially, it's hard to say "Get me a meal"
특히, "밥 좀 줘"라는 말을 하기가 어려워

- I am going to have to learn how to cook and clean a bit after retirement.
  난 퇴직 후에 요리 및 청소하는 법을 좀 배워야 할거야.

- My wife expects me to help out around the house after I retire.
  아내는 내가 퇴직하면 집안일 하는거 도와줄 것을 기대하고 있어.

A: My wife says I'm going to have to help with the housework after I retire. 아내는 내가 퇴직한 다음에는 집안일 하는 것을 도와야 한다고 말해.
B: That's only fair. 공평하네.

04

We will survive on the national pension
우리는 국민연금으로 살아갈거야

- We will have the national pension plus my private pension to live on.
  우리는 국민연금과 개인연금으로 살아가야 될거야.

- He has a great pension which he can live off of comfortably.
  걘 편하게 생계유지를 할 수 있는 멋진 연금이 있어.

A: What will you live on after you retire? 퇴직 후에 뭘로 살아갈거야?
B: I have a nice pension plus a good nest egg. I'll be comfortable.
  밑천 뿐만 아니라 멋진 연금도 있지. 난 편안히 살거야.

05

I try to get out of the house as much as possible
난 가능한한 집밖으로 나오려고 하고 있어

- I plan on doing a lot of traveling and golfing. 여행과 골프를 많이 칠려고.

- My wife wants us to take up gardening. 아내는 우리가 정원을 가꾸기를 원해.

- We plan on spending our winters in Thailand.
  우리는 겨울을 태국에서 보내려고 하고 있어.

A: I heard you bought a small apartment in Thailand.
  태국에다 소형아파트를 구입했다며.

B: Yes, we plan on spending our winters there after we retire.
  어, 퇴직 후에 거기서 겨울을 보낼 생각이야.

Unit 09

건강

I should do something for my health

건강을 위해서 뭔가 해야겠어

퇴직 후에는 충격이 있겠지만 건강을 위해서 뭔가 하는게 바람직하다. 돈안들고 가장 좋은 운동인 하루에 30분간 걷기(walk for 30 minutes a day)를 하는게 어떨까…. 요양원(senior center)에 일찍 들어가지 않으려면 말이다.

01 It seems like my health is wearing down after retirement 퇴직 후에 건강이 나빠지는 것 같아

- **She started having health issues** soon after she retired.
  걘 퇴직 후에 곧 건강문제가 생기기 시작했어.

- **My health has been failing** since I retired. 내 건강은 퇴직이래로 나빠지고 있어.

- **I have been developing health problems** since my retirement.
  퇴직한 후에 내 건강문제가 생겼어.

A: He's in the hospital again? 걘 또 병원신세야?
B: He is. His health has really been failing since he retired.
  그래. 걔 건강이 퇴직 후에 정말 나빠지고 있어.

02 I should do something for my health
건강을 위해서 뭔가 해야겠어

- **I need to start** looking after my health. 내 건강을 보살피기 시작해야 돼.

- **She needs to take** better care of herself. 걘 자기 건강을 더 잘 살펴야 돼.

- **I must start** exercising and eating a bit better.
  난 좀 더 운동을 하고 좀 더 잘 먹기 시작해야 돼.

A: You don't look so well. 넌 썩 좋아보이지 않아.
B: I need to start taking better care of myself. 난 내 건강을 더 잘 살피기 시작해야 돼.

03 I made it a rule to take 10,000 steps a day
하루에 만보걷기를 하려고 해

- I do 50 push ups, 50 sit ups and walk for 30 minutes **a day.**
  난 하루에 푸시업 50개, 싯업 50개 그리고 30분간 걷기를 하고 있어.

- I only eat sweets **once a week.** 난 단 것은 일주일에 한번만 먹어.

- **My wife** is watching what she eats **very carefully.**
  아내는 자신이 먹는 것을 주의깊게 조심하고 있어.

A: What are you doing to take care of yourself better?
자신을 더 잘 살피기 위해 뭐를 하고 있어?

B: I am watching what I eat very carefully. 먹는 것을 아주 주의깊게 조심하고 있어.

04 I sometimes stop by friends and have a game of billiards
때로는 친구들에게 들러서 당구한판 해

- He enjoys playing board games with **his friends regularly.**
  걘 정기적으로 친구들과 보드게임하는 것을 즐겨해.

- **They meet to** play par 3 golf **twice a week.** 그들은 일주일에 두 번 만나서 파쓰리 골프를 해.

A: You need to try and do some fun activities every week.
넌 매주 좀 재미있는 것을 하려고 해봐야 돼.

B: I do. I meet my friends and play board games a few times a week.
그러고 있어. 친구들 만나서 일주일에 몇 번 보드게임을 해.

05 I'm trying my best not to move into a senior center
난 요양원에 들어가지 않으려고 최선을 다하고 있어

- I don't want **to end up in a senior center.** 난 결국 요양원에 들어가는 것을 원치 않아.

- Living in a nursing home **is my worst nightmare.** 요양원 삶은 내 최악의 악몽이야.

- Some retirement homes **are quite nice.** 일부 실버타운은 아주 멋져.

A: I would prefer not to end up in a senior center. 요양원에 들어가게 되지 않기를 원해.

B: Why not? Some of them are quite nice.
왜 안들어가려고? 일부 요양원은 아주 근사한데.

004

Some old couples get divorced to be free

일부 노부부들은 이혼해서 해방되지

퇴직 후 노부부들은 따분해지고(get dull), 서로 부딪힘이 잦아 "Jolhon(a kind of open marriage)"을 하거나 아니면 이혼을 해서(get divorced) 자유를 찾으려고 한다.

01 Most couples get dull after their children move out and get married
대부분의 부부는 아이들이 집에서 나가 결혼하게 되면 따분해지게 돼

- Adjusting to life without children in the home is tough for a lot of couples.
  집에서 아이들없이 사는 삶에 적응하는 것은 많은 부부들에게 힘들어.

- Some couples can't wait for their kids to leave home.
  일부 부부들은 아이들이 어서 빨리 집을 나가 독립하기를 바래.

- My children can't leave home soon enough. 내 아이들은 집에서 나갈 생각이 없어.

A: Adjusting to life without their children at home can be tough for some couples. 집에서 아이들없이 사는 삶에 적응하는 것은 일부 부부들에게는 어려워.

B: It won't be tough for me. My kids can't move out soon enough.
내게는 어렵지 않을거야. 내 아이들은 집에서 나갈 생각이 없거든.

02 The old couples try not to get divorced
그 노부부는 이혼하지 않으려고 노력해

- Divorce is very tough on older couples. 이혼은 노부부들에게는 아주 힘든 일이야.

- My parents got divorced when they were in their 60s and it was very hard on my father. 부모님은 60대에 이혼을 하셨고 아버지에게는 아주 힘든 일이었어.

- If possible, it's better for older couples to stay together and not get divorced. 가능하다면, 노부부들은 이혼하지 않고 함께 사는게 더 좋아.

A: Divorce rates for older couples are going up these days.
요즘 노부부들의 이혼율이 올라가고 있어.

B: It's very tough on older couples to get divorced.
노부부가 이혼하게 되면 되게 힘들어져.

03
We call it "Jolhon", it means a kind of open marriage 우리는 졸혼이라고 하는데 일종의 개방결혼의 한 종류야

- Retirement is a challenging stage of marriage for many couples.
  퇴직은 많은 부부들에게는 아주 힘든 결혼의 단계야.

- Older couples often find retirement a big adjustment.
  노부부들은 종종 퇴직에는 커다란 적응이 필요하다고 생각해.

- My parents had a rough time getting used to living together after my father retired. 부모님은 아버지가 퇴직한 후에 함께 사는데 힘든 시간을 보냈어.

A: Retirement is a challenge for older couples. 퇴직은 노부부에게는 힘든 일이야.

B: My parents had a rough time getting used to each other, especially my mom. 부모님은, 특히 엄마는 서로에게 적응하는데 힘든 시간을 보냈어.

04
Some old couples get divorced to be free
일부 노부부들은 이혼해서 해방되지

- Some older couples realize they have nothing in common after retirement so they get divorced. 일부 노부부들은 퇴직 후에 공통점이 없다는 것을 깨닫고 이혼을 해.

- Divorce is liberating for some older couples.
  이혼은 일부 노부부들에게는 해방이 되는거야.

- Divorce works out for the best for some older couples.
  일부 노부부들에게는 이혼이 최선이 되기도 해.

A: Did you hear that his grandparents got divorced? 걔 조부모님이 이혼하셨다며?

B: That's OK. Sometimes divorce is liberating for older couples.
  괜찮아. 때론 노부부들에게 이혼은 해방이야.

My parents moved to the coast after my father retired

부모님은 아버지가 퇴직하시자 해안가로 이사가셨어

퇴직하면 굳이 서울에 살 필요가 없어지고 그래서 시골 등으로 낙향하는(go back to live in the countryside) 경우가 많다. 낙향은 go down into the country라고 해도 된다.

 One of my friends went back to live in the countryside where she grew up
내 친구들 중 한 명은 자신이 자란 시골로 낙향했어

- My mother moved into a smaller place after we all left home and my father passed away. 엄마는 우리가 모두 출가하고 아버지가 돌아가시자 조그만 집으로 이사가셨어.

- My parents moved to the coast after my father retired.
부모님은 아버지가 퇴직하시자 해안가로 이사가셨어.

- Living in a smaller place is more comfortable for older retired people.
나이든 퇴직한 사람들에게는 조그만 집에서 사는게 더 편안해.

A: Why did they move to the countryside? 걔들은 왜 시골로 이사간거야?
B: They were both retired and wanted a change of lifestyles.
둘 다 퇴직했고 생활방식의 변화를 원했거든.

 It's a good option to go down into the country
시골로 낙향하는 것도 좋은 선택이야

- I want to retire to the country. 난 시골로 낙향하고 싶어.

- I plan on moving to the countryside. 난 시골로 이사할 계획이야.

- They moved to a small mountain town after they retired.
그들은 퇴직 후에 조그만 산골마을로 이사갔어.

A: They have many options after they retire. 그들은 퇴직 후에 많은 선택권이 있어.
B: I heard they are moving to the countryside. 걔네들 낙향한다고 들었어.

Some old couples start a new life together overseas 일부 노부부들은 해외에서 함께 새로운 삶을 시작해

● **My parents** moved to the Philippines after they retired.
부모님은 퇴직 후에 필리핀으로 이주하셨어.

● **There** are many nice places people can retire to overseas.
해외로 이주할 멋진 곳은 아주 많아.

A: Where would you like to retire to? 어디로 이주하고 싶어?
B: Somewhere warm and tropical. Maybe Thailand? 열대지역으로. 어쩌면 태국?

Some want to emigrate but it's not easy for old people 어떤 사람들은 이민을 원하지만 노부부들에게 그건 쉽지 않아

● Moving overseas **when you are older isn't always easy.**
늙어서 해외로 이민가는 것은 항상 쉽지 않아.

● Retiring abroad **can be a challenge for older people.**
퇴직 후 이민가는 건 노인들에게는 어려운 일이야.

A: Immigrating can be hard for older people. 노인들에게 이민은 어려울 수 있어.
B: True. My parents retired to Hawaii but had some problems adjusting
to life there. 맞아. 부모님은 퇴직 후 하와이로 가셨는데 거기 삶에 적응하는데 어려움이 좀 있었어.

But I don't know anything about how to live in the countryside 하지만 난 전원생활에 대해서 아는게 하나도 없어

● They moved to the countryside but really **struggled** getting used to the life
there. 걔들은 낙향했지만 그곳의 삶에 적응하는데 힘겨웠어.

● Moving from a big city to the countryside **is a major adjustment for older
people.** 노인들에게 대도시에서 전원지역으로 이주하는 것은 엄청난 적응이 필요해.

A: I don't know anything about how to live in the countryside.
전원생활에 대해서 아는게 하나도 없어.

B: Changing your lifestyle is difficult when you are older.
나이 들어서 생활방식을 바꾸는 것은 어려운 일이야.

006

I need to pass my real estate license certification test

난 공인중개사 시험을 통과해야 돼

퇴직 후에 무의도식하지 않고 뭔가 자격증을 따서 일을 하려는 것은 바람직하다. 자격 증을 따다는 get certified. 사회복지사가 되다는 become social workers라고 하면 된다.

01 My wife's friend got certified and is still working
내 아내의 친구는 자격증을 따서 아직도 일하고 있어

- **She is a certified teacher.** 걔는 자격증이 있는 교사야.
- **I got my massage therapist certification** this year.
  난 금년에 마사지 치료사 자격증을 땄어.
- **I need to pass my real estate license certification test.**
  난 공인중개사 시험을 통과해야 돼.

A: Is she a good teacher? 걔 좋은 선생이야?
B: I don't know but I know she is certified. 잘 모르겠지만 자격증은 있어.

---

02 Many people try to become social workers
많은 사람들이 사회복지사가 되려고 해

- Social work **is hard but very rewarding.** 사회복지는 어렵지만 매우 보람있는 일이야.
- Social workers **are very important for our society.**
  사회복지사들은 우리 사회에 매우 중요한 사람들이야.
- I have wanted to **become a social worker** ever since high school.
  난 고등학교 이후로 사회복지사가 되려고 했어.

A: Social work is hard but rewarding. 사회복지는 어렵지만 보람있는 일이야.
B: I know. That's why I've wanted to become a social worker since high school. 알아. 그래서 난 고등학교 이후로 사회복지사가 되려고 했어.

03 In this aging society, becoming a social worker is a good option 고령화 사회에서 사회복지사가 되는 것은 좋은 선택이야

- Our society needs more social workers these days.
  우리 사회에는 요즘 더 많은 사회복지사가 필요해.

- Social work doesn't pay well but it is a very important job.
  사회복지는 급여가 많지는 않지만 매우 중요한 일이야.

- That social worker is a very nice person. 저 사회복지사는 매우 착한 사람이야.

A: Society has so many problems. 사회에는 많은 문제들이 있어.
B: That's why we need more social workers. 그래서 우리는 사회복지사들이 필요해.

04 But the pay is very low compared to the one they got before 하지만 그들이 전직장에서 받은거에 비하면 급여가 매우 낮아

- Social workers get very low salaries. 사회복지사들은 급여가 매우 낮아.

- Social work can be a high stress job. 사회복지는 스트레스가 많은 직업일 수 있어.

- Governments don't provide many good benefits for social workers.
  정부들은 사회복지사에게 많은 복지혜택을 주지 않아.

A: Do social workers make good money? 사회복지사가 돈은 많이 버니?
B: No, they get very low salaries. 아니. 급여는 매우 낮아.

007 장사

She is getting into a franchise business

갠 가맹사업에 뛰어들고 있어

퇴직 후에 모아놓은 돈으로 장사를 시작해도 좋은 옵션이다. 커피가맹점을 샀다는 buy into a coffee franchise라고 하고, 편의점을 열다는 open a convenience store라고 말하면 된다.

01 He has run a store for 10 years
갠 10년간 가게를 운영해

- He has had his own business for 30 years. 갠 30년간 자기사업을 해왔어.
- She runs a grocery store. 갠 식료품가게를 운영해.
- She isn't the manager, she's the owner. 갠 매니저가 아냐, 주인이야.

A: Is she the manager? 저 여자가 매니저예요?
B: No, she's the owner and she runs the entire business.
아뇨, 주인이세요. 전체 비즈니스를 운영하고 있어요.

02 She is getting into a franchise business
갠 가맹사업에 뛰어들고 있어

- She bought into a coffee franchise. 갠 커피 가맹점을 하나 샀어.
- He wanted a franchise so he could automatically get customers.
  갠 자동적으로 고객을 확보할 수 있게끔 가맹점을 원했어.
- Buying into a franchise has pros and cons. 가맹점 사업을 하는 것은 장단점이 있어.

A: She is getting into a franchise business. 갠 가맹사업에 뛰어들고 있어.
B: Which one? There are many pros and cons to owning a franchise.
어떤 가맹? 가맹점을 하는데에는 많은 장단점이 있는데.

03 The convenience store is one of the easiest businesses to start 편의점은 시작하기에 가장 쉬운 업종 중의 하나야

- A convenience store can be a good business depending on the location.
  편의점은 위치에 따라 좋은 비즈니스가 될 수 있어.

- She thought it would be easiest to start a convenience store business.
  걘 편의점 장사를 시작하는게 가장 쉬울거라고 생각했어.

A: How did she decide to open a convenience store?
걘 어떻게 편의점을 열기로 한거야?

B: She thought it would be an easy business to run.
운영하기에 쉬운 장사일거라고 생각했어.

04 But the convenience store is not profitable
하지만 편의점은 이익이 나지 않아

- It's hard to make big money running a convenience store.
  편의점을 운영하면서 많은 돈을 벌기는 어려워.

- I thought a convenience store business would make a lot more money than it does. 난 편의점이 현실보다 더 많은 돈을 벌거라 생각했어.

A: Why are you so stressed out? 왜 그렇게 스트레스를 받은거야?
B: The profit margins of my convenience store are much smaller than I thought they would be. 내가 예상했던 것보다 편의점의 수익이 훨씬 적어.

05 Maybe it's best to not do business if you don't want to lose money 돈을 잃고 싶지 않으면 장사를 하지 않는게 최선이야

- You need a good head for business if you want to be successful.
  성공하고 싶으면 장사에 대해 바싹하게 알고 있어야 돼.

- He didn't have a good head for business so he lost a lot of money.
  걘 장사에 대해 잘 몰랐다가 많은 돈을 날렸어.

A: You need a good head for business to be successful.
성공하고 싶으면 사업에 대해 바싹하게 알고 있어야 돼.

B: That's why I'll never own my own business. 그래서 난 내 사업을 하지 않을거야.

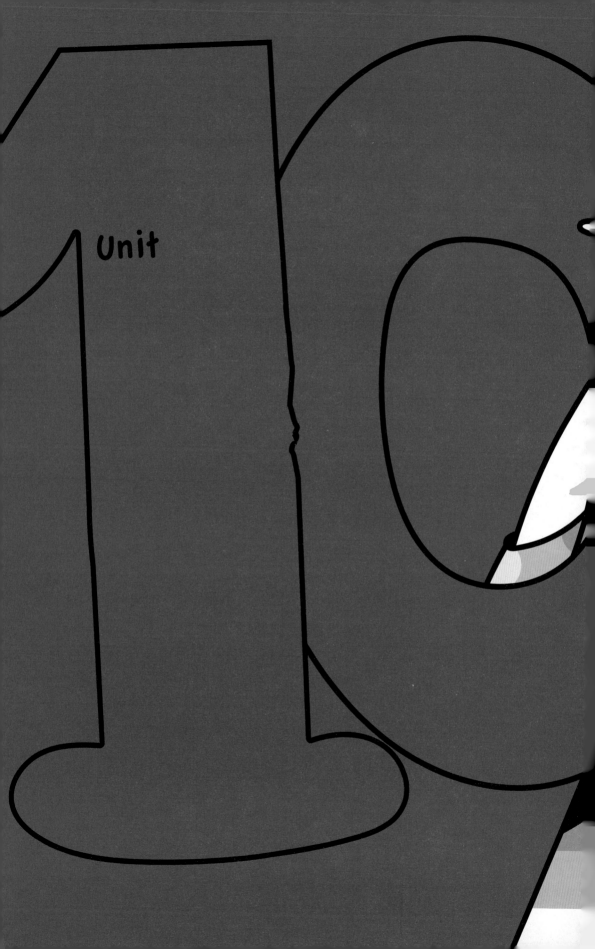

Unit

일상영어 표현사전 3300

Korea

001

You can come with me to hear my fortune
내가 점보러 갈 때 같이 가

현재와 미래가 불안할 때는 꼭 신년이 아니어도 종종 점을 보게 된다. 점을 보다는 go to a fortune teller to see what is in store for you라고 말하고 점괘를 듣는 것은 hear my fortune이나 get my fortune read라고 한다.

01 I wanted to take you to a traditional place
전통이 있는 곳으로 데려가고 싶었어

- I thought you might be interested in learning about some of our traditions and customs. 네가 우리의 전통과 관습을 아는데 관심이 있을거라 생각했어.

- It is customary at the beginning of the New Year to go to a fortune teller to see what is in store for you.
  신년이 되면 사람들이 자신의 앞에 놓인 운명을 알아보려고 점쟁이를 찾는 풍습이 있어.

A: What do you have planned for us today? 오늘 우리를 위해 뭐 준비했어?
B: I wanted to give you a tour of a traditional place. I think you'll find it interesting. 전통이 있는 곳으로 데려가고 싶었는데 흥미를 느낄거라 생각해.

02 They call this place Mi-a-rie
여기는 미아리라는 곳이야

- This area is known for its fortune tellers and palm-readers.
  이 지역은 점쟁이와 손금보는 사람들로 유명한 곳이야.

- From what I remember, it is kind of like a fortune telling district.
  내가 기억하기로는 점보는 지역인 것 같아.

A: What are all of these stalls for? What are people doing here?
이 간판들을 다 뭐야? 사람들이 여기서 뭐하는거야?

B: They are fortune tellers and palm-readers. This area is known as a fortune telling district.
그들은 점쟁이와 손금보는 사람들이야. 이 지역은 점보는 지역으로 알려졌어.

I thought it might be interesting for you to experience some Korean traditions firsthand
네가 한국의 전통들을 직접 체험하는게 흥미있을거라 생각했어

- I figured you may be interested to experience some Korean traditions.
  난 네가 한국전통들에 관심있을지 모른다고 생각했어.

- I heard you are curious about Korean customs and traditions.
  너 한국관습과 전통에 궁금하다며.

A: This palace looks fantastic! Thanks for bringing me here.
이곳은 멋지다! 이곳에 데려와줘서 고마워.

B: Yes, I thought you might like to experience some Korean history and culture firsthand. 어, 난 네가 먼저 한국역사와 문화를 경험하고 싶어할거라고 생각했어.

04

You can come with me to hear my fortune
내가 점보러 갈 때 같이 가

- Would you like to come with me when I go to a fortune teller?
  내가 점보러 갈 때 같이 갈테야?

- Why don't you come with me to get my fortune read?
  나 점볼 때 나와 함께 가는게 어때?

A: Have you ever been to a fortune teller? How about coming with me and getting your fortune read? 점보러 가본 적이 있어? 나와 함께 가서 점을 보는게 어때?
B: I haven't but that sounds fun. Let's go! 난 본 적이 없지만 재미있을 것 같아. 가자!

Have you been coming to this place often?
이 곳에 자주 가?

- These days, we can call a fortune teller and hear my fortune on the phone. 요즘 점쟁이에게 전화해서 전화로 점을 볼 수도 있어.

- Many people can get fortunes read on the Internet these days.
  많은 사람들이 요즘 인터넷으로 점을 볼 수도 있어.

A: How often do you see fortune tellers? 얼마나 자주 점보러 가?
B: I get my fortune read once or twice a year. 일년에 한두 번 점을 봐.

Unit 10

002 신년

The eldest son hosts the party on New Year's Day

설날에는 장남의 집에 가족이 다 모여

요즘은 많이 퇴색했지만 아직 우리의 전통이니 말해보는 연습을 해본다. 음력설은 the Lunar New Year이라고 하고 아직 장남이 모임을 갖지만(host the New Year's dinner) 여행가는(take trips) 사람들이 점점 늘어나고 있는게 현실이다.

01 Am I dressed appropriately for the occasion?
내가 오늘에 맞는 옷차림을 하고 있는거야?

- **Do you think** what I'm wearing is suitable? 내가 입은 옷이 적절하다고 생각해?
- Are these clothes OK for **tonight?** 이 옷들이 오늘밤에 괜찮은거야?
- Is this shirt too casual for **the banquet?** 연회를 하는데 이 셔츠가 너무 캐주얼해?

A: Is this dress suitable for the event? 이 옷이 오늘 행사에 적절해?
B: Yes, it looks lovely. 어, 멋지게 보여.

02 She's busy making the meal for us
걘 우리 저녁 준비하느라 매우 바빠

- **She'll be hard at work** making dinner for us. 걘 우리 저녁을 만들면서 열심히 준비할거야.
- She's going to be very busy preparing dinner for all of us.
  걘 우리 모두의 저녁을 준비하느라 매우 바쁠거야.
- She's in the kitchen right now preparing our dinner.
  걘 우리 저녁을 준비하느라 지금 부엌에 있어.

A: Where is she? 걔는 어디 있어?
B: She's busy making dinner for us. 우리 저녁 준비하느라 바빠.

03 Recently even her husband has been joining her to help prepare dinner 최근에는 남편도 아내를 도와 저녁준비를 해

- This is the Lunar New Year, but we have another one on January 1.
  이건 음력 설이고 1월 1일에도 양력설을 보내.

- Korea has two big holidays every year and one of them is the Lunar New Year. 한국에는 매년 두개의 명절이 있는데 그중 하나는 음력설이야.

A: Is the Lunar New Year a big holiday in Korea? 음력설이 한국에서 명절이야?

B: Yes, Korea has two big holidays every year and one of them is the Lunar New Year. 어, 한국에는 두번의 명절이 매년 있는데 그중 하나가 음력설이야.

04 The eldest son hosts the party on New Year's Day
설날에는 장남의 집에 가족이 다 모여

- In our country, it is customary for the eldest male child to host the New Year's dinner. 우리나라에서, 장남이 설날 저녁을 준비하는게 전통이야.

- The oldest brother always has the rest of the family over for dinner.
  장남은 항상 나머지 가족을 저녁에 초대 해.

A: Why do you always go to his place for New Year's Day?
왜 넌 설날에 그의 집에 가는거야?

B: Because in our country the eldest brother always hosts the dinner on New Year's. 우리나라에서는 장남이 설날저녁을 준비하기 때문이야.

05 A typical Korean food eaten at this time of year is dduck-guk 이건 떡국으로 설날에 먹는 한국의 전통음식이야

- It's called dduck-guk and it is a traditional food that we eat on New Year's Day. 이건 떡국이라고 하는데 우리가 설날에 먹는 전통음식이야.

- Dduck-guk is a traditional New Year's food. 떡국은 전통적인 설날 음식이야.

A: What are some traditional New Year's foods? 전통적인 설 음식으로 뭐가 있어?

B: We always eat dduck-guk on New Year's day. 우리는 설날에는 항상 떡국을 먹어.

Unit 10

003 돌

The first birthday is extra special. It is called "Dol"

첫번째 생일은 '돌'이라고 부르는데 아주 특별해

아이가 태어나고 첫번째 생일이 오면 돌이라고 하고 큰 행사를 한다. 보통 초대된 손님들은 a gold ring을 선물하고, 아이는 잔치상에 놓인 실, 돈, 연필 중에서 하나를 선택하게 된다.

01 The first birthday is extra special. It is called "Dol"
첫번째 생일은 '돌'이라고 부르는데 아주 특별해

- **This is a very important celebration for Korean families.**
  이는 한국에서는 가족들에게 아주 중요한 축하행사야.

- **There are a lot of people that will be there, mostly family, and close friends.** 굉장히 많은 사람들이 모이는데 대부분 가족과 가까운 친구들이야.

A: Why was I invited to their child's first birthday?
왜 내가 걔네들 아이의 첫 생일에 초대된거야?

B: The first birthday is an important milestone for Koreans. The entire family and many friends will be there.
첫 생일은 한국문화에서 중요한 일이야. 가족 전체와 많은 친구들이 참석해.

02 Each guest that arrives presents a gold ring to the parents of the child
잔치에 온 손님들은 모두 아이의 부모에게 금반지를 선물해

- **Everyone gives a gift of a gold ring to the parents.**
  모든 사람들은 부모에게 금반지를 선물해.

- **A gold ring is given to the parents by all the guests.**
  손님들 모두는 부모에게 금반지를 선물해.

- **The customary gift which is given to the parents is a gold ring.**
  부모에게 주는 전통적인 선물은 금반지야.

A: This is the first time I've been invited to a first birthday. What gift should I bring? 첫 생일에 초대된게 처음이야. 어떤 선물을 가져 가야 돼?

B: A gold ring is the customary gift and you give it to the parents.
금반지가 전통적으로 하는 선물이고 부모에게 줘.

03 There has been a strong preference for a male child in Korea 한국에는 남아선호 사상이 있어

● But these days, such trends have been changing. 하지만 그런 경향은 변화하고 있어.

● I mean daughters are preferred to sons. 내 말은 딸들이 아들보다 더 선호되고 있다는거야.

A: Why do Koreans seem to prefer having sons?
왜 한국인들은 아들낳기를 더 원하는 것 같아?

B: Because traditionally, the eldest son takes care of his parents when they are older. 전통적으로, 장남이 부모가 나이가 들었을 때 부모를 돌보기 때문이야.

04 A wife is putting out some thread, money, and a pencil on the table 아내는 탁자 위에 실, 돈, 그리고 연필을 올려놓고 있어

● The baby is going to choose from one of the three things.
아이는 3개 중에서 하나를 선택하게 될거야.

● The pen symbolizes the child will be a scholar, the thread a long life and the money financial success. 연필은 아이가 학자, 실은 긴 수명을, 그리고 돈은 경제적인 성공을 상징해.

A: Why is the mother putting those things in front of the child?
왜 엄마는 아이 앞에 그런 것들을 올려놓는거야?

B: The child will pick from one of the three things and Koreans believe the object they pick will determine their future.
아이는 3가지 중에서 하나를 고를 것이고 한국인들은 아이가 고르는 것이 아이의 미래를 결정한다고 믿고 있어.

05 If the baby picks the thread, he will live a long life
아이가 실을 고르면 아이는 장수할거야

● If he picks the pencil, he will be a scholar. 아이가 연필을 고르면 걘 학자가 될거야.

● If he goes for the money, he will be rich. 돈을 고르면, 걘 부자가 될거야.

● If he takes the thread, he will be healthy and live a long life.
실을 고르면, 건강하고 장수하게 될거야.

A: She picked the money. What does that mean? 걘 돈을 집었어. 그게 무슨 의미야?
B: It means she will be rich when she is older. 나이들어 부자가 될거라는 것을 의미해.

Unit 10

인사동

004 It is the place to buy traditional Korean antiques

이곳은 한국의 전통 골동품을 살 수 있는 곳이야

한국의 골동품을 파는 곳으로 유명한 인사동은 한국적인 선물을 찾을 때(look for a unique gift) 아주 적합한 곳이다. 인사동은 그밖에 paintings나 calligraphy 등으로도 유명한 곳이다.

01 It is the place to buy traditional Korean antiques
이곳은 한국의 전통 골동품을 살 수 있는 곳이야

- It is a popular spot to buy authentic Korean antiques.
  이곳은 한국의 진품 골동품을 살 수 있는 인기있는 곳이야.

- It is known for its traditional Korean antiques.
  이곳은 한국의 전통적인 골동품으로 유명해.

- It has many traditional restaurants and tea shops too.
  이곳에는 전통적인 한식당과 찻집 역시 많아.

A: I need to buy some traditional souvenirs. 난 전통적인 기념품을 좀 사야 돼.
B: Go to Insadong. It's a popular spot for traditional Korean antiques and art work. 인사동으로 가. 그곳은 한국의 전통적인 골동품과 미술품으로 유명한 곳이야.

02 If you're looking for a unique gift, this is the place
특별한 선물을 찾고 있다면 이곳이 가장 적당한 장소일거야

- If you are looking for a special gift for someone back home, this would be the best place to get it.
  고국에 있는 누군가에게 줄 특별한 선물을 찾는다면 이곳이 최고의 장소일거야.

- If you want something uniquely Korean, Insadong is the place to go.
  뭔가 독특한 한국 것을 원한다면 인사동으로 가야 돼.

A: I need to find some good gifts to bring home.
   고국으로 가져갈 뭐 좀 좋은 선물을 찾아야 돼.

B: Insadong is the place to go if you want some good Korean gifts.
   멋진 한국선물을 원한다면 인사동으로 가야 돼.

This place has many specialties such as paintings and calligraphy 이곳에는 서예나 그림과 같은 다른 볼만한 것들도 있어

- There are other things that you might look at, such as some calligraphy or paintings. 서예나 미술같은 네가 눈길을 줄 다른 것들도 있어.

- Korean ceramics are very beautiful and you can get some good deals there. 한국 도예는 매우 아름답고 거기서 저렴하게 살 수 있을거야.

A: What kind of things do they sell there? 거기서 무슨 종류의 것들을 파는거야?

B: It's well known for its variety of art, calligraphy and ceramics. 그곳은 서예나 도예 같은 다양한 미술품들로 유명한 곳이야.

If you're interested, we can take you there sometime 너 관심있으면 언제 한번 그곳으로 데려가줄게

- If you are interested in going there, I'd love to show you around. 거기 가는데 관심있으면 기꺼이 구경시켜줄게.

- If you have free time this weekend, I'll give you a tour. 이번 주말에 시간이 되면, 내가 구경시켜줄게.

A: Insadong sounds very interesting. 인사동은 매우 흥미로운 곳인 것 같아.

B: If you want to take a look, I'll give you a tour of it. 둘러보고 싶으면 구경시켜줄게.

If you like this place, you're going to love Minsokchon 이곳이 맘에 들면, 넌 민속촌을 좋아할거야

- If you want to learn about traditional Korean culture, the folk village is one of the best places to visit. 한국전통문화에 대해 알고 싶으면, 민속촌은 방문할 최고의 장소 중 하나야.

- The folk village shows how Koreans used to live in the old days. 민속촌은 한국인들이 옛날에 어떻게 살았는지를 보여줘.

A: Is there any place I can go to learn about traditional customs? 전통적인 관습에 대해 배우려면 내가 갈 수 있는 곳이 있어?

B: The folk village is the best place to learn about that. It's just south of Seoul. 민속촌이 그걸 배우기에 최선의 장소야. 서울 남쪽에 있어.

Unit 10

005

Have you been to a Korean restaurant before?

전에 한국 식당에서 식사해본 적 있어?

한국식당에서 한식을 먹어봤냐고 대화를 나누는 것이다. 맛이 최고라고 말하려면 have the best food in Seoul. the food is amazing 등으로 표현한다. 특히 …음식을 한번 맛보라고 할 때는 try+음식이라고 한다는 점 기억해둔다.

01 Have you been to a Korean restaurant before?

전에 한국 식당에서 식사해본 적 있어?

- **Have you had any opportunity to eat at a Korean restaurant?**
  한국 식당에서 식사할 기회가 있었어?

- **Have you eaten at a Korean restaurant yet?** 한국 식당에서 식사를 해본 적이 있어?

- **Have you tried going to Korean restaurant?** 한국 식당에 가보려고 한 적이 있어?

A: Have you had a chance to eat at a Korean restaurant?
한국 식당에서 식사할 기회가 있었어?

B: Yes, I ate at one last night. It was fantastic.
어, 지난밤에 한 식당에서 먹었는데 환상적이었어.

02 I wanted to take you to one of my favorite restaurants 내가 좋아하는 식당에 같이 가고 싶었어

- **It's a Korean restaurant that I have been going to for years.**
  그곳은 내가 오랫동안 다니던 한국 식당야.

- **We can walk to it, because we are very close to it right now.**
  지금 그곳 가까이에 있기 때문에 거기까지 걸어갈 수 있어.

- **I'm a regular customer there and the service is great.**
  난 거기 단골고객이고 서비스가 아주 좋아.

A: Can you take me to a Korean restaurant tonight?
오늘 저녁 나를 한국 식당에 데려가줄 수 있어?

B: Sure! It's a restaurant I've been going to for years and the food and service are great. 물론! 내가 오랫동안 다니던 식당인데 음식과 서비스가 아주 좋아.

03 The restaurant might not be very fancy, but in my opinion it has some of the best Korean food around. What would you like to have? 이 음식점이 그렇게 멋져 보이지 않아도 내 생각에는 여기가 한국음식을 젤 잘해. 뭐를 먹을래?

- It may look a little shabby, but I guarantee it has the best Korean food around. 좀 낡아보이지만, 이 근처에서는 최고의 한국 음식을 내놓는다는 것을 내가 보장해.

A: This is the restaurant you recommended? Really? 네가 추천했던 식당이야? 정말?
B: It may look a little shabby, but it has the best food in Seoul.
좀 낡아보이지만, 서울에서 맛은 최고야.

04 Here we are. Let's find a seat. What do you think? 도착했네. 자리를 찾자. 어때?

- I think that we should start out with some Bulgogi and then we'll try something different. 불고기로 시작한 다음 다른 것도 먹어보자.

- Make sure you try some of the side dishes, especially the kimchi. 반찬들, 특히 김치를 꼭 먹어보도록 해.

A: This looks really nice. What should we eat? 정말 맛있게 보인다. 뭘 먹어야 돼?
B: I think we start out with some Bulgogi and make sure you try some of the side dishes too. 불고기로 시작하는데 반찬들도 꼭 먹어보도록 해.

05 Bulgogi is a type of beef that is marinated in soysauce 불고기는 간장소스로 양념된 고기의 형태야

- Kalbi are ribs that are cut very thinly, they just melt in your mouth.
갈비는 매우 얇게 썰어져서 입에서 살살 녹을거야.

- Bibimbop is a mixture of vegetables, rice, meat and a fried egg in it.
비빔밥은 야채, 밥, 고기 그리고 프라이드 에그를 넣고 섞은거야.

A: What is kalbi? 갈비는 뭐야?
B: It's thinly sliced marinated ribs that are grilled and then wrapped in lettuce. 얇게 썰어진 양념된 갈비로 그릴에 구워서 상추에 싸서 먹는거야.

Unit 10

006

I'm a little worried about my singing ability

난 좀 노래 실력이 걱정돼

전국민의 가수화에 일익을 담당하는 노래방. 노래방에 같이 가자는 join us at the noraebang. 노래방에 가자는 go to a noraebang이라고 하면 된다. 노래를 못한다고 할 때는 be not a very good singer, 음치라고 고백할 때는 be tonedeaf 라고 하면 된다.

01 Do you want to come with us to a noraebang after work? 퇴근 후에 우리와 함께 노래방에 갈래?

● Why don't you join us at the noraebang after work for some fun?
재미삼아 퇴근 후에 함께 노래방에 가자?

● Would you be interested in going out with a few of us after work to a noraebang? 일 끝나고 우리들 몇 명이랑 노래방에 갈래?

● How about joining us and going to a noraebang tonight?
오늘밤 노래방 함께 가는게 어때?

A: Why don't you come with us to a noraebang after work?
퇴근 후에 우리와 함께 노래방에 가자.

B: Sure, sounds like fun. 그래, 재미있겠는데.

02 No alcohol is served and many people take their families to noraebang 술은 제공안되고 많은 사람들이 가족을 데리고 노래방에 가

● A noraebang is a great place to take the family because they don't serve alcohol. 술은 판매하지 않기 때문에 노래방은 가족을 데리고 가기 좋은 곳이야.

● It's kind of like karaoke, but completely different from karaoke.
일종의 가라오케 같은 것이긴 한데 가라오케와는 크게 달라.

A: What's a noraebang? 노래방이 어떤 곳이야?

B: It's kind of like a karaoke bar but instead of singing in front of the entire bar, you have a private room.
가라오케랑 좀 비슷하지만, 전체 바 앞에서 노래부르는 대신 개인 방이 있어.

03 I'm a little worried about my singing ability
난 좀 노래 실력이 걱정돼

- I hope people won't laugh at my singing. 사람들이 내 노래에 웃지 않기를 바래.

- I'm completely tonedeaf so please excuse my singing.
난 완전 음치이니 내 노래 양해를 구해.

- I'm not a very good singer so don't expect too much. 난 노래못해 그러니 기대마.

A: Do you enjoy singing? 노래부르는 것을 즐기니?

B: To be honest, I'm tonedeaf so please don't expect too much.
솔직히 말해서 음치이니 너무 기대하지마.

04 There is a new kind of noraebang coming called coin norabang
코인 노래방이라는 신종 노래방이 생겨났어

- There, one can put coins in a karaoke machine and sing alone.
거기서는 노래방 기계에 돈을 넣고 혼자 노래를 부를 수 있어.

- There will be no workers, just singing rooms with coin operated karaoke
machines. 직원들은 없고, 단지 노래하는 방과 코인으로 작동하는 노래빙 기계가 있을 뿐이야.

A: What are the new coin noraebangs everyone is talking about?
사람들이 말하는 신종 코인노래방은 뭐야?

B: They have no workers, just coin operated karaoke machines.
직원들은 없고, 그냥 코인으로 작동하는 노래하는 기계가 있을 뿐이야.

05 Some noraebang are used for illegal activities
일부 노래방에 불법 행위에 이용되고 있어

- They hire girls and let them sing songs with customers.
여자들을 고용해서 고객들과 함께 노래를 부르게 해.

- The girls are actually prostitutes and use noraebangs to sell sex.
여자들은 실제로 매춘부로 노래방을 이용해 성매매하는거야.

A: Do the owners of the noraebang know about it? 주인들은 그에 대해 알고 있어?
B: Yes but they turn a blind eye to it. 알지 하지만 외면하고 있어.

교통체증

I can't believe how terrible the traffic is in Seoul

서울의 교통상황이 얼마나 끔찍한지 놀랄 뿐이야

움직이는 주차장으로 유명한 한국의 교통체증(traffic jam). 차가 많이 막히다고 할 때는 traffic이 bad 혹은 terrible이라고 하면 된다. beat the traffic하면 교통체증을 피하기 위해 일찍 혹은 늦게 차를 운행한다는 의미이다.

01 I had no idea that traffic was this bad in Seoul
서울의 교통상황이 이렇게 나쁜 줄 미처 몰랐어

- I would never have guessed that traffic in Seoul was so bad.
  서울의 교통이 이렇게 나쁜 줄은 생각도 못했을거야.

- I can't believe how terrible the traffic is in Seoul.
  서울의 교통상황이 얼마나 끔찍한 지 놀랄 뿐이야.

- The traffic jams in Seoul are worse than I imagined.
  서울의 교통체증은 내 예상보다 더 나빠.

A: What do you think of rush hour in Seoul? 서울의 러시아워에 대해 어떻게 생각해?
B: I would never have guessed that it would be so bad.
그렇게 나쁘리라고는 절대로 생각도 못했을거야.

02 To tell you the truth, the traffic today is not that bad
솔직히 말하면 오늘은 교통 상황이 좀 좋은 편이야

- I have taken this route hundreds of times and usually it's worse than this.
  난 이 길을 수없이 탔지만 보통은 이보다 더 나빠.

- I can't imagine that it could be any worse. 이보다 더 나쁠거라고는 상상도 못했어.

- This is actually pretty good for Seoul traffic.
  이건 사실 서울의 교통상황에 비해 꽤 괜찮은 편이야.

A: This traffic is horrible! 차가 엄청 막힌다!
B: I take this route every day and usually it's way worse.
난 매일 이 길을 타는데 보통 더 심해.

Many people who commute spend a lot of time in their cars. That may be one of the reasons so many people have cell phones

출퇴근하는 사람들은 많은 시간을 차 안에서 보내지. 아마도 그래서 핸드폰을 가지고 있는 사람이 많은 건지 모르겠어

● To kill time while stuck in traffic, many people use their cell phone.
차가 막히는 동안 시간을 보내기 위해 많은 사람들은 핸드폰을 사용해.

A: How do people cope with rush hour traffic? 출퇴근시 차막힐 때 사람들은 어떻게 해?
B: Using a cell phone to kill time during rush hour is one way.
러시아워에 시간을 보내기 위해 핸드폰을 하는게 하나의 방법이야.

These blue lanes are for buses only during specific hours 이 푸른색 차선은 정해진 시간 동안에는 버스만이 이용할 수 있어

● Only buses are permitted to use the blue lanes during specific hours.
특정 시간에 버스만이 푸른 색 차선을 이용하는게 허용돼.

A: What are those blue lanes for? 푸른색 차선은 뭐야?
B: The blue lanes are for buses during fixed hours.
푸른색 차선은 정해진 시간에 버스만이 다닐 수 있는거야.

I often take the subway because I find that I arrive at my destination more relaxed

목적지까지 더 편하고 느긋하게 갈 수 있기 때문에 자주 지하철을 타

● The subway is a much more relaxing way of commuting during rush hour.
러시아워에 지하철은 훨씬 느긋하게 갈 수 있는 출퇴근 방법이야.

● Taking the subway is cheaper and more convenient during rush hour.
지하철을 타는게 러시아워에 더 싸고 더 편리해.

A: Should I drive to work? 차로 출근해야 할까?
B: Personally, I think that taking the subway is much more convenient, especially during rush hour.
개인적으로, 특히 러시아워에는 지하철은 타는게 훨씬 편리한 것 같아.

Unit 10

008

Thanksgiving and Chuseok have many similarities

추수감사절과 추석은 유사점이 많아

가을에 수확한 곡물에 대한 감사를 한다는 점에서 추석과 추수감사절은 유사하지만, 우리는 '차례'라는 것을 하며 조상에 대한 경의를 표한다(pay our respects to our ancestors)는 점이 다르다.

01 Chuseok is very similar to the American Thanksgiving in some ways

추석은 몇몇 면에선 미국의 추수 감사절과 아주 비슷해

- Thanksgiving and Chuseok have many similarities.
  추수감사절과 추석은 유사점이 많아.

- There are only a few differences between Chuseok and Thanksgiving.
  추석과 추수감사절 사이에는 몇가지 다른 점만 있을 뿐이야.

- Thanksgiving and Chuseok are both traditional harvest festivals.
  추수감사절과 추석은 모두 전통적인 추수를 감사하는 축제야.

A: Is Chuseok the same as Thanksgiving? 추석은 추수감사절과 같은거야?
B: Yes, they are both harvest festivals and have many similarities.
어, 둘 다 추수를 감사하는 축제이고 많은 유사점이 있어.

02 In what ways is it similar?

어떤 점에서 비슷해?

- It's a national holiday to give thanks for the harvest and it is held either in late September or early October.
  추석도 추수한 것에 대해 감사하는 마음을 가지는 공휴일이야. 보통 9월 말이나 10월 초에 있어.

- I have heard some people call the holiday by another name.
  어떤 사람들이 이 날을 다르게 부르는 걸 들었어.

- It is also called Hangawi. 추석은 한가위라고도 해.

A: Chuseok is also known as Hangawi? 추석은 또한 한가위로 알려져 있지?
B: Yes, Hangawi was the original name. 맞아, 한가위가 원래 이름이야.

03 It's a national holiday to give thanks for the harvest

이날은 추수한 것에 대해 감사하는 마음을 가지는 공휴일이야

- Chuseok is a national holiday for giving thanks for the harvest.
  추석은 추수한 것에 감사하기 위한 공휴일이야.

- We celebrate Chuseok nationally in order to give thanks for the harvest in the fall. 우리는 가을에 추수한 것에 감사하기 위해 전국적으로 추석을 기념해.

A: What is the purpose of Chuseok? 추석의 목적은 뭐야?
B: It is a festival to celebrate a good harvest. 풍성한 수확을 기념하기 위한 축제야.

04 One of the differences is that we pay our respects to our ancestors and this is called Charye

다른 점 중의 하나는 우리는 조상에게 경의를 표한다는 점인데 이걸 차례라고 하지

- For Chuseok, one of the major differences from Thanksgiving is we perform an ancestral memorial ceremony called Charye.
  추석이 추수감사절하고 다른 주요한 것은 우리는 차례라고 하는 조상에 대한 제사를 지내는거야.

A: Do all Koreans do the Charye ceremony? 모든 한국인은 차례를 지내?
B: Most do, but some Christian families refuse to do it as it goes against their beliefs. 대부분 그러지만 일부 기독교 집안은 신념에 어긋나기 때문에 하지 않아.

05 We usually go to the graves of our ancestors for a small service. The memorial service is called Sungmyo

보통 조상의 묘를 찾아가 간단한 의식을 지내. 이 기념하는 의식을 성묘라고 불러

- We have a small service at our ancestor's burial ground and it is called Sungmyo. 우리는 조상의 무덤에서 조그만 차례를 지내는데 이를 성묘라고 불러.

- For Sungmyo, the grass around the grave is trimmed and the family puts some food out for their ancestors. 성묘동안 무덤가 수풀들은 다듬고 가족들은 조상에게 음식을 내놓아.

A: What is the Sungmyo ceremony? 성묘가 뭐야?
B: It's when Koreans return to their ancestors' tombs and perform a memorial ceremony. 한국인들이 조상의 묘에 가서 제사를 지내는 것을 말해.

Unit 10

Are there any Koreans playing in the Major Leagues in the US?

한국선수 중에 미국 메이저리그에서 뛰고 있는 선수가 있어?

야구가 가장 인기있는 스포츠(baseball is probably the most popular spectator sport)라고 말할 수 있어야 하고, 손흥민 때문에 프리미어리그를 빠지지 않고 본다고 할 때는 follow the Premier League라고 하면 된다.

01 Is it your first time to see a Korean professional sports event? 이번이 한국 프로팀 경기를 처음 보는거야?

- Have you ever seen a professional Korean team play before?
  전에 한국 프로팀 경기를 본 적이 있어?

- In Korea, baseball is probably the most popular spectator sport and I recommend you go see a game.
  한국에서는 야구가 아마도 가장 인기있게 관람하는 스포츠로 한번 가서 보기를 권해.

A: Does Korea have any good professional sports leagues?
한국에는 프로스포츠 리그가 뭐 좋은게 있어?

B: It has many different leagues but baseball is probably the most popular one. 많은 종류의 리그가 있지만 야구가 아마도 가장 인기있어.

02 Are there any Koreans playing in the Major Leagues in the US? 한국선수 중에 미국 메이저리그에서 뛰고 있는 선수가 있어?

- Do you know of any Koreans playing in the Major Leagues?
  메이저리그에서 뛰고 있는 한국선수 알고 있는 사람있어?

- Years ago there was a famous pitcher by the name of Park Chan-ho, and these days, there are Kim Ha-seung and Choi Ji-man among many others.
  오래전에 박찬호라는 뛰어난 피처가 있었지만 요즘에는 다른 많은 선수들 중에 김하성과 최지만이 있어.

A: Do you know of any Koreans playing in the MLB right now?
지금 MLB에서 뛰는 한국 선수 아는 사람있어?

B: There are many, but Kim Ha-seung and Choi Ji-man are two of the most famous ones. 많지만, 김하성과 최지만이 가장 유명한 선수야.

Soccer has become quite a popular sport due in part to Son Heung-min who played in Tottenham

축구가 상당히 인기있는 종목이 되었는데 그 이유는 토트넘에서 뛰는 손흥민의 활약 때문이야

- These days, Son Heung-min, the world class soccer star, is making Koreans excited. 요즘 축구월드스타인 손흥민이 한국사람들을 흥분케 해.

- Many Koreans follow the Premier League, especially Tottenham Hotspur because of Son Heung-min. 많은 한국인이 PL을 보는데, 특히 손흥민 땜에 토트넘 경기를 꼭 봐.

A: Why is soccer so popular in Korea? 왜 한국에서 축구가 그렇게 인기있는거야?
B: One reason is Son Heung-min, the world class soccer star who plays for Tottenham Hotspur. 한가지 이유는 토트넘에서 뛰는 월드스타 손흥민 때문이야.

It must be exciting for Koreans to watch him play on TV 한국 사람들은 그 선수가 경기하는 것을 TV로 보면서 매우 흥분되겠어

- Especially after Park Seri, Korea has produced many amazing world golf stars, such as Park In-be and many others.
특히 박세리 이후에 한국은 박인비와 다른 선수들 같은 뛰어난 골프 월드스타를 많이 배출했어.

A: Why is golf so popular in Korea? 왜 골프가 한국에서 인기있는거야?
B: After Park Seri won a major tournament, many Koreans started playing and watching golf. 박세리가 메이저 우승한 후에 많은 한국인들이 골프를 하고 시청하기 시작했어.

It's great that young kids have an athlete that they can look up to 아이들이 우러러 볼 수 있는 운동선수가 있다는 건 아주 좋은 일이야

- Korean kids are lucky to have so many athletes to look up to.
한국 아이들에게 우상하는 많은 선수들이 있다는건 행운이야.

- These athletes will be great role models for all of the young children in Korea. 이 선수들은 한국의 모든 어린이들에게 훌륭한 롤모델이 될거야.

A: Who does your son look up to? 네 아들은 누구를 우상화해?
B: He looks up to many different Korean athletes, but especially Son Heung-min. 많은 선수들을 우러러보지만 특히 손흥민이야.

Unit 10

010

I suggest that you try some soju. It's a traditional Korean drink

소주를 마셔봐. 전통적인 한국의 술이야

술한잔 하면서 스트레스를 풀지만, 요즘 젊은 세대들은 예전과 달리 칼퇴근에 동료들과의 회식을 좋아하지 않는다.(don't like drinking with co-workers) 술을 너무 마셨을 때는 해장국이 필요한데 이는 hangover soup이라고 하면 된다.

01 It's not unusual for Koreans to go out drinking during the week with their colleagues or boss

한국에선 주중에 회사 동료들이나 상사와 술집에 가는 건 흔히 있는 일이야

- But recently young workers don't like drinking with co-workers.
  하지만 최근 젊은 직원들은 동료들과 술마시는 것을 좋아하지 않아.

- They tend to want to do things they want to do when work ends.
  젊은 직원들은 일이 끝나면 자기가 하고 싶은 일을 하는 경향이 있어.

A: Do Koreans have to go drinking with their co-workers?
한국사람들은 동료들과 술을 마시러 가야 돼?

B: They used to, but recently young workers are choosing not to do this. 예전에는 그랬는데 최근 젊은 직원들은 그렇지 않아.

02 I think you should have the traditional Korean drink, soju, to start with 우선 한국 고유의 술, 소주를 마셔보도록 해

- I suggest that you try some soju. It's a traditional Korean drink.
  소주를 마셔봐. 전통적인 한국의 술이야.

- If you want to try traditional Korean alcohol, I suggest soju or makkoli.
  한국 전통주를 마시고 싶다면 소주나 막걸리를 추천해.

A: What is a typical Korean drink? 한국의 전형적인 술은 뭐야?
B: Most Koreans drink soju. It's a type of Korean vodka.
대부분의 사람들은 소주를 마셔. 한국판 보드카와 같은거야.

03 Let me pour you a drink
한 잔 받아

- **Can I pour you a drink?** 한잔 따라줄까?
- **Let me** top up your beer. 맥주 가득 따라줄게.
- **Would you like a refill?** 다시 채워줄까?

A: Let me top up your beer for you. 너에게 맥주 가득 따라줄게.

B: Thanks! Can I get you another one? 고마워! 한잔 더 따라줄까?

04 There's a special kind of soup and the name of it is 'hangover soup' '해장국'이라고 부르는 특별한 종류의 국이 있어

- **If you're feeling ill you should** try the hangover soup.
  상태가 안 좋으면 해장국을 먹어봐.

- **After a night of heavy drinking, we always** eat hangover soup.
  밤에 과음한 후에 우리는 보통 해장국을 먹어.

A: Oh, my head is killing me! I drank too much last night.
오, 머리가 아파 죽겠네! 지난밤에 술을 너무 마셨나봐.

B: If you have a hangover, you should try the Korean hangover soup.
숙취가 있다면 해장국을 먹어봐.

05 Drinking is looked upon as stress relief, a time for you to let loose 술을 마시는 건 스트레스를 해소하고 긴장을 푸는 시간으로 여겨져

- **Drinking is something that we do** to relieve the stress from work.
  음주는 직장에서 온 스트레스를 풀기 위해 하는 것이야.

- **One way many Koreans** blow off some steam is by drinking.
  많은 한국 사람들이 스트레스를 푸는 한가지 방법은 술을 마시는거야.

A: Why do I see so many Korean businessmen drinking hard?
왜 그렇게 많은 한국 직장인들이 술을 많이 마시는거야?

B: Drinking is something they do to relieve stress from work.
음주는 직장에서의 스트레스를 풀기 위해 하는거야.

Unit 10

011 Is Christmas a national holiday in Korea?

성탄절이 한국에서 공휴일이야?

믿는 종교와 상관없이 그냥 즐거운 휴일이 되어버린 성탄절. 젊은이들에게는 들뜬 날이겠지만 나이든 사람들은 think the Christmas as a regular day라고 여기며, 이쯤 열리는 망년회는 year-end parties라고 하면 된다.

01 Many Koreans who aren't Christian enjoy the Christmas season 예수를 믿지는 않아도 크리스마스를 즐기는 한국 사람들이 많아

- Many Koreans enjoy the Christmas season, **even though they don't believe in Jesus Christ.** 많은 한국 사람들은 예수를 믿지 않아도 성탄절을 즐겨.

- **Even though Christmas is a Christian holiday,** many Koreans who aren't Christian still have a nice time.
  성탄절은 기독교 휴일임에도 불구하고, 교인이 아닌 많은 한국 사람들은 그래도 멋진 시간을 보내.

A: Is Christmas a national holiday in Korea? 성탄절이 한국에서 공휴일이야?
B: Yes, but even though many Koreans aren't Christian, they still enjoy the Christmas season.
어, 많은 한국 사람들은 기독교인은 아니지만, 그래도 성탄절 시즌을 즐겨.

02 The Christmas season is much more popular among the younger generation

크리스마스는 젊은 세대들 사이에서 더 인기있는 시즌이야

- The younger generation seems to be much more interested in Christmas.
  젊은 세대들은 성탄절에 더 많은 관심을 갖고 있는 것 같아.

- Young Koreans usually go out on Christmas Day and enjoy themselves.
  젊은 한국인들은 보통 성탄절에 밖에 나가서 즐겨.

A: Why aren't any older people out on Christmas Day?
왜 나이든 사람들은 성탄절에 밖에 나오지 않는거야?

B: Younger people are more enthusiastic for Christmas than the older generation. 젊은 세대가 나이든 세대보다 성탄절에 더 열광적이지.

03

Many Korean children get Christmas presents on Christmas day 많은 한국 아이들은 성탄절에 선물을 받아

- These days, many Koreans buy Christmas gifts for their children at Christmas. 요즘, 많은 한국인들은 성탄절에 아이들에게 줄 선물을 사.

- Exchanging Christmas gifts has become more popular than it was a few years ago. 선물교환은 몇년전 그랬던 것보다 더 대중적이야

A: Do Koreans buy each other Christmas presents?
한국인들은 성탄절 선물을 서로에게 사줘?

B: These days many young children receive presents from their parents and some teens exchange gifts too.
요즘 많은 아이들은 부모로부터 선물을 받고 일부 십대들은 선물들을 교환해.

04

There are going to be quite a few year-end parties in the next few weeks 다음 몇 주 동안은 망년회가 꽤 많이 열릴거야

- In December there are usually many year-end parties to attend.
12월에는 보통 참석해야 하는 망년회가 많아.

- I'm getting exhausted from all of the year-end parties I have to go to.
참석해야 하는 모든 망년회를 다녀와 지쳤어.

A: Why do you look so tired? 왜 그렇게 피곤해 보여?
B: I'm getting exhausted from all of the year-end parties this month.
이번 달에 간 모든 망년회 때문에 지쳤어.

People getting older seem to think of Christmas as a regular day 나이들어가는 사람들은 성탄절을 그냥 평범한 날로 생각하는 것 같아

- No more excitement, we usually spend the day without any cakes.
더 이상 들뜨지도 않고 케익도 없이 보통 지내.

- I usually just stay home and watch TV. 난 보통 집에서 TV를 봐.

A: Is Christmas a special holiday for you? 성탄절이 너에게는 특별한 휴일이니?
B: No, it's just a regular day. I stay home and watch TV.
아니, 평범한 하루야. 집에서 TV봐.

Unit 10

나이와 띠

012

It's the year of the snake and that's my sign

올해는 뱀띠 해인데 내가 뱀띠거든

한국에는 12개의 동물로 정하는 띠, 서양에서는 12개의 별로 정하는 별자리가 있다. 별자리는 zodiac sign이라고 하고 띠는 Chinese zodiac sign이라고 하면 된다. 특히 여성들은 나이를 숨기기 위해 tell one's sign하는 것을 꺼리는 경향이 있다.

01 It's the year of the snake and that's my sign
올해는 뱀띠 해인데 내가 뱀띠거든

● This is my year because I'm a snake. 올해는 나의 해야. 내가 뱀띠거든.

● My mother was born in the year of the snake and so was I.
  엄마는 뱀띠해에 태어났고 나도 그래.

● Do you know that this year is the year of the snake which is my sign.
  금년이 내 띠인 뱀의 해인 것을 알고 있어?

A: Happy Chinese New Year! 즐거운 구정보내!
B: You too. This is my year because it is the year of the snake!
  너도. 올해는 나의 해야, 내가 뱀띠거든!

02 What's your sign?
너는 무슨 자리야?

● Are you a Scorpio? 너는 전갈자리야?

● You seem like you're a Libra. Are you? 넌 천칭자리인 것 같아. 맞아?

● A Pisces and a Gemini don't make a good match.
  물고기자리와 쌍둥이자리인 사람은 서로 안어울려.

A: What's your boyfriend's sign? 네 남친 자리는 뭐야?
B: He's a Taurus and I'm an Aquarius so we're a good couple.
  걘 황소자리고 난 물병자리야 그래서 우리는 멋진 커플이야.

03
There are 12 zodiac animals and they change each year 동물로 나타내는 띠가 12개 있는데, 매년 변해

- The zodiac signs change each year and there are twelve different ones.
  별자리는 매년 변하고 12개의 별자리가 있어.

A: What is the Chinese zodiac? 중국식 띠는 뭐야?

B: The zodiac signs change each year and there are twelve different ones. 십이간지가 매년 변하고 12개의 띠가 있어.

04
Korean women are hesitant to tell you their sign because you could guess their age
띠를 알면 나이를 알 수 있기 때문에 띠를 말해주지 않는 한국 여자들이 많아

- Finding out a person's zodiac sign is a way of finding out their age.
  무슨 띠인지 알아내는 것은 나이를 알아내는 한 방법이야.

A: How old is she? 걔는 몇살이야?

B: Ask her what her sign is. You can guess her age if you know her sign. 무슨 띠인지 물어봐. 띠를 알면 나이를 짐작할 수 있어.

05
Koreans consider you to be one year old when you're born and your first birthday is really your second
한국에서는 태어나자마자 한 살이라고 하고 첫번째 생일날은 실은 두 살인거구

- In Korea, you are always one year older than your real age.
  한국에서는 실제 나이보다 한 살이 많아.

- If you ask a Korean how old they are, make sure you ask them if they mean Korean age or Western age.
  한국인에게 나이를 물어보려면 한국나이인지 서양나이인지 구분해서 물어봐야 돼.

A: You're 22 but you were born in 2001? I don't understand!
   넌 22살이지만 2001년에 태어났다고? 난 이해가 안돼!

B: In Korean age, as soon as you are born you are automatically one year old, so Korean age is one year older than other countries.
   한국나이로는 태어나자마자 자동적으로 한 살이 돼 그래서 한국나이는 다른 나라보다 한 살이 더 많아.

Unit 10

하얀 봉투

We also send a wreath at weddings or funerals

우리는 또한 결혼식이나 장례식에 화환을 보내

한국에서 결혼식이나 장례식에서는 선물 등을 주기 보다는 하얀봉투에 돈을 넣어서 주는(give money in a white envelope)것이 관례이다. 물론 화환이나 조화를 보내기(send a wreath)도 한다.

01 People give money to the bride and groom in a white envelope 사람들은 신랑, 신부에게 흰 봉투에 돈을 넣어서 전해

- The bride and groom are given money in a white envelope **at their wedding.** 결혼식에서 신혼부부에게 돈이 들어 있는 흰 봉투가 주어져.
- We give it to the receptionists at the wedding **and they record your name.** 결혼식 접수하는 사람에게 주면 그들은 주는 사람 이름을 기록해.
- You don't usually give gifts at Korean weddings, you give money. 한국 결혼식에서는 보통 선물을 주지 않고 돈을 줘.

A: What should I buy for a wedding present? 결혼 선물로 뭘 사줘야 할까?
B: In Korea we don't give gifts, we give money in a white envelope at their wedding ceremony. 한국에서는 선물을 주지 않아, 결혼식에서 돈을 하얀 봉투에 넣어서 줘.

02 It really depends on how much money you make and how close you are to the person getting married

그건 자신의 소득과, 결혼하는 사람과 얼마나 가까우냐에 달려 있어

- These days the basic rate is 50,000 won **but if you are close to them you give more.** 요즘 기본가는 5만원이고 가까운 사이면 더 하고.
- After you give the money you will **receive a ticket for the wedding meal.** 돈을 주고 나면 결혼식 식사표를 받게 될거야.

A: It's my first Korean wedding so I don't know how much I should give. 한국 결혼식은 처음이어서 얼마를 해야 할지 모르겠어.
B: These days the basic rate is 50,000 won unless you are close friends or family. 가족이나 가까운 친척이 아니라면 요즘 기본이 5만원이야.

03 It also will help them pay for the wedding because getting married in Korea can be really expensive

한국에서는 결혼 비용이 아주 많이 들기 때문에 그 비용을 감당하는 데 그것이 도움이 돼

- One of the reasons people give money instead of gifts is to help pay for the cost of the wedding.

  선물대신 돈을 주는 이유 중의 하나가 결혼식 비용에 쓰는데 도움이 되기 위함이야.

A: Wow! I just heard how much this wedding is costing them.
와! 이 웨딩비용이 얼마나 되는지 방금 들었어.

B: Yes, weddings are super expensive and that is the main reason we give them money instead of gifts.
어, 결혼식은 돈이 아주 많이 들기 때문에 선물 대신에 돈을 주는 주된 이유지.

04 We also give money in a white envelope at funerals

장례식장에서도 흰 봉투에 돈을 넣어 부조를 해

- In addition to weddings, Koreans also give cash to families at funerals.

  결혼식 뿐만 아니라, 한국 사람들은 장례식 가족에 돈을 부조해.

- When someone dies, we also give money at their funeral service.

  누군가 죽게 되면, 우리는 또한 장례식장에서 돈을 부조해.

A: I'm going to my first Korean funeral tonight.
오늘밤 내 첫번째 한국 장례식에 갈거야.

B: Oh, just so you know, it's a custom to give money to the family at funerals. 오. 참고로 말하자면, 장례를 치르는 가족에게 돈을 부조하는게 관습이야.

05 We also send a wreath at weddings or funerals

우리는 또한 결혼식이나 장례식에 화환을 보내

- You will see a lot of wreaths at a funeral service in Korea.

  한국의 장례식장에서 많은 조화를 볼 수 있을거야.

A: Wow! Look at all those wreaths. 와! 저 화환들 봐봐.

B: Yes, unfortunately, the number of wreaths signifies the family's power. 어, 안타깝게도, 화환의 수가 가족의 파워를 나타내.

014 There are many people who practice Buddhism

불교를 믿는 사람들이 많아

종교를 믿고 따른다고 할 때는 동사 practice를 쓴다는 점에 주목한다. 성탄절과 마찬가지로 종교와 상관없이 휴일인 것은 똑같다. 특히 도시마다 연등행렬의 행진이 있다(celebrate the holiday with a parade)는 점이 특이하다.

01 There are many people who practice Buddhism
불교를 믿는 사람들이 많아

- **Many people worship the Buddha.** 많은 사람들이 부처를 숭배해.
- **There are a great many people who are Buddhist.** 불교를 믿는 사람들이 아주 많아.
- **Buddhism is one of the biggest religions here.** 불교는 여기서 가장 큰 종교중의 하나야.

A: What kind of religions are popular here? 어떤 종교가 여기서 일반적이야?
B: Buddhism is one of the main religions here. 불교가 주된 종교 중의 하나야.

02 Buddhism was introduced to Korea in the late fourth century 불교는 4세기 후반에 우리나라에 들어왔어

- **It wasn't until late in the fourth century that Buddhism came to Korea.**
  4세기 후반에서야 한국에 불교가 들어왔어.
- **Buddhism first appeared in the late fourth century in Korea.**
  불교는 4세기 후반에 최초로 한국에 들어왔어.
- **Buddhism was brought to Korea in the late 4th century.**
  불교는 4세기 후반에 한국에 들어왔어.

A: When did Koreans first start practicing Buddhism?
   한국사람들은 언제부터 불교를 믿기 시작했어?

B: It came to Korea late in the fourth century. 4세기 후반에 한국에 들어왔어.

03 Today is the day that we recognize the birth of Buddha 오늘은 우리가 부처님 오신 날이라고 기리는 날이야

- There are many Buddhist temples in Korea and they are very beautiful.
한국에는 많은 절이 있는데 아주 아름다워.

- Today is a national holiday and many people are taking advantage of the day off. 오늘은 공휴일이라서 휴일을 즐기는 사람들이 많은 거야.

- The Buddhists celebrate the holiday with a parade in Seoul and at temples all over Korea. 불교신자들은 서울과 한국의 모든 사찰에서 행진을 하며 석탄일을 기념해.

A: What do Koreans do for Buddha's birthday? 석탄일에 한국사람들은 뭐해?
B: There is a parade in Seoul which many Buddhists attend.
많은 불교신자들이 참석하는 행진이 서울에서 벌어져.

04 You'll notice that many people are carrying a flower shaped lantern 꽃모양의 등을 들고 있는 사람들이 눈에 많이 뜨일 거야

- You may see people carrying flower shaped lanterns.
사람들이 꽃모양의 등을 들고 다니는 것을 보게 될거야.

- At temples you will see many monks and people carrying a lotus flower lantern. 사찰에서 많은 스님과 사람들이 연꽃모양의 등을 들고 다니는 것을 보게 될거야.

A: What are those things the people are carrying? 사람들이 들고 다니는게 뭐야?
B: Those are lotus flower lanterns. 연꽃모양의 등이야.

05 It's a lotus flower, and this represents the truth of Buddha 연꽃인데, 그건 부처의 깨달음을 상징하는거야

- Buddhists believe that the lotus flower represents the truth.
불교신자들은 연꽃이 깨달음을 나타낸다고 믿어.

- The lotus flower is a symbol of the truth for Buddhists.
연꽃은 부처의 깨달음을 상징하는거야.

A: What does the lotus flower mean to Buddhists? 불교신도들에게 연꽃은 뭘 뜻해?
B: It symbolizes the truth for them. 깨달음을 상징해.

Unit 10

Korea was split into two at the 38th parallel

한국은 38선으로 두개로 분단됐어

공동경비구역은 Joint Security Area이고 DMZ의 중간에 위치에 있다. 여기에 있는 판문점은 몇년전 남북한 정상회담이 열렸던 곳이다.(the Inter-Korean summit took place)

This is the "Joint Security Area" between the U.N. and North Korean forces

이곳은 유엔군과 북한군의 '공동경비구역'이야

- JSA is a place where North and South Korea negotiate agreements and is located in the middle of the Demilitarized Zone (DMZ).
  JSA는 남북한이 협정을 맺은 곳이고 DMZ의 중간에 위치해 있어.
- Panmunjeom is the name of the village located in the middle of the DMZ.
  판문점은 DMZ 가운데 위치한 마을이름이야.

A: What is the name of that place located in the middle of the DMZ?
DMZ의 가운데 위치한 장소의 이름이 뭐야?

B: It's Panmunjeom but also known as Joint Security Area or JSA.
판문점이야 하지만 공동경비구역, 즉 JSA로 잘 알려져 있어.

Korea was divided at the 38th parallel

한반도는 38선으로 분단됐어

- Korea was split into two at the 38th parallel. 한국은 38선으로 두개로 분단됐어.
- The 38th parallel marks the division between North and South Korea.
  38선은 남북한의 분단선이야.
- The dividing line between North and South Korea is the 38th parallel.
  남북한을 나누는 선은 38선이야.

A: Where is the DMZ located? DMZ는 어디에 위치해 있어?
B: At the 38th parallel. 38선에.

03

The fighting stopped as a result of the Armistice Agreement that was signed at Panmunjeom on July 27th, 1953

전쟁은 1953년 7월 27일에 판문점에서 조인된 휴전 협정에 의해서 중지되었어

● The fighting ceased when the Armistice Agreement was signed on July 27th,1953 at Panmunjeom.

전쟁은 1953년 7월 27일 판문점에서 조인된 휴전협정에 의해서 중지되었어.

A: Fighting stopped on July 27th, 1953 when both sides signed an Armistice Agreement. 전쟁은 양측이 휴전협정에 조인한 1953년 7월 27일에 중지되었어.

B: That's true but they are still at war until they sign a Peace Agreement. 사실이지만 평화협정을 맺기까지는 아직 전쟁중인거지.

04

This area plays host to ongoing peace talks

이 지역에서 평화회담이 계속 열리고 있어

● JSA is the place where the North and South can have talks about many different issues. JSA는 남북한이 다양한 많은 문제들에 관해 회담을 하는 곳이야.

A: I've never heard of Panmunjeom before. What is it?
판문점은 처음 들어봐. 뭐하는 곳이야?

B: It's located in the DMZ. It's the site where North and South Korea discuss ongoing issues.
DMZ에 위치해 있고 남북한이 현재의 문제들을 논의하는 주요한 장소야.

05

It is the very place where the Inter-Korean summit took place a few years ago 몇년전 남북한 정상회심이 열린 바로 그곳이야

● Even the ex-President of the US, Donald Trump, came here and held a summit talk with Kim Jong un.
미국의 전직 대통령인 도널드 트럼프도 여기 와서 김정은과 정상회담을 개최했어.

A: Have any American Presidents visited Panmunjom? 판문점방문한 미대통령이 있어?

B: Yes, many have, including Donald Trump who visited there to meet Kim Jong un a few years ago. 많아. 몇 년전 판문점에서 김정은을 만난 도널드 트럼프를 포함해서.

Unit 10

016

Jejudo is the largest of Korea's islands

제주도는 우리나라의 섬 중에서 가장 커

한국의 하와이로 불리는 제주도는 신혼여행지로 유명하며(Korea's most popular honeymoon destination), 특히 삼다도, 여자, 돌, 바람이 많은 곳으로 잘 알려져 있다. 요즘에는 제주도를 한 바퀴 도는 올레길(Olle Trail)이 유명하다.

01 Jejudo is the largest of Korea's islands
제주도는 우리나라의 섬 중에서 가장 커

- For many years, Jeju was Korea's most popular honeymoon destination.
  오랫동안 제주도는 한국에서 가장 유명한 신혼여행지였어.

- Jeju isn't just the biggest island in Korea, it is also one of Korea's most popular tourist destinations.
  제주도는 한국에서 가장 큰 섬일 뿐 아니라 한국에서 가장 인기있는 관광명소 중 하나야.

A: What is the biggest island in Korea? 한국에서 가장 큰 섬은 뭐야?

B: It's Jeju. Jeju is also Korea's most popular tourist destination.
제주도야. 제주도는 또한 한국에서 가장 인기있는 관광명소야.

02 It is known as the island of three "many's": many women, many rocks, and many winds
제주도는 삼다도(三多島)로 알려져 있는데, 여자, 돌, 바람이 많아서야

- Jejudo is characterized by three "many's": many women, many rocks, and many winds. 제주도는 삼다도로 특징지워지는데, 많은 여자, 많은 돌, 그리고 많은 바람이야.

- The three things Jeju is famous for are rocks, wind and women.
  제주도가 유명한 삼다는 돌, 바람 그리고 여자야.

- Rocks, wind and women are the 3 things Jeju is known for.
  돌, 바람, 그리고 여자가 제주도가 유명한 3가지야.

A: I heard Jeju is a good place to visit. 제주도는 방문하기에 좋은 곳이라 들었어.

B: Yes, it is very beautiful and famous for three things: rocks, wind and women. 어, 아주 아름답고 3가지(돌, 바람 그리고 여자)로 유명해.

03

It is a dolharubang(stone grandfather), sculptured in large and small sizes from the area's porous lava stone.

이건 돌하르방[石祖]인데, 이 지역의 구멍이 숭숭 뚫려 있는 화산암을 크고 작은 형태로 조각한 것이야

● The stone harubangs are a cultural symbol of the island.
돌하르방은 제주도의 문화적 상징물이야.

● You can see the stone harubangs all over the island.
제주도 곳곳에서 돌하르방을 볼 수 있어.

A: What's that? I keep seeing those things everywhere I go here.
그게 뭐야? 가는 곳마다 그게 계속 보이네.

B: That's a harubang. It's a symbol of Jeju and is made from the local volcanic rock. 하르방이라는거야. 제주도의 상징이고 지역 화산암으로 만들어졌어.

04

It is Mount Halla, which is almost 2,000m

그건 한라산으로, 높이가 거의 2,000미터야

● The only mountain higher than Mt. Halla in Korea is Mt. Paektu which is located in North Korea. 한국에서 한라산보다 높은 유일한 산은 북한에 위치한 백두산이야.

A: How high is Mt. Halla? 한라산의 높이는 어떻게 돼?

B: It's almost 2000m high. It's the highest mountain in South Korea.
거의 2천미터 돼. 남한에서 가장 높은 산이야.

05

Many people come to Jeju to walk the Olle Trail

많은 사람들이 올레길을 걸으려고 제주도에 와

● The growing number of visitors and Jeju Olle Trail's popularity helped Jeju Island get famous. 늘어나는 방문자수와 제주 올레길의 인기가 제주도를 유명하게 해.

● Have you ever walked the Olle Trail in Jeju? 제주도의 올레길을 걸어본 적 있어?

A: What are you going to do when you go to Jeju? 제주도에 가면 뭐를 할거야?

B: Our plan is to hike the Olle Trail and see the entire island that way.
우리 계획은 올레길을 하이크하고 그렇게 섬전체를 구경하는거야.

Unit 10

한국영화

017

Korean films are just as good as Hollywood movies these days

한국영화는 요즘 할리우드 영화 못지 않아

예전에는 할리우드 영화를 선호했으나(preferred Hollywood-produced films). 요즘 한국영화는 have a very good reputation around the world이다. 특히 기생충, 미나리 등이 있으며 시리즈물로는 Squid Game이나 Extraordinary Attorney Woo 등이 각광을 받고 있다.

01

The Korean movie industry is becoming more advanced 한국 영화 산업이 더욱 발전하고 있어

● More movies are being shot in Korea these days.
요즘 한국에서는 많은 영화들을 찍고 있어.

● Korean films are just as good as Hollywood movies these days.
한국영화는 요즘 할리우드 영화 못지 않아.

● Korean cinema has a great reputation among world movie goers.
한국영화는 세계적인 영화광들 사이에서 명성이 자자해.

A: I just love Korean cinema. 난 한국영화를 좋아해.

B: Me too. Korean films are just as good as Hollywood films these days. Maybe even better.
나도 그래. 한국영화는 요즘 할리우드 영화 못지 않아. 더 나을지도 몰라.

02

Koreans usually preferred Hollywood-produced films 한국사람들은 보통 할리우드 영화를 선호했어

● In the 1970s and 80s, Koreans preferred watching American movies to Korean ones. 1970-80년대에 한국사람들은 자국의 영화보다 미국영화를 더 보기를 좋아했어.

● Koreans used to watch more Hollywood movies than Korean ones.
한국사람들은 한국영화보다 할리우드영화를 더 보곤 했어.

A: These days, Koreans love watching Korean movies.
요즘 한국사람들은 한국영화 보는 것을 좋아해.

B: Yes, but they used to prefer Hollywood movies.
그래, 하지만 예전에는 할리우드 영화를 더 좋아했었지.

03 Korean producers will find it easier to get money to make more large-scale movies

제작사들은 보다 규모가 큰 영화를 만들 수 있는 돈을 더 쉽게 구하게 될거야

● **Koreans** are making more large-scale films **than ever before.**
한국사람들은 그 어느때보다 스케일이 큰 영화를 만들고 있어.

A: I heard that the new war film is the most expensive Korean movie ever made. 새로운 전쟁영화가 지금껏 제작된 영화중에서 가장 돈이 많이 든다며.

B: These days many Korean producers are willing to try larger scale productions. 요즘 한국 영화제작자들은 스케일이 더 큰 영화를 만들려고 해.

04 Parasite was a huge revolution, because it won the Academy Award for Best Picture

기생충은 아카데미 작품상을 수상했기 때문에 커다란 충격였어

● **Lee Isaac Chung's "Minari" won Yoon Yuh Jung the Best Supporting Actress Academy Award, making** her the first Korean to win an Academy Award for acting. 리 아이작 정의 "미나리"는 윤여정에게 연기로는 최초로 한국인에게 아카데미 여우조연상을 안겼어.

A: Did you know Parasite won the Academy Award for Best Picture?
기생충이 아카데미 작품상을 탄거 알고 있었어?

B: Of course! The past few years Korean films have done very well at international festivals too. 물론! 지난 몇 년간 한국영화는 국제영화제에서 좋은 성과를 냈어.

05 Korean TV dramas are getting popular worldwide such as Squid Game, Extraordinary Attorney Woo, etc.

오징어게임, 이상한 변호사 우영우 등 한국 드라마가 세계적 명성을 얻고 있어

● **Netflix** is showing a lot of Korean movies and TV shows **these days.**
넷플릭스는 요즘 많은 양의 한국영화와 드라마를 선보이고 있어.

A: I'm really addicted to watching Korean TV shows these days.
요즘 한국 TV 드라마 보는데 정말 중독됐어.

B: Me too. What are your favorite shows? 나도, 좋아하는 드라마가 뭐야?

Unit 10

018

They give the family names of both parents, such as Kim-Park Ji yeon

김박지연처럼 양부모의 성을 아이에게 주기도 해

원래 한국이름은 성이 한 자, 이름이 두 자인 한자로 구성되어 있으나, 요즘에는 김박지연처럼 양부모의 성을 물려받기도 하고, 이름의 경우 순수한 우리말로 짓기도 하는 등 많은 변화가 있다.

01

Korean names are usually three Chinese characters long and the first is the family name, such as Kim, Lee or Park

우리나라 이름은 보통 한자 세 글자로 되어 있는데, 김, 이, 박같은 성(姓)이 먼저 와

- Korean names begin with the last name first, and are made up of three Chinese characters. 한국 이름은 성으로 먼저 시작되고 한자 3개로 구성되어 있어.

- Korean names are made up of three Chinese characters which include one for the family name and two more for the given name.
  한국이름 3개의 한자로 구성되어 있는데 하나는 성을 두개는 이름을 말해.

A: How are babies named in Korea? 한국에서 아이들 이름은 어떻게 지어?
B: You get your family name from your father. Then the parents choose two Chinese characters for the given name.
아버지로부터 성을 받아. 그런 다음 부모는 이름으로 두글자의 한자를 선택해.

02

A given name is two characters and each has a specific meaning 이름은 한자 두 글자로 되어 있는데, 각 한자에는 특별한 의미가 있어

- The meaning of your given name comes from the two Chinese characters. 이름의 의미는 두 글자의 한자에서 유래 돼.

A: Do the Chinese characters mean anything? 한자들이 무슨 의미가 있는거야?
B: Yes, of course. Your given name's meaning comes from combining the meaning of the two characters.
어, 물론. 이름 두 글자의 의미는 2개 한자의 의미를 결합하는데에서 유래 돼.

03
Recently, young couples tend to name their babies with pure Korean names 최근 젊은 부부들은 아이이름을 순수한 우리말로 짓는 경향이 있어

● They give the family names of both parents, such as Kim-Park Ji yeon.
김박지연처럼 양부모의 성을 아이에게 주기도 해.

A: I met a girl who was named Park-Kim Eunhee. That seemed unusual. 박김은희라는 이름의 여자애를 만났는데 이상한 것처럼 보였어.

B: Yes but these days many families are doing that. They are using both the mother and father's family name for their children.
그래 하지만 요즘 많은 가정들이 그렇게 해. 아이들 성으로 부모의 성을 다 사용해.

04
These days we even have name-makers on the Internet thanks to modern technology!
요즘에는 현대 과학기술 덕분에 인터넷으로 이름을 지을 수도 있어!

● There are even Internet sites where you can find services that help you name your child. 아이들 이름짓는데 도움을 주는 서비스를 하는 인터넷 사이트도 있어.

A: Do the parents always name their children? 부모가 항상 아이들 이름을 지어?

B: Usually they do but these days there are many popular internet sites which help parents name their children.
보통 그렇게 하지만 요즘 많은 인터넷 사이트들이 부모들이 아이 이름짓는데 도움을 주고 있어.

05
Unless we are speaking to a close friend or a child, we usually just call each other by our full names and add "ssi" at the end as a term of respect
친한 친구나 어린 아이한테 말할 때가 아니면 보통 성과 이름을 함께 부르고 끝에 "씨"라 는 존칭을 붙여

● If a woman is married and has a child, people will often call them the child's mother. 여자가 결혼을 했고 아이가 있다면 사람들은 종종 아이의 엄마라고 종종 불러.

A: Why are you calling him "Hyeongnim" and not "Sanghee?"
넌 왜 그를 "상희"가 아니라 "형님"이라고 불러?

B: He is older than me, so I call him "Hyeongnim" which means older brother in Korean. 나보다 나이가 많으면 한국어로 형님이라는 뜻의 "형님"이라고 불러.

Unit 10

019

The popularity of K-pop has been rising all over the world

K-pop의 인기는 전세계적으로 올라가고 있어

전세계적으로 유명한 BTS가 be probably the most popular at the moment 일게다. 어떤 K-pop 그룹을 좋아하냐고 물어보려면 Which is your favorite K-pop band?라고 하면 된다.

01 K-pop is one of the most popular types of music around the world
K-pop은 전세계적으로 가장 인기있는 음악 중 하나야

● The popularity of K-pop has been rising all over the world.
K-pop의 인기는 전세계적으로 올라가고 있어.

● K-pop bands like BTS and Black Pink are popular all around the world.
BTS나 블랙핑크 같은 K-pop 그룹은 전세계적으로 인기가 있어.

● Do you enjoy listening to K-pop? 넌 K-pop을 즐겨 들어?

A: What is your favorite K-pop band? 좋아하는 K-pop 그룹은 누구야?
B: I love BTS. 난 BTS를 아주 좋아해.

02 It often blends various musical styles, and is performed by young people who do highly energetic dance moves on stage
그건 종종 여러 음악스타일을 혼합해 아주 혈기 넘치게 춤을 추는 젊은이들이 무대위에서 공연되는 것을 말해

● K-pop is characterized by catchy dance music and young and beautiful singers who can dance very well.
K-pop의 특징은 흥미끄는 댄스뮤직과 춤을 아주 잘 추는 젊고 아름다운 가수들이야.

● Most K-pop bands endorse many different kinds of products.
대부분의 K-pop 그룹은 다양한 제품의 광고를 해.

A: What is K-pop? K-pop은 뭐를 말하는거야?

B: It's characterized by catchy dance music and is performed by young people who do very creative and energetic dance moves during concerts.
흥미끄는 댄스뮤직과 콘서트 동안에 창의적이고 혈기 넘치는 춤을 추는 젊은이들에 의해서 행해지는 것을 말해.

Right now, BTS is the most popular K-pop group, and they hold the record for the best selling music album ever in Korea
현재는 BTS가 가장 유명한 K-pop그룹이고, 한국에서 가장 많은 앨범을 판매한 기록을 보유하고 있어

- There are many popular K-pop bands but BTS is probably the most popular at the moment.
많은 인기있는 K-pop 그룹이 있지만 BTS가 아마도 현재 가장 인기있을거야.

- What K-pop bands are you listening to **these days?**
요즘은 어느 K-pop 그룹의 음악을 들어?

- Have **you** heard any new K-pop bands **lately?** 최근에 새로운 K-pop 그룹을 들어봤어?

A: What K-pop bands are you listening to these days?
요즘 넌 어떤 K-pop 그룹의 음악을 들어?

B: Either BTS or Black Pink. I love listening to both of them.
BTS나 블랙핑크. 난 두 그룹의 음악듣는 것을 좋아해.

020

What is the city doing to help slow down Global Warming?

도시는 지구온난화의 속도를 줄이기 위해 뭐를 하고 있어?

기후변화의 위험을 체험하고 있는 요즘이다. cut down on pollution and greenhouse gas emissions하기 위해서 도시들은 become a green city가 되기 위해 노력하는데 그중 하나가 자전거나 스쿠터의 공유시스템이다.

It has become trendy to cut down on pollution and greenhouse gas emissions 오염과 온실가스방출을 줄이려는 경향이 있어

● Many governments are trying their best to cut down on greenhouse gas emissions to help slow down global warming.
많은 정부는 지구온난화 속도를 줄이기 위해 온실가스방출을 줄이려고 최선을 다하고 있어.

● Many scientists believe that Climate Change is a very serious problem.
많은 과학자들은 기후변화가 아주 심각한 문제라고 믿고 있어.

A: Why are you always reading about Climate Change?
넌 왜 늘상 기후변화에 관한 글을 읽어?

B: Because many scientists believe it is a very serious problem so I want to learn more about it.
많은 과학자들이 기후변화는 매우 심각한 문제라고 믿기 때문에 난 그에 대해 더 많이 알고 싶어서.

As a result, Seoul has been working to become a green city 결과적으로 서울은 녹색도시가 되려고 노력하고 있어

● The Seoul City government is doing a lot of projects to try and be more green. 서울은 더 녹색도시가 되려고 많은 프로젝트를 가동하고 있어.

● Seoul buses are changing from gas to electric to help slow down Global Warming. 지구온난화 속도를 줄이기 위해 서울버스들은 가솔린 차에서 전기차로 바뀌고 있어.

A: Are Koreans concerned about Global Warming?
한국인들은 지구온난화에 관심이 있어?

B: Yes, the Seoul government is doing a lot of projects to be more green. 어. 서울시는 더 녹색도시가 되기 위해서 많은 프로젝트를 하고 있어.

03

One of the steps it has taken was to introduce a citywide bike rental system, for those who want an alternative to driving and riding mass transit

취한 조치 중의 하나는 운전이나 대중교통을 이용하는 대신 대안을 원하는 사람들을 위해 도시 전체에 자전거 대여 시스템을 도입했어

● The government has many different green policies to try and curb carbon emissions. 정부는 많은 다양한 녹색정책을 내놓고 탄소배출을 억제하고 있어.

A: What is the city doing to help slow down Global Warming?
도시는 지구온난화의 속도를 줄이기 위해 뭐를 하고 있어?

B: It has several different policies to try to encourage people to buy electric cars. 사람들이 전기차를 사도록 하기 위한 몇몇 다양한 정책을 시행하고 있어.

04

According to the increasing number of scooters, the number of accidents is also increasing

스쿠터 수의 증가에 따라, 사고나는 숫자도 함께 늘어나고 있어

● The city scooter program has helped ease traffic a little bit.
도시의 스쿠터 프로그램은 교통체증을 조금 감소하는데 도움이 됐어.

A: According to the increasing number of scooters, the number of accidents is also increasing. 스쿠터 수의 증가에 따라, 사고나는 숫자도 함께 늘어나고 있어.
B: Scooter drivers need to drive more safely. 스쿠터를 모는 사람은 안전하게 몰아야 돼.

05

The police enforce helmet laws and require all scooter driver's get a license

경찰은 헬멧착용을 법으로 의무화하고 모든 스쿠터 모는 사람에게 면허증을 요구하고 있어

● Requiring scooter drivers to take lessons might help decrease the number of accidents. 스쿠터 모는 사람들에게 강제교육이수는 사고의 수를 줄이는데 도움을 줄 수도 있어.

A: What can we do to decrease scooter accidents?
스쿠터 사고를 줄이기 위해서 우리가 할 수 있는 건 뭐야?

B: Requiring all scooter drivers to take driving lessons might help.
모든 스쿠터 모는 사람은 운전교육을 강제적으로 이수하는게 도움이 될지 몰라.

Unit 10

021

Serious complaints were ignored

심각한 불만들이 무시되어 왔어

많이 변화하였지만 아직도 문화적 특성상 성희롱이 암암리에 자행되고 이를 신고하지 못하고 극단적 선택을 하는 여성들이 많이 있다. 이를 오픈하자는 미투운동과 성희롱의 헌재에 대해 알아본다.

01

My opinion about the #MeToo movement is that it has been good for combatting sexual harassment and unwanted advances in the workplace

미투운동에 대한 나의 생각은 직장내 성희롱과 원치않는 접촉을 방지하는데 좋다는거야

- Victims of sexual harassment should be compensated by those who commit the crime. 성희롱의 피해자는 죄를 지은 사람들로부터 보상을 받아야 돼.

- The #METoo movement has been educational for both men and women. 미투운동은 남녀모두에게 교육적이었어.

A: I think the #MeToo movement has been great for combatting sexual harassment in the workplace. 미투운동이 직장내 성희롱을 방지하는데 아주 좋았다고 생각해.
B: Yes, it's too bad so many women took their own lives due to sexual harassment. 그래. 많은 여성들이 성희롱으로 극단적 선택을 한 것은 정말 안됐어.

02

For a long time, serious complaints were ignored

오랫동안 심각한 불만들이 무시되어 왔어

- Many bad men got away with serious crimes before the #MeToo movement. 미투운동 전에 많은 못된 남자들은 죄를 짓고도 벌받지 않았어.

- It is hard for abused women to speak up about sexual harassment because they feel ashamed. 희롱당한 여성은 수치스럽기 때문에 성희롱에 대해 공개적으로 말하는게 어려워.

A: Why did so many men get away with sexual abuse?
왜 그렇게 많은 남자들이 성적학대를 하고도 처벌받지 않는거야?

B: Some people blamed women because of the clothes they wore.
일부 사람들은 여성들의 옷 때문이라고 비난했어.

03 I also feel some women may falsely claim they were harassed because they could be rewarded for making a false claim 일부 여성은 거짓주장으로 보상받을 수있기 땜에 희롱당했다고 주장할 수도 있어

● It's possible that some women have accused innocent men of misconduct. 일부 여성들은 죄없는 남자들에게 비행을 저질렀냐고 고소했을 수도 있을거야.

A: There are many bad men who sexually harass women.
여성을 성적으로 희롱한 못된 남성들이 많아.

B: Yes but there are sometimes women who falsely accuse innocent men too. 맞아. 하지만 때로는 죄없는 남성을 거짓으로 고소하는 여성들도 있어.

04 We must be careful when a person is accused of harassment 우리는 어떤 사람이 성희롱으로 고소당했을 때 주의해야 해

● Some comments can be taken as sexual harassment by some and innocent comments by others.
일부 말들은 어떤 사람들에게는 성희롱으로, 어떤 다른 사람들에게는 비성희롱으로 받아들여질 수도 있어.

A: We need to be careful when a person is accused of harassment.
우리는 어떤 사람이 성희롱으로 고소당했을 때 주의해야 해.

B: Yes, it isn't always a black and white issue. 맞아. 그건 항상 흑백의 문제가 아냐.

05 I think that it is important to protect women from men who secretly photograph them
여성들을 몰래 촬영하는 남성들로부터 여성들을 보호하는 것이 중요하다고 생각해

● People who set up secret cameras to take sexual pictures should go to prison. 성적사진을 찍으려고 몰카를 설치한 사람들은 감옥에 가야 돼.

A: With new technology, it's become much easier for men to set up secret cameras to take pictures of women without their knowledge.
신기술에 따라 남성들이 몰카를 설치해서 여성들 모르게 사진을 찍는게 훨씬 쉬워졌어.

B: These men should all go to jail. 이런 남자들은 모두 감방에 쳐넣어야 돼.

Smartphones can be a big distraction for many people

스마트폰은 많은 사람들의 정신을 산만하게 만들 수 있어

많은 사람들이 앉으나 서나, 걷거나 운전할 때 핸드폰을 손에서 못떼는 경향이 있다. 그런 추세에 대해서 그리고 그런 추세가 가져오는 위험성에 대해서 일아본다.

It's easy to get distracted while texting or chatting with someone else on a phone

전화로 누군가와 문자나 채팅하면 정신이 산만해지기 쉬워

- Smartphones can be a big distraction for many people.
  스마트폰은 많은 사람들에게 정신을 산만하게 만들 수 있어.

- Some people can't concentrate on what they are doing because of their smartphones. 일부 사람들은 스마트폰 때문에 하는 일에 집중을 하지 못해.

A: My friend really annoyed me. He wasn't listening because he kept checking his smartphone. 친구땜에 열받았어. 핸드폰 계속 확인하느라 내 말을 듣고 있지 않았어.

B: Yes, smartphones can be a big distraction for many people.
그래, 스마트폰은 많은 사람들의 정신을 아주 산만하게 만들 수 있어.

As a result, there are many accidents related to a distracted person walking out into traffic

결과적으로 차량들 사이로 걸어 들어가는 산만한 사람에 관련된 사고들이 있어

- Smartphones are the cause of many kinds of accidents.
  스마트폰은 많은 종류의 사고의 원인이야.

- Many pedestrians are hurt or killed every year because they are looking at their smartphone instead of where they are walking.
  많은 보행자들은 길을 잘 보고 가는 대신 스마트폰을 보기 때문에 매년 부상을 당하거나 목숨을 잃어.

A: Did you hear about that man who was hit by a car while chatting on his smartphone? 스마트폰으로 채팅하다가 차에 치인 남자 얘기 들었어?

B: Pedestrians need to pay attention to where they are going instead of looking at their phones. 보행자들은 핸드폰보는 대신에 길을 잘 보고 가면서 주의를 기울어야 돼.

 03 **It's important to pay attention to the cars and crosswalks in Korean cities, in order to have a safe visit** 안전한 방문을 하기 위해서 한국 도시에서 자동차와 횡단보도에 주의를 기울이는 것이 중요해

• To be safe when walking around Seoul, you need to watch where you are going. 서울에서 걸을 때 안전하려면 길을 잘 보고 다녀야 돼.

A: Is Seoul a safe city? 서울은 안전한 도시야?

B: Yes, but you need to be careful of traffic when using crosswalks and crossing the street. 어, 하지만 횡단보도를 이용하거나 길을 건너갈 때 차량들을 조심해야 돼.

 04 **I hate it when people text and drive. They start paying attention to their phone and not to the cars around them** 운전 중 문자하는 사람들은 정말 싫더라. 그들은 주변 차들이 아니라 핸드폰에 주의를 기울이기 시작해

• People who text and drive are just as bad as people who drink and drive. 운전 중 문자하는 사람들은 음주하는 사람들만큼이나 나빠.

• My friend was hurt because a driver who was texting hit him at a crosswalk. 운전 중 문자하는 사람이 횡단보도에서 내 친구를 차로 쳐서 다쳤어.

A: I hate it when people text and drive. 운전 중 문자하는 사람들 정말 싫더라.

B: Me too. People who text and drive should lose their license. 나도 그래. 운전 중에 문자하는 사람들은 면허증을 잃게 만들어야 돼.

 05 **I have seen many accidents and many near misses caused by a distracted driver** 산만한 운전자 때문에 생긴 사고와 날 뻔한 사고들을 많이 봐왔어

• Accidents due to texting and driving are increasing every year. 운전 중 문자하다가 발생한 사고가 매년 증가하고 있어.

A: Thousands of people die every year in crashes caused by texting and driving. 운전 중 문자하다가 생긴 충돌사고로 매년 많은 사람들이 목숨을 잃어.

B: The government needs to make a new policy to try and decrease accidents. 정부는 사고를 줄이기 위해 새로운 정책을 만들어야 돼.

Unit 10

023

To deliver food quickly, many scooter drivers break traffic laws

음식을 빨리 배달하기 위해 많은 라이더들은 교통법규를 지키지 않아

무엇이든지 그리고 가장 빨리 배달하려는 업체들의 과잉서비스에 소비자들은 이에 길들여지는데…. 자동차, 오토바이, 스쿠터 등 모든 수단이 동원되며 "빨리빨리"를 외치는 라이더들의 목숨은 더 위태해진다.

01 It is common to see people on scooters, making deliveries in Korea

한국에서 스쿠터를 타고 배달하는 사람들을 보는 것은 흔한 일이야

- Scooters are a very popular vehicle for food delivery in Korea.
  스쿠터는 한국에서 음식을 배달하는데 매우 인기있는 교통수단이야.

- Food delivery drivers usually use scooters in Korea.
  한국에서 음식배달 라이더들은 보통 스쿠터를 이용해.

A: What are all of those scooters I keep seeing with the big steel boxes on them? 커다란 철가방을 뒤에 두고 다니는 계속 보이는 스쿠터들은 뭐야?

B: Those are food delivery scooters. Many restaurants use them to deliver food. 음식배달하는 스쿠터들이야. 많은 식당들이 그들을 이용해서 음식을 배달하거든.

02 This is an efficient way to get something delivered because they can cut between cars and are not held up by traffic jams

스쿠터들은 차들 사이사이로 가고 교통체증에도 막히지 않고 가니 뭔가 배달할 때 효율적이야

- Scooters are much faster than cars for delivery service because they can drive between cars and cut in and out of traffic.
  스쿠터들은 차들 사이사이로 운전하고 차량들 사이를 누비며 달릴 수 있기 때문에 배달에는 차량보다 훨씬 빨라.

- Delivery scooters are fast because they don't get slowed down by heavy traffic. 배달 스쿠터들은 차량이 막혀도 속도를 줄이지 않고 빠져나가기 때문에 빨라.

A: Why don't restaurants use cars to deliver food?
왜 식당은 음식배달하는데 차량을 이용하지 않는거야?

B: Scooters are much faster because they don't get slowed down by heavy traffic. 스쿠터들은 차량이 막혀도 속도를 줄이지 않고 빠져나가기 때문에 훨씬 빨라.

03 Some people complain that they drive too recklessly though 어떤 사람들은 스쿠터들이 너무 난폭운전을 한다고 불평해

- To deliver food quickly, many scooter drivers break traffic laws.
  음식을 빨리 배달하기 위해 많은 스쿠터들은 교통법규를 지키지 않아.

- Delivery drivers have many accidents because they drive so dangerously.
  배달 라이더들은 위험하게 운전하기 때문에 많은 사고를 내.

A: Some people complain that the drivers are very reckless.
일부 사람들은 라이더들이 매우 난폭하게 운전한다고 불평해.

B: Yes, they break many traffic laws because they want to deliver the food as quickly as possible.
맞아. 라이더들은 음식을 가능한 빨리 배달을 하고 싶기 때문에 교통법규를 지키지 않아.

04 Every year a number of them are killed in traffic accidents 매년 많은 라이더들이 교통사고로 목숨을 잃어

- Death rates for delivery drivers are very high in Korea.
  배달 라이더들의 사망률은 한국에서 매우 높아.

- Driving a scooter for a restaurant is considered a very dangerous job in Korea. 식당 배달로 스쿠터를 모는 것은 한국에서 매우 위험한 일로 생각되고 있어.

- I've seen many serious delivery driver accidents here in Korea.
  난 여기 한국에서 많은 심각한 배달 라이더들의 사고를 봤어.

A: Do many of the drivers die? 많은 라이더들이 목숨을 잃어?
B: Yes. Driving a scooter in Korea is considered a very dangerous job.
맞아. 식당 배달로 스쿠터를 모는 것은 한국에서 매우 위험한 일로 생각되고 있어.

Unit 10